The Battle for Los Angeles

The Battle for Los Angeles

Racial Ideology and World War II

Kevin Allen Leonard

University of New Mexico Press ▪ *Albuquerque*

 Published 2006
10 09 08 07 06   1 2 3 4 5

Library of Congress Cataloging-in-Publication Data

Leonard, Kevin Allen, 1964–
The battle for Los Angeles : racial ideology and World War II / Kevin Allen Leonard.
p. cm.
Includes bibliographical references and index.
ISBN-13: 978-0-8263-4047-4 (CLOTH : ALK. PAPER)
ISBN-10: 0-8263-4047-4 (CLOTH : ALK. PAPER)
1. Los Angeles (Calif.)—Race relations—History—20th century.
2. Racism—California—Los Angeles—History—20th century.
3. World War, 1939–1945—California—Los Angeles.
4. World War, 1939–1945—Social aspects. 5. Japanese Americans—California—Los Angeles—Social conditions—20th century. 6. Mexican Americans—California—Los Angeles—Social conditions—20th century.
7. African Americans—California—Los Angeles—Social conditions—20th century. I. Title.
F869.L89A2535 2006
305.8'00979494—dc22
2006008564

Book and cover design and typography: Kathleen Sparkes
This book was typeset using Utopia 9.5/14, 26P6
Display type is Officina Sans and Officina Serif

To the memory

of Bill Hill

Contents

Illustrations

Acknowledgments

Although I have spent thousands of hours by myself working on this book, it owes its existence to the generous assistance and support of many teachers, colleagues, librarians, institutions, and friends and family members. This project began fifteen years ago as a doctoral dissertation in the history department at the University of California, Davis. In my research and writing I was fortunate to have the guidance of Michael L. Smith, Vicki L. Ruiz, Clarence Walker, and David Brody, each of whom offered both support and constructive criticism. After we left Davis, Vicki continued to offer advice and encouragement. In the years I spent at Davis, I gained tremendously from a community of graduate students who were supportive at all times but critical when they needed to be. I am pleased to be able to thank Tom Adams, Marie-Pierre Arrizabalaga, James F. Brooks, Jeff Kolnick, Jenny Levine, Frank Malaret, Nikki Mandell, Margarete Myers, Salwa Nacouzi, Rich Negron, Kathy Olmsted, Jim Rose, Lil Taiz, and David Vaught. I would not have completed the graduate program without advice and assistance from Karen Hairfield. I am especially grateful to Lil and her husband Chris for offering me a place to stay in Los Angeles as I returned to work on this project in 2003.

During my final year in California, my oldest friend, Kent Ono, joined the faculty at Davis. Kent has always expected more of me than anyone else. It gives me great pleasure to be able to thank him for his high expectations and the example he has provided. Kent also exposed me to important theoretical writings about "race," and he helped me to understand his disciplinary training. Conversations with Kent's partner, Sarah Projansky, further helped me to understand how to approach and analyze discourse. After I left California, Kent and Sarah provided me with lodging and companionship on several return visits while I pursued additional research.

In the 1993–94 academic year I had the good fortune to be a visiting assistant professor at the University of New Mexico. The students in my graduate seminar and my colleagues Virginia Scharff and Elizabeth Jameson all influenced my thinking about "race." Since that year both Gingy and Betsy have offered unwavering emotional and intellectual support. Both have addressed questions in their own research that shaped my approach to my topic. From the fall of 1994 until the spring of 1997 I taught at Antioch College in Yellow Springs, Ohio. Although Yellow Springs is a long way from Los Angeles, my students and colleagues helped me to continue to think carefully about what happened in southern California during World War II. Robert Fogarty, Jean Gregorek, and Melinda Kanner helped me to rethink this book at a critical moment in my personal and intellectual development. Bob especially served as a model scholar and teacher, and he and his wife Katherine Kadish provided me and my partner Bill much-appreciated hospitality and stimulating conversation.

On a number of visits to Los Angeles I derived benefit from a group of scholars who welcomed me into their community. Howard Shorr helped me to find sources and shepherded me through the Huntington Library during my first visit there. Mike Engh shared with me sources about the Catholic Interracial Council, listened patiently to my ideas, and offered advice and encouragement. Doug Flamming shared some of his ideas with me and directed me to source material relating to the history of African Americans in Los Angeles before the war. Unfortunately, three of the people who advised and assisted me at the Huntington have not survived to see this work's completion. Wilbur Jacobs and Martin Ridge freely offered their advice to me, and Clark Davis inspired all of us who had the honor of knowing him.

Since 1997 I have taught at Western Washington University. Although my teaching and service have often prevented me from working on this book, the history department has consistently supported my research. I am grateful for the support and advice I have received from department chairs George Mariz and Chris Friday. Conversations with my colleagues Susan Costanzo and Nancy van Deusen helped me to negotiate the writing process. George, Chris, Susan, Nancy, Cecilia Danysk, Peter and Kari Diehl and their family, Amanda Eurich, and the late Tom Horn provided emotional support at a critical point in my life. I am fortunate to have a colleague whose research engages many of the same questions and problems as my research. Chris Friday has read drafts of several of the chapters of this book, and he has spent countless hours in conversation with me. No one else has had a greater influence on the content of this book. I am very pleased to be able to thank Chris for his guidance throughout the project.

A number of scholars have read portions of this book, usually in the form of conference papers, and provided helpful and much needed comments and criticism. I would like to thank Quintard Taylor, Alice Yang Murray, María Montoya, Brian Hayashi, and the participants in the Los Angeles History Research Group at the Huntington Library. I am especially appreciative of Peggy Pascoe's willingness to read a conference paper that represented an important effort to rethink my interpretation of Japanese Americans and racial ideology.

Historians would not be able to conduct their research without librarians and archivists. Many librarians and archivists have assisted me in my research. Unfortunately, I cannot list every individual librarian whose efforts helped me to complete this book. I would like to thank the librarians and archivists at the Huntington Library, the Department of Special Collections of the Charles E. Young Research Library at UCLA, the Department of Special Collections of the Stanford University Libraries, the National Archives in Washington, the National Archives, Pacific Region in Laguna Niguel, and the Manuscript Division of the Library of Congress. Sarah Cooper of the Southern California Library for Social Studies and Research went out of her way to assist me in conducting research in the Charlotta Bass papers. Joe Cali and Jan Miller of the Olive Kettering Library at Antioch College made it possible for me to examine newspapers from Los Angeles while I was in Ohio. Carolyn Kozo Cole of the Los Angeles Public Library and Simon Elliott of the Department of Special Collections of the Young Research Library at UCLA provided invaluable assistance in locating and providing photographs.

The research and production of this book would have been impossible without the generous support of a number of different institutions. A UC Davis Humanities Grant funded research travel, and a year-long position as a graduate fellow of the UC Davis Washington Center allowed me to conduct research in the National Archives and the Library of Congress. A John Randolph and Dora Haynes Foundation fellowship supported two months of research at the Huntington Library in the summer of 1990. Faculty Fund awards from Antioch College offset the cost of research trips to California in the summers of 1995 and 1996. A Huntington Library/ National Endowment for the Humanities fellowship allowed me to spend six months at the Huntington Library in 1997. A Summer Research Grant from Western Washington University supported my research in the summer of 1998. The writing of the second half of the book occurred in 2003–4, while I was supported by a year-long professional development leave from WWU. Finally, the WWU Bureau for Faculty Research provided a grant to cover the costs of photographs for the book.

Durwood Ball initially convinced me that the University of New Mexico Press should publish this book. David Holtby has displayed unending patience and offered kind words of encouragement. Floyce Alexander copyedited the manuscript. Maya Allen-Gallegos answered a number of my questions, and Sonia Dickey shepherded the book through the production process. Jeanne Broussard dramatically improved the quality of the images of the editorial cartoons that appear as illustrations.

Finally, friends and family have sustained me throughout the many years during which I have been working on this book. My parents, Charles and Ruth Ann Leonard, always had faith in me, and they provided much appreciated financial support. My siblings, Scott, Kris, and Jamie, have provided encouragement and inspiration. Jamie and his wife Yvette Aparicio also offered me a place to stay and good company on several research trips to California. Kris and her husband Abelardo Barrantes offered me a place to stay when professional conferences took me to Chicago. In Bellingham, the friendship of Sibyl Sanford, Doug Wadkins and David Webster, Carrie Seidl, Matt and Alona Christman, Steven and Vicky Garfinkle and their children, and the members of the Bellingham Unitarian Fellowship has allowed me to complete this book. My dear friends, the pianists Ford Hill and Jeffrey Gilliam, have inspired me with their music and the discipline it requires to prepare a recital or to write a book. The love of my first partner, Bill Hill, sustained me through the writing of the dissertation and the rethinking of my ideas that led me to write this book. Bill's unexpected death in January 1999 filled me with sadness and uncertainty. I soon decided, however, that I had to complete the book to honor his faith in me. This book is dedicated to Bill's memory. For the last five years my partner Tim Fitzpatrick has offered me the encouragement and love that I needed to continue my research and writing about "race" and World War II in Los Angeles. I could not have finished this book without his support.

INTRODUCTION

Earl Warren, Racial Ideology, and History

The Japanese attack on Pearl Harbor left Earl Warren in a difficult position. The Republican attorney general of the state of California received from military officers reports that alarmed him. One admiral told him, for example, that the navy did not have any ships with which to defend the Pacific Coast. Warren replied, "Well, my God! We have thousands and thousands of Japanese here. We could have an invasion here."[1] Despite his suspicions about people of Japanese ancestry, the attorney general was not at first a leader in the movement to have all people of Japanese ancestry removed from the coastal area. Warren was a member of the American Legion and the Native Sons of the Golden West, but he made no public statements in support of those organizations' anti-Japanese positions. When Warren was elected attorney general in 1938, he became an ex-officio member of the outspokenly anti-Japanese California Joint Immigration Committee. He never attended a meeting, however, and he resigned from the committee in the summer of 1939.

Although Warren was not an outspoken leader of the post–Pearl Harbor anti-Japanese movement, he did work behind the scenes to accumulate and disseminate information that supported the arguments of other anti-Japanese leaders. At a meeting in San Francisco in early February 1942, for example, Warren told law enforcement officials from around California that the fact that there had been no instances of sabotage or espionage in California was an ominous sign. It showed that Japanese "fifth columnists" were simply waiting to act until the Japanese imperial forces attacked. He also encouraged district attorneys to prepare maps that identified land owned by people of Japanese ancestry. Many of these officials drew the conclusion that Japanese Americans had intentionally purchased or leased land in the vicinity of every facility "of strategic military importance."[2]

When Warren did publicly endorse the removal of all Japanese Americans, his words may have carried more weight because he had not previously distinguished himself as an outspoken proponent of this course of action. In fact, Warren had defended the rights of Japanese immigrants to possess business and professional licenses.[3] Warren argued forcefully that all people of Japanese ancestry, including U.S. citizens, should be incarcerated when he appeared before the U.S. House Select Committee Investigating National Defense Migration on February 21, 1942. Warren told this committee, usually known as the Tolan Committee because it was chaired by U.S. Representative John H. Tolan of Oakland, that the "opinion among law-enforcement officers of this State is that there is more potential danger among the group of Japanese who are born in this country than from the alien Japanese who were born in Japan." Warren also told the committee that law enforcement officials could determine the loyalty of members of "the Caucasian race." "But when we deal with the Japanese we are in an entirely different field and we cannot form any opinion that we believe to be sound."[4] By this time President Roosevelt had already signed Executive Order 9066, which gave the army the authority to incarcerate and remove all of the Pacific Coast's residents of Japanese ancestry.

For more than two years after the Tolan Committee hearings, Warren maintained in public his position that all people of Japanese ancestry should be kept away from the Pacific Coast. In May 1943, for example, Warren, now the governor of California and the head of the California War Council, said that "we can't meet danger if we have potential traitors and saboteurs in this area." Warren's statement supported the action of the

California War Council. According to the *Los Angeles Times*, the War Council had "expressed vigorous opposition to any plan for the return of Japanese citizens or aliens to the West Coast for the duration of the war." The governor also said that "it's our right and duty to keep the people of the nation conscious as to the dangerous position California is in."[5] In private correspondence, however, Warren at times expressed doubts about the wisdom of the position he had taken.[6]

By the time the army announced its rescission of the exclusion orders in December 1944, Warren's position had changed. He was the most prominent of the anti-Japanese leaders who encouraged California residents to accept the army's decision and to honor and protect Japanese Americans' civil rights. "Any public unrest that develops from provocative statements, or civil disturbances that result from intemperate action will of necessity retard the war effort," Warren said.[7]

The popular governor was reelected in 1946 and again in 1950. He was the Republican party's vice-presidential nominee in 1948. In 1953, after the Republicans had regained the White House, President Dwight D. Eisenhower appointed Warren the chief justice of the U.S. Supreme Court. In his sixteen years as chief justice, Warren presided over a court that issued many opinions that dramatically reinterpreted U.S. law. Many of these rulings, such as the 1954 decision in *Brown v. Board of Education* and the 1967 decision in *Loving v. Virginia*, dealt with the role of "race" in U.S. society. The *Brown* decision declared school segregation unconstitutional, and the *Loving* decision struck down state laws that prohibited marriage across "racial" boundaries.

Warren's later opinions in cases dealing with "race" may seem to suggest that his beliefs about "race" had changed between 1942 and 1954. Warren argued otherwise. In his memoirs, published in 1977, three years after his death, Warren offered an interpretation of his actions thirty years before. His interpretation began with a statement of regret. "I have since deeply regretted the removal order and my own testimony advocating it, because it was not in keeping with our American concept of freedom and the rights of citizens," Warren wrote. Warren connected his regret to the fact that the removal of Japanese Americans affected innocent children. The retired chief justice confessed that "whenever I thought of the innocent little children who were torn from home, school friends, and congenial surroundings, I was conscience-stricken." He declared bluntly, "it was wrong to react so impulsively, without positive evidence of disloyalty, even though we felt we had a good motive in the security of our state." Warren admitted that "racial antagonism" influenced the incarceration and removal of Japanese Americans from their Pacific Coast homes. "It demonstrates the cruelty of war when fear, get-tough military psychology, propaganda, and racial antagonism combine with one's responsibility for public security to produce such acts," he wrote. Warren, however, depicted this "racial antagonism," on his part at least, as a wartime aberration. "I have always believed that I had no prejudice against the Japanese as such except that directly spawned by Pearl Harbor and its aftermath," Warren declared. He pointed out that when he was the district attorney of Alameda County in the 1920s and 1930s "I had great respect for people of Japanese ancestry, because during my years in that office they created no law enforcement problems. Although we had a sizable Japanese population, neither the young nor the old violated the law."[8]

The example of Earl Warren offers historians one way to understand the effect of World War II on racial ideology in California and, more broadly, the United States. As Warren's biographers and Warren himself depicted his actions, he was someone who did not harbor any prejudice toward Japanese Americans until Pearl Harbor. Then he lent his authority to the movement to incarcerate and remove all people of Japanese ancestry from the Pacific Coast. Even though in public Warren was a strong advocate of the removal of Japanese Americans from coastal areas, in his private correspondence he expressed some doubts about the wisdom of this course of action. By the time Japanese Americans were allowed to return to the coast, Warren had overcome the prejudices that had been inspired by Pearl Harbor, and he publicly urged all Californians to respect the rights of Japanese Americans. Later he expressed regret for his role in the incarceration and removal of Japanese Americans from the Pacific Coast. It is tempting to suggest that Warren's wartime thoughts and actions were in some ways representative of the thoughts and actions of many Californians or even Americans more generally. From this perspective, changing beliefs about "race" within U.S. society would result from millions of people, like Warren, struggling quietly and internally with their prejudices and ultimately abandoning some of them.

There is merit to such an argument. To some extent social change does occur as a result of millions of individual internal conflicts. Such an interpretation, however, raises a critical interpretive question: How can historians know what people thought or believed? When I first began the research for this project fifteen years ago, I thought that I knew the answer to that question. I strode confidently into archives and libraries and collected documents that I thought showed what people believed about "race." Many years of research, thought, and reading, however, convinced me that I did not truly know what any single individual thought about "race." I knew what many people had written and said about "race," but I could not know what they really believed. Every document I held in my hands had been crafted by someone whose words might have been shaped by a number of influences, many of which are unknowable to historians, such as the author's motivation for writing; the author's perception of the person or people for whom she or he was writing; the author's desire to present herself or himself in a certain light; even the limitations of language itself to convey subtle and complex emotions.

More than seven years ago I decided that it was impossible to salvage the initial result of my research, my doctoral dissertation, and I began writing an entirely new and different book. After several years of additional thinking and writing, I finally realized that I could not draw conclusions about changes in people's thoughts or beliefs about "race." However, I could draw some conclusions from what people said and wrote about "race." My goal in this book, then, is not to assess changes in people's beliefs about "race," even if I think that changes in people's writing and speaking about "race" hint at changes in their beliefs. Instead, my goal is to trace and interpret changes in what people wrote and said about "race" immediately before, during, and immediately after the Second World War.

My focus on what people wrote and said about "race," however, does not simply reflect my conviction that it is impossible for me to know what people truly thought. It also reflects my belief that "race" itself was created and remade in the public debates about the meanings of differences among people. People's actions are no doubt influenced by feelings that cannot be expressed in words, and it is possible that some beliefs about "race" cannot be expressed in words. However, it seems to me that even these feelings have been shaped by words. Moreover, Americans have been writing and speaking about "race" for much of the nation's history. The meanings of this term, which I think constitute "race" itself, changed over time as the term was used by different people who understood the term in different ways. People often argued publicly about what "race" meant, hoping to persuade others to abandon their positions.[9]

As historian Peggy Pascoe has argued, the dominant narrative that explains changes in "mainstream twentieth-century American racial ideologies" emphasizes cultural anthropologists' assault upon scientific racism in the 1920s and 1930s. This narrative suggests that social scientists' critique of scientific racism gradually spread throughout U.S. society in the 1940s, 1950s, and 1960s.[10] Many scholars failed to recognize the ideological shift that occurred in the 1940s and 1950s in the United States because they were intimately involved in the debates about "race." From their perspective, the spread of their ideas was "natural." Steeped in a rationalist, social scientific tradition, they saw older ideas about "race" as outmoded.

In her critique of this dominant narrative regarding changes in mainstream racial ideologies, Pascoe points out that writing about "race" has tended to focus on the ideas of intellectual elites.[11] In focusing on the words of intellectual elites, scholars often depict racial ideologies as if they were simply created and maintained by the Anglo Americans who derived the greatest benefit from them. My reading of newspapers in Los Angeles has convinced me that the creation and maintenance of racial ideologies has been much more complicated. People from a variety of ethnic and class backgrounds participated in the process of "racial formation." Of course, not all people had the ability to participate as equals in the debates about the meanings of "race," but this does not mean that we should simply ignore the words of African Americans, Asian Americans, and Mexican Americans. Members of all of these groups publicly expressed their beliefs about "race" and at times challenged the statements of members of other groups.

Los Angeles is an ideal setting in which to examine these debates about "race." As the previous paragraphs suggest, Japanese Americans were frequently at the center of these debates, and Los Angeles before the war was home to more Japanese Americans than any other city. According to the 1940 census, nearly thirty-seven thousand Japanese Americans lived in Los Angeles County in 1940. This number constituted nearly one-quarter of all the people of Japanese ancestry living on the U.S. mainland at that time.

The fact that riots erupted in Los Angeles during the war also makes the city an ideal venue in which to examine debates about the meanings of "race." Observers on the local and national level disagreed about whether or not the Zoot-Suit Riots were race riots, but these very disagreements meant that people in Los Angeles were debating the meanings of "race" more than they might have if rioting had not occurred there. The rioting in Los Angeles generally involved attacks by navy and army personnel upon young Mexican American and African American men. Los Angeles was the home to the largest Mexican American community in the United States and the largest African American community in the West. According to the 1940 census, almost sixty-three thousand African Americans lived in the city of Los Angeles, and another twelve thousand African Americans lived outside the city limits in Los Angeles County. The size of the Mexican American community is more difficult to determine, since the Census Bureau did not define Mexican Americans as a "race." The census counted just over thirty-eight thousand Mexican-born residents in the city of Los Angeles in 1940 and more than fifty-nine thousand Mexican natives in Los Angeles County. The 1940 census also found more than seventy thousand U.S.-born Mexican Americans in the city.[12] Some historians have suggested that the Census Bureau seriously undercounted the number of Mexican Americans in the Los Angeles area.

The Japanese American, Mexican American, and African American communities in Los Angeles were large enough that they supported newspapers and organizations that allowed members of these communities to attempt to participate in the debates about the meanings of "race" during the war. Even after Japanese Americans were removed from Los Angeles and other coastal regions in 1942, Japanese Americans continued to observe the ongoing debate about "race" in Los Angeles. Some Japanese Americans even attempted to participate in these debates by publishing editorials and columns about events in Los Angeles, although many of these editorials and columns appeared in the *Pacific Citizen*, a Japanese American newspaper that was not widely read in Los Angeles during the war.

Just as Los Angeles's diversity makes the city an ideal venue for a study of debates about the meanings of "race," the critical issues involved in World War II make the war years an excellent time period in which to study such debates. For many Americans the Second World War was a conflict with Hitler and everything he represented. Many Americans found Hitler's ideas about "race" and the policies based upon those ideas repugnant, especially as it became clear during the war that Hitler had embarked on a program of genocide. Opponents of racial prejudice and discrimination during the war began to compare the people who supported and defended discrimination with Hitler. As this study will show, some people who defended discriminatory practices during the war backed away from direct and explicit appeals to racial prejudice.

At the same time, however, World War II was also a conflict between the United States and the Japanese empire. Some Americans argued that the war with Japan was a "race war"—a struggle between two separate and incompatible peoples. Even some people who opposed Hitler and backed away from explicit appeals to racial prejudice continued to express hostility to all people who were "racially" Japanese. It is this complexity that I think makes this subject both fascinating and important. This study does not tell a simple story of people rejecting racism. Instead, it shows people struggling with each other and with themselves about racial ideology. Some people expressed contradictory positions. For example, even as the *Los Angeles Examiner* argued that the United States was engaged in a "race war" with Japan, it published an editorial that suggested that racial prejudice should not affect the experiences of people in the United States. The editorial declared that the United States was "one country—neither race nor creed count." Celebrating the fact that "a Protestant rector, a Jewish rabbi and a Catholic priest had jointly officiated" at a memorial service for three navy men, the *Examiner* contrasted "Hitler-ridden, hate-infested Europe" with the United States.[13] A later editorial published in the Hearst newspaper also opposed racial and religious discrimination. "In the United States, as in Europe, campaigns and practices of racial and religious disparagement and discrimination never STOP with the Jews," the editorial stated. "Once the practice of intolerance was accepted in Nazi Germany and the Jews were made to suffer, Catholics and Protestants suffered alike." The editorial predicted that "the United States will have the same tragic experience, if it ever makes the same fatal mistake."[14] In a July 1944 editorial protesting the Nazi persecution of Jews, the *Examiner* stated that "when the Axis defeat in Europe is accomplished, it is the hope and expectation of the civilized world that the persecution of racial and religious minorities will end."[15]

After the *Examiner* and other Hearst newspapers denounced racial discrimination, some Japanese Americans ridiculed the newspapers for their failure to recognize that in their anti-Japanese stand they had supported racial discrimination. Japanese American Citizens League President Saburo Kido suggested that "Orientals, Mexicans, Negroes and others of the colored races may not be human beings in the eyes of the Hearst papers. Otherwise, the same reasoning should apply. If the citizens of Japanese ancestry can be pushed around and their rights violated with the approval of the Supreme Court, it is going to boomerang against some other group one of these days."[16]

The changes I trace in the debate about the meanings of "race" were often subtle, complex, and contradictory. These changes in people's words and the ways in which they used those words help to explain not only the successes of the postwar civil rights struggles but also the failures of those movements. As a result of the war, explicit expressions of racial prejudice became unacceptable in much of the United States. The changes in the ways in which Americans talked about "race" clearly reflected some ideological change. Courts struck down certain discriminatory practices, lawmakers passed legislation to guarantee the rights of citizens, and some policies changed. Yet much discrimination persisted.

Influences, Methods, and Sources

Some of the previous paragraphs may suggest that my approach to this subject has been strongly influenced by my reading of the works of Michel Foucault and other postmodernist theorists. I will not deny that I have read several of Foucault's works, but my sense is that I have been much more deeply influenced by other historians of the United States and Canada. Philip J. Ethington's *The Public City: The Political Construction of Urban Life in San Francisco, 1850–1900,* and Karen J. Sawislak's *Smoldering City: Chicagoans and the Great Fire, 1871–1874,* convinced me of the value of analyzing public debates in a single city and provided impressive models for doing so. Barbara Dianne Savage's *Broadcasting Freedom: Radio, War, and the Politics of Race, 1938–1948,* also led me to think more carefully about the ways in which people presented their arguments about "race" during World War II. Two books that helped me to approach my sources with a critical eye are Elizabeth Vibert's *Traders' Tales: Narratives of Cultural Encounters in the Columbia Plateau, 1807–1846,* and Frieda Knobloch's *The Culture of Wilderness: Agriculture as Colonization in the American West.*[17] The single most important influence in this research, however, was Peggy Pascoe's pathbreaking article "Miscegenation Law, Court Cases, and Ideologies of 'Race' in Twentieth-Century America." Pascoe's work provided me with terminology and, more importantly, a framework that helped me to begin to understand the changes over time that I had noticed but not yet understood in the sources I had examined.[18] From Pascoe I have borrowed the terms *American racialism* and *modernist racial ideology.* According to Pascoe, racialists believed that "race, understood as an indivisible essence that included not only biology but also culture, morality, and intelligence, was a compellingly significant factor in history and society." The adherents of modernist racial ideology, Pascoe notes, saw biology and culture as separate. To modernists racial differences between people were merely biological and therefore superficial. They believed that "the eradication of racism depends on the deliberate nonrecognition of race."

The University of California Press has recently published several monographs that deal with the history of "race" and of racialized groups in Los Angeles. Each of these works has provided me with valuable background information and has led me to ask new questions of many of the articles and editorials that I have examined. Taken together, Douglas Flamming's *Bound for Freedom: Black Los Angeles in Jim Crow America* and Josh Sides's *L.A. City Limits: African American Los Angeles from the Great Depression to the Present* constitute the first complete history of African Americans in Los Angeles for most of the twentieth century. Because both Flamming and Sides set out to trace the broad contours of African American experiences, their studies differ fundamentally from mine, which focuses on a limited time period and a much narrower topic. Nonetheless, I hope that this study intersects in valuable ways with these larger, sweeping narratives of African American history. The experiences that Flamming and Sides describe influenced the African Americans who participated in the debates that I analyze.[19]

Recent monographs by Eric Avila and Mark Wild are more comparable to this study, although both deal with events that occurred and with sources produced over a longer number of years. In some ways, Wild's *Street Meeting: Multiethnic Neighborhoods in Early Twentieth-Century Los Angeles* ends where my study begins, with the U.S. entry into World War II. It draws upon a wide range of sources, such as oral histories, research papers, and theses from the early twentieth century, government reports, and some newspaper articles, to examine the effects of the mixing of people from different ethnic groups in many of Los Angeles's neighborhoods. Wild's work helps to explain why members of one group sometimes claimed the right to speak for members of another group. In some ways, Avila's *Popular Culture in the Age of White Flight: Fear and Fantasy in Suburban Los Angeles* begins where my study ends, with the end of the war. His work analyzes the stories people told about the transformation of the Los Angeles area after the war. Avila draws upon a wide range of sources—motion pictures, letters to elected officials, magazine articles, and murals, to name a few. He shows how racialized depictions of urban space encouraged not only "white flight" but also an effort to remake parts of the city in the mold of suburbia. Rarely, however, do these historians draw upon the newspapers as I do. As I will explain in greater detail shortly, I think that newspapers represent an especially valuable and increasingly underused source for historians.[20]

The book that is most similar to this study is Eduardo Obregón Pagán's *Murder at the Sleepy Lagoon: Zoot Suits, Race, and Riot in Wartime L.A.* Pagán's topic, however, is more narrowly defined than mine. In his thoughtful and thorough analysis of the trial transcript in the so-called Sleepy Lagoon trial (discussed here in chapter three) and other sources, Pagán addresses many important questions about the meanings of "race" in wartime Los Angeles. Like Mauricio A. Mazón's earlier psychohistorical study, *The Zoot-Suit Riots: The Psychology of Symbolic Annihilation,* Pagán's monograph places the Sleepy Lagoon case and the Zoot-Suit Riots in the context of a city in which wartime changes had increased class and "racial" antagonism. Pagán's attention to interaction across "racial" boundaries in places such as the Central Avenue jazz clubs is especially provocative. Nonetheless, like Mazón, Pagán still tends to tell a story in which most of the subjects are either Mexican Americans or Anglo Americans.[21]

One of my overarching goals is to address the fact that Los Angeles during the war was a multicultural city. As previous paragraphs have noted, Los Angeles had large Japanese American, Mexican American, and African American communities, even though the combined populations of these groups amounted to less than 10 percent of the population of Los Angeles County. Members of these communities often responded to events in the city that involved members of other groups or that dealt more generally with "race." My method in tracing and then analyzing the debates about "race" involved the identification of events or episodes that generated public discourse about "race" and the examination of the articles and editorials about each episode in as many newspapers as were available. This method has produced a study that is episodic, but the character of the study also reflects the character of the debate about the meanings of "race." This debate was not a constant, steady, ongoing exchange. Instead, it flared up when something happened that led some public officials, journalists, or concerned citizens to react.

As I read and reread the articles, editorials, and statements of people who participated in each episode, I asked a series of questions. Rather than assuming that each article or editorial presented its author's thoughts, I tried to avoid questions such as "why would this person have said or written these words." Instead, I asked questions such as: How does this person describe "race"? How does this description of "race" compare with other people's descriptions of "race"? What are the implications of this person's description of "race"? What does this source reveal about the debate about "race" in Los Angeles during World War II?

The research for this study involved the careful reading of as many newspapers as were available. Unfortunately, copies of many newspapers have not survived. In some cases it was possible to reconstruct arguments by reading carefully articles or editorials that challenged statements that were printed in newspapers that do not survive. I have examined every issue of three daily newspapers, the *Daily News*, the *Los Angeles Examiner*, and the *Los Angeles Times*, for most of the period between October 1941 and November 1946. I have examined selected issues of another daily newspaper, the Spanish-language *La Opinión*. I have read the English-language section of every issue of *Rafu Shimpo*, a Japanese American daily newspaper, from January 1940 until it was forced to suspend publication in March 1942. I have also read every issue of *Rafu Shimpo* from the time it resumed publication in 1946 until November 1946. I have perused every issue of the *California Eagle*, an African American weekly newspaper, from October 1941 until November 1946. Unfortunately, issues of two other African American weekly newspapers, the *Los Angeles Sentinel* and the *Los Angeles Tribune*, have not survived for this entire period. Scattered issues of the *Tribune* from 1943 through 1945 have survived, and I have examined those, as well as all the available issues of both the *Sentinel* and the *Tribune* from 1946.

A more complete description of each of these newspapers will prove helpful to the reader. The *Times* was the oldest of the daily newspapers I examined. It began publication in 1881, as the *Daily Times*. Harrison Gray Otis, a Civil War veteran and printer who had moved to California in 1876, and his wife Eliza bought a one-quarter interest in the struggling new paper in 1882. The Otises reaped the benefits of a real estate and population boom in southern California. Otis's son-in-law, Harry Chandler, assumed control of the *Times* in 1914. From its inception, the *Times* had been a Republican newspaper. It was also fiercely anti-union. Its editorial policy did not change dramatically over time. By the early 1940s the *Times* remained rigidly Republican and anti-union. It opposed President Franklin D. Roosevelt's New Deal and Communism, and at times it suggested that the New Deal was essentially communistic. In 1941 Norman Chandler had assumed editorial control of the newspaper from his father Harry, but there was no perceptible shift in editorial policy. By 1940, the *Times*'s daily circulation was 226,395.[22]

William Randolph Hearst began publishing the *Los Angeles Examiner* in 1903, when the *Times* was engaged in a struggle with the International Typographical Union. In contrast to the anti-union *Times*, the *Examiner* promised support for organized labor. By the 1940s, however, it had largely abandoned its support for organized labor, although it still attempted to appeal to working-class readers. Its pages contained a number of articles and photographs designed to appeal to readers' emotions, such as photographs of dogs demonstrating loyalty to other dogs that had been hit and killed by cars. The *Examiner* boasted a circulation of 240,000 copies every morning and more than 600,000 every Sunday. Although the *Examiner* published more feature articles intended to appeal to working-class readers than did the *Times*, its editorial policy was not remarkably different from that of its rival. The *Examiner*, like the *Times*, was unremittingly hostile to the Democratic party, the New Deal, and Communism.[23]

The *Daily News* was the only "liberal" daily in Los Angeles in the 1940s. Cornelius Vanderbilt, Jr., founded the newspaper as the *Illustrated Daily News* in 1923 and experienced immediate success as a champion of organized labor and an opponent of the city's dominant business interests. The newspaper's photographs also undoubtedly helped it to surpass all of its established rivals in circulation. Vanderbilt soon began publishing other, similar newspapers in San Francisco and Miami. When his family decided that the chain was too expensive, however, Vanderbilt lost those newspapers. The *Illustrated Daily News* went into receivership in 1926. With support from some influential investors, Manchester Boddy gained control of the newspaper. At the time Boddy, a native of Washington state and a veteran of World War I who had come to Los Angeles in 1920, was managing the book division of the Times-Mirror Company, the parent company of the *Los Angeles Times*. After six years during which Boddy supported Republican candidates and policies, he shifted course during the Depression. The *Daily News* became a reliably Democratic, pro–New Deal newspaper. In local politics, however, the newspaper at times remained neutral, apparently to avoid alienating advertisers. In the late 1930s the *Daily News*, which appeared on newsstands in the mornings, absorbed the evening *Post-Record*, and the transformed *Daily News* boasted of being "a 24 hour newspaper." Editions of the newspaper appeared throughout the day. In

1942 the circulation of the *Daily News* was nearly equal to that of the *Times* and the *Examiner*, at 221,000 copies daily.[24]

Ignacio Lozano began publishing the Spanish-language daily *La Opinión* in 1926. Lozano had come with his family to San Antonio, Texas, from Mexico in 1908. Lozano had begun publishing *La Prensa* in San Antonio in 1913. By the early 1940s *La Opinión* was well established. The content of the newspaper reflected the middle-class background and interests of its publishers. Unlike the *Examiner*, *La Opinión* did not publish sensational or sentimental articles. Although *La Opinión* published some local news, much of what it covered was national news and news from Mexico.

Rippo Iijima, Masaharu Yamaguchi, and Seijiro Shibuya began publishing *Rafu Shimpo* in April 1903. At that time the newspaper was a mimeographed news bulletin entirely in Japanese. The newspaper began to grow when H. T. Komai took over in 1914. In 1926 *Rafu Shimpo* began publishing an English-language section. This section became a daily feature in 1932. By 1941 *Rafu Shimpo* had a daily circulation of eighty-five hundred. Prior to Pearl Harbor the Japanese-language newspapers in general published articles that supported the actions and policies of the Japanese imperial government.[25] The English-language section of *Rafu Shimpo*, however, devoted little attention to support for these policies. The Nisei who worked for the newspaper tended to be Democrats in their personal politics, and some of their columns and editorials express a preference for the Democratic party.

The *California Eagle* in the 1940s was synonymous with Charlotta A. Bass. Little is known about Bass's life before she arrived in Los Angeles in 1910; a number of sources provide conflicting information about the year and place of her birth. These sources, including an autobiography that Bass wrote in 1960, provide little insight into Bass's career before she came to California. Bass claimed that John Neimore founded the *Eagle* in 1879, but that information is misleading. Neimore did begin publishing a newspaper, the *Owl*, in 1879, but the *Eagle* did not begin publication until the mid-1890s.[26] When Neimore died in 1912, Charlotta Spears took over the publication. The next year Joseph Bass, who had experience in the newspaper business, assumed management of the newspaper's business operation and married Charlotta. Joseph and Charlotta Bass operated the newspaper together until Joseph Bass died in 1934. Bass continued to publish the newspaper until 1951, when she sold it to Loren Miller, who had worked for the newspaper in the 1930s and had then become a prominent civil rights attorney. Although Bass insisted

FIG. 1. *Charlotta A. Bass, publisher of the* California Eagle *from 1912 until 1951. Although Bass retained some ties to the Republican party, during World War II her political position moved leftward. In 1952 she was the vice-presidential candidate of the Progressive party. Security Pacific Collection, Los Angeles Public Library.*

that she maintained her affiliation with the Republican party through the war, her paper's editorial position moved progressively leftward. By the middle of the war, some members of the African American community accused the *Eagle* of being an organ of the Communist party.[27]

Leon Washington came to Los Angeles in 1928. He originally worked for David Taylor's short-lived *California News* and then published a free newspaper, *Town Talk*, before he went to work as the advertising manager at the *Eagle*. After working at the *Eagle* for a year and a half, Washington left to establish the *Los Angeles Sentinel* in 1933. Advertising revenue allowed Washington to distribute the *Sentinel* at no charge.[28] The *Sentinel* did not embrace radicalism as the *Eagle* did. Instead, it tended to support the Democratic party.[29] Less information is available about the *Los Angeles Tribune*. It was founded in 1940 by Lucius Lomax, Jr., the son of a newcomer from Chicago whom Douglas Flamming identifies as "a gambler who quickly established black L.A.'s first significant numbers game." Flamming points out, however, that Lomax "had high status" because he used some of his money to assist the community. He bought the Somerville Hotel, the city's first hotel owned by an African American, and he assisted the *Eagle* and the *Sentinel* in the 1930s.[30] It is not clear why his son established the *Tribune* in 1940. During the war Almena Davis edited the *Tribune*. An outspoken critic of her competitors at both the *Sentinel* and the *Eagle* and of the African American press in general, Davis won the first Wendell Willkie Award for Journalism. Historian Lee Finkle argued that the Willkie awards were established by "Southern white liberals" who sought "to control the black press." Finkle pointed out that, in the year in which she was honored, Davis had "joined Westbrook Pegler in denouncing the black press, and had characterized most of the reporting in the press as 'nauseating.'"[31]

Argument and Organization

This book suggests that modernist racial ideology spread in wartime Los Angeles as a result of repeated verbal conflicts about the meaning of "race." I have referred to these verbal conflicts as the "battle for Los Angeles," because the participants in these conflicts frequently compared their rhetorical battles to the life-and-death struggles occurring in Europe, North Africa, and the Pacific. As chapter one shows, this "battle" did not begin until late in 1941, when President Roosevelt's newly appointed Committee on Fair Employment Practice, usually known as the FEPC, held its first hearing in Los Angeles. Prior to that time, many African Americans and Japanese Americans had protested racial discrimination and other public displays of racial prejudice, but no officials or journalists responded to their protests. The FEPC hearings revealed why few people in positions of power had paid attention to these protests: they insisted that the fact that few African Americans, Asian Americans, or Mexican Americans worked in aircraft factories was not the result of discrimination.

As chapter two argues, the debate about the meanings of race intensified immediately following the attack on Pearl Harbor. Japanese Americans did not argue that all people of Japanese ancestry were loyal to the United States. In fact, some conceded that there were some people within the Japanese community in the United States who were not loyal to this country. Their fundamental point, though, was that "race" was not an indicator of loyalty. It was not possible to conclude that a person was loyal to Japan simply because that person was "racially" Japanese, many Japanese Americans argued. In response to this argument, a number of public officials and newspaper editors advanced an array of arguments that rested on the fundamental assumption that "race" did determine loyalty. Although these arguments did not in and of themselves lead to the incarceration and removal of Japanese Americans from the Pacific Coast, they did provide ideological justifications for these actions by federal officials.

Few Los Angeles residents came to the defense of Japanese Americans in the months following Pearl Harbor. By the summer of 1942, however, a number of people responded vocally to the statements of law enforcement officers. A number of law enforcement officers argued in August 1942 that Mexican Americans were racially inclined toward criminality. In response to these arguments, and especially in response to the Sleepy Lagoon trial, some opponents of racial prejudice and discrimination organized and advanced their belief that discrimination against Mexican Americans rather than a racial proclivity toward criminality were responsible for any increase in juvenile delinquency in Los Angeles. Chapter three examines this episode in the "battle for Los Angeles."

By the end of 1942, as chapter four shows, Japanese Americans had returned to the center of the debates about the meanings of "race." A number of the people who had supported the incarceration and removal of Japanese Americans continued to attack the loyalty of the imprisoned people and opposed any efforts by the War Relocation Authority or the army to release any Japanese Americans. In April 1943 Lt. Gen. John L. DeWitt, the commander of the Western Defense Command, told a congressional committee that U.S. citizens of Japanese ancestry were no more loyal to the United States than the residents of Japan. "A Jap's a Jap," DeWitt declared. Nonetheless, by June 1943 the army had increasingly refused to base its policies on the racial ideology that DeWitt had embraced.

Although opponents of racial prejudice and discrimination began attacking the racialists' depiction of juvenile crime among Mexican Americans in 1942, as chapter five argues, it was not until the Zoot-Suit Riots erupted in June 1943 that many influential individuals began to reject explicit statements of traditional racial ideology. The riots drew the attention of the nation and the world to Los Angeles. Even though many officials and newspaper editors resolutely insisted that the riots were not racially motivated attacks upon young Mexican Americans, prominent leaders throughout the United States and Latin America argued just as forcefully that the riots reflected racial prejudice and discrimination in Los Angeles. As a result of the riots, the opponents of racial prejudice and discrimination began to form organizations and to push for changes in policy.

Throughout the war anti-Japanese leaders continued to argue that Japanese Americans were, because of their racial origin, loyal to Japan and a threat to the security of the United States. These leaders lobbied elected and military officials to keep all people of Japanese ancestry in concentration camps and away from the Pacific Coast for the duration of the war. As chapter six shows, these anti-Japanese leaders failed in their efforts to influence federal policy relating to Japanese Americans. The opponents of discrimination, many of them Japanese Americans, instead succeeded in employing powerful symbols of Japanese American loyalty to the United States, particularly the military service of Japanese Americans, in order to render powerless most of the anti-Japanese accusations.

The "battle for Los Angeles," however, did not result in an unqualified victory for advocates of modernist racial ideology. As chapter seven shows, opponents of prejudice and discrimination did not achieve all of their goals. Many people expressed their agreement with modernist ideology, but few Anglo Americans were willing to give up what they considered the privileges of whiteness. Many Anglo Americans defended their right to live in segregated neighborhoods, and an overwhelming majority of Los Angeles residents voted against a fair employment practices initiative that appeared on the November 1946 ballot.

ONE

"This Fair Land where the East Meets the West"

"Race" in Los Angeles before Pearl Harbor

Twenty members of the Ku Klux Klan gathered on the steps of City Hall on the evening of March 31, 1940. Clad in robes and hoods, they marched through the streets of downtown, distributing pamphlets that called upon legislators to outlaw Communism. Los Angeles newspapers responded in different ways to the Klan's march through downtown. The *Los Angeles Times* printed a six-paragraph article about the march. The article described the route of the march and noted that "scores of plainclothes Klansmen joined the hooded group along the line of march." The *Times* did not quote any Klan members or mention the presence of people protesting the demonstration.[1] The *Times* did not publish an editorial about the demonstration or any articles about people who objected to the Klan's march. Neither the *Los Angeles Examiner* nor the *Daily News* published an article about the march.

The *California Eagle*, one of the city's African American weekly newspapers, in contrast, published a front-page article that reported that "shock quivered through Negro Los Angeles this week as news spread that Ku Klux Klansmen marched Saturday night from the steps of City Hall thru-out the downtown section." The article also noted that "prominent leaders" "severely lashed" the police for their failure "to halt the parade of Kluxers." The *Eagle* indicated that the march "was the first blatant indication of active local participation" in the Klan, whose rebirth "has been heralded for more than two years."[2] In her column, *Eagle* publisher Charlotta A. Bass declared that the Klan march "is an astounding blow to those citizens of the community who had believed Southern California to be outside the area bounded by the Mason-Dixon line." Bass also wrote that "those of us who have fought the battle against intolerance here over the years had deemed our victory won with regards to this vicious organization. If we were mistaken, very well; the battle will be started all over again."[3]

The *Eagle* published an editorial about the Klan in addition to a news article and Bass's column. The editorial insisted that "lest the precedent of this Klan demonstration become settled in the minds of our city gendarmerie, it is necessary that all those who are opposed to the Klan and Klan principles immediately register protests against the countenancing of the body 'in our fair city.'" The editorial declared that "the Ku Klux Klan is the perfect embodiment of all the things which it supposedly denounces—communism, fascism, nazism; these, aside from purely original notions of intolerance." Although the *Times* had simply depicted the Klan demonstration as an anti-Communist statement, the *Eagle* pointed out that the Klan viciously opposed and had committed outrages against "Catholics, Jews, Negroes, labor unions, and the foreign-born."[4]

The articles, column, and editorial discussed in the preceding paragraphs reveal that the Klan march in downtown Los Angeles at the end of March 1940 meant different things to different people. To the journalists at the *Los Angeles Times*, the march seems to have been merely a demonstration against Communism. To the African Americans who produced the *California Eagle*, however, the march was a sign that a group of people were trying to import patterns of race relations from the South to southern California. The march was also a call to action for these African Americans, who insisted that Klan activity must be met with vigorous protests.

The response of Los Angeles newspapers to this demonstration also reveals some important characteristics of public discourse in the city before World War II. Neither the *Times* nor the *Eagle* suggested that elected officials had expressed any concern about the march. This suggests that public officials, like the *Times*, did not see the presence of the Klan in the city as cause for concern. The fact that the *Times* did not mention the outrage of African Americans also suggests that African Americans were largely excluded from public discourse in the city. African Americans published several weekly newspapers, and some people outside the African American community may have read those newspapers. Journalists at the daily newspapers, however, apparently did not deem it necessary to report on the effects of the Klan demonstration on people who had historically been the targets of Klan violence.

In the chapters that follow, this book will examine a debate about the meanings of "race" that occurred during and after World War II. The response to the Klan march in 1940, however, suggests that this debate had not begun at that time. Two of the daily newspapers did not even report on the Klan march. The *Times* did not comment editorially on the march or publish any articles about protests against the Klan presence. Elected officials did not issue condemnations of the Klan or statements that contradicted those published in the *Eagle*. Instead, the daily newspapers and officials simply ignored the words published in the *Eagle*. Less than two years later, a lively debate about "race" would play out in the pages of the city's newspapers. Opponents of racial discrimination could not make a public statement without evoking responses from newspaper editors or elected officials. This was not the case, however, in 1940.

The response to the Klan march also suggests the presence of a hegemonic racial ideology. This set of beliefs held that discrimination was not a serious problem in Los Angeles, if it existed at all. At the heart of this hegemonic, traditional ideology, which the historian Peggy Pascoe has identified as "American racialism," was the belief that the differences among "races" of people were fundamental and immutable.[5] Within this ideology it was natural for members of different groups to live in separate neighborhoods, to work in different occupations, and to pursue recreational activities in different places. These phenomena simply reflected the fundamental differences among these groups of people. American racialism was the ideology of the Klan, and the fact that the *Times* did not mention the Klan's racial ideology suggests that there was nothing unusual or noteworthy about it.

Even though residents of Los Angeles did not engage in an open, public debate about the meanings of "race" until the second half of 1941, the responses to the Klan suggest that some residents of Los Angeles spoke and wrote about "race" prior to that time. This chapter will explore the ways in which people spoke and wrote about "race" before Pearl Harbor. It will draw on a number of examples, most notably the October 1941 hearing of the President's Committee on Fair Employment Practice, to show that daily newspapers rarely published articles directly about "race" or that quoted the words of African Americans, Mexican Americans, or Japanese Americans. The newspapers' refusal to allow members of these groups to express themselves implies a rejection of their arguments and suggests support for the traditional ideology of American racialism. The words of African Americans, Japanese Americans, and Mexican Americans, however, suggest a different set of beliefs about "race." Members of all these groups used the term *race*, which implies that they accepted the notion that people could be divided into separate groups on the basis of biological characteristics. At the same time, however, many rejected the idea that these characteristics made one "race" superior or inferior to another. Some expressed the belief that "racial" characteristics were superficial and that the existing social hierarchy based upon racial ideology should be eliminated. This set of beliefs tends toward what Pascoe has termed "modernist racial ideology."[6]

African Americans, Japanese Americans, Mexican Americans, and "Race"

In the months before Pearl Harbor, readers of any of the English-language daily newspapers would have found little mention in these papers of the city's African American, Japanese American, or Mexican American residents. The articles that most frequently mentioned African Americans were those that identified suspected criminals by their "race." The section of these newspapers that most often mentioned "race," however, was the classified advertisements. In the "help wanted" advertisements, readers would find requests for "Negro" maids, Japanese gardeners, and "white" secretaries. These advertisements suggest that a person's "race" meant that she or he was by nature suited for a particular occupation. Combined with the absence of African Americans, Japanese Americans, and Mexican Americans from other sections of the paper, these advertisements suggest the hegemony of traditional racialist ideology in Los Angeles before U.S. entry into World War II.

Complaints about racial discrimination were as common in the city's African American newspapers as they were absent from the mainstream press. These complaints frequently dealt with discrimination in different places around the United States, especially in the South. These frequent complaints suggest that most African Americans disagreed with the Anglo Americans who embraced traditional racialist ideology. African Americans rejected the notion that their "race" made them inferior to Anglo Americans and suited only to certain low-status occupations. Few articles and editorials, however, directly and explicitly criticized this ideology. Instead, they most forcefully criticized the discrimination based upon this ideology.

Even though African Americans most frequently mentioned "race" when they complained about Anglo Americans' discrimination against African Americans, their presence in Los Angeles sometimes led them to focus on the broader ramifications of racialist ideology. Los Angeles's multicultural character led some African Americans to compare their community with other groups. In a November 1939 radio broadcast, Charlotta A. Bass compared the "Oriental" and "Negro" communities in Los Angeles. Bass set out to explain why African Americans had not achieved the kind of economic success that Asian Americans had. Bass did not say explicitly that Asian Americans' racial characteristics had made them successful in southern California. She did, however, argue that heredity explained their success. "The remarkable fidelity to work found among most Orientals, their painstaking and earnest labor at any project, may be explained by the fact that most of them in the Los Angeles area are descendants of the ancient laboring classes, trained by ruthless overlords for centuries into a submissive acceptance of their duties," Bass said. On the other hand, she argued, African cultures had been destroyed by slave owners in North America. The destruction of African cultures meant that "the philosophy of Negroes differ with almost every individual . . . *there is no typical Negro*." The "remarkable sameness of thought and action" that had led to "the economic advancement of L.A.'s Orientals" was "at this time a rank impossibility for Negroes," Bass insisted. "Just now we are too occupied in a great psychological effort to adjust ourselves to the paradoxes of American life—the bewildering civilization that says we are free in one breath, and lynches us in the next. We are a people in search of a soul."[7] Even though

Bass's insistence that "there is no typical Negro" suggests that it made little sense to generalize about African Americans as a "race," Bass continued to depict African Americans as a distinct "people." Because Bass insisted that it was possible to generalize about "L.A.'s Orientals," her words bear comparison with the words of proponents of traditional American racialism. Like almost all other African American leaders, Bass rejected the notion that African Americans were inferior to "whites." However, she suggested that "racial" groups were characterized by certain inherited traits, even if slavery had prevented African Americans from inheriting the positive traits of their African ancestors.

Whereas Bass emphasized the differences among Asian Americans and African Americans, other African American community leaders recognized similarities among Los Angeles's racial minority groups. The most visible of these leaders was Floyd Covington. A native of Denver, Covington had come to Los Angeles after he graduated from Washburn University in Topeka, Kansas. He began serving as executive director of the Los Angeles Urban League in 1928, and he held that post for twenty-five years. In the late 1930s, Covington had developed a working relationship with some leaders of the Mexican American community in Los Angeles. Covington's annual reports to the National Urban League indicate that he argued for industrial training and employment for African Americans, Mexican Americans, and Asian Americans throughout the 1930s.[8] Members of other communities recognized Covington's interest in discrimination against all minority groups. He was asked to chair a session at the first meeting of El Congreso de Pueblos de Habla Española, the Spanish-Speaking People's Congress, in April 1939.[9]

Although Covington's presence at El Congreso suggests that he might have made public statements about the similarities among the experiences of African Americans, Mexican Americans, and Asian Americans, I have not found evidence of such public statements before October 1941. However, Covington did point out these similarities in a report he wrote in 1940 for the study that resulted in Gunnar Myrdal's *An American Dilemma.* Covington noted that "Mexicans, Orientals, and Negroes" were "very largely shunted together in the twilight zone areas and the problems of each parallel, although they are not identical." Covington further suggested that the physical proximity of these groups and their parallel problems opened "the possibility of working toward a tri-minority relationship."[10] Although

Covington's statement was not part of the public discourse about "race," it does provide insight into racial ideology in Los Angeles before Pearl Harbor. It is worth pointing out that Covington noticed similarities among the problems faced by African Americans, Mexican Americans, and Asian Americans but did not explicitly connect these similarities to racial ideology. When Covington did explicitly address racial ideology in his report, he cast it in terms that emphasized the origin of Anglo Americans' beliefs in the South. Covington blamed the decline in employment opportunities on the hundreds of thousands of Anglo Americans from the South who had moved to southern California in the 1930s. "The southernizing of California," he wrote, "is becoming a real factor in mitigating against employment opportunities for the Negro." Covington thought that California was "becoming a state as southern in influence as the states largely contributing to its population; namely, Texas and Oklahoma. On all sides can be sensed a general change of attitude toward the Negro, due to the impress of this southern influence on almost every activity within the community."[11]

Bass and Covington used the term *Oriental* to describe all of the Asian immigrants and their descendants in Los Angeles. Japanese Americans, however, more often described themselves as members of a distinct "Japanese race." Most Nisei writers used the term *Japanese* to describe all people of Japanese ancestry and the term *American* to describe a specific group of Americans—Anglo Americans.[12] Belonging to "the Japanese race," however, had different meanings for different people. Some Japanese Americans believed that the "Japanese race" was superior to other races. Historian David Yoo concluded from his study of Japanese American newspapers in the 1930s that many Japanese Americans saw themselves as superior to Filipinos.[13] Not all Japanese Americans, however, described the "Japanese race" as superior to other groups. Some, like Nisei columnist Mary Oyama, criticized Japanese Americans for their prejudices, particularly toward other Asian American groups. "It's about time we Nisei and we Japanese got over our prejudices. You must admit that a lot of us have them, too," Oyama wrote.[14] Some Japanese Americans, such as Oyama, seem to have recognized that the discrimination that they encountered as Japanese Americans rested on a racial ideology that was similar to if not exactly the same as their beliefs toward other Asian American groups. Some Japanese Americans seem to have been exposed to these new ideas about "race" in the courses they took in the social sciences at universities such as UCLA and USC.[15]

Statements of racial superiority and denunciations of racial prejudice among Japanese Americans were not as common as criticism of discrimination against Japanese Americans. The Japanese Americans who criticized housing discrimination did not argue that Japanese Americans should not endure such discrimination because they were better than other groups. At the same time, they generally did not explicitly challenge the racial ideology that underlay such discrimination. In a letter to *Rafu Shimpo*, for example, John F. Aiso did not dwell on the beliefs of people who had filed suit to enforce restrictive covenants. Instead, he suggested that Japanese Americans faced discrimination in part because they had not fully accepted their rights and responsibilities as Americans. Aiso urged Japanese Americans, especially members of "the Issei Community"—immigrants from Japan—to "blend ourselves into the main currents of American life." The welfare of Japanese Americans, Aiso argued, depended on their "shouldering our full measure of duties and demanding the correlative enjoyments which belong to every American citizen."[16]

Some Japanese Americans recognized that their experiences were in some ways comparable to the experiences of other racialized groups, but they more frequently described their situation as unique. One editorial in the English-language section of *Rafu Shimpo*, for example, acknowledged that the problem of restrictive covenants "cannot be studied apart from the larger issues of restrictions affecting other races." Most of this editorial, however, focused only on housing discrimination against Nisei—the second generation whose parents had come to the United States from Japan. Moreover, instead of suggesting that racial prejudice against Japanese Americans was similar to or related to prejudice against African Americans or other groups, the editorial stated that "one of the difficulties in solving the problem has been the outmoded conception of the American citizen nisei in the eyes of the average American citizen. That conception is generally 30 years behind the times and in nearly every particular inaccurate."[17]

Mexican Americans' statements about "race" reveal conflict within the community about the meaning of "race." This conflict reflected the ambiguous position that people of Mexican ancestry occupied within U.S. society. The federal government, whose policies to some extent mirrored societal attitudes about "race," did not characterize Mexicans as a distinct racial group. Instead, federal officials generally classified people of Mexican ancestry as "white" or "Caucasian." Some Mexican Americans embraced this classification and did not challenge the U.S. system of racial classification so long as they enjoyed the privileges of "whiteness." Others, however, did not accept the idea that they were "white," especially since most Mexican Americans faced discrimination in the United States.

People who saw themselves as members of a "Mexican race" tended to interpret the discrimination they confronted as racial discrimination. Some people, however, did not acknowledge the existence of a "Mexican race." Some of these people described discrimination against Mexican Americans as discrimination on the basis of nationality. Leaders of El Congreso de Pueblos de Habla Española—the Spanish-Speaking People's Congress, which was organized in 1938—generally avoided describing Mexicans as a "race." What Mexican immigrants, Mexican Americans, and Spanish-speaking residents of New Mexico, who generally described themselves as "Spanish Americans," had in common, organizers argued, was not racial; it was a cultural characteristic—they all spoke Spanish as their native tongue.[18] Communist party positions also influenced El Congreso's leaders' descriptions of Mexican Americans. Many of El Congreso's organizers were party members or had close ties to the party. The Communist party's position on Mexican Americans was enunciated in 1939, when Emma Tenayuca, a Mexican American Communist from Texas, and her husband, Homer Brooks, published "The Mexican Question in the United States" in *The Communist,* the party's theoretical journal. Tenayuca and Brooks identified ethnic Mexicans in the United States as an "oppressed national group" within the United States; they did not refer to Mexicans as a "racial" group. Instead, like most Communists, they argued that "racial" oppression was simply a form of class oppression and that Mexicans' "economic, and hence, their political interests are welded to those of the Anglo-American people of the Southwest."[19] El Congreso's positions often echoed those expressed by Tenayuca and Brooks. Delegates to the first national congress, held in Los Angeles in April 1939, approved a resolution that declared that "the Spanish-speaking people of the United States well recognize the fact that racial prejudice is caused by false theories of race supremacy based on biological and blood concepts and the low economic status of a racial group." This racial prejudice could be eradicated by education, the resolution said. The congress also endorsed "legislation outlawing all racial distinctions against the Spanish speaking people by public institutions, schools, neighborhoods and commercial enterprises."[20]

El Congreso, as an entity whose participants represented more than one hundred different organizations among Spanish-speaking people, found it difficult to maintain ideological purity. Some participants did describe Spanish-speaking people as a race. One banner at the first congress in April 1939, for example, said "We Ask for Justice and Equality for La Raza Latina [the Latin race]."[21] This use of the term *race* suggests that El Congreso participants had expanded the "Mexican race" to include other people of Latin American ancestry. This undoubtedly reflected the fact that many "Spanish Americans" from New Mexico refused to describe themselves as "Mexicans." Delegates to the second congress of the Spanish-speaking peoples of California, held in December 1939, were invited to participate in a cultural sub-session whose goal was the establishment "of a true CULTURAL COMMITTEE that will work towards elevating our CULTURAL standards and gaining recognition, merit and worth as a Cultured Race."[22] This statement suggests that some Spanish-speaking people continued to see themselves as a "race."

As the preceding paragraphs suggest, many African Americans, Japanese Americans, and Mexican Americans protested racial discrimination before U.S. entry into World War II. With a few exceptions, however, most people who protested discrimination focused exclusively on discrimination against members of their group. Moreover, these discussions rarely attacked the racial ideology that lay beneath all prejudice toward and discrimination against a single group.

The Beginnings of the Battle for Los Angeles

The debate about the meaning of "race" in Los Angeles began sometime after June 25, 1941. On that day, President Franklin D. Roosevelt issued Executive Order 8802, which outlawed discrimination on the basis of race, creed, or national origin by firms holding defense contracts with the U.S. government. The March on Washington Movement, an effort to have 100,000 African Americans gather in Washington, D.C., for a protest march, prompted Roosevelt to issue the executive order. A. Philip Randolph, the longtime leader of the Brotherhood of Sleeping Car Porters, had devised the March on Washington, which was canceled in response to the executive order. Executive Order 8802 created the President's Committee on Fair Employment Practice, more commonly known as the Fair Employment

Practice Committee or FEPC. The FEPC was empowered to investigate allegations of discrimination, to decide if discrimination existed, and then to urge offending employers and unions to comply with its rulings.[23]

The FEPC decided to conduct its first hearing in Los Angeles. According to the National Association for the Advancement of Colored People (NAACP), Los Angeles was chosen because of "the virtual exclusion of colored workers here from the booming industry." The committee's decision to hold its first hearing in southern California evoked an enthusiastic response from African Americans in the region. Every week the *Eagle* reminded its readers of the hearing and encouraged them to report all incidents of discrimination. The articles and editorials in this African American newspaper warned readers not to expect too much from the FEPC, but they also expressed the hope that the committee's ability to draw attention to discrimination would lead employers to hire more African Americans. As the following paragraphs indicate, articles and editorials in the *Eagle* did not clearly and explicitly depict supposedly racial differences between people as merely biological and superficial. Instead, they usually focused narrowly on the issue of discrimination. Some of these articles and editorials even suggested that in some cases an employer might be justified in denying employment to a person on the basis of racial characteristics.

The Eagle reported on September 18 that the hearing would occur on October 1 and 2, and it indicated that the NAACP, the National Negro Congress, and the Allied Organizations against National Defense Discrimination would collect testimony from people who had endured discrimination in local aircraft plants and shipyards.[24] By this time the NAACP, founded in 1909, had emerged as the leading national organization working against discrimination against African Americans. Its Los Angeles branch had been founded in 1914 and had a distinguished history of defending the rights of southern California's African Americans.[25] The National Negro Congress emerged from a 1935 conference on the economic status of African Americans held at Howard University. The organizers of the Congress tried to bring together all elements of the African American community, from ministers and business owners to members of the Communist party. Its supporters in Los Angeles included a number of African Americans who also maintained their affiliation with organizations such as the NAACP. The Allied Organizations against National Defense Discrimination had emerged from a January 1941 mass meeting sponsored by the Interdenominational Ministers' Alliance, the Baptist Ministers' Union, the NAACP, and the Twenty-eighth Street YMCA. The Allied Organizations included women's clubs, business and professional associations, unions, veterans' organizations, and several African American newspapers.[26]

In early October, when the *Eagle* reported that the hearing had been postponed so that local organizations had more time to gather evidence of discrimination, it also noted that the Allied Organizations against National Defense Discrimination and the NAACP had embarked an "an all-out community campaign to file and register every individual complaint of defense industry discrimination." According to representatives of these organizations, "the entire success of the investigation depends upon the immediate co-operation of all citizens who have been victimized by racial prejudice in defense employment." In order to facilitate this gathering of evidence, people who had encountered discrimination could register their complaints at the offices of the *Eagle*, the Urban League, and attorneys Thomas L. Griffith, Jr., and Loren Miller. Griffith was the president of the local branch of the NAACP. Complaints could also be lodged at the Twenty-eighth Street branch of the YMCA. The *Eagle* pointed out how important it was for its readers to document cases of discrimination. "The local hearings will be the first conducted by the federal FEPC since the President's formation of the body through his executive order outlawing defense employment discrimination several weeks ago," the *Eagle* stated. "Los Angeles' ability to establish a factual case against West Coast industry will set the national standard for FECP [*sic*] hearing."[27]

The *Eagle* reiterated this point in an editorial. The editorial declared that "the full blaze of a national spotlight is upon Los Angeles" because the West Coast had been the "loudest of all sections of the nation . . . in its cry of unfair discrimination against Negro workers in national defense industries." On the Pacific Coast "massive aviation plants which manufacture the greatest proportion of America's fighting aircraft have slammed shut their doors in the face of black labor." The editorial declared that the treatment of African Americans by California military contractors was "scandalous." "This we know," the *Eagle* stated.

It was not enough, however, to know that discrimination had occurred. According to the newspaper, "the city's responsibility reaches far beyond 'knowing' that Negroes have been subjected to unfair treatment." Los Angeles's African American residents had to prove that they had encountered discrimination—to "put up or shut up," according to the editorial. The *Eagle*'s editorial revealed the many ways in which discrimination might have influenced the hiring process. It published a list of questions that people needed to answer: "If we are discriminated against, just who has been discriminated against, individually? At what date? What time? Did he have witnesses? Was he really fit for employment? Did he fail the company's mathematics test? How much education did he have? How did he rate on the personality tests?" Although it may not have reflected a conscious decision on the part of the newspaper's editor and publisher, this set of questions depicted African American men as the victims of discrimination. Its exclusive use of masculine pronouns suggests that only men had applied for and been denied work in defense industries. The set of questions also makes clear how narrowly "discrimination" was being defined. An applicant apparently could fail "personality tests" and therefore not be suitable for employment. At this point, at least, the *Eagle* accepted the validity of a "mathematics test" and "personality tests" as measures for employment without raising questions about whether or not these tests measured any abilities that were essential to the jobs being filled. The *Eagle* editorial urged its readers to come forward with evidence of specific cases in which a person was not hired because *and only because* that person was an African American. "Now the fullest responsibility remains, as always, upon the mass of people. Every single case of asserted discrimination must be brought to the attention of persons qualified to present it before the FEPC." The editorial concluded with a reiteration of the historic significance of the FEPC's decision to hold its first hearing in Los Angeles. "The choice of Los Angeles as the first source of investigation by the President's specially appointed Committee on Fair Employment Practices has placed upon us the burden of proof. This proof we possess in full measure. We must not hesitate in bringing it to light."[28]

The next week the *Eagle* published a short article that identified the members of the FEPC and a longer article that explained the hearing process for its readers. The shorter article included descriptions of the position on "racial affairs" taken by each of the committee's members. The article suggested that four of the members of the committee were strongly opposed to racial discrimination, but the other three members' commitment to racial equality was suspect. It described Mark S. Ethridge, the editor of the *Louisville Courier-Journal* and the chair of the committee, as "an outstanding example of the 'young South's' revulsion against ante-bellum prejudices." Lawrence W. Cramer, the committee's secretary, the article noted, was "known for his liberal viewpoint on racial affairs." Two of the committee's members, Earl B. Dickerson and Milton T. Webster, were clearly identified as African Americans. Of Dickerson, a Chicago alderman, the article stated that "he battled successfully before the U.S. Supreme Court in the Hansberry residential restriction case, which smashed healthily at jim-crow housing in Chicago." The article described Webster only as "the right-hand man of A. Philip Randolph" in the Brotherhood of Sleeping Car Porters. The article reported that William Green, the president of the American Federation of Labor "works with Negro labor leaders, but to date has failed in effective opposition to race hatred within the AFL." In its mention of Philip Murray, the head of the Congress of Industrial Organizations, the article noted that the CIO "is active against racial discrimination in employment, though often 'talking louder' than it acts." Finally, the article indicated that David Sarnoff, the president of the National Broadcasting Company "is not well known as a liberal."[29] This article, then, suggested that African Americans in Los Angeles should trust a bare majority of the seven members. Two of the remaining three, while stating their opposition to discrimination, had not effectively prevented or eradicated discrimination within the organizations they headed.

In the longer article, John Kinloch reported that the "function of the committee is to corral factual data on discrimination against Negroes in firms holding government defense contracts and in the Federal civil service." Kinloch informed his readers that they could not, therefore, report complaints against private industry without military contracts or against state, county, and city agencies. Kinloch also noted that "it is assumed that the FEPC is convinced that Negroes should be employed without discrimination in defense industries and that they should be given all available defense training. Therefore speeches on the subject will be ruled out." Kinloch pointed out that individuals could present evidence of discrimination before the committee, but "it is felt that a more effective presentation can be made through one of the racial organizations gathering data and prepared to present it to the best legal advantage."

After describing what the hearing would be like, Kinloch then presented a "survey of conditions at the various plants" in "the Southland's phenomenal aircraft industry." He reported that "Douglas Aircraft was the first major aircraft firm in this area to open its doors to skilled Negro labor."

As of October 1941, however, Douglas had only "about 9" African American employees. Kinloch quoted North American Aviation's "crusty president, J. H. Kindelberger," who had announced several months earlier that "I will not hire Negroes in skilled positions regardless of their qualifications." According to Kinloch, "it is believed Kindelberger's flat, fascistic announcement hastened Mr. Roosevelt's executive order 'outlawing' National Defense discrimination and setting up the FEPC." Kinloch noted that "there are something less than 10 Negroes employed as janitors at North American." Kinloch identified the recent elimination of discriminatory practices at Lockheed-Vega's four southern California plants as "the bright spot of local aircraft employment." Lockheed-Vega employed twenty African Americans in skilled positions.

Kinloch's article concluded by offering an answer to the question "What good will the FEPC do?" Kinloch pointed out that the FEPC had the power to cancel government contracts, but "it is generally believed that the FEPC holds no real threat against biased Big Business. Tying up of production schedules on vitally needed defense equipment as a punitive measure for racial discrimination is something which it is not now believed the government will do." However, the FEPC hearing might "serve to re-emphasize the President's executive order and to marshall [*sic*] an impressive array of facts upon the American Negro's true economic position."[30]

On October 9 the *Eagle* published another editorial about discrimination in the aircraft industry and the scheduled FEPC hearing. This editorial marveled at the transformation of the aircraft industry in Los Angeles, declaring that "there is a magnificence in the energy of America, once she swings into action. There is an unbounded power, a sort of practical genius, at the heart of this nation." It was, however, "heartbreaking to realize that in the midst of such superb industry and ingenuity there are the poisonous germs of racial hatred and discrimination. In the midst of material plenty there is a spiritual drought." The *Eagle* insisted that "every tenet of the supposed American Way of Life is smashed in the practice of race prejudice." When "a man" was denied "his rightful place within industry because his skin is dark," the American commitment to "sportsmanship" rang hollow. Laws such as the "poll tax law" undercut the American commitment to democracy.

The *Eagle* blamed "the triumph of prejudice over America's conscience" on both hatred and indifference. "Those who have the vile initiative to engage in active propaganda against Negroes, to spill over with indignant repulsion at the thought of 'social equality,' are not much worse than the countless millions of indifferent Americans who stand by permitting the pollution and degradation of our fondest beliefs," the *Eagle* declared. The editorial then criticized what it depicted as the timid actions of the federal government. "Without seriously assaulting the basic lie of prejudice—white supremacy—the government attempts to mollycoddle industry into a recognition of ordinary human rights." The *Eagle* suggested that the FEPC hearing was an attempt to "mollycoddle industry into a recognition of ordinary human rights," although it acknowledged that the FEPC's accumulation of evidence of discrimination "will be eminently worthwhile." The editorial warned African Americans not to "raise their hopes too high; for, with all its aura of Federal authority, the FEPC has little real power."

The editorial concluded by arguing, contrary to the statements of U.S. officials, that it was possible to change "the customs of a people." "If all the agencies of a powerful central government are brought to bear upon some vital item of public education, the public is educated!" As evidence that racial discrimination could be obliterated quickly, the editorial pointed to the Soviet Union. "Twenty years ago, Russia was a hodgepodge of racial enmity more vicious and complex than anything we have in America today," the *Eagle* declared. "Yet today all the people of Russia fight their common enemy with a mutual devotion and a courage equal to anything in world history." The editorial argued that the elimination of racial hatred in the Soviet Union was not the result of a "gradual shift in 'the customs of the people.'" Instead, "it is the product of deliberate education and militant laws against the practice of race chauvinism and discrimination." Quoting a letter from Soviet diplomat Andrei Gromyko, the editorial pointed out that "all attempts at introducing racial discrimination" in the Soviet Union "are punishable by law." The *Eagle* insisted that "the United States, though opposed to many of the Russian economic innovations, can well mimic the U.S.S.R. in her uncompromising and victorious battle against racial bigotry."[31]

It would be easy to dismiss this editorial in the *Eagle* as evidence of support for Communism among the newspaper's staff. In fact, over the course of the war, many people in Los Angeles did tend to dismiss the pro-Communist position of the oldest of Los Angeles's African American newspapers. Yet this editorial also reveals something important about the meaning of "race" in Los Angeles. This editorial implicitly suggested that African Americans were equal to Americans of European ancestry. It explicitly declared that the notion that European Americans were superior to African Americans was a "lie." In its statement that people faced discrimination because their "skin is dark," the editorial implied that all people were equal "under the skin," although it did not state this explicitly.

In the last issue it published before the hearing, the *Eagle* reported that FEPC member Earl B. Dickerson had already arrived in Los Angeles and that "a great number of complaints are being made alleging discrimination on account of race, creed, color and national origin in local defense industry." The *Eagle* also expressed the expectation that "the names of companies and government agencies allegedly practicing discrimination will be released before the end of the week."[32] The *Eagle* published nearly a full page of photographs that it said portrayed the "FEPC Problem." Two of these photographs, however, showed African American workers at the Lockheed plant in Burbank. Three others depicted generic scenes of aircraft and ship production.[33] In her October 16 column, *Eagle* publisher Charlotta Bass declared the FEPC hearing in Los Angeles "the biggest news of the year." The hearing, she wrote, "will write history that may well govern the national policy of Negroes for the next several years." The hearing meant that "a terrifying responsibility rests upon Los Angeles. We must present such a wall of factual data on discrimination in national defense industry that the Committee will have no excuse for not taking immediate militant action against those who offend the principles of equal opportunity upon which this government is supposedly founded." Bass insisted that "every Angeleno who has the slightest information concerning specific cases of discrimination against Negroes in local defense industries" should "BRING THAT INFORMATION TO THE ATTENTION OF INVESTIGATORS IMMEDIATELY." Bass stated that "the Federal government has set up the machinery of a thorough-going inquiry at huge expense and after the greatest minority group 'pressure' campaign in U.S. history. The ball is now in our hands—we, the citizens of Los Angeles. WE CANNOT FUMBLE IT."[34]

In contrast to the *Eagle,* which publicized the hearing for weeks in advance and urged African Americans to report evidence of discrimination, the daily newspapers published only brief notices of the FEPC hearing. The *Daily News,* for example, simply noted in a brief October 10 article that "a series of OPM [Office of Production Management] committee hearings to investigate alleged discriminatory practices of California firms in the employment of labor because of race or creed will be conducted here

October 20 and 21."[35] The *Daily News* published another short article on October 16, but it never offered its readers information about how to contact the officials who were in charge of the hearing.[36] The day the hearing began the *Daily News* published a longer article noting that "racial groups who have long complained that defense industries, particularly aircraft, will not employ their members, will get a chance to unburden themselves today." The article identified the members of the FEPC and the Los Angeles residents who were scheduled to speak before the committee. It also explained the purpose of the hearing, as expressed by Ethridge.[37] The *Times* published a similar article the day before the hearing began.[38] The *Los Angeles Examiner* also published a brief article on October 16 and another on October 19. These articles simply reported when and where the hearing would take place.[39]

The FEPC Hearing

Although the *Eagle* had depicted the FEPC hearing as part of an investigation of discrimination specifically against African Americans, more than twenty-five witnesses from several different ethnic groups appeared before the committee on October 20, the first day of its two-day hearing. Seven of these people represented military contractors. Most of the rest came to argue that these contractors and some unions discriminated against African Americans, Japanese Americans, and Mexican Americans. Some of the witnesses indicated an awareness of the diversity of Los Angeles's population. Several drew attention to discrimination against several different racial and religious groups. Most, however, focused quite specifically on discrimination against members of a specific group. Several African Americans described employers who practiced racial discrimination as "fascists" or "Nazis." These witnesses, however, generally did not challenge the idea that "race" was a meaningful concept, even though they rejected the belief that African Americans, Japanese Americans, and Mexican Americans were inferior to Anglo Americans.

In their statements to the committee, these witnesses, most of whom were African Americans, sometimes described Los Angeles as a unique place. Hugh Macbeth, an attorney and the Liberian Consul in Los Angeles, for example, described Los Angeles as "this fair land where the East meets the West, and the South brings the soft color and romance of Latin America to temper the rush and materialism of the North."[40] Dorothy Guinn, the executive secretary of the Twelfth Street Branch of the YWCA, suggested that Los Angeles's unique character could help to end discrimination. She told the committee that "Los Angeles is a melting pot of races and nationalities. It is a great city in which live and are coming to live large groups of minority people against which much prejudice exists." Guinn also described Los Angeles as "a new and growing community where the pattern of hatred has not yet been set." She praised many of the city's Anglo residents, saying that "in Los Angeles there are many of the finest, most genuine white Americans, native Californians, who are as gracious and friendly to minority groups as is our sunshine." Ironically, Guinn did not regard the FEPC's presence in Los Angeles as a sign of serious problems within the city. Instead, she told the committee that "it is indeed an honor and privilege that has been conferred upon Los Angeles to have been selected as the first place for the hearings on fair employment practices."[41]

In describing Los Angeles as a "melting pot," some of these witnesses claimed to speak for people other than African Americans. Macbeth, for example, said that

> it should be borne in mind that the American Negro of today comprises all colors, creeds and racial strains of mankind. We leave [*sic*] in peace and happiness with Jew and Gentile, Catholic and Protestant, English and Germans, Italians and Japanese, Mexican and Chinese and all others. In short, we have been impregnated with the blood of all peoples, and we have never refused any race, creed, or nationality the hospitality of our homes, our neighborhoods and our living, meager as it is. We do not hate any race, creed, or color of mankind. We are of them all.[42]

Floyd Covington, the executive director of the Los Angeles Urban League, did not claim that he was of all races, creeds, and colors, but he said that he could speak for members of other groups "by virtue of the large number of friends and acquaintances in both the Negro group and the second generation Japanese group, Filipino and Spanish-speaking group."[43] In claiming to speak for members of other groups, these African American community leaders insisted that the problem of discrimination was not simply a problem endured by African Americans.

Some witnesses directly attacked white supremacist ideology. In his statement before the committee, for example, Laurence F. La Mar of the Eastside Chamber of Commerce, an association of African American business owners, declared that "the American has No Color, but is a component of all colors" and that "the American has no particular religion, but has all religions." Therefore, La Mar argued, "the setting up of an aristocracy or 'elite' of 'white skin,' is a presumption, that has no foundation in fact. Conversely, we argue the segregation, separation, ostracism or discrimination of any particular race, color or creed by and into involuntary groups is Un American and unlawful." La Mar insisted that "we are Americans; not Italians, Englishmen, Irishmen, or Germans, or Negroes. To stand aloof as any one of the above group is to be an 'isolationist' of the lowest sort. To force or intimidate the individual into any one of these groups against his will is un-American and cruel."[44]

Several of the African American witnesses described specific incidents of racial discrimination and identified discriminatory hiring policies. Rev. J. L. Caston of Trinity Baptist Church, for example, told the committee about "two Negro youths" who had completed a National Youth Administration job training program. When these two young men were referred to the Consolidated aircraft plant in San Diego, they "were told to go get one year's work experience."[45] La Mar referred to a memo indicating that only "unmarried white youth" would be accepted into aircraft training schools and a letter signed by the president of Douglas Aircraft that "declares the intention of that company to never hire Negroes, Mexicans, etc."[46] C. E. Pearl, representing the National Negro Congress, quoted from an August 1940 letter from W. Gerard Tuttle, the industrial relations manager at Vultee Aircraft, indicating that "it is not the policy of this company to employ people other than of Caucasian Race." Like other witnesses, Pearl pointed out that not only African Americans faced employment discrimination. At one time, Pearl said, "the National Youth Administration, whose policy was made to conform to the policy of aircraft, did not refer for training Negro, Jewish, or dark-skinned Mexican youths."[47]

One witness, however, rejected the notion that individuals should have to prove that they had endured discrimination. Baxter Scruggs, the executive secretary of the Twenty-eighth Street YMCA, told the committee that "the mere fact that national defense firms are unable to show a reasonable number of non-white workers in the different job classifications is sufficient evidence of racial discrimination." Companies accused of discrimination "cannot escape their guilt by answering the cry of race discrimination with a demand for legal proof. The four freedoms we defend not only carry a legal implication but, above all, they demand a moral fulfillment of the obligations of democracy." Like Pearl, Scruggs did not focus exclusively on African Americans. He insisted that "the impact of this race discrimination is insidiously breaking the dikes of morale for thousands of minority group citizens," and he mentioned "firms which flatly refuse to employ any Negro, Japanese or Mexican."[48]

Several witnesses did not confine their remarks to specific incidents of discrimination or specific discriminatory policies that violated Executive Order 8802. Some witnesses also criticized state agencies and programs and the U.S. military, over which the FEPC had no jurisdiction. Caston, for example, pointed out that California state policies had exacerbated the problem of employment discrimination. He mentioned that state officials had "seized upon the expanded defense work opportunities to make drastic regulations and reductions" in the state's relief program. State officials did not acknowledge the existence of employment discrimination. Because officials assumed that "all persons had equal opportunity to be employed," Caston said, "hundreds of Negroes were cut off by the State and County, working tremendous hardships on many Negro families and shattering the morale and sometimes the health of those workers affected."[49] La Mar suggested that the FEPC inquiry would not have any real or lasting results unless it also involved an investigation of segregation in the U.S. military.[50] In response to La Mar's suggestion that the FEPC should investigate segregation in the U.S. military, committee member Earl Dickerson pointed out that Executive Order 8802 did not give the committee jurisdiction over the military.[51]

Guinn and Miss Jessie Terry both pointed out that women as well as men faced employment discrimination. Terry told the committee that "if men are generally discriminated against in defense industry, then women are discriminated against more so." She reported that "it is very, very hard at any time for women to find employment in the sphere for which they are fitted, and I don't believe there has been but one woman integrated into the defense program in Los Angeles, and that happened I think last week." Terry also said that "we do feel very keenly the fact that women are being discriminated against, and we want something done to assure us that you are going to integrate into defense industry the unemployed women, especially single women." Although Terry suggested that employment was more important for single women than for women with families, she did point out that "there are many women who are heads of families and who are breadwinners for their families."[52] When she was questioned by Dickerson, Terry pointed out that many aircraft manufacturers employed "women generally," but none of them employed African American women.[53] Guinn told the committee that African American girls and "girls who happen to be of the Oriental race or who are Mexican" all faced job discrimination in Los Angeles. She also argued that "the young man who marries the Negro girl cannot attain the full stature of manhood as head of the family because in industry and in government service he is barred from work in spite of training because of color." As a result of "the inadequate wage of her husband," "the Negro wife is overburdened with the need to leave her home and children to seek employment," Guinn said. The YWCA official warned that discrimination could lead African Americans "to become easy prey to cults and causes, inimicable to the American way of life," and this would be a "social waste of manpower."[54]

African American witnesses frequently connected employment discrimination with fascism. Caston, for example, referred to employers who practiced discrimination as "American fascists" and told the committee that "we will not desert the citadel of democracy. We propose to defend it against Hitlerism here or abroad."[55] Scruggs also referred to discrimination as "Hitlerism."[56] Macbeth referred to employers who discriminated against African Americans as "elements of Fascism and Nazism." He also insisted that "it were far better to have one-half the guns, airplanes, tanks and other instruments of death for our arsenal of democracy created by democratic, fair employment processes, than to produce twice the amount under Nazi, Fascistic racially intolerant processes."[57]

Not all the witnesses who appeared before the FEPC were African Americans. One Japanese American, Mike Masaoka, testified before the committee. Masaoka was a field secretary for the Japanese American Citizens League (JACL). The JACL had emerged at the end of the 1920s from a number of Japanese American "loyalty leagues" in Pacific Coast cities. JACL leaders tended to be older Nisei born at the end of the nineteenth century or in the first years of the twentieth century. They were often professionals, such as lawyers, doctors, and dentists, or the owners or managers of small businesses that served the Japanese American community. Throughout the 1930s the JACL tended to depict the Nisei as loyal, patriotic Americans.[58] In his testimony, Masaoka pointed out that international tensions had exacerbated employment discrimination against Japanese Americans. "Even in normal times," he pointed out, "the lot of the Japanese Americans in securing and retaining employment is a difficult one." During the tense days of 1941, he said, "our position is even more difficult, for not only are we up against the prejudices which were rampant in normal times but also against a fallacious type of reasoning which either suspects our loyalty and allegiance to the United States or assumes that we are responsible for the activities of the Imperial Japanese government."

Masaoka emphasized the fact that Japanese Americans were "racially" Japanese by contrasting them with other ethnic groups. He argued that "because of our physical make-up we cannot camouflage our racial identity by changing our names, as certain other nationality groups may have done, and so, we are branded wherever we may go." He declared discrimination against Japanese Americans "un-American and undemocratic." Masaoka described a number of ways in which employers discriminated against Japanese Americans: some cited policies against the hiring of "Orientals," while others "reject Japanese after giving oral examinations of technical and difficult nature on unrelated subjects." Masaoka pointed out, however, that almost all Japanese Americans who reported discrimination refused to come forward publicly. "Most of these persons are afraid of unfavorable publicity, personal embarrassment, and future repercussions."

Like most of the African American witnesses, Masaoka emphasized the importance of eliminating discrimination. He told the committee that "these are times when national unity, solidarity, and mutual confidence and respect are most vital to the common cause of preserving liberty and freedom here in these United States. In this great task, there cannot be race, color, or creed—there can be only Americans." Without referring to people who practiced discrimination as "fascists," Masaoka warned that "we cannot expect unstinted loyalty and allegiance from those to whom we refuse the right to 'life, liberty, and the pursuit of happiness.' We cannot expect a unified nation when we discriminate against certain individuals and races on the basis of color and creed, and not on the basis of personal merit and worth."[59]

Attorney Manuel Ruiz appeared before the committee as a representative of Mexican Americans in Los Angeles. The son of immigrants from Mazatlán, Ruiz was born in Los Angeles in 1905. He graduated at the top of his class from Manual Arts High School in 1923. Ruiz earned his law degree from the University of Southern California in 1930 and established his own practice in Los Angeles in the same year. He began his statement to the committee by contrasting Mexican Americans with other groups. "Unlike some other racial groups, the American of Mexican extraction has never been a pressure group," he said. He reported that even though there were about 250,000 people "of Latin American extraction" in Los Angeles, "the largest concentrated minority group by far," there were "no judges of Latin American extraction on the local or Superior Court bench." Ruiz suggested that many judgeships were filled "by persons who have been usually pushed forward by other minority groups." Ruiz attributed the fact that there were no Mexican American judges in Los Angeles to "the fact that assimilation of these people into our body politic is occurring at a greater speed than can be checked by consciousness of national and racial origin." Ruiz suggested that this rapid assimilation was a result of the fact that "we are a little more fortunate than the Japanese in that many of our people are not stamped physically, . . . and some of us get lost in the general social setup."

Even though Ruiz suggested that most people "of Latin American extraction" had rapidly "assimilated," he admitted that there were "those who are caught in the throes of discriminatory practices. Although they consider themselves as Americans, they are treated by thoughtless citizens as distinct and inferior. They are victims of frustration and inhibitions and all of the consequent evils which all of us aware [*sic*] result from that." Ruiz pointed out that the FEPC's complaint form was published in the Sunday edition of *La Opinión*, and he suggested that it would be a good idea to have one member of the committee be "of Latin American extraction." He also suggested that companies that refused to abandon discriminatory practices should be fined.[60]

Ruiz's lack of focus on employment discrimination troubled John Brophy, the CIO representative on the FEPC. In response to a question from Brophy, Ruiz identified one specific instance of discrimination. In this case, the applicant "was told very definitely that by reason of the fact that he was a dark Mexican he was not wanted."[61] Ruiz also said that he understood that some people "of Latin American extraction" were employed in the defense industries, but he added that "insofar as local Mexicans are concerned, I personally do not know of any that are being employed." Brophy said to Ruiz, "I am sure that you appreciate the fact that your statements have been pretty general." The CIO representative on the FEPC also told Ruiz, "I think it is very important that your group so organize its activities as to emphasize this particular complaint as to discrimination as it affects national defense plants and industries."[62]

Dr. Victor M. Egas, speaking on behalf of "the large Spanish-American colony of Los Angeles," presented testimony that differed from Ruiz's testimony. He began by stating that "it is with regret that the citizens of this community confess the patent existence within its borders of deleterious racial, religious and nationality discrimination." Most of Egas's testimony, however, dwelled on the difficulty of convincing victims of discrimination to come forward to complain. "A long and sad experience," he said, "demonstrates that the complaints of a victim have frequently been punished with additional cruel pressures or indirect ostracism by the powers that be, resulting often in provoking a cataclysm in the victim's family." Egas said that Spanish Americans were hopeful about the FEPC's hearing. "Some members of the colony, based on prior experience, are dubious; but they are hopeful for the best; nevertheless, they are not desirous of speaking up. There have been too many martyrs for the cause in the past without avail."[63]

The Employers Respond

After representatives of minority groups testified before the committee, employers and union leaders offered rebuttals. Some of the managers and public relations officers who testified before the FEPC admitted that their firms employed few members of minority groups. Douglas Aircraft's Perry A. Neal, the personnel director, and A. M. Rochlan, the public relations director, told the committee that only ten of the company's thirty-three thousand employees in its four plants were African Americans. Douglas also employed "four or five Japanese, four or five Chinese, seven or eight Indians, a large number of Mexicans, and several hundred Jewish people." Neal and Rochlan did not attribute the small number of minority employees to discrimination. Neal said that the airplane manufacturer's personnel officers were aware of Executive Order 8802 and had "been told specifically in their interviews with men, that the color of their skin, religion or race should not be considered." Douglas Aircraft had few minority employees, Neal and Rochlan said, because only a handful had applied for jobs.[64]

Some managers and union representatives expressed surprise when told that people had filed complaints of discrimination against their firms or unions. Rodney Edward Van Devander of the Bethlehem Shipbuilding

Corporation acknowledged that only two African Americans—both hired the day of the hearing—were among his firm's nearly three thousand employees, and he said that no Japanese Americans had applied for jobs. According to an FEPC summary of the hearing, Van Devander "was surprised to hear that an affidavit had been filed by a Japanese alleging that he had been refused employment at the San Pedro yard and promised to investigate and report to the Committee."[65] Southern California District Council of Laborers representative James J. Bardwell "was surprised at the complaints of discrimination against Negro workers. He agreed to work with the Committee to straighten out the complaints."[66]

One military contractor blamed its discrimination on the prejudices of white workers. The Hercules Foundry Company employed between 175 and 200 people, 40 percent of whom were African Americans and Mexican Americans. Walter P. Spreckels, labor relations counsel for the company, said that white workers threatened not to work with African Americans if they were promoted from laborers to core makers and molders.[67]

Two witnesses rescinded earlier statements and insisted that their companies no longer practiced discrimination. Dick Coleman, an industrial relations counselor representing the Paulsen and Nardon Company, retracted a statement by the company's president, who had vowed that "he would not hire Negroes if he could help it." Coleman pledged that the company would not discriminate.[68] W. G. Tuttle, the director of industrial relations for Vultee Aircraft, had told the National Negro Congress in August 1940 that Vultee would only hire "Caucasians." At the time of the hearing, however, he reported that Vultee's policy "is definitely to hire on the basis of the applicant's qualifications for the job for which they are to be employed regardless of race, color, creed or origin." Although Tuttle said that Vultee no longer engaged in employment discrimination, he did report that ten to fifteen African Americans had applied for work since June 1941. All were rejected on the basis of their qualifications for the jobs. As a result, Vultee had no African American employees at the time of the FEPC hearing.[69]

Representatives of two corporations told the committee that they had embarked on programs to attract minority workers. Leland R. Taylor, assistant to the president of North American Aviation, said that North American "was working with the State Employment Bureau and the Urban League in an effort to comply with Executive Order 8802 and had indicated to the Employment Bureau its desire to employ Negroes in clerical as well as production work."[70] R. Randall Irwin, industrial relations director for Lockheed Aircraft Corporation and Vega Airplane Company, said that "the problem of integrating Negroes with a minimum of confusion was studied for many months before affirmative steps were taken." Lockheed-Vega officials consulted the Urban League before they implemented their "affirmative action" program. Corporate executives made certain that application forms did not ask for race or creed, implemented a system in which each job applicant was interviewed by at least two interviewers "to minimize the possibility of personal prejudices," and informed supervisors that they would not tolerate discrimination. According to Irwin, the program had yielded impressive results. After one month Lockheed-Vega had more African American employees than any other large military contractor in Los Angeles. Fifty-four of Lockheed-Vega's forty-eight thousand employees were African Americans at the time of the hearing.[71] North American's program appears to have had less dramatic results. Only eight employees in its Inglewood Plant were African Americans.[72]

The small number of minority workers in aircraft plants and shipyards seems to have impressed FEPC members more than military contractors' expressions of compliance and surprise. In its "Recommendations and Findings," the committee said that companies with an insufficient number of minority employees had most likely practiced discrimination. The FEPC insisted that these companies had to take action to increase the number of minority employees. The committee declared that employers could not require job applicants to reveal their race or religion, and it insisted that companies that had previously announced discriminatory policies had to make the public aware that their policies had changed. In addition to making the public aware of changed policies, the FEPC said, employers needed to review the attitudes of their personnel interviewers and examiners. They also needed to establish procedures by which claims of discrimination could be investigated. Finally, the committee reiterated that labor unions that excluded minorities and had contracts with military contractors were in violation of Executive Order 8802.[73]

Newspapers and the FEPC Hearing

The newspaper coverage of the FEPC hearing is also revealing. The daily newspapers tended to emphasize employers' denials of discrimination more than the statements of African Americans, Mexican Americans, or

Japanese Americans. In an article describing the hearing, for example, the *Daily News* quoted Neal, the personnel manager for Douglas Aircraft; Taylor, of North American Aviation; and Spreckels, of Hercules Foundry. After twenty-eight paragraphs describing the testimony of these witnesses, the article quoted the words with which Ethridge had opened the hearing. The article's final five paragraphs described the testimony of the first two witnesses, Caston and David Coleman of B'nai B'rith, who had described discrimination against Jews.[74]

After the second day of the hearing, the *Daily News* did publish the statements of some people who reported specific incidents of discrimination. The newspaper also inadvertently revealed the ways in which racial prejudice might have influenced the hiring process. It quoted the words of Randall Irwin, industrial relations manager for Lockheed. "In hiring a man the first requisite that we look for and the major requirement is the man's attitude or temperament," Irwin stated. "He must have a healthy outlook on life and be well adapted to work with a large group of individuals." Irwin's words reveal the degree to which hiring was based on subjective criteria. In an environment in which many people undoubtedly expected certain attitudes or behaviors to be associated with a person's "race," it seems likely that the people who interviewed and hired employees for Lockheed interpreted certain attitudes or behaviors as unsuitable for the company's employees.[75]

Like the *Daily News*, the *Examiner* emphasized the statements of representatives of military contractors, who denied that their companies had engaged in discrimination. The *Examiner* quoted at length the statement of David Coleman of B'nai B'rith, but it did not identify by name any of the fourteen African American witnesses who appeared before the committee. It did report that "representatives of numerous Negro organizations constituted a majority of speakers" "during the morning session" of the hearing, but it devoted only three paragraphs to these speakers' statements about discrimination.[76] The *Examiner*'s coverage of the FEPC hearing graphically reveals the fact that daily newspapers in Los Angeles tended to silence the voices of African Americans.

Unlike the *Daily News* and the *Examiner*, which emphasized employers' denials of discrimination more than the charges brought by African American, Japanese American, and Mexican American community leaders, the *Times* identified by name and briefly mentioned the statements of

George Beavers, Rev. J. L. Caston, Baxter S. Scruggs, Laurance F. La Mar, Hugh Macbeth, and C. E. Pearl. The final ten paragraphs of the article in the *Times* reported on the words of the representatives of military contractors. All of these representatives denied that their firms engaged in racial discrimination.[77]

In contrast to the daily newspapers, the *Eagle* placed the emphasis in its article on the words of FEPC Chair Mark F. Ethridge. As the hearing opened, the *Eagle* reported, Ethridge announced "all of us feel that we are engaged in an effort in which every hand that can run a machine must be used; an effort in which every skilled and loyal workman must have an opportunity to participate in the common defense." The *Eagle* also dwelled upon Ethridge's statement that the FEPC had determined that discrimination did exist. It reported that Ethridge had announced that "during the short life of this committee, we have received and investigated complaints in sufficient numbers to indicate that discrimination does exist." Repeating the words of several of the African Americans who had appeared before the committee, Ethridge said that "we cannot afford to play Hitler's game of indulging in Fascism and prejudices while we are attempting to destroy him." The article pointed out that "the major aircraft companies were given definite orders that they were to follow out the orders of President Roosevelt in hiring all men, regardless of race, creed or color in their industries." The *Eagle* also noted that representatives of the aircraft manufacturers agreed not to discriminate, "with the exception of the Vultee Company, which was scored by chairman Mark Ethridge as being 'the most negative company toward this investigation of discrimination in industries of any that has been cited here for these hearings.'"[78]

Conclusion

The statements made by African American, Japanese American, and Mexican American community leaders and by Anglo American employers, as well as the newspapers' reports on the FEPC testimony, reveal the contours of the public discourse surrounding "race" in Los Angeles before Pearl Harbor. The words of most employers and the reports in the English-language daily newspapers show that many powerful Anglo Americans did not characterize their refusal to employ African Americans, Asian Americans, or Mexican Americans as discrimination. These employers argued that their refusal to hire specific employees was not a result of racial prejudice. Newspaper articles lent support to the statements of employers by repeating them and failing to report the statements of people who insisted that discrimination had occurred. Taken together, the statements of employers and newspaper articles hinted at the existence of a hegemonic racial ideology. According to this ideology, discrimination did not exist; African Americans, Asian Americans, and Mexican Americans simply did not have the abilities needed to work in aircraft factories. The words of African Americans, Asian Americans, and Mexican Americans showed that they rejected this ideology, which they associated with Hitler. Most argued that the fact that so few members of their groups worked in the aircraft industry constituted proof of discrimination. As the FEPC hearing suggests, the impending war had already begun to change how Los Angeles residents spoke and wrote about "race." A cataclysmic event—the Japanese attack on Pearl Harbor—led to an even more noticeable debate about the meanings of "race."

TWO

"While We Are at War with their Race"

Pearl Harbor, "Race," and Japanese Americans

Japanese fighter planes and bombers attacked the U.S. naval base at Pearl Harbor, in the U.S. territory of Hawai'i, just before 8 AM (10 AM in Los Angeles) on Sunday, December 7, 1941. An hour and a half later, the major radio networks broadcast the news of the attack. According to the *Los Angeles Times*, "every man and woman" in the city was "electrified by the news that Japan had struck at this country." The *Times* also reported that the city was "stunned at first, incredulous that Japan actually had bombed Pearl Harbor defenses" and "set buzzing as the news flashed through the streets."[1] The Los Angeles residents who expressed shock at the news of the attack on Pearl Harbor included many Japanese Americans. Gongoro Nakamura, the president of the Central Japanese Association in Los Angeles, told a *Daily News* reporter that he was "stunned" by news of the attack.[2] The *Times* reported that "a Japanese of about 50" who had read a bulletin pasted to a wall said, "I can't believe that the Japanese government would order such an attack." He suggested that Germans might have "got hold of Japanese planes and carried out the bombing."[3]

Not all Los Angeles residents seem to have reacted to the news of the attack with shock or concern. Correspondents for *Time, Life,* and *Fortune* magazines observed that "there was no hue and cry on the public streets where the outdoor loving were bound for their Sunday pleasures."[4] "Generally speaking," these correspondents concluded, "people went about their usual Sunday night routines without outward evidence that 'the news' had overwhelmed them. . . . But they weren't just being blasé, they were simply gradually accepting a fact that they had been long expecting."[5] The *Daily News* also reported that "potential incidents were few and quickly ended" in Little Tokyo, where "Japanese American merchants went on with their work of decorating their stores for the Christmas trade."[6] A caption beneath a photo of a Little Tokyo store noted that the extra police officers assigned to Little Tokyo "found little to do aside from examining Japanese bibelots in store windows."[7] (A *bibelot* is a curio, antique, or work of art.)

The *Times* also noted that "'business as usual' prevailed in Little Tokyo" on December 7. "Cafes, newsstands and bars were open and the Japanese populace went about its ordinary Sunday activity with an air of resigned calm," the *Times* reported.[8] Within a few hours after they received news of the attack at Pearl Harbor, a number of Los Angeles residents and organizations had begun to take action. FBI agents, assisted by local police officers and deputy sheriffs, took into custody "close to 200 suspicious Japanese," according to the *Los Angeles Times*.[9] Southern California leaders of the Japanese American Citizens League (JACL) also took action. A few hours after they heard the news about the attack at Pearl Harbor, Los Angeles JACL leaders met and formed a committee to convince officials and the general public that Japanese Americans were loyal Americans. To emphasize their loyalty to the United States and their opposition to Japanese military policy, these community leaders decided to name their organization the Anti-Axis Committee.

The Anti-Axis Committee was an important participant in the beginning of a debate about Japanese Americans that lasted from December 7, 1941, until 1946. A number of elected and appointed officials, leaders of civic organizations, journalists, and Japanese American community leaders argued about the loyalty of Japanese Americans. Some insisted that Japanese Americans

FIG. 2. *The* Daily News *published this photograph showing Little Tokyo on December 7, 1941, the day of the attack on Pearl Harbor. The caption said: "Two of the many extra policemen assigned to Little Tokyo keep their eyes open. They found little to do aside from examining Japanese bibelots in store windows."* Daily News, *Dec. 8, 1941, p. 3.* Los Angeles Daily News *Photographs (Collection 1386), Department of Special Collections, Charles E. Young Research Library, University of California, Los Angeles.*

were by nature inclined toward loyalty to Japan and therefore should be subject to incarceration and removal from the region. Others argued that Japanese Americans were not naturally loyal to Japan and should be treated as all other U.S. residents. This chapter will explore the first portion of this debate. (Chapters four, six, and seven will deal with later portions of this debate.) Although this debate was ostensibly about the loyalty of Japanese Americans and about government policy toward Japanese Americans, it was also clearly a debate about racial ideology. The point of this chapter is not to argue that this debate decisively influenced the decision to incarcerate Japanese Americans. That decision was made far away from Los Angeles, and, although some people from Los Angeles attempted to influence the decision, it is beyond the scope of this study to determine how the debate in Los Angeles influenced decisions made by military officers and civilian officials in San Francisco and Washington, D.C. This chapter will show that many Japanese American leaders insisted that their "race" did not make them loyal either to Japan or the United States. They argued that U.S. policy toward Japanese Americans should not be based on assumptions about "race." In the weeks following Pearl Harbor, many elected officials and journalists expressed support for this position. In January 1942, however, many of these officials and journalists began to argue that U.S. policy toward Japanese Americans should be based upon "race." Eventually these officials and journalists came to dominate the debate about Japanese American loyalty. Their dominance in this debate suggests that traditional American racialism remained hegemonic through the early months of 1942.

An Apparent Consensus

In the days following Pearl Harbor there did not seem to be much of a debate at all about the loyalty of Japanese Americans. Instead, most people seemed to agree with the JACL's Anti-Axis Committee, which first enunciated its position in the hours following the Pearl Harbor attack. In a statement of its objectives and program, the committee, which included more than forty JACL members from several different southern California communities, announced "our unequivocal repudiation of Japan" and promised to "bend our energies to the common objective of an American victory and the defeat of the Axis powers." The committee's stated goals included cooperation "with all national, state, and local government agencies," the coordination of "the activities of all citizens and alien residents in the successful prosecution of this war," and the securing of "National unity by fair treatment of loyal Americans." Running beneath these stated goals, of course, was a more fundamental objective: to convince people that Japanese Americans, despite their ancestry, *could be* loyal to the United States.

The committee did not insist that all Japanese Americans were loyal to the United States. Committee Chair Fred Tayama suggested that some people of Japanese ancestry in the United States were loyal to Japan. "Every man is either friend or foe," Tayama said. "We shall investigate and turn over to authorities all who by word or act consort with the enemies," he said, promising that the Anti-Axis Committee would "do all in our power to help wipe-out vicious totalitarian enemies."[10] It is important to note that Tayama's words and the actions of the Anti-Axis Committee exacerbated divisions within the Japanese American community. Some of the people who were arrested in the days following Pearl Harbor blamed Anti-Axis Committee "informers." Members of the committee did provide information to the FBI, and some boasted about their role in the raids.[11] In the larger context of public discourse about "race," however, Tayama's words represented an important statement. Tayama's words implied that "race" did not determine loyalty. Since "race" was not a reliable indicator of loyalty, Tayama said, patriotic Americans should not lash out at all people of Japanese ancestry. He warned that such anti-Japanese sentiment could undermine the war effort. "Every loyal American must be permitted to render his services. The enemy will try to sabotage our usefulness by inciting race hysteria. Let us be vigilant."[12] The *Times*, the *Examiner*, and the *Daily News* quoted Tayama's statement in full, and the *Times* published a photograph of JACL leaders meeting with Mayor Bowron and declaring their loyalty to the United States.[13]

In the aftermath of Pearl Harbor, many prominent individuals, including some elected officials, expressed their agreement with the Anti-Axis Committee. All of the distinguished guests the committee invited to its December 8, 1941, meeting reassured Japanese Americans that they believed that Japanese Americans were loyal to the United States. The statements of these officials and civic leaders, however, depicted loyalty as something that Japanese Americans had to prove. This tendency would become increasingly important as the debate about Japanese American loyalty unfolded. John Hartsock, the county council commander of the American Legion,

FIG. 3. *On December 8, 1941, leaders of the Japanese American Citizens League met with Los Angeles Mayor Fletcher Bowron and pledged their loyalty to the United States. A year and a half later, Bowron said that all people of Japanese ancestry were "a race apart" and that they "could never be Americans in the true sense." This photograph in the* Times *appeared beneath the headline "Citizens Offer Loyalty Pledge to Flag," and the caption said: "Fealty Pledge—left to right are Mayor Bowron, Ken Matsumoto, Fred Tayama, Kay Sugahara, Shigemi Aratani, George Inagaki, Frank Kito and Togo Tanaka as members of Japanese-American Citizens League declare to Mayor that the American Flag is theirs."* Los Angeles Times, *Dec. 9, 1941, pt. 1, p. 19.* Los Angeles Times *Photographic Archive (Collection 1429), Department of Special Collections, Charles E. Young Research Library, University of California, Los Angeles.*

read a statement "commending the true Americanism record of the citizens of Japanese ancestry and Japanese alien residents of this community." The statement also pledged the American Legion's "fullest protection and cooperation to them in this emergency." Lt. Commander Kenneth Ringle, of the Eleventh Naval District, expressed his faith in Japanese Americans, who, he expected, would "prove yourselves all Americans." Mayor Fletcher Bowron appeared at the meeting and told the committee that he harbored no doubts about the Nisei's "sincerity and patriotism." He also promised that the city government would provide Japanese Americans with the same protections accorded every citizen.[14]

Although the newspapers did not report on the December 8 Anti-Axis Committee meeting, they did publish later statements of officials who expressed support for the idea that Japanese Americans could be and were loyal to the United States. Some of the statements issued by these leaders emphasized the "racial" difference between Japanese Americans and other Americans and continued to depict loyalty as something that Japanese Americans, but not members of other "racial" groups, had to prove. On December 9, for example, the Los Angeles County Board of Supervisors passed a resolution urging the county superintendent of schools to make certain that "American born children of Japanese blood" were not mistreated in the county's schools. The resolution pointed out that many Japanese Americans "have proven their loyalty to the United States by service in the World War and in other ways."[15]

On occasion the daily newspapers kept their readers abreast of the actions of the Anti-Axis Committee. In an article published a week after Pearl Harbor, the *Times* pointed out that most of the businesses in Little Tokyo were closed. "But there was plenty of activity at headquarters of the anti-Axis committee of the Japanese American Citizens League." In the office, "volunteer workers were busily mailing copies of the committee's loyalty pledge to government officials, Army and Navy officers, veterans' organizations and civic welfare groups." This article was accompanied by a photograph of the Anti-Axis Committee's headquarters.[16]

In the week following Pearl Harbor, as many elected officials and civic leaders expressed the belief that Japanese Americans were loyal to the United States, many Japanese Americans praised "the fairness of white Americans." Thomas Koichi Kido, a Japanese American student at Los Angeles City College, for example, told a *Los Angeles Times* reporter that "we

American students of Japanese blood have confidence in the fairness of white Americans." Kido added, "Everyone I know has been sympathetic in recognizing our position. There will be no trouble."[17] The *Daily News* reported that two hundred Japanese American students at UCLA had issued a statement pledging their loyalty to the United States and pleading that "our friends will accord us the same impartiality and tolerance they have shown in the past."[18] At a December 12 meeting of the Los Angeles County Defense Council, Ken Matsumoto, speaking on behalf of the Anti-Axis Committee, "expressed deep gratitude on behalf of the 40,000 Japanese for the tolerance and deep understanding of the American people."[19]

"Race" and Doubts about Japanese American Loyalty

Although most officials and journalists warned people not to attack Japanese Americans, and many civic leaders expressed the belief that most Japanese Americans were loyal to the United States, some newspapers sounded ominous notes soon after Pearl Harbor. In an editorial published the day after Pearl Harbor, for example, the *Los Angeles Times* advised its readers not to resort to violence against Japanese Americans. "Panic and confusion, even Jap tactics themselves, serve the enemy," the editorial declared. The term *Jap tactics* suggests a connection between biological characteristics of Japanese soldiers and their behavior. In addition to racializing certain "tactics," this editorial raised doubts about the loyalty of many Japanese Americans. The editorial acknowledged that "some, perhaps many" Japanese Americans were "loyal Nisei, or good Americans, born and educated as such." Emphasizing what it saw as a racial penchant for "treachery," the editorial stated that "what the rest may be we do not know, nor can we take a chance in the light of yesterday's demonstration that treachery and double-dealing are major Japanese weapons."[20] Although this editorial cast suspicion upon Japanese Americans, the *Times* emphasized the citizenship and loyalty of Japanese Americans in photo captions. Many residents of Little Tokyo "are loyal Americans," said a caption beneath a photograph of people reading bulletins in Japanese.[21]

Articles and photographs as well as editorials in the daily newspapers also served to raise doubts about Japanese Americans' loyalty to the United States. Even though articles and captions mentioned that many Japanese Americans were U.S. citizens, others emphasized the fact that federal officials had closed banks and businesses that had a connection to Japan and rounded up "suspicious" Japanese aliens.[22] Other articles emphasized the possibility that Japanese immigrant farmers might have poisoned the vegetables that they produced. One article, for example, pointed out that "hundreds of chemical tests have revealed no poisoning in Japanese grown vegetables." Instead of absolving Japanese immigrants of the charge of desiring to poison vegetables, however, this article suggested that Japanese immigrant farmers could not be trusted. "No alien Japanese vegetables can now be marketed. Alien custodians are being appointed to take care of the Japanese ranches, most of which are now being patrolled by government agents."[23] The newspapers did report when many of the restrictions were lifted, but they did not explicitly draw the conclusion that the lifting of the restrictions proved that most Japanese Americans were loyal to the United States.[24]

Less than two weeks after Pearl Harbor, daily newspapers began to publish articles that depicted all people of Japanese ancestry as a threat to the security of the United States, and some elected officials and journalists began to suggest that drastic action should be taken to reduce or eliminate the threat of sabotage posed by Japanese Americans who were at least potentially loyal to Japan. On December 19, 1941, the *Times* and the *Examiner* both published front-page articles reporting that Dr. Rikita Honda, who had killed himself while in U.S. custody a week after Pearl Harbor, had been "the head of a society directing a vast network of espionage on the Pacific Coast." The *Times* noted that the FBI, the Gardena police, and U.S. Senator Guy Gillette of Iowa had confirmed the existence of this "vast network." The senator said that this organization, the Imperial Comradeships Society, "had 4800 members in California and Arizona and other Western States." The *Times* also suggested that this "vast network of espionage" still posed a threat to the security of southern California and the nation by reporting that Gardena police and FBI agents had only arrested fifteen Japanese aliens.[25]

This front-page story presented apparent evidence of a Japanese threat, but it did so in a way that this evidence was removed from the Californians who had led an anti-Japanese campaign for more than thirty years. Instead of citing the words of these anti-Japanese leaders, the article emphasized that the FBI and a U.S. senator from Iowa had uncovered evidence of a Japanese threat to the security of the Pacific Coast. Because this evidence came from apparently disinterested parties rather than anti-Japanese organizations, it made it difficult if not impossible for Japanese Americans and their allies to discredit this report. Although the portion of this article that appeared on the front page claimed that the FBI had confirmed the existence of this "Jap Spy Ring," the continuation of the article, on page 8, was more ambiguous. This portion of the article pointed out that "F.B.I. agents admitted here that investigation of the society was continuing but would disclose no details of its operation." The article did not identify the sources of some of the information about the "spy ring." The article resorted to the passive voice in reporting that "during recent years, Dr. Honda's office, it was learned, became something of a gathering place for Japanese in the Gardena area." The article also said that "it was reported that sabotage had also been one of the principal interests of the Comradeships Society, and that strong-arm methods were used against recalcitrant Japanese who declined to take orders from the society."[26]

It may appear that this article reflected a conscious decision on the part of newspaper editors and reporters to raise doubts about the loyalty of Japanese Americans. It is impossible for me to determine whether or not the reporters and editors consciously decided to present this information as they did. From my perspective, however, there is little value in trying to determine whether or not there was any kind of "conspiracy." Whether or not the content of this article and the way it was presented reflected conscious decisions or unconscious inclinations, it depicted a substantial number of Japanese Americans as a threat. Such depictions of Japanese Americans became increasingly common in late December 1941 and January 1942.

Although the newspapers published articles raising doubts about the loyalty of Japanese Americans, they did not immediately stop publishing articles that suggested that Japanese Americans posed no significant threat to the U.S. war effort or to the security of the United States. A December 19 article in the *Times*, for example, noted that "with a total of 442 Japanese, German and Italian aliens rounded up in Los Angeles since the outbreak of war, Federal agents have about completed the huge job which has been accomplished efficiently because of years of planning." The article reported that years before the United States entered the war "the F.B.I. was working secretly in tabulating and checking those aliens who were either known agents of foreign powers or working closely with such agents."[27] Follow-up articles about the people detained after Pearl Harbor did not emphasize the threat posed by people who were still at large.[28]

Even as the daily newspapers began to print more and more articles and editorials that questioned the loyalty of Japanese Americans, some

Japanese Americans continued to praise "white" Americans for their tolerance. In one editorial, *Rafu Shimpo* declared that "we must never forget that in our greatest hour of need the American people had not forgotten us or our immediate problems. The Japanese attack was dastardly but their feelings toward us were indeed sympathetic. We had friends among them even when our own race inflicted such great sorrow."[29] Another editorial insisted that "the resident Japanese, ever since the war began, have been very cordially treated by Americans everywhere." "Americans" were "indignant at Japan's perfidy in attacking Pearl Harbor," but "they realize that the Japanese in America had nothing to do with instigating the attack." The newspaper, "speaking on behalf of the resident Japanese," thanked "the American people for their kindness and generosity."[30]

Although these editorials praised "the American people" generally, other editorials criticized Chinese Americans and Filipino Americans who had begun wearing badges so that people could distinguish them from Japanese Americans. Editorials and columns in *Rafu Shimpo* declared that the wearing of badges was "quite contrary to the democratic spirit." These badges perpetuated the notion that Japanese Americans were responsible for Pearl Harbor and obscured the fact that "the nisei are innocent of the crime committed by the Japanese military."[31] Another editorial insisted that "people from all parts of the world came to this country to lose their racial identity, to become Americans all." By wearing identification badges, other Asian Americans were encouraging people to think that "Orientals are unassimilable." Badges also raised questions about the loyalties of these Asian Americans, "for no identification buttons or badges mention loyalty to America, only victory first for their homeland!" *Rafu Shimpo* advised the people who were wearing badges "to forget that they are Chinese or Filipinos or Koreans and think [of] themselves as true Americans. . . . We want everyone to forget his racial identity in order to fight the enemies of America."[32]

Many Japanese Americans may have sincerely believed that people needed to "forget" their racial identities in order to win the war. Editorials and columns in *Rafu Shimpo*, however, also allowed Japanese Americans to depict members of other Asian groups, particularly Filipinos, as backward, misguided, unenlightened, or dangerous. As noted in chapter one, a number of Japanese Americans had depicted Filipinos in this negative light in the 1930s. One editorial criticized the actions of Filipino farm laborers who "refused to work for the Japanese farmers because Japanese troops invaded the Philippine islands."[33] Although *Rafu Shimpo* criticized Filipino workers, it praised "level-headed Filipino leaders up and down the coast with sound university training" who had acknowledged that the "Japanese community is certainly not responsible for the present situation" and were working to "create friendships between the two peoples."[34]

In early January 1942 a *Rafu Shimpo* editorial criticized the "perverted patriotism" that had led some Filipinos to attack Japanese Americans. The murder of "an American of Japanese ancestry who had been honorably released from the U.S. Army hardly brought succor to the gallant Filipino cause in the Far East," the editorial said. Instead, this murder "has worked to bring less respect for Filipinos hereabouts generally. It has tended to picture the Filipinos here as less civilized, less emotionally stable, knife-wielding sinister individuals." The newspaper conceded that the picture of Filipinos as unstable, "knife-wielding sinister individuals" was unfair, but "there have been enough killings, enough stabbings, enough attempted murders by Filipinos against innocent persons that a halt to this misguided, perverted patriotism ought to be called."[35]

The complaints of *Rafu Shimpo* apparently had little effect on the efforts of Chinese Americans to make certain that people did not mistake them for Japanese Americans. On January 6, 1942, the *Times* reported that new stickers depicting the flags of the United States and China had been prepared for display in Chinese Americans' businesses, homes, and automobiles. "They are to avert misunderstanding and embarrassment for America's allies," the *Times* noted.[36]

Late in December the daily newspapers published other articles suggesting that people disloyal to the United States were still at large in the Pacific Coast states. These articles reported that all "enemy aliens" in the "seven Pacific Coast States" (California, Oregon, Washington, Montana, Idaho, Utah, Nevada, and Arizona) had to surrender all of their shortwave radio equipment and cameras to police authorities. These articles suggested that some of these aliens may have been engaged in sabotage or espionage. The article in the *Times*, for example, noted that "military and naval authorities are checking reports that illegal radio messages have been intercepted in the Pacific Coast area, it was learned unofficially, and bootleg stations are understood to have been discovered by Federal Communications Commission monitoring stations." Like previous articles, this article did not clearly identify the sources of information about this suspicious activity. This article did not single out Japanese aliens, nor did it suggest that there was a "racial" basis for loyalty to any nation. In fact, the same article quoted from a statement by Attorney General Francis Biddle, who was "irritated by reports of discrimination and unwarranted discharges from jobs on 'vague suspicion.' Biddle reminded the nation that dangerous aliens have been apprehended."[37] In a follow-up article on the Justice Department's order that all enemy aliens surrender two-way radios and cameras, the *Times* emphasized Japanese immigrants' compliance with the order.[38]

In this period of confusion in the first month following Pearl Harbor, some newspaper articles did not suggest that the "racial character" of Japanese Americans posed any threat to the United States, but others did accentuate the notion that Japanese people displayed certain negative, "racial" characteristics. One article in the *Times*, for example, described a Chinese restaurant operator who "disclosed how he differentiates his countrymen from Japanese." This unnamed restaurateur told a reporter that it was easy for him to distinguish between Chinese and Japanese people, "but for native Americans to apply the rules safely takes time and study." In describing how he differentiated Chinese from Japanese people, this Chinese restaurant owner suggested that "American-born Japanese" were different from people born in Japan. "Natives of Japan," he said, "toe out more than either Chinese or American-born Japanese. Japanese walk and talk faster, seldom strolling along in a relaxed manner." He also said that "few alien Japanese are taller than 5 feet 3 inches," whereas "Japanese born in this country usually are considerably taller." Although this restaurant proprietor did not paint all Japanese Americans with the same brush, he did ascribe negative characteristics to immigrants from Japan. In addition to walking and talking quickly, he said that "with the exception of the 'upper crust,' Japanese faces tend to be coarser featured with thicker lips and wider and flatter noses" than those of Chinese people. The restaurateur also noted that "Chinese don't try to put on impressive faces. Their expressions are natural, neither artificially genial nor artificially aggressive." Near its conclusion, this article indicated that "there is a small group of Japanese of a more refined racial type. They have thinner and higher noses, more slanting eyes and smaller mouths. The skins of this group are almost white in the better classes."[39] This article seems to reflect the ambiguity and confusion surrounding Japanese people as a racialized group in the month following

Pearl Harbor. On the one hand, it suggests that some Japanese people were "almost white," at least in terms of their skin color. The article describes most Japanese people, however, in negative terms. It did not, however, explicitly depict Japanese people as a threat to U.S. security. The article never clearly indicated why it might be useful for "native Americans" to know how to tell Japanese people from Chinese people.

A New Consensus Emerges

The ambivalent but often positive depictions of Japanese Americans in the daily newspapers began to disappear in January 1942. In that month the newspapers increasingly published articles and photographs that depicted Japanese Americans as people of questionable loyalty to the United States and as potential threats to the nation's security. On January 3, 1942, the *Times* and the *Examiner* reported that two Japanese Americans, Tomio Ambo and Shigeki Kayama, were arrested after one of them allegedly spat at a woman who criticized them for "applauding scenes of the bombing of Pearl Harbor and hissing pictures of Roosevelt and Churchill" in a downtown motion picture theater.[40] The article in the *Times* raised doubts about both the citizenship of the arrested Japanese Americans and the loyalty of all Japanese Americans; it said that Ambo and Kayama "are said to be American citizens." Although the article indicated that Ambo and Kayama *were accused of* applauding pictures of the attack on Pearl Harbor, the caption beneath their photo insisted that they were guilty of the charge: "They laughed at Pearl Harbor Pictures." The article included only the statements of the person who filed the complaint and of police officers; it included no statements by the Japanese Americans who were arrested.

Rafu Shimpo protested the metropolitan newspapers' coverage of this alleged incident, pointing out that Ambo and Kayama "vehemently denied they hissed & booed & laughed." Ambo and Kayama's "side of the story, which probably won't be printed in the downtown newspapers, won't be known very widely," and "the repercussions on other nisei and issei theatergoers, to say the least, will not be favorable," the Japanese American newspaper lamented.[41] The *Times* did report that Ambo and Kayama's accuser never appeared to press charges, but it never allowed the Japanese Americans to defend themselves.[42]

FIG. 4. *The* Los Angeles Times *published this photograph above the following caption: "They laughed at Pearl Harbor Pictures–Tomio Ambo, left, and Shigeki Kayama, American-born Japanese youths, charged by Winifred J. Stephens with spitting on her when she remonstrated with them for applauding Pearl Harbor bombing and hissing Roosevelt."* Los Angeles Times, *Jan. 3, 1942, pt. 2, p. 1.* Los Angeles Times *Photographic Archive (Collection 1429), Department of Special Collections, Charles E. Young Research Library, University of California, Los Angeles.*

For the most part, Japanese American efforts to defend themselves reached only the readers of community newspapers such as *Rafu Shimpo*. In early January 1942 a *Rafu Shimpo* editorial responded to a letter from Frank Kelly of Los Angeles to the editor of the *Herald and Express*. In the letter, Kelly wrote, "a Japanese is a Japanese, no matter where he was born. He is taught from infancy the religion of Japan, which is: Be polite and nice to everybody because some day you will help stick them in the back." Kelly expressed the opinion that "every Japanese in the United States should be rounded up along with every other alien enemy and placed in a concentration camp until after the war, then send them back home and lock the gates on them for good." The *Rafu Shimpo* editorial replied to Kelly by noting that "it's a common weakness of all unthinking persons to say 'a Japanese is a Japanese, no matter where he was born.'" The editorial also invoked President Roosevelt's call for employers not to discriminate against loyal aliens. It also asserted that "we do not feel compelled to ask for the privileges of American citizenship," because "we were born with them. We'll die for them."[43]

In the second half of January, Japanese American public employees found themselves at the center of the debate about the treatment of Japanese Americans. Some officials and journalists depicted public agencies' employment of Japanese Americans as Japanese infiltration of U.S. institutions. Newspaper accounts presented the statements of these officials as if they were unimpeachable facts presented by disinterested parties. On January 20, 1942, for example, the *Times* reported statements about Japanese Americans made by agents of the Dies Committee—the U.S. House Committee on Un-American Activities, chaired by Representative Martin Dies of Texas. Dies Committee investigators claimed that thirteen Japanese Americans were "slipped into important spots" in the Department of Water and Power "after city officials, at the suggestion of the Justice Department, refused to supply details requested by the Japanese Consulate a few years ago about the city's power and water systems."[44] In commenting on the Dies Committee's investigation, a *Times* editorial noted that "many of our Japanese, whether born here or not, are fully loyal and deserve sympathy rather than suspicion." Other Japanese Americans, both aliens and U.S. citizens, however, "hold to a foreign allegiance and are dangerous, at least potentially," the *Times* argued. The editorial insisted that "it would sometimes stump an expert to tell which is which and mistakes, if made, should be made on the side of caution." The *Times* acknowledged that it "might be a mistake and promote injustice" if all Japanese American employees were to be fired, "but on the other hand a mistake in the other direction could be very costly." The editorial ended by declaring that "if there is evidence that Japanese-Americans were slipped into the Water and Power Department here to obtain information for the Japanese Consulate, as Dies committee agents intimate, no chances should be taken with any of them."[45]

No evidence to support the claim made by Dies Committee investigators was made public, but the actions of the city and the county governments suggested that there was in fact evidence of disloyalty. By the last week of January, the City of Los Angeles had dismissed all of its Japanese American employees.[46] In a statement to reporters, Mayor Fletcher Bowron defended the city's action. In a revealing error, Bowron referred to the discharged workers as "employees of Japanese birth." Most if not all of the city's Japanese American employees were born in the United States. Bowron explained that the dismissal of these employees "is not the result of hysteria." Bowron's words are intriguing, for they seem to suggest that someone had suggested that the city had acted as a result of hysteria. Yet no one publicly claimed that the officials or the public had been seized by hysteria. Bowron also said that the dismissal of Japanese American employees was "not to be construed as any indication that any of them are dangerous or that their loyalty has been questioned." Instead, thirty-nine Japanese American municipal employees were forced to leave their jobs because "certain embarrassing situations might develop by reason of their continued connection with the various departments of city government."[47] Despite Bowron's elaborate disclaimer, the city's actions indicated that some Japanese Americans were in fact disloyal to the United States and were dangerous to the nation.

At the same time the Los Angeles County Board of Supervisors ordered department heads to dismiss all of the county's Japanese American employees. The Board's explanation for its actions revealed the influence of racialist ideology in the decision. The Board explained that "it was unfeasible to detail Americans to shadow all 56 Japanese employees to make sure of their loyalty to the United States."[48] This statement implied that all "Americans" are unquestionably loyal to the United States, while all "Japanese" are potentially disloyal.

In dismissing all of the county's Japanese American employees, the Board of Supervisors was undoubtedly influenced by Los Angeles Chief

Administrative Officer Wayne Allen. Allen had fired the Japanese Americans in his department before the Board took its more sweeping action. Allen, a native of Denver, had spent twenty years working as a purchasing agent for San Francisco Bay Area railroads before he was hired as a purchasing agent for Los Angeles County in 1936. The Board of Supervisors appointed Allen as the county's first chief administrative officer in 1938. John Anson Ford, who served on the Board of Supervisors from 1934 until 1958, recalled that Allen "brought to his new responsibility vigor, open-handed methods, boundless energy, and a determination to put the county's huge operations more firmly on a business basis." Ford also noted that Allen's introduction of more efficient procedures "relieved the supervisors of arduous and time-consuming responsibilities. They soon gave him almost a free hand."[49] Ford's description of Allen is pertinent to the debate about Japanese Americans in Los Angeles after World War II. Allen presented himself and was accepted by many politicians as an expert who was not influenced by politics. Allen's pronouncements about Japanese Americans, then, appeared to be based upon careful reasoning and research and not on political considerations or personal prejudices.

When Allen fired all of the Japanese American employees on his staff, he explicitly denied that he suspected that his employees were disloyal. Allen's explanation for the dismissals, however, clearly implied that some were disloyal. He explained that "in my own department I have discharged Japanese not because I doubted their loyalty, but because the possible loss of reserve supplies should one single act of sabotage occur would be my responsibility."[50] In other words, Allen stated that he had to assume that some Japanese American employees were saboteurs.

The Demands for Incarceration and Removal

By the third week of January, some people had begun to call publicly and explicitly for the incarceration of Japanese Americans in "concentration camps." In that week U.S. Representative Leland M. Ford of Santa Monica asked U.S. officials to move "all Japanese, native born and alien, to concentration camps."[51] Ford, a Republican, was for a few years in the late 1930s and early 1940s an important figure in Los Angeles politics. Born in Eureka, Nevada, in 1893, Ford was peripatetic as a young man. He began working for the Southern Sierras Power Company in 1909. Two years later he was working for the Southern Pacific Railroad in California. He was in New York in 1912 and 1913. Ford moved to Los Angeles in 1915, but he did not stay long. By the end of the year he was farming in Lynchburg, Virginia. Ford settled permanently in Santa Monica, on the ocean west of Los Angeles, in 1919, and began working in real estate. Ford served on the Santa Monica Planning Commission for four years in the 1920s, but he catapulted into public office in 1936, when he landed a coveted seat on the Los Angeles County Board of Supervisors. Ford won election to Congress in 1938.

In Congress Ford was an anti-labor, anti–New Deal Republican. LaRue McCormick, the Communist party candidate who opposed Ford in 1938, recalled that Ford "was one of the most vitriolic, outspoken reactionaries—public officials—that we had at that time." McCormick remembered that the Board of Supervisors apologized to her "because Leland Ford stuck out his tongue and made an obscene gesture when he saw me in the supervisors' room preparing to speak in behalf of the unemployed." McCormick also recalled that Ford "was sort of the darling of the *Los Angeles Times*, of the open shop, and represented all of those things that we, the ordinary people, were against."[52] After Pearl Harbor, Ford publicly declared that the federal government should arrest International Longshoremen's and Warehousemen's Union leader Harry Bridges as part of its effort to round up "dangerous aliens."[53]

In August 1942 the *Daily News* revealed that Ford had served on the executive committee of the Citizens Committee to Keep America Out of War. This committee was investigated by a federal grand jury. Although none of the members of the committee were charged with a crime, "the jurors did return indictments against the alleged Nazi agents and seditionists who are charged with using Ford, [U.S. Rep. Hamilton] Fish [of New York] and other congressional obstructionists of the administration's war and defense policies," the newspaper reported. On the basis of this indictment, the *Daily News* referred to the committee as a "'Nazi stooge' group." The *Daily News* also noted that Ford had "based his extensive billboard campaign for reelection upon claims of 'complete cooperation' with the administration" and suggested that disclosure of his membership on the Citizens Committee would "prove the deciding factor in the approaching election."[54] Ford failed in his bid for reelection in 1942. He lost his seat to Democrat Will Rogers, Jr.

In calling for the incarceration of Japanese Americans, Ford did not argue that all people of Japanese ancestry were definitely loyal to Japan, but he did state that "native-born Japanese may not be any more loyal than are the foreign born." If any Japanese Americans were really loyal citizens of the United States, Ford argued, they "should be willing to acquiesce in the movement of all Japanese people to whatever location the military authorities think they ought to be in." Despite Ford's words, at this point no military authorities had publicly suggested that Japanese Americans should have been moved. In suggesting that "loyal citizens" should be willing to move wherever military authorities wanted them to be, Ford was both defining any resistance to removal as evidence of disloyalty and equating loyalty with obedience to authority. Ford depicted Japanese Americans as men who were unwilling to serve in the U.S. military. He compared Japanese Americans with "other loyal Americans" who were "enlisting in the Army and Navy and Air Forces and are willing to give their lives for their country." Comparing military service with imprisonment, Ford declared that "it is not asking too much of the Japanese" to make a wartime sacrifice by "permitting themselves to be placed in concentration camps."[55]

Other proponents of incarceration soon joined Ford. Their calls for internment appeared prominently in Los Angeles's daily newspapers. On January 22 the United Fresh Fruit and Vegetable Association adopted a resolution calling for the internment of "enemy aliens" in California, Arizona, Oregon, and Washington. Newspaper reports on the resolution, which was passed at a convention in Florida, emphasized the "bad feeling between Filipino and Japanese labor." The newly elected president of the association, Norman K. Evans of Los Angeles, declared that Japanese immigrants were "a menace in this country and sooner or later they're going to lead to open shooting."[56] Although it is clear that some members of this association stood to benefit economically from the removal of Japanese American competition, more important from my perspective is that this statement was published by newspapers whose editors considered the statement newsworthy. Beginning in mid-January 1942, the *Times* and the *Examiner* published a substantial number of articles like this one, endorsing the incarceration and removal of some or all people of Japanese ancestry from the coastal states. These articles tended to depict the calls for drastic action as the result of careful deliberation rather than as expressions of economic self-interest.

Some articles also drew conclusions that did not seem to be supported by the statements of the officials quoted in the articles. On January 27, for example, the *Times* reported that naval officers were worried about "the presence of Japanese on Terminal Island." The article focused on the testimony of Admiral Harold R. Stark, the Chief of Naval Operations, before the House Appropriations Committee. Stark was asked a series of pointed questions by U.S. Representative Harry R. Sheppard of Yucaipa, a small town located east of San Bernardino. Sheppard, who was born in Mobile, Alabama, in 1885, had worked for the Santa Fe Railway and had managed a business before he was elected to Congress as a Democrat in 1936. Sheppard was an important leader of the anti-Japanese movement in Congress during and after the war. The *Times* noted that Stark "confessed" that "he would have preferred to remove the fish canneries and Japanese colony" from Terminal Island, even though he felt that "the Japanese fishing fleet is under control." The article, however, also quoted from Stark's testimony, and none of the quotations seem to reflect the "worry" mentioned in the headline. Stark told the committee that "I would have felt more comfortable if we were able to transfer this entire situation to an area clear of naval activities." He also said that naval authorities had decided that "fencing, surveillance and police control" were "adequate to prevent any damage to naval facilities."[57]

Although U.S. Representative Leland Ford had called for the removal of both aliens and citizens, most of the proponents of incarceration and removal initially focused their attention on Japanese aliens. Near the end of January 1942, Wayne Allen, the chief administrative officer for Los Angeles County, informed the Board of Supervisors that "it would be advisable for the Federal Government to transfer Japanese aliens away from Pacific Coast areas and care for them at inland points where they could till the soil far removed from airfields, power and water and other strategic defense plants." Allen wrote that "Japanese aliens are a possible danger to our interests as a nation, state and county." He presented his recommendation as "fair and logical," neglecting the hardships it would work on many Japanese American families. He argued that "it would seem only fair and logical that those Japanese who are loyal to the United States would understand the wisdom" of removal and incarceration, "while those disloyal would object and thereby prove their disloyalty."[58] In response to Allen's recommendation, the Board of Supervisors passed a resolution asking federal authorities to evict "all Japanese aliens" "immediately from Los Angeles Harbor and from the vicinity of defense plants and aircraft factories." This resolution conceded that some Japanese aliens were loyal to the United States but stated that "it is difficult if not impossible to distinguish between loyal and disloyal Japanese aliens." The resolution argued that Japanese Americans' religious beliefs, not their race, made them a potential threat to the security of the United States. It stated that Japanese aliens were a threat because "80% of Japanese residents here retain their native Buddhist and Shinto religions." The resolution also pointed out that "the Shinto religion is that of the Emperor of Japan and includes worship of ancestors and the belief that soldiers who die for Japan become spirits to be worshiped." Although the resolution attempted to distinguish between "race" and religion, it depicted religion as a fundamental characteristic of human beings. The resolution's description of religion bore a striking resemblance to many popular beliefs about "race." "The strong ties of religious beliefs are often so implanted in humans that they are prone to revert to original or native allegiance in periods of stress or emotion," the resolution stated. Because there were so many Buddhists and Shintoists among the Japanese American population, "in the event of an invasion of California by forces of Japan, the civil population . . . would be unable to cope with the large Japanese population which would constitute a potentially dangerous fifth column enemy."[59]

As the Board of Supervisors' resolution suggests, before the end of January 1942 there was little explicit mention of "race," even though many statements revealed racialist assumptions. This changed dramatically in the last few days of January. At this point in time, participants in the debate about Japanese Americans began to describe the war in the Pacific as a war between two incompatible "races." An editorial in the *Times*, for example, referred to "members of enemy races." By describing the Pacific war as a "race war," the *Times* implicitly explained why all people of Japanese ancestry, not simply aliens, should be removed. The *Times* acknowledged that the removal of U.S. citizens would violate their civil liberties, but it argued that civil rights were a luxury that the United States could not afford when the nation was at war. It said that all proponents of the removal of Japanese Americans wanted "to respect civil liberties and to protect members of enemy races from persecution or unnecessary hardship. But this is war. And in wartime, the preservation of the nation becomes the first duty." This editorial argued that Japanese Americans should submit to these drastic actions because of the ways in which the *Times* editors supposed Americans were treated in Japan. The *Times*, for example, drew attention to Terminal Island in Los Angeles Harbor, where "both alien and second-generation Japanese are enjoying virtually unrestricted freedom today despite the United States naval and military movements taking place under their very eyes." The *Times* argued that "it is certainly unthinkable to suppose that in Japan at this moment any Americans are permitted to reside unmolested in an area adjacent to vital military zones." The *Times* editorial stated that "the mounting wave of demands . . . that the Federal government remove Japanese from vital military areas represents no sudden burst of hysteria." Instead, the editorial continued, "it is the calm, common-sense conclusion of patriotic citizens who are determined there shall be no Pearl Harbor here."[60]

The actions and words of the Board of Supervisors and the *Times* editorial reflect a significant shift in the debate about Japanese Americans. At the end of January 1942 expressions of concern about the civil rights of U.S. citizens gave way to increasingly strident demands for the removal of all Japanese Americans from sensitive areas along the Pacific Coast. On January 29, syndicated columnist Henry McLemore plunged into the debate. McLemore, who was born in Macon, Georgia, in 1906, had worked as a sportswriter, correspondent, and columnist since the 1920s. By 1942 his column was syndicated by the McNaught Syndicate. McLemore wrote his January 29 column after he had spent a day in Los Angeles. In the column he urged Americans to "have no patience with the enemy or with anyone whose veins carry his blood." McLemore declared, "personally, I hate the Japanese. And that goes for all of them." McLemore suggested that, in a national emergency, a commitment to equality should give way to hatred. "I know this is the melting pot of the world and all men are created equal and there must be no such thing as race or creed hatred, but do these things go when a country is fighting for its life? Not in my book," McLemore wrote. McLemore asked rhetorically, "How many American workers do you suppose are free to roam and ramble in Tokyo? Didn't the Japanese threaten to shoot on sight any white person who ventured out-of-doors in Manila?"[61]

In addition to claiming that all people of Japanese ancestry were "racially" loyal to Japan, writers and politicians claimed that the behavior of Japanese Americans conformed with Japanese military strategy. Kyle Palmer, the Washington, D.C., correspondent for the *Times*, suggested that the fact that there had been no sabotage in California since Pearl Harbor showed that Japanese Americans were simply obeying orders from Tokyo. Palmer reported that "known plans of the Japanese military heads include instructions to Japanese in this country to observe the most loyal and circumspect attitude toward the United States until war developments reach a stage where sabotage can be made an active part of a military campaign."[62]

The *Times* also reported on January 29 that Martin Dies, the representative from Texas who chaired the House Committee on Un-American Activities, had warned his colleagues that "unless the government adopts an alert attitude there will occur on the West Coast a tragedy that will make Pearl Harbor sink in significance." Although Dies apparently did not question the loyalty of all Japanese Americans, he did imply that his committee had accumulated a great deal of information about "Japanese espionage." He also promised to "make public within a week or two a full and complete report on Japanese espionage and sabotage in this country."[63]

By the end of January 1942, the repeated attacks on Japanese Americans' loyalty had led some Japanese Americans to admit that they would not question government actions, no matter how drastic those actions might seem. Yasushi Sakimoto of the Southern California Japanese Fishermen's Association, for example, told the *Times* that "the Japanese here, including the first generation are here with a desire to live here permanently and to live the lives of good Americans. I think all suspicious Japanese already have been picked up by the government and I doubt if there are any remaining in liberty who would do harm to America." Sakimoto, however, admitted that "if I were a white American in Japan now, I would not expect to be allowed to stay in the vicinity of defense facilities. The American government has been very tolerant toward us, both first and second generation, and when the order comes, if it comes, we will be reconciled to comply with it." O. Hara, a native of Japan who had lived in the United States for thirty years and the father of two sons "soon to be drafted in the Army," said that "he believes that all of the Japanese here are law-abiding and trying to cooperate with the government. He believes the Federal Bureau of Investigation is doing a good job. He believes some Japanese were rounded up who were harmless." Hara admitted, however, that "I don't know what the F.B.I. knows."[64] These Japanese Americans, then, were repeating statements made by advocates of removal who continued to compare "Japanese" people in the United States with, as Sakimoto said, "white Americans" in Japan. They also left open the possibility that there might be good reasons for federal officials to relocate Japanese Americans. It is worth noting that in this article the *Times* quoted only Japanese Americans who had come to accept the possibility that they might be forced to move. The newspaper had stopped paying attention to any Japanese Americans who asserted their rights as citizens and residents of the United States.

Proponents of the removal of Japanese Americans from certain areas claimed victory on January 30, 1942, the day after Attorney General Francis Biddle announced that Japanese, German, and Italian aliens would be evicted from "vital areas in Los Angeles and San Francisco." The area in Los Angeles County from which aliens were to be removed included the cities of Inglewood, Hawthorne, and Lennox, and a portion of the city of Los Angeles. Two aircraft factories, the Los Angeles Municipal Airport, and oil tank farms were located in this zone.[65] The *Times* applauded Biddle's announcement in an editorial but also stated that it represented only "a start in imperative precautionary restrictions." The editorial insisted that "it undoubtedly will become necessary, too, for the Federal government to deal with the immediate descendants of enemy aliens, particularly the Japanese in strategic sections here."[66] In this editorial, then, the *Times* did not explain why it was necessary for the "descendants of enemy aliens" to be moved. By using this term, the editorial avoided acknowledging that these "descendants" were born in the United States and were entitled to civil rights.

"Race" and Removal

By early February the cautious statements of December 1941 had given way to unabashed expressions about the "racial" character of Japanese Americans. In an editorial published in the February 2, 1942, issue of the *Times*, W. H. Anderson said that Japanese Americans were "born of Japanese parents, nurtured upon Japanese traditions, living in transplanted Japanese atmosphere and thoroughly inoculated with Japanese thoughts, Japanese ideas and Japanese ideals." As a result, the "Japanese-American, . . . notwithstanding his nominal brand of accidental citizenship, almost inevitably and with the rarest of exceptions grows up to be a Japanese, not an American." Although Anderson's editorial seems to emphasize the influence of Japanese culture rather than biology on Japanese Americans, the degree to which Anderson conflated biology and culture can be inferred from the editorial's insistence that "a viper is nonetheless a viper wherever the egg is hatched" and "a leopard's spot and its disposition is the same wherever it is whelped." Anderson also wrote that all Japanese

Americans should be treated as enemies "while we are at war with their race."[67] In December and January, most officials and journalists had conceded that most Japanese Americans were loyal to the United States. Even Henry McLemore estimated that "80 per cent or 90 per cent of the California Japanese" were loyal to the United States.[68] But Anderson insisted that most Japanese Americans were in fact loyal to Japan. "It might cause an injustice to a few to treat them all as potential enemies," he wrote.[69]

Despite their increasingly explicit statements about "race," supporters of the removal and incarceration of Japanese Americans frequently insisted that they were not motivated by racial prejudice or hysteria. They also depicted the forced removal of tens of thousands of U.S. citizens as "ordinary precautions." These denials are more remarkable because few people publicly defended the loyalty of Japanese Americans after December 1941. "There is no hatred for the Japanese on the Pacific Coast," one member of Congress said, "and the demands for ordinary precautions in this situation represent neither hysteria nor reprisal for what happened at Pearl Harbor."[70]

By early February even those officials who had promised Japanese Americans that they would protect their rights had begun to change their positions. Los Angeles Mayor Fletcher Bowron's reversal was the most telling. Bowron had assured the Anti-Axis Committee on December 8 that the city government would protect Japanese Americans. By the beginning of February, however, the mayor had defended the city's decision to discharge its Japanese American employees and embraced a program of forced removal of Japanese Americans. Mayor Bowron said in early February 1942 that Japanese Americans who were loyal to the United States "will not object to making the sacrifice that moving entails—even as American young men are called upon to make the sacrifice of entering the armed services of this country and meeting the enemy face to face on land or sea."[71] A few days later Bowron proposed "a form of internment, but without the necessity of closely continued incarceration," for Japanese aliens and labor conscription for "American-born Japanese." Bowron said that he "could not conceive that Japanese residents are entitled to any more consideration than young American men on the threshold of a career, taken from colleges or places of employment, given $21 a month, placed in uniform, trained, and sent to face danger and death."[72]

Even as federal authorities identified new areas from which Japanese aliens were to be removed and federal agents rounded up aliens living in these areas, some officials continued to clamor for even more drastic action. On February 2, for example, the Los Angeles County Defense Council, which consisted primarily of elected officials in the county, unanimously approved a resolution calling for "immediate internment of all enemy aliens, including American-born Japanese unable to prove they do not hold dual citizenship."[73] Members of Congress from California said that they acknowledged "the formidable obstacles presented by the constitutional rights of citizens of Japanese ancestry," but many also argued that all West Coast residents understood Japanese Americans, whereas officials in Washington, D.C., did not. In depicting Pacific Coast residents as unified, these members of Congress and journalists who repeated their statements simply denied the existence of disagreement about the treatment of Japanese Americans. "West Coast members took the position that the people on the Pacific Coast fully understand the problem and are merely insisting that it be treated firmly and realistically by Washington authorities," the *Times* reported. The members of Congress used the words of Japanese Americans, who had praised the restraint of "white Americans," to counter the charge from federal officials that a "state of public hysteria and near panic exists on the Pacific Coast." Officials denied that they were calling for drastic actions against Japanese Americans. One unidentified member of Congress from California insisted that "all that we are preaching here is prudence and all we are asking for is preparedness."[74] These articles show how rapidly and without any debate the concern about "enemy aliens" had expanded to include all people of Japanese ancestry.

For several days in early February banner headlines on the front page of the *Times* drew readers' attention to the evidence assembled by the Dies Committee. Both the committee and the newspaper declared that this evidence showed conclusively that Japanese aliens had sent strategic information to Japan. Although these articles claimed that there was abundant evidence of spying by Japanese aliens, most of the evidence that was presented in the articles focused on a request by the Japanese Consul in 1934 for information pertaining to the city's water system. The articles did not identify by name any of the leaders of "Japanese military associations," nor did they provide specific examples of acts of espionage by the eight thousand people who were supposedly members of these military associations.[75]

The *Times* insisted in an editorial that U.S. policy should be based upon the statements made by officials such as the Dies Committee investigators, even if these statements were "inaccurate in minor detail." The

Times pointed out that the Dies investigators incorrectly identified the position held by Kiyoshi P. Okura. The investigators described Okura as "chief examiner of the city Civil Service Bureau," but the *Times* pointed out that Okura "was merely 1 of 10 junior personnel technicians." Despite the fact that Okura was not in a position to "insert" Japanese Americans into city jobs, the *Times*, obscuring its sources by relying upon the passive voice, indicated that "it is admitted he could have influenced the obtaining by Japanese of ratings entitling them to be considered for appointments to city jobs." Despite these inaccuracies, the *Times* characterized the Dies Committee's investigators' statements as "unassailable."[76]

Without any public discussion of evidence relating to the loyalty of U.S. citizens of Japanese ancestry, some elected officials had come to the conclusion that the Pacific Coast faced what some officials and journalists referred to as "the native-born Japanese problem." These officials expressed the belief that "American-born Japanese" should be removed from "Pacific Coast defense areas." Most of the statements about this "problem" did not explicitly argue that "American-born Japanese" were loyal to Japan because of their "race," but they did imply that Japanese Americans posed a threat to the security of the coastal region.[77]

The *Times* repeated and summarized many of the arguments in favor of removal of Japanese Americans in an editorial published on February 7. In criticizing Attorney General Francis Biddle's reluctance to sanction internment, the editorial said that Biddle's concern for freedom and rights "would be highly commendable in time of peace." The editorial argued that "there have been few voices calling for internment of all enemy aliens. What we on the Pacific Coast are calling for is removal of enemy aliens, particularly Japanese, inland to nonmilitary areas where their potential capacity for mischief will be slight." The *Times* insisted that "children of enemy aliens" should also be removed. The editorial conceded that these children were "citizens and in many cases loyal to the United States," but it concluded that they "are nevertheless suspect." The *Times* declared that enemy aliens and their children should be removed because of "the intrigue and the spying indulged in by some members of the Axis alien community, as revealed by the Dies committee." The editorial conceded that there was some risk of reprisal by Axis nations, but this "is a risk that must be taken; the safety of the United States, not of the handful of its citizens living abroad, is the paramount consideration." The *Times* also repeated its speculation that similar restrictions had already been imposed upon Americans living in Axis countries. "Certainly Japan would not permit an American colony to live near important military and industrial establishments."[78]

Dissenting Voices

For much of January and early February, the statements of officials and editorialists went unanswered. Finally, however, some people responded to these statements about the disloyalty of Japanese Americans. The opponents of the removal or incarceration of Japanese Americans, however, did not find their words in articles in daily newspapers such as the *Los Angeles Times*. The *Times* did not publish an article about Japanese American opposition to removal until February 20. Only the readers of newspapers such as the Japanese American *Rafu Shimpo* were exposed to most of the opposition to the movement for removal. In attacking the campaign for removal, some people challenged the idea that the war was a conflict between "races." An editorial in *Rafu Shimpo*, for example, insisted that "we are fighting a war of systems, of ideology. We are fighting for the principle that the state exists for the individual, as in our American democracy, and not that the individual exists for the state, as in the totalitarian axis nations. This is a war for the preservation of the free way of life."[79]

Many opponents of removal or incarceration drew attention to the similarities between Fascist racial ideology and the racial ideology embraced by the advocates of incarceration. One reader of the *Times*, for example, pointed out that the newspaper's position on Japanese Americans was incompatible with its previous position on the persecution of Jews in Germany. George Clark called W. H. Anderson's column "the denial of everything for which you have stood up to this moment." Clark pointed out that the *Times* "ably stated the American doctrine of human rights and dignities" when Hitler embarked upon his policy of persecuting Jews in Germany. Yet the *Times* decided to publish Anderson's statements "with no sign of editorial disagreement." Clark wrote that Anderson "blithely damns everybody regardless of individual background who was so unfortunate as to choose the wrong grandparents." In his letter, Clark pointed out that "the Jew has no rights in Germany simply because he is a Jew. Mr. Anderson would empty the Bill of Rights and the Fourteenth Amendment of all meaning in the case of everyone who happened to have a parent born in Japan.

If this is not Hitlerism, what is it?"[80] Although Clark was criticizing a *Times* editorial decision, the editors of the newspaper apparently refused to print Clark's letter. It was published instead in *Rafu Shimpo*.

Some Japanese Americans pointed out that the fact that they were not "white" made them less of a threat than German or Italian spies. A Nisei who wrote a letter to *Rafu Shimpo* in early February 1942 noted that "many who are sent from Germany look just like ordinary citizens. We don't. When we walk on the street people stick their necks out and watch us. We're too easy to identify to do a thing."[81]

Some opponents of removal warned that such a course of action could harm other groups. In one editorial, for example, *Rafu Shimpo* noted that "the same excuse of expediency used to deal with the resident American Japanese" could be "turned against some other so-called 'minority' group."[82] Organizers of a mass meeting to protest the movement for incarceration said that "dangerous precedents are being set up in the treatment of the citizen minority that may pave the way for similar treatment of other groups."[83]

When protests did not stem the movement for removal, some Japanese Americans blamed disunity within the community for their failure to persuade officials that they should not be incarcerated. *Rafu Shimpo* presented this criticism of the community in quotations attributed to unidentified local officials. "You just can't seem to get organized among yourselves. You're always bickering. There's no recognized leadership."[84] Another *Rafu Shimpo* editorial quoted "one very influential City Hall official," who told Japanese Americans, "you're mostly a bunch of bickering adolescents. You've been led around by anyone and everyone so long as you were satisfied that no one of you was considered outstanding. You can't stand any leadership that IS leadership because of petty jealousies."[85] Although the Japanese American community may have been disunited, there is little evidence to suggest that greater unity within the community would have led many influential officials to abandon their commitment to a policy of removal and incarceration. After all, a number of these officials had previously expressed the belief that most Japanese Americans were loyal and that the rights of all U.S. citizens must be protected. Within two months, however, many of these officials had changed their position. It is possible that their position changed because they encountered evidence that indicated that many Japanese Americans were not loyal to the United States. No such evidence, however, was made public at this time. And, there were serious problems involved in officials' reliance on the "evidence" presented by the Dies Committee. One major problem was that the "evidence" presented by the Dies Committee directly contradicted statements made not only by the Federal Bureau of Investigation and the Department of Justice but also by military officers who had investigated Japanese Americans.

On February 20 the *Times* printed the first article in several weeks in which Japanese Americans themselves were quoted. It reported on a meeting of more than fifteen hundred Japanese Americans who were organizing to "fight the threatened evacuation of Japanese-Americans, as well as all enemy aliens, from the Pacific Coast defense areas for the duration of the war." The article quoted several Japanese American leaders. Larry Tajiri said, "we need action and need it now. The Federal authorities have been very fair in their treatment of us despite tremendous pressure from certain interests. We know we are loyal to the American Flag but race hatreds are being stirred up now in the Fascist pattern." The depiction of Tajiri as a "former correspondent for a Japanese news service" served to raise doubts about his loyalty to the United States. Kay Sugahara, who was identified as a "produce merchant and civic leader of 'Little Tokyo,'" said, "if the Army and Navy say we are a menace, let's get out, but if it's merely a question of fighting politicians that would gain favor by hopping on 'those defenseless Japs,' we should fight them to the last ditch." This position conceded that Japanese Americans were in an untenable situation. Already, to the delight of anti-Japanese politicians and journalists, the power to make decisions about Japanese Americans had been moved from civilians to the military. In wartime, however, no one had anything to gain from opposing policies implemented by the military, even if those policies were heavily influenced by racial prejudice. The article also quoted Joseph Shinoda, who pointed out that Japanese Americans "have done all that we could to prove our loyalty. We have donated to the Red Cross, we have bought Defense Bonds and Stamps and offered our services wherever we thought them needed."[86] All of these actions, however, did not constitute proof of loyalty to people who described U.S. citizens of Japanese ancestry as "Japanese" and as members of an "enemy race."

The day after this meeting, President Franklin D. Roosevelt signed Executive Order 9066, which "gave the Army authority to establish military zones anywhere in the United States from which any person, citizen or alien, may be evacuated and excluded."[87] The *Times* praised the order, although it also reiterated its claim that the military should have been given this authority immediately after Pearl Harbor. The order, however, did not satisfy all of the proponents of the removal of Japanese Americans from coastal areas. Some politicians and journalists demanded an "immediate evacuation," despite the fact that the army and other federal agencies had to determine how to remove Japanese Americans from coastal areas. After a Japanese submarine surfaced and shelled an oil field near Santa Barbara, the *Times* reported that "Southern Californians yesterday demanded summary evacuation of all enemy aliens to inland points." As was the case in previous articles, the *Times* depicted all southern Californians as united behind this policy. This article emphasized statements made by U.S. Representative A. J. Elliott of Tulare. After reports of the submarine attack circulated, Elliott told the House that "we must move the Japanese in this country into a concentration camp somewhere, some place, and do it damn quickly." Claiming that Japanese Americans on shore had attempted to signal the submarine, Elliott advised his colleagues, "Don't kid yourselves and don't let someone tell you there are good Japs. . . . Perhaps, one out of 1000." The article also quoted Santa Barbara County District Attorney Percy Heckendorf, who said that "enough has been learned as to shore signals in Monday night's Japanese submarine attack" to make removal "more imperative than ever before." Heckendorf also said that "we want absolute control of aliens and American-born Japanese alike. It is up to the Federal government. We are giving all the warning we can."[88]

In the two months following Pearl Harbor, then, advocates of the incarceration and removal of all people of Japanese ancestry had come to dominate not only the debate about Japanese Americans' loyalty but also the related debate about the meanings of "race." I cannot determine the degree to which the debate in Los Angeles influenced U.S. policy. It is clear, however, that the leaders of the movement for incarceration and removal in Los Angeles were pleased that U.S. officials had embarked on the policy they recommended. Not all of the arguments advanced by the proponents of incarceration and removal reflected traditional American racialism, but many did, and the policy of the U.S. Army clearly rested upon the racialist idea that all people who were "racially" Japanese were potentially loyal to Japan.

By mid-March 1942 it was clear that the army would force all people of Japanese ancestry to leave their homes in certain designated zones of the Pacific Coast states. Even as they accepted and obeyed the army's orders, however, some Japanese Americans vowed that they would continue to fight for their rights as U.S. citizens. "You can rob us of all our worldly goods. You can drive us from our homes. You can herd us into concentration camps. You can kill incentive for clean, hard work. You can do all these and more. But you CANNOT stop us from thinking. You CANNOT crush the spirit of liberty and the American traditions on which we were nurtured and raised," Togo Tanaka wrote in a March 13, 1942, editorial in *Rafu Shimpo*. "Our sacrifice in cooperating with Army authorities surpasses that of our boys on the battlefields, because we want the opportunity they have to prove their loyalty. We are asked to accept a denial of that privilege in the name of patriotism. Who else would do that except those who deeply love America?" Tanaka insisted, "we're not giving up our birthright of American citizenship without a fight."[89]

African Americans, Pearl Harbor, and the War

One of the most striking characteristics of the debate about Japanese Americans' loyalty was that it involved only Anglo Americans and Japanese Americans. Surviving evidence suggests that African Americans and Mexican Americans did not participate in this debate. The attack on Pearl Harbor, however, did affect African Americans' statements about "race." The *California Eagle* declared that "an era in American life died" on December 7, 1941. As long as the security of the United States was at stake, the "'Negro' problem . . . can no longer dominate our thoughts." Instead of demanding their rights, the *Eagle* editorial declared, African Americans would have to exercise their duties as citizens, as they had always done during "times of military emergency." The *Eagle* insisted that its opposition to discrimination and segregation—even in the armed forces—had not waned. "But the common sense knowledge of all American Negroes is that black people in this nation have today more liberty, greater power and truer freedom than any equal concentration of black people on the face of the earth." African Americans owed their liberty, power, and freedom to black soldiers. "We must defend this democracy, for it is the child of our blood and suffering. . . . It is the noble service of colored citizens during every national calamity which has earned for us the right to demand full and equal rights to citizenship." Although the primary duty of African Americans was to ensure victory for the United States, the *Eagle* promised that

"Negroes will continue to petition their rights throughout the conflict so long as it does not interfere with the vigorous prosecution of an all-out war."[90]

Despite the *Eagle*'s initial reaction to Pearl Harbor, U.S. entry into the war allowed African Americans to link clearly and forcefully their struggle against discrimination with U.S. war aims. African Americans argued that racial discrimination was hindering the war effort. One editorial in the *Eagle*, for example, declared that "when the United States is threatened hourly with bomb attack and the multiple horrors of all-out warfare, what nonsense it is to dilly dally with the niceties of complexion!" The *Eagle* also argued that discrimination would cause African Americans to grow bitter, and "every act which embitters a citizen of the United States against his own government is treachery not only to the Constitution and its noble provisions but to the very defense of the nation."[91]

The *Eagle* also warned that racial discrimination would hinder the war effort by damaging relations between the United States and many of its allies. In a February 5, 1942, editorial, for example, the *Eagle* warned that U.S. efforts to cement an alliance with Latin American nations might fail unless U.S. officials understood "that fully one-fourth of the Latin American population is out and out Negro and the rest rather thoroughly mixed." These Latin Americans would be offended by "the U.S. conception of democracy as a white man's invention, to be ladled to darker races at some future period." In order to avoid alienating not only the "American Negro but his 23,692,000 blood brothers in Latin America," the *Eagle* insisted, "Uncle Sam's nieces and nephews had better change some of their notions about 'inferior, dark races.'"[92]

In responding to efforts to keep African Americans from moving into the suburban community of Maywood, Charlotta Bass asked her readers how they thought the slogan "Keep Maywood White" would affect Filipinos, Chinese, and Indians in Asia as well as African Americans around the United States. Bass suggested that most Asian people felt an affinity for African Americans, because they were "members of the darker races" and "colored peoples." "The overwhelming majority of our South American neighbors are dark people also, and have to be convinced by our actions that we are in truth fighting for the freedom and equality of all peoples regardless of race, color or creed."[93]

African Americans' concerns about the effects of white supremacist ideology on wartime alliances seems to have translated into greater concern with discrimination against Mexican Americans in Los Angeles. In a February 1942 radio broadcast, for example, Charlotta A. Bass applauded the opening of a federal office in downtown Los Angeles "to concern itself with the problems of our city's Latin-American population." Bass said that "the privations of our Mexican citizens as the result of racial prejudice far exceed those suffered by my own people in this area" and that "there are parts of California where the treatment and general condition of the Mexican people can be compared only with that meted out to the blacks of the deep South." Shipyards and aircraft manufacturers had hired few Mexicans or Mexican Americans, Bass said. "Establishment of an office in Los Angeles to insist upon the proper, democratic treatment of our Mexican citizenry is a vital, encouraging step in the direction of all-out warfare against our fascist enemies and their native American allies."[94]

African Americans' concerns about discrimination against "the darker races," however, did not extend to concerns about the treatment of Japanese Americans. The *California Eagle* did not participate in the metropolitan press campaign to force federal officials to remove Japanese Americans from coastal areas. The *Eagle*, however, did encourage African Americans to take advantage of opportunities offered by the removal. Throughout the spring of 1942, *Eagle* editorials repeated the claim that the evacuation of Japanese Americans offered African Americans "a tremendous agricultural opportunity." One editorial asked, if the agrarian "empire" that Japanese Americans had constructed "must be lost to them, why shouldn't it fall into our hands?" According to the *Eagle*, the movement of African Americans into agriculture would help solve some of the problems facing the community, such as juvenile delinquency. "If nothing else," farming "KEEPS FAMILY UNITS TOGETHER. The big city in which black parents are hired out day and nite, to whites is the most potent threat to Negro youth."[95] Another editorial said that "there is no simpler or more direct way toward solution, in some measure, of the Race's overwhelming economic problem."[96] Members of the Los Angeles NAACP branch's executive committee discussed "the question of getting in control of produce now under control of Japanese" and appointed a committee to "look into this matter."[97] According to the *Eagle*, many African Americans responded with indignation to an article in the *Los Angeles Examiner* that indicated that Japanese American farmers in southern California would be replaced "with 'white Americans' only." Actually, the *Eagle* reported, Japanese American farmers would be replaced by "qualified American farmers."[98]

Mexican Americans, like African Americans, generally seem to have remained silent during the debate about the incarceration or removal of Japanese Americans. Mexican American organizations such as the Coordinating Council of Latin-American Youth investigated and protested discrimination against Mexican immigrants in the months after Pearl Harbor. These organizations, however, generally objected to discrimination on the basis of nationality rather than to "racial" discrimination. They apparently did not agree with African Americans such as Charlotta Bass, who argued that Mexican Americans were victims of even more pernicious racial discrimination than African Americans faced in southern California. Mexican American organizations did not begin to argue that discrimination against Mexican immigrants undermined the U.S. war effort until June 1942, when the Coordinating Council of Latin-American Youth passed a resolution that said that "the unity of the United Nations and the government's program of Pan-American solidarity are endangered by discriminatory treatment of nationals of allied countries."[99]

Conclusion

As this chapter has shown, in the months following the Japanese attack at Pearl Harbor, a struggle raged in Los Angeles over racial ideologies and the policies based on those ideologies. On the one hand, Japanese Americans and a small number of allies argued that, although Japanese Americans were racially Japanese, their "race" did not determine their loyalty to the United States. At first, they received support from many European American politicians, who seemed to agree with Japanese Americans that Japanese Americans could be loyal to the United States and that most were. By insisting that biology did not determine behavior, however, some Japanese Americans did raise questions about the loyalty of other Japanese Americans. While many Japanese Americans advanced a fairly nuanced interpretation of what it meant to be Japanese and American, a growing number of Anglo Americans with a variety of motives argued forcefully that "race" was not superficial—biology determined beliefs and behaviors, and, these people argued, all Japanese were "vipers," even if some appeared to be loyal U.S. citizens. Clearly most people fell somewhere between these two extremes, as ideas about race in the United States were slowly changing. Most people who participated in this struggle agreed that a substantial number of Japanese Americans, perhaps a majority, were good, loyal Americans. There was, however, they insisted, falling back on their older racialism, no way to distinguish these loyal Japanese from disloyal Japanese. For the sake of the nation, then, all Japanese had to be rounded up and, most officials eventually agreed, interned for the duration of the war.

Perhaps nothing is more important than the fact that the most important struggle over the meanings of "race" in Los Angeles in late 1941 and early 1942 involved only Japanese Americans and Anglo Americans. African Americans and Mexican Americans did not actively participate in the debates about whether or not Japanese Americans were or even could be loyal to the United States. Many African Americans and Mexican Americans did not argue that their status in U.S. society was related to the treatment of Japanese Americans. African Americans and Mexican Americans, however, did continue to pursue political strategies that they had largely embraced before the war. African Americans continued to argue that the United States could be a society composed of distinct but equal "races," and they continued to wage a war against employment discrimination and housing discrimination. The rhetoric used by many African Americans, however, did begin to change after Pearl Harbor. Increasingly African Americans began to argue that their struggle for equality and dignity in the United States could not be separated from the U.S. war against fascism in Europe and Asia. The treatment of African Americans in the United States, they said, would let the "colored people" of the world know if the United States really stood for democracy and against fascism. African Americans also increasingly made overtures toward Mexican Americans in Los Angeles.

Mexican Americans, however, seem to have been less affected by U.S. entry into the war than African Americans or Japanese Americans. The Mexican American newspapers and the records of Mexican American organizations contain few discussions of how the war had changed the position of Mexican Americans within the United States. These organizations continued to work against discrimination, but without using the kind of war rhetoric that Charlotta Bass and some other African Americans employed. In the second half of 1942, however, Mexican Americans would move to the center of the debate about "race" in Los Angeles.

THREE

"Due to Social Factors Rather than to Biologically Inherited Traits"

"Race," Mexican Americans, and Juvenile Delinquency

In early August 1942, less than six months after President Franklin D. Roosevelt issued Executive Order 9066, the *Los Angeles Examiner* published a front-page article that reported that "vicious gangs of Mexican youths—one group including girls—left a trail of death and injury in two forays yesterday." The article briefly mentioned that "one man was beaten to death at a birthday party broken up by the hoodlums" and then described a "brawl" involving "11 Mexican youths" and "five white boys at a gravel pit swimming pool in Baldwin Park." The *Examiner* reported that the "Mexican youths" "chased an unidentified boy into the water, beating him with chains until he disappeared, and beat up the quintet of white youths." Although county lifeguards from Hermosa Beach spent several hours dragging the pool the day after the alleged drowning, they failed to locate a body. The newspaper noted that sheriff's deputies arrested eleven Mexican American men, who ranged in age from sixteen to eighteen years, "several of whom... admitted they were in the rock pit vicinity, but denied the assaults."[1]

The first event described in this article—the death of twenty-two-year-old José Díaz—has deservedly received a great deal of attention from journalists and scholars since it occurred in 1942. The Grand Jury returned murder indictments against twenty-nine young men, six of whom had not been identified or arrested at the time. One of these six unidentified defendants eventually came forward. Twenty-four young men actually faced charges. Two requested separate trials, but twenty-two were tried in a single trial. After a trial that lasted three months, nine of the defendants were convicted of second-degree murder and sent to prison at San Quentin. Five were convicted of assault; they served their sentences in the Los Angeles County Jail. This case became known as the "Sleepy Lagoon" case due to its association with a gravel-pit swimming hole nicknamed "Sleepy Lagoon." The Sleepy Lagoon case prompted a number of people in Los Angeles to organize to correct what they perceived as a grave miscarriage of justice. Their efforts led to the reversal of the convictions and the release of the young men who had been convicted of murder.[2] The sensational trial and the mobilization following the verdict in the Sleepy Lagoon case have allowed historians to ignore the other event described in this article—the alleged attack by "Mexican youths" upon "white boys." The debates surrounding the meanings of "race" in Los Angeles in the second half of 1942, however, tended to focus more broadly on what was perceived as an increase in gang violence among "Mexicans" than on the Sleepy Lagoon case in particular. The *Examiner*'s depiction of this "brawl" reveals a good deal about meanings of race in Los Angeles in August 1942. The newspaper article contrasted "Mexican youths" with "white boys," clearly suggesting that "Mexicans" were a racial group and that the "Mexican" character of the alleged assailants helped to explain their actions.

This article in the *Examiner* prompted a response from Mexican American attorney Manuel Ruiz, Jr., in his capacity as the secretary to the trustees of Cultura Panamericana, Inc. Ruiz and other leaders in the city's Mexican American community established Cultura Panamericana in 1940. The organization worked to "stimulate and promote interest in Inter-American culture, bring about a closer relationship between nations of the

Western Hemisphere, and develop American continental solidarity."[3] In an August 6, 1942, letter to the editor of the *Examiner*, Ruiz drew attention to the article's reference to "a melee between 'Mexican' and Whites." Ruiz characterized this reference as a "blunder" and declared it "incomprehensible." Although Ruiz had referred to Mexicans as a "racial group" when he appeared before the FEPC in October 1941 (see chapter one), he informed the editor that "the word 'Mexican' denotes a nationality, not a race." Recasting the complex meanings of "race" and patterns of racial interaction in Mexico to conform to those in the United States, Ruiz explained that "there are White Mexicans, Mexican-Indians, and a few Mexican-Negros [*sic*], a negligible number of the latter however in proportion to Americans of negro [*sic*] extraction." He further insisted that "the alleged 'Mexican Youths' involved in the gang fights are 'American Youths' born and reared in this vicinity," and he concluded: "Western-hemispheric solidarity will have to be preceded by a more clear understanding upon the part of the editors of our newspapers, of pertinent historical and geographical data."[4] The newspaper's managing editor, sensitive to charges that his publication might be undermining the war effort, apologized for "this error." He indicated that "instructions have been issued to all of our staff so that there will be no repetition of this statement in the future," and he assured Ruiz that "it is our desire at all times to foster good neighborly relations."[5]

Although the *Examiner* did not publish Ruiz's letter, the exchange between Ruiz and the *Examiner*'s managing editor suggests that by the summer of 1942 a new site of contention had emerged in the ongoing debate about the meanings of "race." Most of the daily newspapers continued to publish articles and editorials that reiterated the idea that Japanese Americans' racial characteristics made them a threat to the security of the United States. In the second half of 1942 and for much of 1943, however, elected officials, civic leaders, and journalists also argued about what most agreed was an increase in juvenile delinquency among young Mexican Americans. By insisting that "Mexicans" were not a racial group, Ruiz had at least obliquely challenged the dominant construction of "race" in Los Angeles. If "Mexicans" did not constitute a "race," any increase in juvenile delinquency among Mexican Americans could not be rooted in biology. In the months following Ruiz's correspondence with the *Examiner*'s editor, many law enforcement officers and some elected officials argued that a natural or genetic proclivity toward criminality on the part of people of Mexican ancestry had led to the increase in juvenile delinquency among Mexican Americans. In response, the Mexican consul, a number of Mexican American community leaders, union officials, Communist party members, elected officials, scholars, and social workers joined Ruiz in insisting that people of Mexican ancestry were not by nature inclined toward criminal behavior. Although this disagreement did not lead either side to abandon its position, it did make clear that there were many people in Los Angeles who rejected the idea that "race" determined how a person acted. It also set the stage for a more decisive disagreement about the meanings of "race" that followed the outbreak of rioting in June 1943.

The Grand Jury Investigates

Many officials in Los Angeles did not see José Díaz's death as the result of an isolated crime. Instead, they interpreted it as the logical result of a crime wave among organized gangs of young men and women. Law enforcement agencies in Los Angeles responded to José Díaz's death by rounding up hundreds of suspected gang members.[6] In addition to returning indictments against twenty-nine young men suspected of killing Díaz, the Los Angeles County Grand Jury responded to Díaz's death by conducting an investigation into juvenile delinquency. The Grand Jury provided an opportunity for people with very different perceptions of juvenile delinquency to express their opinions. The first group of people to present their opinions to the Grand Jury were law enforcement officers. High-ranking officers from both the Los Angeles Police Department and the Los Angeles County Sheriff's Department appeared before the jury ten days after Díaz died. Some officers also sent letters to Ernest W. Oliver, the Grand Jury foreman. These officers made it clear that they believed that there had been a startling increase in juvenile crime among Mexican Americans. They offered a number of different explanations for the rise in juvenile delinquency. One argued that the existing recreation program in the city had led to the increase in juvenile crime. Capt. Vernon Rasmussen of the Los Angeles Police Department explained that young Mexican Americans "who congregated at the various recreational centers developed into a clannish, self-centered group and refused to associate with the other recreational groups." Members of one center would not invite members of other centers to their functions, and this led to conflicts between centers, he insisted.

Rasmussen also indicated that he had contacted supervisors of some of the existing recreation facilities. These supervisors told him that "the Mexican youths who used these centers were very destructive" and demonstrated "absolutely no appreciation of the efforts put forth for their betterment."[7]

The highest-ranking official to appear before the grand jury was Police Chief C. B. Horrall. Clement B. "Jack" Horrall was a native of Indiana who had served as an officer in the U.S. Army during World War I. He joined the Los Angeles Police Department in 1923. Like Mayor Fletcher Bowron, Horrall was a Republican. Bowron appointed Horrall the chief of the department after his reelection in 1941, and Horrall remained loyal to the mayor.[8] Horrall argued that the class status of Mexican immigrants led their children to join gangs and commit crimes. These immigrants, Horrall stated, "were the poor class of Mexicans and have not been able to acquire or accept the standards of living that exist in this country." Because their children were educated in the United States and noticed "the differences between their standard of living and that of the majority of persons in this country," they had "lost respect for their parents and their parents have lost the ability to properly control them."[9]

All of these law enforcement officers argued that Mexican Americans were biologically inclined toward criminal behavior. Lt. Ed. Duran Ayres, the head of the Foreign Relations Bureau of the Los Angeles County Sheriff's Department, expressed this idea most clearly and explicitly. Duran Ayres, a native of San Francisco, had served in the merchant marine in the First World War. He joined the sheriff's office in 1924 and served in the Robbery and Homicide bureaus before he was appointed head of the Foreign Relations Bureau.[10] In his statement to the grand jury, Duran Ayres acknowledged that "economics, lack of employment, and small wages" led some young Mexican Americans to commit theft and robbery. He also acknowledged that "discrimination and segregation as evidenced by public signs and rules such as appear in certain restaurants, public swimming plunges, public parks, theatres and even in schools, causes [*sic*] resentment among the Mexican people." Duran Ayres, however, insisted that poverty and discrimination were not the fundamental causes of crime among young Mexican Americans. "To get a true perspective of this condition we must look for a basic cause that is even more fundamental than the factors already mentioned," he said. Duran Ayres argued that "the biological basis" was "the main basis to work from."

Duran Ayres insisted that "there is practically as much difference between the races of man" as there is between wild and domesticated animals. "Although a wild cat and a domestic cat are of the same family they have certain biological characteristics so different that while one may be domesticated the other would have to be caged to be kept in captivity," he said. Duran Ayres quoted Rudyard Kipling's maxim, "East is East and West is West, and never the twain shall meet," which he said "gives us an insight into the present problem because the Indian, from Alaska to Patagonia, is evidently Oriental in background—at least he shows many of the Oriental characteristics, especially so in his utter disregard for the value of life." Duran Ayres concluded from the fact that Aztecs sacrificed as many as "30,000 Indians" in a single day that "this total disregard for human life has always been universal throughout the Americas among the Indian population, which of course is well known to everyone." Duran Ayres conceded that it would be unfair to conclude that all Mexicans were like the "Oriental" Aztecs. He did point out, however, that "less than 20%" of Mexico's population "are pure Caucasians or White. The remaining population are Indian and Mextizos [*sic*]." Duran Ayres claimed that "the Mexican Indian is mostly Indian—and that is the element which migrated to the United States in such large numbers." In Los Angeles, Duran Ayres argued, Mexicans' styles of fighting revealed their racial origin. "The Caucasian, especially the Anglo-Saxon," relied upon his fists in fights. Kicking an opponent "is considered unsportive," Duran Ayres said. "But this Mexican element considers all that to be a sign of weakness, and all he knows and feels is a desire to use a knife or some lethal weapon. In other words, his desire is to kill, or at least let blood."

Duran Ayres noted that "representatives of the Mexican colony" would be reluctant to admit that there was a biological basis for criminality among Mexican Americans. He argued that the fact that "Chinese and Japanese in California" had "always been law abiding" proved that Mexican Americans were biologically inclined toward criminal behavior. Like Mexican Americans, Chinese Americans and Japanese Americans had endured discrimination, "but such acts of violence as now are in evidence among the young Mexicans has been entirely unknown among these two Oriental peoples." Although Duran Ayres's statement about Chinese Americans and Japanese Americans seemed to contradict his earlier statement about the "Oriental" character of American Indians, he explained that Indians were more closely related to "Malays" than to "Mongolians." According to Duran Ayres, then,

Mexican Americans had more in common with the violent Filipinos, whom he claimed were Malays, than with the law-abiding Chinese and Japanese.[11]

Horrall and Rasmussen embraced Duran Ayres's racialist argument. Horrall stated that Duran Ayres "gave an intelligent statement of the psychology of the Mexican people, particularly the youths."[12] Rasmussen supported Duran Ayres's argument that "Mexicans" needed to be punished severely because they were different from "Caucasians." According to Rasmussen, Mexican gang members admired other gang members who had committed crimes but received suspended sentences. "This is exactly contrary to the attitude adopted by the respectable Caucasian element," Rasmussen insisted. To undercut this apparently racial tendency, Rasmussen recommended that "as little publicity or notoriety as possible should be given any of these Mexican violators, and, that if possible, no pictures or other general information should be published by the press."[13]

Although all of these law enforcement officers agreed that Mexicans were biologically inclined toward criminality, none of them suggested a solution that would actually address this supposed inclination. They did not call for the expulsion of all Mexicans from Los Angeles. Nor did they call for a program of sterilization. They also disagreed strongly with reformers who called for more job training and recreational facilities for young Mexican Americans. "I do not feel that additional recreational facilities will in any way assist in the solution of the problem," Rasmussen wrote.[14] Instead, they insisted that the only way to reduce crime among Mexican Americans was to make certain that lawbreakers received "swift and sure punishment such as proper incarceration." Mexican American lawbreakers, Duran Ayres said, interpreted any lenience by authorities as "evidence of weakness or fear." Duran Ayres argued that "it is just as essential to incarcerate every member of a particular gang, whether there be 10 or 50, as it is to incarcerate one or two of the ring leaders. In other words—take them out of circulation until they realize that the authorities will not tolerate gangsterism."[15]

Duran Ayres's, Horrall's, and Rasmussen's statements were not presented publicly to the Grand Jury. No mention of their statements was published in the Los Angeles press. Their statements, however, must be considered, because they inspired a detailed response a few months later. Even though the statements of Duran Ayres and Rasmussen were not publicized, they were similar to arguments presented by some journalists. A week before Duran Ayres appeared before the Grand Jury, an editorial in the

Times blamed the rise in juvenile delinquency on the "efforts of professional mollycoddlers to prevent or mitigate the punishment of young criminals." The *Times* argued that "the community, in self-defense, needs to try the deterrent effect of some severe punishment. . . . The only way to cure tough crime is to be tough with perpetrators, which is a lesson some of our State and local prosecutors and judges could take to heart."[16] *Times* reporter Timothy G. Turner later criticized "the mush-headed sentimentalists" who thought of the "zoot-suit gangsters" as "'naughty boys' who should not be punished too severely."[17]

The Grand Jury Investigates Again

Two months after Duran Ayres, Horrall, and Rasmussen testified before the Grand Jury, another group of witnesses appeared before a special committee of the Grand Jury. Carey McWilliams noted in *North from Mexico* that Harry Braverman, one of the members of the Grand Jury, was distressed by Duran Ayres's testimony and arranged to have witnesses rebut Duran Ayres's arguments about the racial disposition of predominantly Indian Mexicans to engage in criminal activity.[18] It is not clear, however, why this rebuttal did not occur soon after Duran Ayres testified. By the time this second set of witnesses appeared before the Grand Jury, the Sleepy Lagoon trial had begun, and Los Angeles newspapers had begun to devote more space not only to the trial but also to what reporters and editors characterized as the continued problem of juvenile delinquency.[19]

The people who responded to the statements of Duran Ayres, Horrall, and Rasmussen were all prominent men. They included Carey McWilliams, the chief of the Division of Immigration and Housing of the state of California; Harry Hoijer, a UCLA anthropologist; Guy T. Nunn, a representative of the Minority Groups Service of the War Manpower Commission; Manuel Aguilar, the Mexican consul in Los Angeles; Eduardo Quevedo, a leader in the Mexican American community; Oscar R. Fuss, the director of legislation and research for the Congress of Industrial Organizations; and Walter H. Laves, an employee of the Office of Inter-American Affairs.[20] These men came from a variety of backgrounds. McWilliams, for example, was an attorney, an author, and a public official. Born in Steamboat Springs, Colorado, in 1905, he moved to Los Angeles in 1922 and enrolled in the University of Southern California. After he earned his law degree, he joined a Los Angeles law firm. In his spare time, McWilliams pursued his desire to be a writer. He published a biography of Ambrose Bierce in 1929. The Depression led McWilliams to become increasingly concerned about poor people in California. He investigated the experiences of farm laborers in the state, and his efforts attracted the attention of leaders in the state's Democratic party. After Democrat Culbert Olson was elected governor in 1938, he appointed McWilliams to head the Division of Immigration and Housing. McWilliams's book on California farm labor, *Factories in the Field,* was published a few months after he assumed public office. At the time he appeared before the Grand Jury in October 1942, McWilliams had begun work on a book about racial groups in the United States. This book, *Brothers under the Skin,* was published in 1943.[21]

Unlike McWilliams, Harry Hoijer had spent only two years in Los Angeles. Hoijer was born in Chicago in 1904. Both of his parents were Swedish immigrants. As an undergraduate at the University of Chicago, he studied mathematics and engineering. Hoijer decided against a career as an engineer; in 1927 he began his graduate study in anthropology at the University of Chicago. As a graduate student and throughout his career, Hoijer studied languages. His doctoral dissertation focused on the Coahuiltecan language, Tonkawa, of Oklahoma. Hoijer completed his doctorate in 1931 and taught for several years as an instructor at Chicago. UCLA hired Hoijer as an assistant professor in its new Department of Anthropology and Sociology in 1940.[22]

Guy T. Nunn was still in his twenties when he appeared before the Grand Jury. Nunn was born in New Orleans, but his father worked for railroads, and the family moved often during his childhood. Nunn graduated from Occidental College in Los Angeles in 1936. He was awarded a Rhodes Scholarship and spent two years studying at Oxford. Nunn also studied in Paris before he returned to the United States, where he worked as a field examiner for the National Labor Relations Board and as a labor economist for the Federal Reserve System before he began working for the War Manpower Commission. Nunn joined the army later in the war and served as a paratrooper in Europe. He was captured and spent thirteen months as a prisoner of war.[23]

It is significant that only these officials and community leaders were allowed to speak before the Grand Jury. No gang members were allowed to tell the Grand Jury why they joined gangs or participated in the acts they did. The people who testified before the Grand Jury did not indicate that they had talked with any gang members. Instead, they relied largely upon the work of social scientists and social workers, some of whom had drawn conclusions from their observations of and conversations with members of minority groups. A number of common themes emerged in the testimony of these individuals.

All of the witnesses accepted the law enforcement officers' argument that there had been an increase in juvenile crime among Mexican Americans. Most also agreed with Duran Ayres's statement that discrimination against Mexican Americans had led to this increase in juvenile crime. However, they rejected Duran Ayres's claim that discrimination was "a contributing factor, but not the main one." Consul Aguilar, for example, said that discrimination was "the basis of the whole problem." He argued that juvenile crime could only be eliminated by the adoption of "effective and legal means and ways of stopping once and for [all] racial prejudice and bigotry of all sorts and forms."[24]

Some of the witnesses warned Grand Jury members about the international ramifications of law enforcement actions in Los Angeles. Nunn, for example, said that some Latin American newspapers interpreted the police roundup of suspected gang members as evidence that Latin Americans "could expect nothing but abuse from the United States." Nunn described the publishers of these newspapers as "hostile to full Pan-American cooperation and aggressive prosecution of the war."[25]

Some of the witnesses challenged Duran Ayres's depiction of American Indians and Mexicans. Hoijer, for example, rejected Duran Ayres's claim that Los Angeles's Mexican residents were the descendants of bloodthirsty savages. Hoijer argued that Los Angeles's Mexicans were descended from "American Indians of a high degree of civilization." The Mayas, he said, had "developed a civilization rivaling in splendor and complexity that of the ancient Egyptians. . . . North of these peoples lived the Aztecs and many other tribes only slightly less advanced than the Maya." Hoijer conceded that the Aztecs practiced human sacrifice. He said it was "ridiculous," however, to conclude from the fact that the Aztecs practiced human sacrifice that they "were inherently indifferent to human life or had an inherent desire to kill." Hoijer pointed out that Americans "kill several thousands of persons a year in traffic accidents and are now sacrificing thousands more in the war against fascism." These facts, however, did not demonstrate that Americans were inherently indifferent to human life.

Hoijer also pointed out that most Mexicans were not direct descendants of the Aztecs but instead "mixtures of Caucasoids" and Indians, and he insisted that "nowhere among these people . . . do we find any lust for blood, any human sacrifice, or any inborn desire to kill." He asked rhetorically, "can it be that this so-called inborn desire to kill has been found only twice in this history of the Mexican people—once among the relatively pure Indians of the Aztec Empire and the second time among a certain element of the Mexican population of Los Angeles?" Hoijer suggested that it was more sensible to conclude that both human sacrifice among the Aztecs and any crimes committed by Mexicans in Los Angeles were "due to social factors rather than to biologically inherited traits."[26]

Most of the witnesses directly attacked Duran Ayres's statements about the "biological basis" of crime among young Mexican Americans. "I know of no scientific warrant for the doctrine that there is any biological predisposition on the part of any race toward certain types of behavior," McWilliams told the Grand Jury. "Even the very term 'race' has generally come to be regarded as being almost meaningless. Tendencies toward certain types of behavior are to be found, not in the blood stream of people, but in their cultural heritage."[27] Aguilar insisted that any study of crime and delinquency in Los Angeles "should be made from a sociological point of view and not from a biological basis."[28] Nunn told the Grand Jury that "delinquency is not a monopoly of any racial or national group; it is a monopoly of poverty, excessive housing concentration, social and economic discrimination. These, far more than juvenile delinquency, characterize our Spanish-speaking minority."[29] Hoijer offered the most detailed critique of Duran Ayres's statements. He told the Grand Jury that the research of physical anthropologists proved that "there are none other than anatomical differences distinguishing the races of man; all differences in intelligence, character, personality, mentality, or in any other non-physical aspect are the result of differences in civilization, education, and training."[30]

As Hoijer's statement suggests, these witnesses relied heavily upon the research of social scientists, and they appealed to science in their testimony. McWilliams supported his statements with references to research by "our leading anthropologists," including Dr. Ruth Benedict.[31] Aguilar noted that he had consulted sociologists and psychologists, all of whom agreed with his assessment of juvenile delinquency.[32]

In addition to drawing upon scientific research, Duran Ayres's critics used the implications of his statement to attack the premise upon which it rested. Aguilar, for example, said that Duran Ayres's statement led logically "to the conclusion that there cannot be any possible harmony between people of our two nationalities." The "mutual understanding and mutual respect" that lay beneath wartime cooperation between the United States and Mexico, the Consul said, demonstrated that Mexicans were not racially inferior to Americans.[33]

In attacking Duran Ayres's arguments about "race," these witnesses suggested that immigrants wanted to and should assimilate into U.S. society. Most of these witnesses did not depict U.S. society as capable of accommodating different groups of people with different cultures, values, and patterns of behavior. When discrimination frustrated immigrants' efforts to assimilate, they argued, the frustration of the immigrants and their children led to antisocial behavior. Hoijer, for example, argued that prejudice and discrimination left "our Mexican citizens" as isolated from "the white members of our community as if they lived in Timbuctoo or some other equally remote place. As a consequence they are driven in on themselves and only the rare individual succeeds in adjusting himself completely to our language, customs, and ideals." In addition to being angry at those people who denied them access to "a place in our society equivalent to that enjoyed by their white contemporaries," Hoijer said, young Mexican Americans were "ashamed of their parents' language, behavior, and ideals; these are foreign and therefore scorned, the youth want to behave as other Americans do." Because they did not embrace their parents' values and they were not accepted by European Americans, "the youth have no recourse but to band together in gangs for their mutual protection. In the gang the Mexican youth finds an opportunity to expand his ego and to strike back at his oppressors."[34] Hoijer's statement suggests that juvenile crime among Mexican Americans would only disappear when they were allowed to assimilate into "white" society. As McWilliams pointed out, however, the prospect of such assimilation was remote. McWilliams argued that Mexicans faced discrimination because of their "degree of color visibility." He also quoted sociologist Robert E. Park of the University of Chicago, who explained that "the races of high visibility are the natural and inevitable objects of race prejudice."[35]

Because these officials and community leaders disagreed forcefully with law enforcement officers about the causes of juvenile delinquency, their recommendations to the Grand Jury also differed. Since they depicted juvenile delinquency among Mexican Americans as the "natural" and "inevitable" result of discrimination, they suggested that an end to discrimination would lead to a decline in criminal behavior. McWilliams recommended surveys and studies of conditions in Mexican American communities, greater federal attention to "improving the living and working conditions among the 3,500,000 Spanish-speaking people resident in the United States," and revision of citizenship and naturalization programs.[36] Hoijer pointed out that "the gangsters are already responding violently to repression, segregation, and defeat" and argued that "the imposition of more severe penalties and a more stringent regulation of these gangs would not only fail to solve the problem as it exists but would actually aggravate the difficulties to a point where even more serious outrages may result." Instead of being punished for their activities, Hoijer suggested, young Mexican Americans should be educated about their "rights and privileges as American citizens," and they should "have the opportunity to exercise these rights and privileges. Let us, in short, practice the democratic ideal as well as fight for it; the winning of several wars for democracy will avail us but little if we lose that democracy in our dealings with our next door neighbors."[37] Hoijer provided few details, however, about how Mexican Americans could be guaranteed the opportunity to exercise their rights and privileges as U.S. citizens.

In contrast to Hoijer and McWilliams, Nunn advocated sweeping changes in U.S. society. Nunn suggested that the war had already begun these changes. It "has set in motion a gigantic leveling force in our society," he said. "This war is teaching us lessons in interracial democracy which a hundred years of wistful pedagogy have not brought home to us. We are faced by the alternatives of taking these lessons to heart or losing the war," he added. Nunn argued that the war "demands that the crusts of our social caste structure be broken through, not only in employment but on all other levels in civilian life." He called upon federal agencies to change their policies and to recruit Spanish-speaking people as war workers and volunteers. He also urged the elimination of school segregation and housing discrimination.[38]

The daily newspapers devoted a small amount of space to the statements of some of the people who appeared before the Grand Jury. The *Times*, for example, devoted two paragraphs each to the statements of Nunn and Aguilar. The article pointed out that Nunn blamed juvenile gang violence on "caste and color discriminations, coupled with exceptionally low annual incomes." It also mentioned Nunn's criticism of "strong-arm tactics" as a way to eliminate gang violence, and it pointed out that Nunn also argued that the elimination of school segregation and other forms of discrimination would alleviate the problem of gang violence. The *Times* article mentioned that Aguilar agreed with Nunn that discrimination led to the emergence of antisocial gangs and that the consul "favored playground activities with proper supervision, Boy Scout troops, boys' clubs and night-school classes for parents." The article noted that Quevedo "praised the hearing for recognizing existing discrimination, prejudice and lack of opportunities." The article concluded with a four-paragraph summary of Hoijer's statement. Although the *Times*'s coverage of the hearing did not mention all of the ideas expressed by the men who appeared before the committee, it did faithfully convey their tendency to blame gang violence on discrimination and their argument that the elimination of discrimination would alleviate gang violence.[39]

It is not clear if the testimony of McWilliams, Hoijer, and other Grand Jury witnesses influenced some officials and journalists. It is clear, however, that some public officials and journalists agreed with these witnesses about juvenile crime among Mexican Americans. Karl Holton, the chief probation officer for Los Angeles County, for example, told members of the Kiwanis Club in late October 1942 that "this is merely one of the second-generation problems that every American city has had due to maladjustments in homes of foreign parents in low economic conditions." Holton was born in Blaine, Kentucky, in 1897. Due to the depressed economy, his family left Kentucky and moved first to North Dakota, then to Spokane, Washington, and then to a homestead near Stettler, Alberta. Holton served in France in the First World War. After the war he finished high school in Seattle and attended the University of Washington. In 1924 he rejoined his parents, who had moved to southern California, and began working for the county's probation department.[40] Holton also agreed with these witnesses about discrimination. "The Mexicans have suffered from prejudices which have prevented them from going into anything but common labor. High school graduates say: 'What's the use of our going through school, if you can only pick prunes?'" Holton insisted that young Mexican Americans should not be "arrested indiscriminately, and innocent ones branded as guilty." Holton, however, did not embrace McWilliams's and Hoijer's statements about the meaninglessness of race. He said that "Mexicans generally have very fine racial qualities and cultures from which we can profit."[41]

Los Angeles Times journalist Timothy G. Turner, who wrote that he "has had a lifetime of association with Mexicans," explained the growth of "gangsterism" in terms strikingly similar to those employed by McWilliams and Hoijer. Turner wrote that the principal cause of gangsterism "lies in the social problem of first generation Americans." Encounters with prejudice led these children of immigrants to wage war on the society that rejected them. Turner argued that this "first generation problem" was "compounded by color prejudice. Most of these young Mexicans have much Indian blood. There is a definite caste system against them." Turner pointed out that Mexicans did not face the same discrimination that African Americans faced. "Like Orientals they can go into restaurants and theaters. But a young Mexican American finds the economic bars up against him. He or she cannot get a job in stores or offices, even as a waiter or waitress in restaurants. The Mexican, however, can be a bus boy." Since Mexicans were excluded from most white-collar jobs, "we have graduated a whole generation of young Mexicans out of high school, educated sons and daughters of Mexican laborers into a middle class which for them does not exist," Turner wrote. Turner concluded by pointing out that he had "no solution to offer for these disturbances." Like Holton, he suggested that "the first thing to do is to punish the young men found guilty by fair trial of these atrocities, but to avoid anything savoring of persecution of the innocent. In other words, the authorities should be just." Like Holton, too, Turner rejected McWilliams's and Hoijer's statements about the meaningless of the term *race*. Turner characterized Mexicans as "a kindly, polite and goodhearted people." As a result of the revolution, however, "some classes of Mexicans lost much of their fine culture and the restraining influences of the Catholic religion." Turner asserted that many of the juvenile criminals "come from homes of recent immigrants of the worst kind, and our lavish relief system has not helped matters." Turner also blamed "our culture" for exposing young Mexican Americans to "an idealization of gangsterism which has existed since the days of prohibition, the evil effects of which are not yet over. These young men thus represent the worst of both races, and the shame of it should be mutual."[42]

McWilliams, Hoijer, Nunn, and Aguilar seem to have persuaded members of the Grand Jury that discrimination against Mexican Americans was having a negative effect on the conduct of the war. As a result of its investigation, the Grand Jury sent letters to a number of federal officials in

November 1942. The Grand Jury asked the Coordinator of Inter-American Affairs to establish a regional office in Los Angeles, the Office of War Information to create a unit to produce publicity for Spanish-speaking people, and the Secretary of War to make Mexican aliens eligible for defense work. These letters indicated that jury members believed that "raising the social and economic levels and promotin [*sic*] the full community integration of this minority is no longer a reformist or humanitarian movement but a war-imposed necessity."[43]

The Grand Jury's investigation into juvenile delinquency in Los Angeles offered a number of different people the opportunity to present their interpretations of what they all agreed was an increase in juvenile crime among Mexican Americans. The witnesses before the Grand Jury, however, did not represent all possible interpretations of recent events in Los Angeles. Most of the witnesses interpreted these events from similar perspectives. Except for Aguilar, all of the witnesses were Anglo Americans, and all of the witnesses were men. Many Mexican Americans, some African Americans, and women from a variety of ethnic groups responded to the reports of gang warfare, the death of José Díaz, and the Sleepy Lagoon trial in ways that differed from the responses of McWilliams, Hoijer, and Nunn.

The Citizens' Committee for the Defense of Mexican-American Youth

Although Mexican immigrants and Mexican Americans did not appear before the Grand Jury, some did express publicly their interpretation of recent events in Los Angeles. In early September 1942, for example, one hundred Mexican employees of California Mill Supply, all of whom were also members of ILWU Local 26, adopted a resolution that they sent to elected officials.[44] As the Sleepy Lagoon trial began, other Mexican American community leaders, union leaders, and Communist party leaders spoke up about the trial and the larger issue of juvenile delinquency. In mid-October 1942, the Spanish-Speaking People's Congress appointed LaRue McCormick to investigate the conditions within the Mexican American community that led to the emergence of "so-called 'boy gangs'" and to assist in the defense of young men and women who had been arrested.[45] LaRue McCormick was born LaRue Manby in 1909 in La Grange, Kentucky, a small town near Louisville. As a result of economic conditions, her parents moved the family to southern California. LaRue married Lester McCormick, her first cousin and a sailor in the navy, when she was sixteen. By 1930 the McCormicks had two children. She became involved in the revolutionary movement in the early 1930s. She joined the Communist party in 1934 and served as the executive director of the International Labor Defense in southern California from 1937 until 1950. In 1938 McCormick had been the Communist candidate for the congressional seat won by Leland Ford. In 1942 she was the party's candidate for the state senate seat occupied by Jack B. Tenney.[46]

One of McCormick's first acts was to call a meeting of people concerned about the Sleepy Lagoon case. Most of the people whom McCormick invited to the meeting were either members of the Communist party or friendly to it. They included California State CIO President Philip M. Connelly and *Eastside Journal* editor Al Waxman. Two CIO unions were represented. Several Mexican Americans came to the meeting: Josephine Fierro de Bright, the executive secretary of El Congreso de Pueblos de Habla Española (the Spanish-Speaking People's Congress), screen actor Anthony Quinn, and Bert Corona, the president of the Warehousemen's Union, Local 26, all attended. Fierro and Quinn both served as bridges between Hollywood and the Mexican American community. Fierro, who was born in Mexico, was married to the screenwriter John Bright. Quinn was a Mexican immigrant, born in Chihuahua in 1915, who began appearing in Hollywood pictures in 1936. Corona was born in El Paso in 1918. Corona's mother was a teacher, and he finished high school in El Paso. He came to Los Angeles to enroll at the University of Southern California in 1936. Soon after he became active both in community organizing and labor organizing for CIO unions.[47] The meeting ended with the creation of a committee to investigate the issues involved in the trial.[48] That committee eventually became the Citizens' Committee for the Defense of Mexican-American Youth, which was later reorganized and renamed the Sleepy Lagoon Defense Committee.

The statements of the Mexican workers and of the organizers of the Citizens' Committee for the Defense of Mexican-American Youth, as well as the statements issued by the committee itself, often conflicted directly with the statements of law enforcement officers. Some of these people and groups offered recommendations identical to those presented to the Grand Jury by McWilliams, Hoijer, and Nunn. The resolution passed by the California Mill Supply employees, for example, called upon local governments to provide "adequate and more ample recreational facilities" and to establish "more defense job training schools" in Mexican neighborhoods. The resolution also encouraged the U.S. Employment Service to do more "to procure jobs for the unemployed Mexican youth" and criticized the police for their "mass jailings, unnecessary arrests and beatings of Mexican youth." These "iron-handed methods will only create a worse and more bitter feeling among the Mexican people," the resolution predicted.[49]

Even as they disagreed with police responses to gang violence, some participants in the October 22 meeting described Mexicans as a racial group and suggested that they shared certain "natural" characteristics. *Eastside Journal* publisher Al S. Waxman, for example, declared in an editorial that "Mexicans as a race are easy-going, peace-loving people." He also argued that "the 20th century Mexican" was also committed to democracy, anti-Fascism, and organized labor. "They are a progressive people, and, if not hampered, would go far in the history of the United States," Waxman wrote. Waxman's concern with discrimination against Mexican Americans indicates that a person did not have to embrace modernist racial ideology in order to oppose discrimination. He pointed out that Mexican Americans, especially in southern California, "have had to face every sort of discrimination that can be heaped upon a minority group." Waxman's recommendations, however, overlapped with those offered by people such as McWilliams and Hoijer, who largely rejected the idea that Mexicans were a racial group. He suggested that greater recreational and employment opportunities would reduce crime among young Mexican Americans.[50]

Most of the union leaders and community activists, however, did challenge the racial ideology expressed by law enforcement officers. At the October 22 meeting, for example, some people demanded that Duran Ayres "be ousted from his position as head of the foreign relations bureau of the County Sheriff's office" because of his "vicious 'biological' theory to explain the incidence of crime among Mexican youth."[51]

At first, some of the founders of the Citizens' Committee seemed skeptical toward the assimilationist arguments advanced by people such as McWilliams and Hoijer. Philip Connelly, for example, did not accept the idea that Mexican Americans engaged in crime because they had not been allowed to assimilate into U.S. society. Connelly expressed doubt that there had been an increase in juvenile delinquency among Mexican Americans. "Crime waves are turned on and off by newspapers like water in a spigot,"

Connelly said at the October 22, 1942 meeting.[52] By March 1943, however, the committee's press releases began to borrow heavily from the Grand Jury testimony of Nunn, Hoijer, and McWilliams. One such release, for example, repeated Hoijer's statement that young Mexican Americans "are ashamed of their parents' language, behavior, and ideals. These youths want to behave as other Americans do, but it is evident that they suffer from prejudice."[53] It is not clear if the committee's apparent acceptance of this assimilationist strain of racial ideology was a direct result of Carey McWilliams's presence on the committee. McWilliams, however, was invited to join the committee when it was first organized, and he seems to have become increasingly important in its operations in 1943.

In their public statements these unionists and activists emphasized the threat to wartime unity posed by the juvenile crime wave, the police response to the crime wave, and the press coverage of the crime wave. They insisted that "fifth columnists" both were responsible for the crime wave and sought to manipulate the press coverage of juvenile delinquency. The resolution passed by the California Mill Supply employees, for example, argued that the "wave of juvenile vandalism and delinquency being carried on by Mexican youths," which included "anti-American activities, such as defaming our American flag," was "inspired and directed by the Sinarquista Youth Movement." These workers called upon all Mexican Americans to reject the Sinarquistas and "to rally around a real program of winning the war by joining the pro-war forces in our country, the labor movement, our national and state administration and the Spanish-Speaking People's Congress to push for the full integration of the Mexican people in our country's war effort."[54]

Unionists and community leaders also argued that racial prejudice and discrimination threatened U.S. alliances with Latin American nations. "Mexicans in the United States offer a testing-group for the sincerity of American attitudes towards Latins to the South," the Citizens' Committee for the Defense of Mexican-American Youth declared. The "long series of mass arrests, persecutions and police brutalities against Mexican-American people" could jeopardize "hemispheric solidarity," the committee insisted.[55]

The Citizens' Committee's emphasis on U.S. relations with Latin America offered it some protection from its opponents. The committee had many critics, most of whom were hostile both to unions and to the Communist party. These critics, however, had to exercise caution in their attacks on the committee, because the committee's allies included not only the Mexican consul but also some prominent Mexican leaders. Unrestrained criticism of the committee and all of its arguments could have been interpreted as offensive to these wartime allies. After the Citizens' Committee declared that the verdicts in the Sleepy Lagoon case resulted from prejudice, the *Los Angeles Times* blandly defended the jury. An editorial argued that the fact that the jury "acquitted five of the defendants, and in the case of others made what seems to have been a careful discrimination in their degree of guilt, offers a strong presumption, if not proof, that there was neither prejudice nor persecution, and that the court and jury considered the evidence on its merits."[56] The editorial did not identify the committee by name, nor did it directly criticize any of the committee's more general statements about the treatment of Mexican Americans.

The Citizens' Committee's strategy also offered it some protection from anti-Communists. In December 1942 the California legislature's Fact-Finding Committee on Un-American Activities, chaired by Jack B. Tenney of Los Angeles, announced its desire to investigate the claims that Sinarquistas had ties to the Nazis and had instigated juvenile crime in Los Angeles. Tenney, a World War I veteran and pianist, had put himself through law school in the early 1930s. In 1936 he won a seat as a Democratic member of the California State Assembly. At almost the same time he was elected president of Local 47 of the American Federation of Musicians. Until 1939 Tenney was a liberal Democrat. After he lost the presidency of the union in 1939, however, he set out to expose and destroy Communists, whom he blamed for his defeat. In 1941 the California legislature created a permanent committee to investigate "un-American activities." Tenney dominated this committee from its creation until 1949, when a bitter legislative battle over his tactics and over legislation he had introduced led to his resignation from the committee.[57]

In investigating the claims that Sinarquistas had ties to the Nazis, Tenney had to exercise caution. His investigation could have provoked an international incident, as a representative of the Mexican government had already declared that "Axis agents were using the National Sinarquista Union, a Fascist, anti-administration underground organization in Mexico, to stir up Mexican hate against 'Yankee imperialism.'"[58] In a long statement published in its entirety in the *Times*, Tenney assured the public that "the Mexican people and Americans of Mexican origin are not under investigation." He pointed out that "Mexico and the United States are Allies in the present world struggle," and he insisted that "the members of the committee investigating subversive activities hold Mexico, its people, its government and the Americans of Mexican origin in our community in the highest esteem and affection." Tenney further declared that "no doubt of the loyalty of the Mexicans or Mexican-Americans exists in the mind of anyone conversant with these splendid people." Instead, Tenney explained, his committee was interested in a group of "American Communists and close fellow travelers" that had "continuously demanded an investigation of the so-called Sinarquista movement, alleging that recent disturbances among Mexican-American youth in Los Angeles is the result of the Sinarquistas." Tenney contrasted these "Communists and close fellow travelers" with "outstanding citizens, whose patriotism cannot be questioned." According to Tenney, "recent articles in the public press" quoted these "outstanding citizens," who charged that "Communists are attacking the Sinarquista movement solely because of its anti-Communist character." Tenney insisted that his committee "intends to determine the facts" about any links between Hitler and the Sinarquistas and about the reasons for Communists' hostility toward the Sinarquistas.[59] Philip M. Connelly, Oscar Fuss, and LaRue McCormick appeared before the Tenney Committee on December 19, 1942. Tenney announced that they had "admitted under oath that they had no information of evidence linking the Sinarquistas with Hitler or his agents."[60] Tenney's investigation, limited as it was by concerns about U.S. relations with Mexico, seems to have had little effect on the words or actions of the Citizens' Committee and its leaders.

African Americans and Juvenile Delinquency

African Americans as well as unionists and Mexican American activists expressed concern about the reported increase in juvenile delinquency among Mexican Americans. In their statements African Americans clearly rejected the argument that young Mexicans were biologically predisposed toward criminality. At the same time, they did not argue that "race" was a meaningless category, and they did not directly criticize the statements of law enforcement officers such as Edward Duran Ayres. Like the organizers of the Citizens' Committee for the Defense of Mexican-American Youth, African Americans expressed concern about the effects of the campaign against "boy gangs" on wartime unity. Some African Americans also argued that some Anglo Americans were so afraid of democracy that they would work actively to hinder the war effort.

Like McWilliams and Hoijer, some African Americans argued that criminal activity represented "the revolt of urban Mexican youth" against widespread discrimination. They also embraced McWilliams's, Hoijer's, and Nunn's recommendations to the Grand Jury. An editorial in the *Eagle*, for example, endorsed "proper public housing," "adequate defense training for Mexican young people," and "immediate placement in those very industries which howl long and loud about the shortage of manpower."[61]

Some African Americans, however, broke with McWilliams and Hoijer and raised doubts about the reported increase in juvenile crime among Mexican Americans. The most outspoken of these community leaders was John S. Kinloch, Charlotta Bass's nephew and the managing editor of the *California Eagle*. Kinloch had come to Los Angeles in 1936, when he was fourteen, and lived with his aunt. He graduated from Polytechnic High School and studied at USC. In addition to studying and helping Bass produce the *Eagle*, he served as the president of the Junior Council of the NAACP. He was inducted into the army in November 1943 and died in combat in Germany on April 3, 1945.[62] Kinloch accused the "vermin press"—William Randolph Hearst's *Los Angeles Examiner* and *Herald-Express* and Harry Chandler's *Los Angeles Times*—of manufacturing the "phoney 'crime wave.'" Kinloch insisted that "the 'crime' has existed all along, just as the revolting system out of which it grows has existed." Deplorable housing conditions, employment discrimination, and race prejudice had led "kids of slum belts all over America" to engage in gang warfare, Kinloch argued. Newspaper publishers only became interested in this warfare, he suggested, when it could serve their political purposes.

Kinloch explained that there was "a gang of pro-Fascists in this country who are scared sick at the prospect of victory for the United Nations, the kind of victory charted by President Roosevelt, Wendell Willkie, Senator Pepper, Joseph Stalin, and Chiang Kai-Chek." These "pro-Fascists" drew their inspiration from Hitler, "and Hitler says that 'America is a country permanently on the brink of revolution,'—that its minorities may be used to divide and disrupt the nation's war effort." "Pro-Fascist" newspaper publishers ordered city editors in New York, Detroit, and Los Angeles to "whip up a phoney 'crime wave' among Negro kids in Harlem, Negro kids in

Detroit and Mexican kids in Los Angeles," Kinloch wrote. By publicizing these crime waves, Kinloch suggested, "pro-Fascist" newspaper publishers sought to destroy "the fundamental prerequisite of a victorious America: national unity."

Kinloch also explained why the "vermin press" in Los Angeles focused upon juvenile delinquency among Mexican Americans rather than African Americans. "In Los Angeles, we have a peculiar situation," he wrote. "The Negro people here, through magnificent organization . . . have blasted a gaping hole in the wall that formerly dammed us into paths of restricted employment." Most young African Americans, Kinloch argued, had found jobs in defense plants, and "THE DECREASE IN JUVENILE DELINQUENCY HAS BEEN ASTOUNDING!" The "militance and organization of Negroes in Los Angeles" would have made a press campaign against African Americans ineffective. "So the Hearst-Chandler press looked around for a more likely target, and they leveled a lousy typewriter barrage at the Mexican population."

Kinloch contrasted the "militance and organization" of African Americans in Los Angeles with the lack of such militance and organization in the Mexican American community. He pointed out, as had racial modernists such as McWilliams and Hoijer, the "real cleft between the first and second generations," and he suggested that the Catholic Church controlled Mexican American political activity. Kinloch also insisted that "the other wing of the Axis propaganda machine, the pro-Fascist Sinarquistas," had gained some influence in the Mexican American community. A few Mexican Americans believed Sinarquista propaganda, Kinloch said, "but only as the police crusade and the lying press campaign force them to desperation."[63]

A number of editorials and columns in the *Eagle* explained why African Americans should be interested "in what happens to our Mexican neighbors." Like Mexican Americans, Kinloch wrote, African Americans had "felt the whip-lash of oppression and we know how and where it stings." Moreover, he argued, African Americans would have been the target of the press campaign "if the Mexicans weren't more convenient. It's us in Harlem and Detroit."[64] An *Eagle* editorial further explained that "so long as the principle of discrimination may be employed to cheat ANY group of justice, our achievements are not safe. Any division of the American people today is fraught with danger for us all. The fight for the rights of Mexican citizens is part of the struggle of Negro America. It is also part of WINNING THIS WAR!"[65]

Conclusion

Many of the ongoing debates about the meaning of "race" within Los Angeles between the summer of 1942 and December 1942 revolved around the Sleepy Lagoon case and the closely related issue of "juvenile delinquency" among Mexican Americans. Historians since the late 1940s have generally accepted the arguments advanced by people such as John S. Kinloch and have interpreted the Sleepy Lagoon case as the result of an anti-Mexican campaign waged by the Los Angeles metropolitan newspapers. They have also tended to interpret the Sleepy Lagoon case as an important indicator of the attitudes that spawned the Zoot-Suit Riots. None, however, have carefully examined the rhetoric that surrounded the case and the larger anti–juvenile delinquency campaign to see what that rhetoric reveals about changes in the meanings of "race." As this chapter suggests, officials and scholars such as Carey McWilliams and Harry Hoijer became concerned with the Sleepy Lagoon case only after Sheriff's Department Lt. Ed Duran Ayres told the Grand Jury that Mexicans were violent criminals by nature. Perhaps because defending their ideas and Mexicans involved only a struggle with local officials and not federal or military officials, these officials and activists were more vocal in the weeks and months following the Sleepy Lagoon arrests than they had been in defending Japanese Americans earlier in 1942. Drawing upon research by anthropologists and sociologists, McWilliams and Hoijer argued that a person's "race" was not a reliable indicator of how that person would behave. By emphasizing the threat posed to wartime unity and to U.S.–Latin American relations by Duran Ayres's ideas, these activists and their allies received some support from local officials, most notably the Grand Jury. The Sleepy Lagoon case, the police campaign against Mexican American "juvenile delinquency," and the response to these events by officials and activists attracted the attention of some African American community leaders in Los Angeles. African Americans, while emphasizing the similarities between the experiences of Mexican Americans and those of African Americans, do not seem to have embraced wholeheartedly the racial ideology expressed by people such as McWilliams and Hoijer. Their statements and writings, unlike those of McWilliams and Hoijer, do not contain sweeping statements about the meaninglessness of "race" as a category. This may have reflected their ambivalence about the abandonment of "race" as a concept that could be used to encourage unity among the diverse group of people who were lumped together under the term *Negro* in the 1940s. By the end of 1942, however, events in the concentration camp at Manzanar had attracted the attention of many Los Angeles residents. For much of the rest of the war the debate about the meanings of "race" in Los Angeles would focus once again on Japanese Americans.

FOUR

"EVERY Person with Jap Blood in his Veins"

"Race" and Japanese Americans from Sleepy Lagoon to the Zoot-Suit Riots

One week after the Sleepy Lagoon trial began, the *Los Angeles Times* published an article about a new controversy surrounding "race." At the center of this controversy was a twenty-page pamphlet, "Japanese on the Pacific Coast," written by Dr. George Gleason, the executive secretary of the Los Angeles County Committee for Church and Community Cooperation. A long-time resident of Los Angeles, Gleason had worked for the YMCA in Japan from 1901 until 1919. At the beginning of this pamphlet, Gleason wrote, "At the outset of such a study as this tribute should be paid to the splendid loyalty of the great majority of the Japanese, both alien and American-born." Gleason declared that "their patriotic services to the American nation are numerous and well known. Their acceptance, also, of the government's program for evacuation has been not only prompt, but marked with a genuine spirit of co-operation."

Drawing upon the reports of lawmakers and law enforcement officers, Gleason dismissed rumors that people of Japanese ancestry had committed acts of sabotage on December 7. In discussing the reasons for the incarceration and removal of Japanese Americans, Gleason quoted other observers, one of whom wrote that "the Army actually yielded to the clamor of the extremists . . . led by irresponsible radio commentators and by politicians bent on catering to mass prejudices, and by business interests eager to crowd out Japanese rivals." Another wrote that "there is an uncomfortable parallel between Nazi and American practices." Gleason, however, did not simply report the words of people who were critical of the decision to remove Japanese Americans from coastal areas. He also reported on the statements of Secretary of the Navy Frank Knox, the Dies Committee, and Mayor Bowron, all of whom supported the decision. Gleason urged "friends of the Japanese" "to study and plan for a solution of the problem of dual citizenship, abolishment of all organizations in America directed from Japan, continued support of Japanese churches, and study and revision of the present immigration and naturalization laws."

Even though this pamphlet quoted both people who had supported and those who had opposed the incarceration and removal of Japanese Americans, its appearance sparked a protest by the American Legion. Legion officers argued that Gleason's pamphlet defended "the Japanese" and was "laudatory to Japanese, aliens and American born, and a part of the appeasement program designed to prepare Americans for a stalemate peace." Legion officials also said that the pamphlet "should not be circulated at a time when we are fighting the people that stabbed America in the back at Pearl Harbor." Walter J. Sullivan, the commander of the Los Angeles County Council of the Legion, said, "We think, from our present understanding, that Dr. Gleason's pamphlet is a good-will builder for the Japs and we don't need and we don't want that. We in the Legion want to nip in the bud any movement, no matter how small, that starts building America up for another stab in the back by anybody."

In response to the Legion's attack, Gleason "quickly offered his full cooperation in the inquiry and said he hoped the Legion officials would call him so that all the facts could be made public." Gleason took "sole responsibility" for the contents of the pamphlet, which he had showed to two members of the Board of Supervisors, "Mayor Bowron, representatives of the Department of Justice, Army officials connected with the evacuation of Japanese and religious leaders from several faiths." "I don't say they all approved of it entirely but no one asked me not to publish it," Gleason told the *Times*. "I meant it to be a factual report on the question."[1]

As soon as the American Legion raised objections to the pamphlet's publication, county officials decided not to publish additional copies. The *Times* reported that Gleason wrote a letter to Roger Jessup, the chair of the Board of Supervisors, explaining that the pamphlet's "sole purpose was to give a factual study of events." Gleason also noted that he "had no intention of making the pamphlet pro-Japanese." Karl Holton, the chief of the county's Probation Department and Gleason's supervisor, defended Gleason, describing him as "a sincere American who is trying to promote a better understanding of President Roosevelt's evacuation of the Japanese." Jessup told reporters that he thought that "citizenship should be taken away from all Japs."[2]

As the controversy surrounding Gleason's pamphlet suggests, the incarceration and removal of Japanese Americans from the coastal area did not end the public debate about Japanese Americans. In fact, although a number of people in Los Angeles argued about the relationship between "race" and juvenile delinquency in the summer and autumn of 1942, this argument only dominated the ongoing debate about the meaning of "race" for a few months. The daily newspapers reported on the "crime wave" among young Mexican Americans, but, by December 1942 newspapers consistently devoted more space to articles and editorials about Japanese Americans than to articles and editorials about Mexican American gangs. For the remainder of the war, the daily newspapers published countless articles describing the threat to national security posed by the release of Japanese Americans from concentration camps. Most of these articles reported on the statements of anti-Japanese politicians.

The Legion's criticism of Gleason's pamphlet is particularly revealing, because it focused on how Gleason depicted Japanese Americans. Many of the attacks on people like Gleason in the two years following the publication of his pamphlet also challenged any depictions of any people of Japanese ancestry that did not emphasize "treachery" or other negative, supposedly racial traits. This episode suggests not only that the fundamental issue in the debate about Japanese Americans was the significance of "race" but also that anti-Japanese leaders would use all the power they could muster to silence the voices of people with whom they disagreed.

This chapter traces the debate about Japanese Americans from the summer of 1942 until the Zoot-Suit Riots of June 1943. It would be impossible to discuss all of the anti-Japanese articles that were published in the Los Angeles newspapers during this period. Many of the articles about the efforts to confiscate farm equipment, trucks, and tires owned by Japanese Americans and stored in warehouses included very little about Japanese Americans themselves, although they did imply that Japanese Americans should not enjoy the right to make decisions about the use of their property.[3] Instead of attempting to discuss all of these articles, this chapter will identify trends in the debate about Japanese Americans, focusing particularly on arguments that were not simply about Japanese Americans but were also about "race." It will show that anti-Japanese leaders, such as the Legionnaires who attacked Gleason's pamphlet, dominated this debate through the end of 1942. They continued to argue not only that all people of Japanese ancestry should continue to be excluded from the Pacific Coast area but also that they should be further punished for being Japanese. Even though this debate was one-sided during late 1942, the voices of anti-Japanese leaders were often strident. They often lashed out at federal officials in the East who they insisted did not truly understand the Japanese as only anti-Japanese Californians could. In the first six months of 1943 the voices of anti-Japanese leaders grew even louder and more insistent as federal officials, including high-ranking military officers, announced actions and policies that anti-Japanese leaders opposed. The words of people who believed that Japanese Americans should be treated fairly and not punished for their ancestry also became more visible in the first six months of 1943.

An article published in the *Los Angeles Times* in February 1943 succinctly captured the essence of the debate in Los Angeles. Although the article was about conditions in Hawai'i, it could have been describing conditions in southern California. The author of this article was Kyle Palmer, who was usually identified as the *Times*'s political editor or correspondent. Palmer, however, also represented the Chandler family, which owned the *Times*, in backroom political dealings.[4] According to Palmer "the one big menacing question" in Hawai'i was "the loyalty of approximately 100,000 American citizens of Japanese ancestry." The article pointed out that there were two groups of people on the islands: those who believed that Japanese

Americans were loyal U.S. citizens and those who believed that Japanese Americans were disloyal. The article pointed out that "all sides are agreed that no single act of known sabotage occurred coincidentally with the arrival of Japan's hit-and-run surface, air and subsurface craft on Dec. 7, 1941." Some people, however, did not believe that this fact meant that Japanese Americans would not rise to support the emperor's troops if they invaded the islands. The fact that people disagreed about how Japanese Americans would respond in the case of an invasion reflected "a fundamental disagreement concerning the basic character of the Japanese as a race." On one side were people who believed that "the Japanese is inherently treacherous, fanatic, wholly incapable of breaking through a shell of tradition and inherited race motives and influences. From this viewpoint it is obvious that a Japanese cannot comprehend true democratic principles; cannot be assimilated into a democracy." On the other side were people who viewed the Japanese "as being no different from any other member of the human family, feels he is well along the road—in Hawaii—of development as a true lover of liberty; thinks of him here as being misunderstood, unappreciated—the innocent victim of circumstances."[5] Articles in the Los Angeles newspapers and the statements of many politicians and activists suggest that Los Angeles residents disagreed about the loyalty of Japanese Americans in much the same way that residents of Hawai'i disagreed about the loyalty of Japanese Americans.

Japanese Americans and Racial Ideology

The imprisonment and later removal of all Japanese Americans from the coastal area effectively prevented Japanese Americans from participating in the debate about their treatment. The daily newspapers rarely mentioned the statements of Japanese Americans. If any of the journalists who wrote for these papers read the Japanese American Citizens League's weekly newspaper, the *Pacific Citizen,* which was published in Salt Lake City during the war, they did not mention it. Even though the Los Angeles papers ignored their words, Japanese Americans continued to write about "race" both in camp newspapers and in the *Pacific Citizen.*

Japanese Americans often criticized the racial beliefs of people who had supported their incarceration and removal. In the June 18, 1942, issue of the *Pacific Citizen,* for example, Tom Hirashima, the president of the

Santa Barbara branch of the JACL, accused supporters of the Japanese American incarceration of embracing "Hitlerism" and "fascist race theories." Hirashima also argued that the treatment of Japanese Americans was a threat to members of "other minority groups." Hirashima asked rhetorically, "if citizenship of those of Japanese ancestry can be taken away today for whatever reason or reasons the would-be takers have, what is to prevent the taking away tomorrow of the citizenship of other minority groups in this country—of the Negroes, the Chinese, the Filipinos, the Mexican, etc."[6]

Many Japanese Americans expressed ideas that resembled those presented before the Grand Jury by men such as McWilliams and Hoijer in October 1942. In one column, for example, *Pacific Citizen* editor Larry Tajiri pointed out that science had failed to uncover some "natural" basis for hostility between "races." Quoting an article by historian of psychiatry and newspaper columnist Albert Deutsch, Tajiri told his readers that "there is 'no scientific or physical basis for race discrimination,' in terms of 'natural aversion.'" Tajiri wrote that "the nisei can accept race prejudice for what it is: a weapon in the hands of selfish and greedy people."[7]

Because it was published in Salt Lake City by people who were not incarcerated, the *Pacific Citizen* did not endure direct censorship. The federal officials who operated the concentration camps, however, did censor the newspapers that were published by the people imprisoned in these camps. Due to direct censorship or the threat of censorship, these camp newspapers usually did not publish articles or editorials that directly criticized either the decision to incarcerate and remove Japanese Americans from coastal areas or the execution of the incarceration and removal. These newspapers did, however, publish a number of articles that criticized racial prejudice and discrimination. After former Republican presidential candidate Wendell Willkie spoke in Los Angeles in July 1942, for example, the *Santa Anita Pacemaker* published excerpts from his speech. "We are learning in this war that it is not racial classifications nor ethnological considerations which bind men together," Willkie said. "It is shared concepts and kindred objectives. We are learning that the test of a people is their aim, not their color." The *Pacemaker* commented on Willkie's address, stating that "it is encouraging to note that America's leaders are not only aware of, but voice publicly, this fundamental essence of true democracy—that epidermal pigmentation is, after all, only skin deep; that democracy includes all peoples, or it negates itself." To accept "the myth of racial superiority," the newspaper said "is to revert once more to the days of witch doctors, pyromancy and nescience." Unfortunately, the editorial continued, "the great tragedy during this struggle out of primitive ignorance has been that the victims of this perverted theory have, in turn, sought other people over whom they could lay claim to superiority. The nisei, of any American today, has the most to lose by this."[8] This warning was the forerunner of many later articles in camp newspapers and in the JACL's *Pacific Citizen* that urged Japanese Americans not to think of themselves as superior to any other racial group. A week later Mary Oyama more explicitly cautioned Japanese Americans not to indulge in anti-Semitism, "that peculiarly fascistic phenomenon," that "has a closer relation to Americans of Japanese ancestry and to their issei parents than most of us realize." When "thoughtless" Japanese Americans make "derogatory remarks about the Jewish people in general, or about any other racial minority group, whether it be Negroes, Mexicans or Filipinos," they are "toying with a dangerous boomerang," Oyama wrote. "To indulge in any form of race-baiting is to play directly into the hands of the Axis. Any person guilty of race-baiting is participating in a definitely fascistic act." Before making a critical remark about "any people of any race or nationality," Oyama advised, "it would be wise to stop, count to ten, and ask yourself, 'Is this true?' 'Is this necessary?' 'Is it discreet?'"[9]

Later in August, the *Pacemaker* encouraged Japanese Americans to exercise their right to vote by absentee ballot. This call for participation in U.S. politics was combined with an attack on people who discriminate against other people on the basis of race. "There are those on the outside who would deny to us on a racial basis the right" to vote, the *Pacemaker* said. "Those who would discriminate against a race on a racial basis alone are enemies of America. For us to passively lose the right of franchise by non-exercising of that right would be aiding in the victory of America's enemies. It thus becomes incumbent on us to fight for America, in our way, on the home front."[10]

The *Pacemaker*'s editorials against racial distinctions and stereotypes were sometimes undermined by other articles in the newspaper. On August 15, 1942, for example, the newspaper reported a scheduled "Southern Jamboree," sponsored by the "Girls' club department." "Mammy lapel pins advertising the event are being worn by all girls' club members." The program, which began with the Pledge of Allegiance, included "Ole Southern Songs," "Southern Fun," and "More Ole Southern Songs." Although the program itself did not suggest that the evening's performances would include stereotypes of African Americans, the choice of this theme and the idealization of the Old South suggest that some Japanese Americans were much like European Americans in southern California and around the country, who, consciously or unconsciously, perpetuated vicious stereotypes about African Americans in the celebration of the Old South. The story was accompanied by an illustration of a "mammy" with big, white lips, apparently similar to the lapel pins being worn by girls' club members.[11]

Even though Japanese Americans were not able to participate in debates about their treatment, they were sometimes portrayed sympathetically in daily newspapers. As Japanese Americans boarded trains at Santa Anita and were transported to other camps around the country in the summer of 1942, Los Angeles newspapers published articles that did not depict the tens of thousands of imprisoned men, women, and children as threatening. One report on the movement of "500 inmates" of the Santa Anita Assembly Center, for example, stated that "except for the slanted eyes and flat noses of nearly all the evacuees, the departure could easily have been that of an equal number of Americans of Caucasian blood." The reporter apparently drew this conclusion from the fact that "not a word of Japanese was heard, except among the small proportion of Issei, or first-generation Nipponese." The reporter also indicated that "the Japanese youths wore the nondescript garb of American high school and college students." When the young Japanese called out the names of their friends, those names were "'Joe,' 'Pat,' 'Betty,' 'Rose,' and the like." At the same time as this article emphasized the "Americanness" of young Japanese Americans, it also depicted them in stereotypical fashion—they had "slanted eyes" and "flat noses," and they displayed "Oriental stoicism" until the train departed. The article's headline, moreover, referred to the "American" Japanese as "Japs."[12]

The Manzanar Riot

On December 6, 1942, violence erupted in the War Relocation Authority's concentration camp at Manzanar, about 225 miles north of Los Angeles in the Owens Valley. The outbreak of violence at the camp was a complex event that historians have been debating for more than thirty years. The details of the event are not relevant to this study, because they were not particularly relevant to the Los Angeles newspapers. It is important, however, to note that the violence was related to the December 5 beating of JACL leader Fred Tayama and to hostility on the part of some inmates toward people suspected of being spies for camp administrators.[13] The daily newspapers in Los Angeles tended to depict the violence as evidence that Japanese Americans were disloyal to the United States. The violence also offered editors and politicians the opportunity to attack the War Relocation Authority. Some of their attacks on the WRA clearly reflected disagreement about racial ideology.

The *Times* and the *Examiner* published reports of the violence at Manzanar on their front pages. These reports noted that some of the Japanese Americans were loyal to the United States. They noted, for example, that "pro-American Japanese"—specifically Fred Tayama and Tad Uyeno—had been beaten and later removed from the camp for their own protection. In its coverage of the violence at Manzanar, the *Los Angeles Examiner* presented a glowing portrait of Fred Tayama as an American patriot. The *Examiner* described Tayama as "one of Los Angeles' best-known Japanese and a militant anti-Axis leader here." The Hearst newspaper quoted from a speech that Tayama had delivered before Pearl Harbor, in which he declared that all Japanese Americans, "as good Americans, will be willing to lay down our lives for this our native land!" It also quoted from a letter Tayama had written in Manzanar to Assistant U.S. Attorney Atillio di Girolamo. In this letter, Tayama wrote, "if this is one way for us to prove our loyalty and worth as Americans, our sacrifice is really small in comparison to what others are going through."[14] In printing these words, the *Examiner* suggested that loyal and patriotic Japanese Americans had accepted that incarceration was necessary.

The *Examiner* and the *Times* also published articles about Japanese American Boy Scouts at Manzanar who prevented "pro-Axis" inmates from hauling down the U.S. flag at the camp. According to the article in the *Examiner*, the Scouts, "armed only with 'stones the size of baseballs,' defied a mob leader and his cohorts." In praising the Scouts, Director Ralph Merritt said, "the Flag was not hauled down, as these Scouts, their faces grim with determination, formed a phalanx at the base of the pole and had arms cocked ready to stone the first rioter who would dare draw near."[15]

Even though these articles acknowledged the loyalty of some Japanese Americans, the newspapers dwelled on the "pro-Axis group" in their editorials. The first of two *Times* editorials about the riots at Manzanar declared that the attacks on loyal Japanese Americans seem "to show that American kindness to the disloyal does not pay." The editorial insisted that "the Japs" in the camps "have been afforded the very best of treatment, together with food and living quarters far better than many of them ever knew before, and a minimum amount of restraint." The editorial compared U.S. citizens of Japanese ancestry to Americans who had become prisoners of war in Asia. This editorial did not explicitly say that Japanese Americans were by nature loyal to Japan. Instead, it conceded that some Japanese Americans were loyal to the United States. The *Times*, however, did not indicate that there was any problem with the fact that "disloyal" and "loyal" Japanese Americans were both incarcerated. Instead of calling for the release of "loyal" Japanese Americans, the editorial endorsed "close internment" or punishment for "rioters and troublemakers."[16] The second editorial also refused to admit that the existence of "pro-Axis" and "loyal" factions meant that all Japanese Americans should not have been treated as if they were all "pro-Axis." Instead, it declared that the riot proved "up to the hilt the necessity of Gen. DeWitt's order clearing all persons of Japanese ancestry out of the Pacific Coast military areas." According to the *Times*, the riot made apparent that "the feeling of too many Japanese was entirely unfriendly to the United States, and that considerable numbers of Japanese born here were included in the unfriendly group." If these "unfriendly" Japanese Americans had "been left at large, it would have been impossible to prevent spying and sabotage on a large scale, on one hand, and probably undiscriminating mob violence against all Japanese on the other."[17] Despite its admission that some Japanese Americans were loyal to the United States, then, the *Times* implicitly expressed support for continuing to treat all people of Japanese ancestry as potentially disloyal.

The editorials in the *Times* acknowledged that some Japanese Americans were loyal to the United States. The newspaper published letters, however, that drew no distinction between "loyal" and "disloyal" Japanese Americans. One letter to the editor depicted the violence at Manzanar as an expression of support for Japan and compared the treatment of the rioters with what would happen "if Americans in a concentration camp in Japan were to riot for their American love of country." The writer insisted that "if the Japanese demons did not sit them upon their haunches until their feet rotted off, or other tortures unbelievable to Christian minds, they would run a sword through their bellies." The letter called upon authorities to "punish these vultures who have preyed upon the rights of our glorious freedom" and to "place them under military jurisdiction so strong and so drastic that the exponents of infamy, treachery and cruelty shall never be able to raise their voices within our beloved land again."[18]

In the aftermath of the riots, some members of Congress blamed not only the Japanese Americans but also the federal government's War Relocation Authority for the unrest at Manzanar. In their attacks on the WRA, these members of Congress, unlike the articles and editorials in the newspapers, depicted all Japanese Americans as disloyal saboteurs. They also expressed hostility toward bureaucracy. Rep. Harry Sheppard, a Democrat from Yucaipa, suggested that the WRA had "coddled" Japanese Americans in the camps; this "coddling" had fostered the conditions that led to the riots. Sheppard warned that, in the excitement surrounding another riot "the evacuees might easily make a break from the camp to commit acts of sabotage." Leland Ford, the Republican U.S. Representative from Santa Monica who had been one of the most outspoken advocates of incarceration and removal of Japanese Americans, also blamed the leniency of the WRA for the outbreaks at the camp. He referred to the policies of the WRA as "social experiments." He told reporters that "months ago, officials of the War Relocation Authority were warned very bluntly that if they tried to carry out social experiments in these camps there would be trouble."[19] Ford also referred to WRA policies as "socialistic experiments." He said that "the Japanese were told by these socialistic experimenters to move about freely, and the people of the surrounding country do not know whether or not the Japs they see on the loose are escapers bent on sabotage or are abroad by permission."[20] Ford urged federal officials to "adopt a policy of rigid control."[21] In a somewhat confusing antibureaucratic statement, Ford said, "instead of the Federal government having jurisdiction over these camps, jurisdiction has been handed to one more civil bureaucracy which is making socialistic experiments in the camps."[22] In calling for "rigid control," Ford's and Sheppard's arguments were similar to the arguments advanced by law enforcement officers in their defense of police use of force to control juvenile gangs. All of these officials presented themselves as hard-nosed realists and their opponents as dreamers who wanted to conduct "social experiments" at the risk of public safety.

Although the statements of anti-Japanese politicians appeared frequently in the daily newspapers in Los Angeles after the riot at Manzanar, defenders of Japanese Americans were not entirely excluded from the debate. A few days after the riot, for example, the *Examiner* reported that some members of the Los Angeles County Grand Jury refused to support a resolution that called upon the California legislature to "prohibit any Japanese, alien or American-born, from occupying agricultural lands in California." This minority on the Grand Jury, led by Harry Braverman—the same person who had arranged for McWilliams, Hoijer, and Nunn to testify in October 1942—revealed the contradictions in the positions taken by anti-Japanese politicians and publications. Although the *Times* had admitted that some Japanese Americans were loyal, it had not argued that they should be treated as loyal citizens. Instead, it suggested that all people of Japanese ancestry, because they were "racially" Japanese, should continue to be treated as people whose loyalty was suspect. The minority on the grand jury insisted that a distinction had to be drawn between "loyal" and "disloyal" Japanese. "There are now 5000 loyal Japanese now serving in the United States Army and the minority did not believe that they or their children should be subject to exclusion from citizenship rights," Braverman told the *Examiner*.[23]

"Coddling and Pampering"

Throughout the first five months of 1943, politicians continued to repeat and to elaborate on the charges first leveled by U.S. Representatives Sheppard and Ford in December 1942. Members of Congress and the California state legislature insisted that the War Relocation Authority was not treating Japanese Americans as it should. Like the editorials published in the *Times* after the violence at Manzanar, these politicians argued that all Japanese Americans should be treated as potential saboteurs, whether or not they were U.S. citizens or loyal to the United States. Some suggested that all Japanese Americans were comparable to Americans imprisoned in Japan. The *Times* published one article in January 1943 reporting that several different members of the U.S. Senate had expressed concern that "the internees are not rationed on food, are permitted to govern and police themselves, can obtain release on parole to take outside jobs, and enjoy many privileges denied Americans in Japan." According to the *Times*, Sen. Hiram Johnson of California "complained that building materials denied American citizens are being released by Federal authorities to the camps." As a result of the reports of "coddling and pampering," the Senate Military Affairs Committee empowered a subcommittee, headed by Sen. A. B. "Happy" Chandler of Kentucky, to investigate conditions in the camps.[24]

The hearings of Chandler's subcommittee produced few startling revelations.[25] In fact, when the subcommittee released its recommendations in April 1943, those recommendations were at odds with the positions taken by anti-Japanese leaders in Los Angeles. The subcommittee recommended that "loyal" and "disloyal" Japanese Americans should be segregated and the "loyal" ones released from the camps. In a revealing statement, Chandler warned that the WRA could become a bloated bureaucracy like the Indian Bureau, and the camps could become like reservations, if the agency did not release loyal Japanese Americans.[26] The Chandler subcommittee's hearings did, however, allow politicians to continue to depict Japanese Americans as spies and saboteurs. After WRA Director Dillon S. Myer appeared before the subcommittee, for example, Sen. Chan Gurney, a South Dakota Republican, criticized the WRA for not monitoring more closely the contact between incarcerated people and people outside the camps. "Nobody knows who they write or telephone or send money to. They may be sending money to other Japs or to Germans or to other spies or saboteurs," Gurney said.[27] Some of the concerns about "coddling," however, actually led the newspapers to print articles that dispelled these reports. In response to the senators' concern that food was not rationed in the camps, for example, the *Times* contacted the director at Manzanar and reported that "the Japs get no eggs, no butter, less sugar than the civilian quota, and one cup of coffee per day."[28]

Many of the politicians who decried "coddling and pampering" in the camps implied that all people of Japanese ancestry should be treated as potential spies and saboteurs because of their "race." A few, however, explicitly expressed this idea. The most notable among these politicians was U.S. Rep. John Rankin. Born in Itawamba County, Mississippi, in 1882, Rankin graduated from the University of Mississippi with a degree in law in 1910. He moved to Tupelo in 1911 and served as a prosecuting attorney before he served in the U.S. Army during the First World War. A Democrat, Rankin was elected to the U.S. House of Representatives in 1921. At the end of January 1942 Rankin pledged "to the West the support of the South in emphasizing the immediacy of the Japanese threat," reminding his fellow representatives that "the South always supported the Far West in the latter's resistance to Japanese encroachments."

Rankin depicted the war in the Pacific as a "race war." He warned that if the United States did not counteract Japan's increasing strength, "it may well be that white civilization is entering its twilight." Rankin said that Americans might "get along" with Germans after "we have destroyed the Hohenzollern school of thought," "but we can never hope to get along with the Japanese people." Rankin insisted that "we can never hope to change Japanese thought-processes, which have not been modified by so much as one democratic Western concept in the 88 years that have passed since Admiral Perry opened the world, and the weapons thereof, to a tribe of savage feudalists." The "dean of the Mississippi delegation" succinctly summarized his position: "It is Japan or us, life or death for one or the other." Rankin lamented the fact that "Western civilization" did not remember history. He argued that "throughout the past warlike peoples among the yellow race have at almost regular intervals descended on the Whites—Attila, Tamerlane, Genghis Khan and Kublai Khan and Batu Khan of the horde."

Rankin connected Japanese Americans to the war in the Pacific. He told Ray Richards of the *Examiner*'s Washington bureau that he was preparing a speech for delivery to the House in which he would recommend that "after the Japanese Imperial government has been broken and the Japanese race once again confined to its aboriginal islands, all those of Japanese blood in the United States be sent back there." Rankin also said that he wanted to test in the Supreme Court "the claim that no Japanese is a citizen of the United States, even though he was born here." Rankin insisted that "Japan has always claimed these American-born Japanese as citizens unless they foreswear allegiance to Japan at Japanese consulates. The claim that such an oath means anything in a legal sense can be annihilated in any court, as great lawyers have told me."[29]

A few days later both the *Times* and the *Examiner* published reports of Rankin's speech before the House. Rankin told the House that "in this conflict Japan is our most dangerous enemy, our most insidious and treacherous enemy, and in peace or war she is our permanent enemy." Rankin declared that "this war is but one of the many conflicts we shall have to fight with her—conflicts that may extend for centuries and in which the whole Caucasian race may in the end be vanquished—unless we halt her advances now." Rankin continued to connect the war in the Pacific with the WRA's treatment of Japanese Americans. He insisted that "the American people are sick and tired of this policy of pampering the Japs in the relocation camps. Those camps should be turned over to the Army, and every one of them should be put under strict military control." Rankin suggested that the WRA's treatment of Japanese Americans represented a continuation of "that maudlin policy toward them that resulted in, if it did not invite, Pearl Harbor." Such a policy should not be pursued "while our boys are being butchered by these brutal apes in the Pacific, and while these savages are now on our soil in the Aleutian Islands," the Mississippian argued.[30]

Perhaps more significant than the fact that Rankin refused to distinguish between residents of Japan and U.S. citizens of Japanese ancestry or between "loyal" and "disloyal" Japanese Americans is the fact that Los Angeles newspapers prominently reported his words. The first article about Rankin's statements in the *Examiner* appeared above the newspaper's nameplate on the front page. It covered the entire width of the page.[31] Neither the *Examiner* nor the *Times* offered editorial comments about Rankin or his position. They expressed no embarrassment about the fact that their position regarding Japanese Americans had been endorsed by one of the nation's most ardent supporters of racial segregation. Instead, they enthusiastically accepted his support.

Rankin's depiction of the war in the Pacific seemed to resonate especially with the publisher of the *Examiner*. A few weeks after it published Rankin's remarks, the *Examiner* published an editorial that warned that "Japan might unite Asia in opposition to the Occident and include India and even China in a renascence of Asiatic power and policy." The editorial noted that "the Asiatics have tried before to impose their dominion upon the Occidental race and inevitably will try again as the course of empire wends its westward way." The *Examiner* declared that "we should see that this Asiatic renascence does not happen NOW, when the Occidental races are divided among and against themselves and are thus exposed to possible Oriental invasion."[32]

Anti-Japanese Leaders, the Army, and the War Relocation Authority

Throughout early 1943 anti-Japanese leaders consistently depicted the U.S. Army as their ally. They frequently suggested, as Rankin did in his speech before the House, that the army should take over the management of the WRA camps in order to end "coddling" and "pampering." Even though these leaders insisted that the army understood "the Japanese," however, on a number of occasions they discovered that army policies were not consistent with their goals. In these cases, however, they did not attack the army. Instead, they blamed the War Relocation Authority and other civilian authorities for pressuring the army into taking actions that anti-Japanese leaders deemed unwise. In criticizing the WRA and other officials, these anti-Japanese leaders often implied that all Japanese Americans were potentially dangerous because of their "race."

Near the end of January 1943, the army announced that it had decided to form a combat team of Japanese Americans. In announcing this decision, Secretary of War Henry L. Stimson clearly suggested that some Japanese Americans were loyal to the United States. He also indicated that loyal Japanese Americans should not be treated as if they were potentially disloyal. Stimson said that "the War Department's action is part of a larger program which will enable all loyal American citizens of Japanese ancestry to make their proper contribution toward winning the war through employment in war production as well as military service." Stimson also said that the decision to form the combat team reflected the army's recognition of "the inherent right of every faithful citizen, regardless of ancestry, to bear arms in the nation's battle."[33] The *Pacific Citizen* interpreted the army's action as military authorities' expression of "faith in the loyalty of the nisei."[34] On February 6, 1943, newspapers reported that the army had begun to accept Japanese American volunteers.[35]

Anti-Japanese leaders and organizations decried the army's decision. In their statements, they frequently argued that people of Japanese ancestry were by nature loyal to Japan and could not be loyal to the United States. A Los Angeles parlor of the Native Sons of the Golden West, for example, adopted a resolution stating that the "enrollment of Japanese would be inimical to the welfare of California, the United States and will undoubtedly create a dangerous threat to a proper and adequate defense of this country." The Native Sons insisted that all people of Japanese ancestry, "regardless of protestations otherwise, inherently are loyal only to Japan."[36] The Veterans of Foreign Wars post in Torrance adopted a resolution in March opposing the acceptance of Japanese Americans in the army. The resolution declared that the acceptance of Japanese Americans "is very dangerous to our national welfare and embarrassing to our troops." The resolution explained that Japanese Americans were fundamentally different from people of European ancestry and by nature loyal to Japan. "We have no doubt that should we be invaded these Japs would certainly go with their own race. They are Orientals," the resolution stated. The resolution further suggested that the army's decision was influenced by "pacifists of the East Coast who naturally would not be familiar with Jap tactics." Army officials should instead heed the warnings of war veterans on the Pacific Coast, who were "familiar with Jap tactics," the resolution implied.[37] U.S. Rep. John E. Rankin also protested the army's plans. "I was shocked beyond expression to learn a few days ago that the Secretary of War was organizing a Jap unit in the American Army," Rankin said in a speech on the floor of the House. "Such a unit would not only be dangerous, but it would do much to injure the morale of the men in our fighting forces and to shake the confidence of their people at home."[38]

Not all Los Angeles residents, however, opposed the army's acceptance of Japanese Americans. On February 19, 1943, the *Times* reported that the East Los Angeles Breakfast Club supported a resolution that declared that a Japanese American unit in the army "would be a menace to California and the nation." The club heard from Walter B. Odemar, a leader of the Native Sons of the Golden West, and from Judge E. P. Woods, who said, "we cannot afford to take a chance with the Japanese—their treachery at Pearl Harbor ought to teach us that we would be foolish to be betrayed again." C. D. Enfield, a local school principal, however, declared that he "did not believe in discriminating against the Japanese any more than against the Germans or Italians as an entire group." In the end, with Enfield and other members "emphatically opposed" to the resolution, "it was decided that individual members should send Representative Chet Holifield of the Nineteenth District their opinions on the resolution." Although the article clearly indicates that the club did not agree to pass the resolution, the *Times* emphasized the support of the resolution more than it did the opposition to it. The newspaper published its article under the misleading headline, "Ban on Japs in Army Backed."[39] The protests did not sway army officers. Not only did the army allow Japanese Americans to volunteer for service, but it also soon began drafting them.[40]

Even though the army had decided to allow Japanese Americans to enlist and soon thereafter began drafting Japanese American men, some high-ranking officers continued to express doubt about the loyalty of any Japanese Americans. In mid-April 1943 Gen. John L. DeWitt, who as head of the Western Defense Command had recommended and supervised the incarceration and removal of Japanese Americans from coastal areas, appeared before a U.S. House Naval Affairs subcommittee and declared that all people of Japanese ancestry were essentially Japanese and could not be Americans. "A Jap's a Jap," and "it makes no difference whether he is an American citizen or not," DeWitt said. "You can't change him (a Japanese) by giving him a piece of paper." DeWitt's statements supported his emphatic opposition to "the sentiment developing to bring back some of the Japanese to the West Coast." DeWitt further emphasized the importance of "race" by admitting that he was not worried about Germans or Italians on the West Coast "except in specific cases." In contrast, he said that "the Japs we will be worried about all the time until they are wiped off the face of the map."[41]

Japanese Americans responded to DeWitt's statement with anger and disbelief. The *Pacific Citizen* pointed out that DeWitt's statement undercut the claim that the imprisonment of all Japanese Americans on the coast was a result of military necessity. "It now appears . . . that wholesale evacuation and the abridgment of the citizenship rights of an entire American minority group was born of the blind race prejudice of a single individual." DeWitt's statement further made it seem as if the evacuation of Japanese Americans from the Pacific Coast could legitimately be "compared to the Nazi evacuation of Jews from Germany since both were carried out on the basis of racial ancestry alone."[42]

The daily newspapers did not immediately comment on DeWitt's statement, although they later embraced his position. Three days after DeWitt declared that "a Jap's a Jap," however, anti-Japanese leaders had to confront disturbing news. The *Times* reported on its front page on April 17 that the "return of 'loyal' Japanese and Japanese-Americans to Pacific Coast areas from which they were removed a year ago was under consideration." Although this article's first paragraph did not identify who was considering allowing Japanese Americans to return, it suggested that the War Relocation Authority was promoting the return. The article indicated that the WRA "and other interested Federal agencies" were discussing "various plans for releasing trustworthy evacuees." The *Times*, however, did report that the acting head of the WRA "denied reports his agency is exerting pressure on the War Department." The *Times* article noted that some officials argued that "if a man is good enough to die for us, he ought to be able to go where he wants." The article also stated that War Department officials had not commented officially on the reports, "but The Times learned various high military authorities are inclined toward 'gradual' easing of present bans."

In addition to reporting that some unnamed officials were considering allowing some Japanese Americans to return to the Pacific Coast, the *Times* article offered two prominent anti-Japanese members of the U.S. House of Representatives the opportunity to denounce the proposal. U.S. Rep. John M. Costello of Hollywood said, "I don't think anything of this sort should be done. It would create a tremendous furor and there is no way of deciding which Japanese is trustworthy." According to the *Times*, U.S. Rep. Harry R. Sheppard of Yucaipa "questioned whether any of the evacuees should be released and said that under no circumstances should they be allowed inside the forbidden area." Sheppard claimed that his beliefs were completely consonant with those expressed by General DeWitt, and he suggested that all residents of the Pacific Coast opposed the return of Japanese Americans. "The general is in the best position to judge whether the Japanese would be dangerous in California, and his opinion should carry great weight. I think the people on the Coast would resent it very much if the bars are let down."[43]

Even though only the army and perhaps the Supreme Court had the authority to rescind any of the exclusion orders, Costello refused to criticize military authorities. Instead, he continued to attack the War Relocation Authority. In an April 17 speech on the floor of the House, Costello argued that WRA officials did not have the experience with Japanese Americans to determine whether or not they were loyal to the United States. "Those in charge of the War Relocation Authority, after a few months of experience, feel capable of judging the loyalty of these people (evacues) [*sic*] without having had any previous experience with the Japanese," he declared.[44] Instead of noting that the army would be responsible for the consequences if it relaxed the exclusion orders, Costello insisted that "if the proposal to return the so-called loyal Japanese to the Pacific Coast is carried out, the responsibility of even one act of sabotage or for one life lost due to secret information being given to the enemy will rest entirely with the War Relocation Authority."[45]

The next day, April 18, General DeWitt, the hero of the anti-Japanese leaders, decreed that U.S. soldiers of Japanese ancestry on furlough could move freely throughout the states of the Western Defense Command. The Associated Press article reporting DeWitt's orders pointed out that "the nature of the order contrasted sharply with convictions expressed only last Tuesday by Gen. DeWitt when he told a House Naval Affairs subcommittee here that he didn't want any Japanese on the West Coast." In that hearing, the article reported, DeWitt had said that "there is developing a sentiment on the part of certain individuals to get the Japanese back to the Coast. I am opposing it with every means at my disposal."[46] Assistant Secretary of War John J. McCloy later explained the rationale behind the order: Japanese American troops should not be expected "to fight in combat against the enemy" while they were denied "the privileges that all other American soldiers have."[47]

General DeWitt had issued the proclamation allowing Japanese American soldiers on furlough to move freely in areas that were off-limits to all other people of Japanese ancestry, but anti-Japanese leaders did not attack DeWitt. They insisted that the general if not the entire army had been pressured into issuing this order.[48] In a long editorial the *Times* made explicit that it was not criticizing DeWitt's relaxation of the exclusion orders for Japanese American soldiers. The *Times* even downplayed the significance of the order. It pointed out that there were not very many Japanese American soldiers, they would be in uniform, and their furloughs on the Pacific Coast would be "of too-short duration to permit of much damage-doing, were those enjoying them so disposed or had they the civilian accomplices with whom to carry it out." Instead, the editorial attacked "the eastern leaders, official and other, of the movement to release from evacuation centers and return to their former homes thousands of Pacific Coast Japanese." The editorial insisted that people of Japanese ancestry had spied for Japan in Hawai'i before Pearl Harbor and on the Pacific Coast before their incarceration and removal. The editorial suggested that all people of Japanese ancestry shared negative "racial" traits, and it insisted that all people of Japanese ancestry should be judged and treated "as a race." It declared that "the Japanese are among the most clannish people on earth." Even though U.S. citizens of Japanese ancestry were supposed to be loyal to the United States, "there has been no published instance in which a 'loyal' Jap has given information of enemy activities on the part of any of his countrymen," the editorial stated. "As a race, the Japanese have made for themselves a record for conscienceless treachery unsurpassed in history," the *Times* declared. Like many of the other statements by anti-Japanese activists, this editorial argued that "the people of the Coast States, who know the Japanese by long personal contact with them, are virtually a unit in opposition to their return." The *Times* declared that a decision to allow Japanese Americans to return to the Pacific Coast would be "stupid and dangerous."[49]

Although the *Times* indicated that the order allowing Japanese American soldiers on furlough to enter the restricted zones was not too objectionable, many anti-Japanese politicians disagreed. The *Times* reported that members of Congress from California, Oregon, and Washington formed a committee in early May to convince the War Department not to allow any Japanese Americans to return to the coastal zone. Members of this committee repeated the charge that "pressure from civilian sources" had led the army to decide that Japanese American soldiers should be allowed to enter the area. Other members of Congress warned that Japanese American soldiers might be the victims of violence if they returned to the coastal area. U.S. Rep. Chet Holifield, a Montebello Democrat, for example, argued that Japanese American soldiers should not be allowed into the coastal zone because they might encounter Filipinos "who have a vicious hatred toward the Japanese." Holifield warned that Filipinos might kill Japanese American soldiers and that race riots involving Filipinos and Japanese Americans might erupt.[50] *Times* political editor Kyle Palmer agreed with members of Congress that Japanese Americans "should not come back for the very plain reason that their own persons would be placed in jeopardy."[51]

One of Costello's many attacks on the War Relocation Authority may help to explain why anti-Japanese leaders continued to focus on the army's decision to allow U.S. soldiers of Japanese ancestry into the coastal zone. Costello suggested that the army's decision was part of a larger plan by the WRA. In words that were prominently reported in the *Times*, Costello said that "he understood War Relocation Authority officials had the idea of breaking down West Coast prejudice against return of the Japanese by first permitting the soldiers to return, then allowing their families to join them and ultimately allowing all loyal Japanese to return."[52] Costello clearly opposed the "breaking down [of] West Coast prejudice," and he opposed the return even of "loyal Japanese" to their former homes. He did not explain why "loyal Japanese" should not be allowed to return, but his opposition to their return suggests that he refused to acknowledge that any person of Japanese ancestry could actually be loyal to the United States.

Before the Zoot-Suit Riots, then, it was clear that the army was not playing the role that anti-Japanese leaders had hoped it would. In fact, some army officers directly challenged the arguments of the anti-Japanese leaders. On May 12 the *Times* reported that Col. William P. Scobey of the War Department's general staff had sent the Los Angeles County Board of Supervisors a letter reassuring them that the War Department would not engage "in any action that would jeopardize the security of the West Coast, or any other coast, or the safety of its military expeditions." In the letter, however, Scobey explicitly declared that "the mass evacuation of Japanese did not imply disloyalty on the part of all Japanese and it does not appear either right or in accordance with the American conception of democracy to retain these loyal ones in restricted custody."[53] Despite Scobey's words, many anti-Japanese leaders expressed hope that General DeWitt would remain in charge of the Western Defense Command and his policy, reflected in his statement that "a Jap's a Jap," would remain in effect.

"The Color of the Skin or Shape of the Eyes Has Nothing to Do with Character"

It is difficult to disentangle anti-Japanese leaders' support for General DeWitt from their opposition to the War Relocation Authority and people who did not accept that "a Jap's a Jap." Not all Los Angeles residents, however, agreed with the statements of anti-Japanese leaders. Some southern Californians defended the rights of Japanese Americans. These people who defended Japanese Americans' rights often referred to themselves as advocates of "fair play." They frequently expressed concern about what they saw as unfair treatment of Japanese Americans. In January 1943 a group of "fair play" advocates in the San Francisco Bay Area formed the Pacific Coast Committee on American Principles and Fair Play, which was often known as the Fair Play Committee. This organization, however, was not as active in southern California as it was in northern California, especially during the first half of 1943. None of the articles about the people who defended the rights of Japanese Americans published through May 1943 mentioned the Fair Play Committee. Nonetheless, it makes sense to refer to people who defended the rights of Japanese Americans as advocates of "fair play."

The advocates of fair play offered a number of different arguments. None called for immediate release of all people of Japanese ancestry. Few criticized the army's exclusion orders. Most called for the gradual release of people who were determined to be loyal to the United States. A number criticized the statements of anti-Japanese politicians and journalists. The statements of fair play advocates and the vitriolic response to some of those statements by anti-Japanese leaders suggest that the disagreement between these two groups was fundamentally a disagreement about the meaning of "race." Fair play advocates insisted that Japanese Americans could be loyal to the United States and that most were; "race" did not make them inclined toward loyalty to Japan. Anti-Japanese leaders, on the other hand, consistently argued that "race" made all people of Japanese ancestry predisposed to loyalty to Japan.

The ranks of fair play advocates included a substantial number of religious leaders and organizations. These leaders and organizations argued that anti-Japanese actions were incompatible with the teachings of Christianity and Judaism. At the end of January 1943, for example, the Church Federation of Los Angeles and the Southern California Council of Churches protested against efforts to restrict the rights of Japanese American citizens and urged that "a spirit of justice, fair play and far-sighted deliberation may be exercised." These religious organizations argued that "discriminatory legislation against the members of one race causes anxiety, restlessness and friction among all racial minorities which look to the spirit of democratic justice as their security." They also warned that "if racial groups cannot depend on the understanding, the tolerance and the good will of Christian democracy, their hope is gone. The hope turned to despair will rise in global conflagration and racial warfare."[54] This statement was published in the *Pacific Citizen*; the daily newspapers tended to ignore the words of fair play advocates in late 1942 and early 1943.

By April 1943, however, a number of prominent individuals had begun to endorse fair play, and the daily newspapers could not ignore their words and actions, especially since these words and actions seemed to have the potential to influence U.S. policy toward Japanese Americans. In mid-April Secretary of the Interior Harold L. Ickes announced that he had hired three Japanese Americans to work on his Maryland farm. Ickes told reporters that his hiring of the workers reflected his belief that "we should do all we can to ease the burden that the war has placed upon this particular group of our fellow citizens." Ickes also said that he did "not like the idea of loyal citizens, no matter of what race or color, being kept in relocation centers any longer than need be."[55] The *Times* and the *Daily News* both reported on Ickes's action.

The *Times* and the *Examiner* did not denounce Ickes's actions in editorials, but they did publish articles that reported on one group that did condemn Ickes for hiring Japanese Americans. Russ Avery, a prominent attorney and the president of the Pacific League, and Frederic T. Woodman, a former mayor of Los Angeles (1916–1919) and the chair of the league's alien problems committee, sent Ickes a request to fire the Japanese Americans and return them to concentration camps. The letter presented arguments that had become or were becoming common among anti-Japanese leaders. It rejected the notion that U.S. citizenship made Japanese Americans loyal to the United States: it described Ickes's action as "this strange employment of subjects of a nation with which we are bitterly at war." It admitted that "a few" Japanese Americans might "possibly" be "loyal to the United States as the land of their birth," but it suggested that most were unquestionably loyal to Japan. The letter also compared Japanese Americans to U.S. soldiers in the Pacific and suggested that no Japanese Americans had served in the U.S. Army. "It is unfortunate," the letter stated, that a handful of loyal people "must suffer because of the known disloyalty of the many. But what is their suffering compared to the suffering of our American boys who fought the Japs at Bataan and Corregidor?" The letter characterized Ickes's employment of Japanese Americans as "coddling of the Japs," and it implied that all parents of U.S. soldiers, sailors, and marines in the Pacific harbored hatred toward all people of Japanese ancestry. "How do you think the mothers and fathers of these gallant lads . . . will feel about your coddling of the Japs on your farm?" they asked.[56]

The day after the *Times* reported Ickes's hiring of Japanese Americans, it printed an article about a speech by John W. Powell, assistant chief of the community services division of the WRA's Poston camp in Arizona. Powell told the National Conference of Social Work in St. Louis that Japanese Americans "were not, and are not dangerous." Powell said that "in spite of rumors, repeatedly denied by all official sources, there is no record of a single act of sabotage either in California or Hawaii, where tens of thousands (of Japanese) are working on secret military preparations and where 10,000 of them have volunteered for the Army." He also criticized the supporters of the incarceration and removal of Japanese Americans from coastal areas, noting that they were motivated by greed. Powell stated that Japanese Americans' "major crime" in California "was to have created millions of dollars of agricultural wealth which some of their neighbors sought to control by forcing the racial issue under the forced draught of war fears."[57]

The *Times* editors did not allow Powell's statements to pass without comment. The newspaper attacked Powell in an editorial, calling him a "soft-minded," "ultrasentimental" "bleeding heart." "If Powell really believes what he says he is unfit to hold the post he does; if he doesn't he should be fired for lying," a *Times* editorial declared. The editorial admitted that Powell was correct in stating that no Japanese Americans had committed acts of sabotage or espionage but insisted that "there unquestionably were dangerous spies and saboteurs among them." The fact that both Gen. John L. DeWitt and President Roosevelt had endorsed the removal of Japanese Americans from coastal areas proved that Japanese Americans were dangerous. These officials knew more about the threat posed by Japanese Americans than did Powell, the editorial asserted.[58] The implications of this editorial are clear: anti-Japanese leaders were masculine realists who remained unmoved by appeals to sentiment, while fair play advocates were feminine "sentimentalists" who refused to believe the awful truth about the "Japanese race." Mayor Fletcher Bowron later used similar terms in his criticism of fair play advocates: he referred to people who wanted Japan-ese Americans to be released from the concentration camps as "well-intentioned American men and women who have a disproportionate sense of justice." He said such people "are sorry for the Japanese," and their feelings grew out of a "mushy, sickly sentimentality."[59]

Although some of the daily newspapers ignored Ickes's actions and Powell's statements, they could not ignore the words of First Lady Eleanor Roosevelt. On April 26 the First Lady arrived in Los Angeles after visiting the WRA camp at Gila River, Arizona. Roosevelt's words reveal how cautious advocates of "fair play" were. She told reporters that she had wanted to see for herself what conditions were like in the camps. Some letters she had received, she said, had indicated that "conditions in the camps were outrageous, something like concentration camps in Nazi Germany; others had written that the Japs were being pampered." After visiting Gila River, Roosevelt decided that "the truth is somewhere between." In a revealing statement, Roosevelt compared the WRA camps to Indian reservations. She argued that "the sooner we get the young Japanese out of these camps the better. Otherwise we will create another Indian problem. I think it is bad to institutionalize anybody." The First Lady did not call for indiscriminate releases of Japanese Americans from the camps. Instead, she said that "the citizen Japanese in these camps should be checked carefully but then I think they should be put to work at locations where they are welcomed and where government officials are willing they should be."[60]

The *Times* did not criticize Roosevelt's position in an editorial, but it did publish letters from readers who attacked the First Lady. Some of these letters reveal the degree to which hostility toward Japanese Americans was connected with hostility toward the Roosevelt administration. Mrs. J. C. Thomas of Los Angeles, for example, declared that "by joining the bleeding hearts club for the assistance of the poor misguided Japanese, Mrs. Eleanor Roosevelt has finally reached the apex of her activities against the people of the United States." Thomas listed all of what she described as Roosevelt's "anti-American" actions, which included support for Communists and "her stirring up of racial hatred," but none of them were as bad as her "bemoaning the plight of the treacherous snakes we call Japanese (with apologies to all snakes)." Thomas insisted that Roosevelt had "reached the point where she should be forced to retire from public life."[61]

Thomas and another *Times* reader suggested that it made no sense to distinguish between loyal U.S. citizens of Japanese ancestry and the residents of Japan. They also implied that all U.S. military personnel in the Pacific and all of their relatives harbored hatred for all people of Japanese ancestry. Thomas deemed Roosevelt's concern for Japanese Americans "unbelievably insulting to our men who are fighting and their families."[62] W. C. Simmons of Long Beach wondered what Roosevelt "thinks fathers, mothers, wives, sisters and sweethearts would do who have lost loved ones in the war." Simmons reported that many workplace conversations revolved around the desire to kill "Japs." If the participants in these conversations "mean what they say, and I think they do, there would have to be a special detail to bury the dead Japs who would be found every morning." In a statement reminiscent of the *Times*'s attack on "sentimentalism," Simmons concluded, "It's nice to be sympathetic but better leave them where they are."[63]

Although the *Times* published a number of vitriolic anti-Japanese letters, it also published letters from people who criticized the newspaper's anti-Japanese position and called for fair play for Japanese Americans. After the *Times* published an editorial, discussed above, that declared that it would be "stupid and dangerous" to allow Japanese Americans to return to the Pacific Coast, Wendell L. Miller, the minister of the University Methodist Church in Los Angeles, wrote a letter of protest to the editor. "There is no good to come from going into my reasons with you as we know your deep-dyed prejudice. I simply want you to know that I think your expressions are very immature and are so expressed," Miller wrote.[64] Leonora Vickland of Los Angeles compared the "ugly and vicious expressions" in letters published in the newspaper with "mouthings of Nazi spokesmen or what might be expected from anyone who had never heard of or had entirely renounced the precepts that have served as guides and ideals at the heart of most of us." Vickland pointed out that Americans could not claim to be "better than our enemies" or that "right is on our side if such hysterical diatribes are encouraged by would-be leaders of the people's 'thinking.'" She also argued that "a grave injustice is being done to hundreds of kindly Christian and loyal Americans of Japanese ancestry as well as to thousands of Christians of Caucasian ancestry who are convinced that the color of the skin or shape of the eyes has nothing to do with character."

In an editorial response to Vickland's letter, the *Times* insisted that it "has no prejudice about color of skin or shape of eyes, but it most decidedly has a vigorous and growing distrust of the black hearts of the Japs, singly and collectively."[65] This response reveals as much about anti-Japanese leaders as Vickland's letter does about fair play advocates. Vickland's letter suggested that "race" was simply "the color of the skin or shape of the eyes." The brief editorial comment, on the other hand, suggested that anti-Japanese leaders did not think that "race" was simply "the color of the skin or shape of the eyes." What united all people of Japanese ancestry as a racial group, the *Times* suggested, was their "black hearts."

The *Times* also published a letter from a Japanese American criticizing the newspaper's depiction of Japanese Americans. "We feel that you are not doing us justice," Tom Saki wrote from the Poston camp in Arizona. Saki pointed out that "not even one proven act of sabotage" had occurred in Hawai'i or California, and he mentioned that Japanese Americans did not protest their incarceration and removal "because we were law-abiding." He also wrote that "here in camp with very few exceptions we have tried to conduct ourselves in an exemplary way. Those who do not like the American way of life are already known and are dealt with as such." Saki suggested that "if you knew our story, if you saw the hundreds of fellows volunteering for the Army, if you were here to see how we desire to go out and do our share in this great struggle of ours that perhaps you would not feel the way you do." The *Times* responded to Saki's letter with a note declaring that it "does not question the loyalty of some Japanese. It does, however, contend that it is impossible to distinguish between the loyal and nonloyal, and that for the good of everybody a system of detention is best."[66]

Perhaps in response to the criticism of readers such as Miller, Vickland, and Saki, later in May the *Times* published articles that reported on the words of fair play advocates. At the same time, however, the *Times* and other newspapers continued to publish a large number of anti-Japanese articles. On May 12, 1943, for example, the *Times* published two articles that portrayed Japanese Americans in a positive light. The first one reported on the words of Charles F. Ernst, the director of the WRA's Topaz camp in Utah. On a visit to Los Angeles, Ernst stated emphatically that the WRA's goal was to train Japanese Americans "for jobs in which they can be useful and to get them out over the United States on those jobs. Anything resembling idleness on the part of Americans these days is a foolish waste of money we need for something else." Ernst consistently referred to Japanese Americans simply as "Americans." "America needs these Americans. Among them are highly educated and trained men and women and others of all shades of usefulness. Let us get them out over the United States as rapidly as possible in order that they may really pull the weight they are so eager to pull," he said.[67] The second article described how "thousands of American citizens of Japanese descent are being systematically moved into essential jobs." The article reassured readers that Japanese Americans were thoroughly investigated before they were allowed to leave the camps.[68] A brief article in the May 16 edition of the *Times* reported that the executive council of the Los Angeles Church Federation had condemned "the fostering of race hatred." The council issued a statement indicating that "we deplore that on the home front there should be so much evidence of attempts to generate hatreds, and that there are those who would foster hatred against American citizens of Japanese ancestry, even when there is no well-founded evidence as to their disloyalty to our country."[69]

Even though the daily newspapers published mostly anti-Japanese articles and editorials, then, advocates of fair play were not entirely excluded from the public debate about the meanings of "race" in Los Angeles. Their words reveal that they disagreed with anti-Japanese leaders about

U.S. combat troops. As will become evident in chapter six, this tendency to depict all Japanese Americans as men undermined the anti-Japanese position in 1944, when the army allowed Japanese American women to return to the coastal area.

In addition to attacking Japanese Americans, a number of people who responded publicly to the news of executions in Japan also attacked "New Dealers" who disagreed with their demands for harsh treatment of Japanese Americans. One reader of the *Times,* for example, expressed the opinion that the news of executions would discourage Americans from following "Mr. Ickes' puerile example and take the Japanese into our homes." "C. R. C." from Seal Beach also argued that "turning the Japs over here loose as some CRACKPOTS suggest" would be to "betray our brave flyers."[80] Another *Times* reader wrote that the United States needed to deport Japanese Americans "before the Ickeites and a few other sob sisters get some New Deal law put over which would put the F.B.I. on our trail if we did not take these SKUNKS to our bosom as the ICKEITES are doing."[81]

The *Times* echoed the anti-New Deal sentiments of its readers in editorials. In one editorial, for example, the newspaper declared that "it has been a mistake to put the relocation centers under the control of civilian theorists who have used them for social experiments; the Army should have been boss of the job throughout."[82] *Times* political editor Kyle Palmer declared that "the social planners and advanced thinkers in Washington should leave strictly alone" the issue of Japanese exclusion from the Pacific Coast. Palmer also implied that fair play advocates were "meddling sentimentalists and scheming social uplifters," and he insisted that they "should be thrown out of any discussions looking to a logical solution" of the "Japanese problem."[83] Another *Times* editorial revealed a connection between gender ideology and anti-New Deal sentiment. This editorial argued that federal policy concerning Japanese Americans should be based upon the attitudes of "the people of the Pacific Coast" rather than "ex parte conclusions reached in Washington on theoretical grounds and the reports of sob-sister social workers."[84]

These attacks on Harold Ickes and other "New Dealers" were essentially expressions of disagreement about the meaning of "race." The authors of these anti-Japanese letters and editorials fumed at Ickes and other "New Dealers" because these government officials insisted that "race" did not make Japanese Americans loyal to Japan.

Conclusion: "Gen. DeWitt Has Proved Wisdom in Jap Policy"

On May 19, 1943, the *Times* reported that the U.S. House Committee on Un-American Activities—the Dies Committee—would soon release "a set of special reports throwing new light on Japanese organizations in the United States and dealing with subversive activities in war relocation camps."[85] The next day the newspaper published a front-page article that quoted committee member J. Parnell Thomas, the New Jersey Republican who later chaired the committee and served time in prison for embezzlement. According to the *Times*, Thomas, who had recently arrived in Los Angeles, offered reporters "an amazing revelation of a Los Angeles-Tokyo Japanese spy system, the operations of a Nipponese woman who secretly collected information from San Pedro fishermen about the navy and other startling anti-American trickery by Japs here," the *Times* reported.[86]

The *Times* greeted Thomas's statements with enthusiasm. An editorial in the newspaper pointed out that Thomas "cannot be accused of sectional prejudice against Japanese." The editorial characterized Thomas's statements about "Jap spy activity" as "a full answer to the sentimentalists who want the Japs turned loose to wander at will throughout the United States." The *Times* declared that "it is noteworthy that every official investigation of the relocated Japanese adds up to the same thing: that the Japs are not safe as unrestricted residents of any part of the United States, and particularly that none should be returned to the Pacific Coast."[87]

The articles and editorial about the House committee's investigation are significant in that they reveal a shift in the tactics of anti-Japanese leaders. The army had turned out to be an unreliable ally. According to anti-Japanese leaders in Los Angeles and throughout California, the army had succumbed to civilian pressure, allowing Japanese Americans to serve and weakening its own exclusion orders in order not to discriminate against Japanese American soldiers. From May 1943 until 1945 the efforts of anti-Japanese leaders focused on investigations by legislative committees dominated by anti-Japanese politicians. In the final seven months of 1943 the Dies Committee, the California Legislature's Joint Fact-Finding Committee on Un-American Activities in California, chaired by State Sen. Jack B. Tenney of Los Angeles, the California Senate's Committee on Japanese Resettlement, and the California Assembly's Committee on Japanese Problems held hearings in various places around California. These hearings received a good deal of attention in Los Angeles's daily newspapers.

As anti-Japanese leaders turned away from the army and toward anti-Japanese legislators, they thanked General DeWitt for his actions in incarcerating and removing Japanese Americans from the coastal zone. On May 21 the California War Council, headed by Governor Earl Warren, "expressed vigorous opposition to any plan for the return of Japanese citizens or aliens to the West Coast for the duration of the war" and commended DeWitt "for evacuating the Japanese to relocation centers after Pearl Harbor." The council also praised DeWitt for attempting to keep Japanese Americans away from the Pacific Coast. Warren told reporters that "we can't meet danger if we have potential traitors and saboteurs in this area."[88]

In a long editorial published on May 28, the *Times* praised Gen. John L. DeWitt and addressed the "intimations" that DeWitt was being recalled to Washington due to his "uncompromising opposition to any Japs whatever being sent back to this region." This editorial suggests that some anti-Japanese leaders were unwilling to embrace unequivocally and publicly DeWitt's statement of racial ideology—"a Jap's a Jap." At the same time, however, it also reveals that these same leaders' support for policies based on that ideology had not wavered, even as the voices of fair play advocates became more audible in the first six months of 1943. In praising DeWitt, the *Times* acknowledged that some Japanese Americans were clearly loyal to the United States and that "keeping the Japs in the relocation centers is undoubtedly an injustice to some of them." No people of Japanese ancestry should be released, however, because "it defies anybody to produce an infallible method of sorting out the good from the bad." Unlike DeWitt, then, the *Times* did not say that all "Japs" were "bad." Its insistence that there was no "infallible method of sorting out the good from the bad," however, reflected a set of ideas about "race" closely related to those reflected by DeWitt's statement. Instead of indicating that all people of Japanese ancestry were loyal to Japan, the *Times* argued that all people of Japanese ancestry shared racial traits that made it impossible to determine whether or not they were loyal to the United States. This editorial suggests, then, that it had become less acceptable to express racial prejudice openly. However, people who endorsed the policies based on racial prejudice tried to find ways to maintain those policies while distancing themselves from explicit statements of prejudice.

In arguing for continued incarceration of all people of Japanese ancestry, the *Times* also passed the mantle of leadership in the anti-Japanese movement from DeWitt to two legislators—U.S. Rep. John M. Costello of Hollywood and State Sen. Jack B. Tenney of Los Angeles. The editorial quoted Costello, who criticized WRA officials who "have been in contact with the Japanese for the 'grand space of 12 months' and think they know all about them." The editorial also repeated Tenney's "unanswerable argument": "if any Japs at all are permitted to return to the Pacific Coast, even in the uniform of United States soldiers, the introduction of Jap spies into this region will be made easy." The *Times* noted that "the Japs, through their captures at Bataan and elsewhere, have an unfortunately large supply of United States Army uniforms and nothing could be easier than to slip uniformed spies ashore from submarines."[89]

Although the *Times* supported policies based on racial prejudice while avoiding explicit statements of prejudice, the *Examiner* did not express any reluctance to embrace both the policies and the prejudice that undergirded them. In an editorial published in mid-May 1943, the *Examiner* declared that the war between the United States and Japan "is truly a race war, in which a grasping, cruel and insanely ambitious race is determined to exterminate whoever opposes its dream of conquest and its plan of world dominance." Lest anyone misconstrue this statement, the *Examiner* offered a sentence to clarify it: "Japan is that aggressor, and America is that opponent."[90]

In the months preceding the Zoot-Suit Riots, then, people in Los Angeles and Japanese Americans who had been forcibly removed from the city debated the treatment of people of Japanese ancestry in the United States. At their roots these debates were about the meaning of "race." Many anti-Japanese leaders argued that all people of Japanese ancestry were members of an "enemy race" and should be treated as dangerous enemies and punished for the actions of Japanese troops. Some anti-Japanese leaders, however, had begun to move away from crude statements of these ideas. They masked their racial ideology behind apparently more practical concerns, such as how allowing Japanese American soldiers into the Pacific Coast area would allow the Japanese military to slip spies and saboteurs ashore in U.S. Army uniforms. On the other hand, fair play advocates argued that "racial" differences were superficial—simply differences in "the color of the skin or shape of the eyes." They called for an end to policies based on these superficial differences. This debate would continue until the end of the war. In the first half of June 1943, however, most participants in the debate about "race" focused their attention on rioting in Los Angeles.

FIVE

"A Criminal Is Not a Criminal Because of Race"

"Race" and the Zoot-Suit Riots

On the first page of the second section of its May 10, 1943, edition, the *Los Angeles Examiner* published an article beneath the headline, "Brown Race Danger Seen by Scientist." The article consisted mostly of quotations of Dr. Albert Edward Wiggam. The article pointed out that Wiggam was the creator of "Let's Explore Your Mind," a syndicated feature that the *Examiner* published, a director of the American Eugenics Society, and "one of the 25 members of the top-flight Science Writers' Association." The article did not point out that Wiggam, who was born in 1871, was the author of several books, including *The New Decalogue of Science, The Fruit of the Family Tree,* and *The Next Age of Man,* all of which dealt with heredity and eugenics. *The New Decalogue of Science* was one of the best-selling nonfiction books of 1924. According to the article, Wiggam, "one of America's foremost scientists," was in Los Angeles for a speaking engagement.

In the article Wiggam warned that "unless all the white races look to their biological problems, they are certain to fade before the brown races."

Wiggam claimed that the "population of the white races" was decreasing by fifteen million a year, while "the brown races" were increasing by fifty million a year. He expressed special alarm that "in America, and generally in the white countries, it is the better educated and more able groups that are dying out most rapidly." He pointed out that "not a single group in America earning over $1000 a year replaced its parents prior to 1940."[1]

This article in Los Angeles's most widely read morning newspaper offers a revealing glimpse into the ongoing public debate about the meanings of "race" in mid-1943. Wiggam clearly expressed the notion, widely accepted among adherents of eugenics, that economic success reflected hereditary superiority. He suggested that people who earned the most money were most fit to reproduce. Wiggam also referred to the United States as a "white country," ignoring the significant and apparently growing numbers of Americans who could not claim to be "white." Wiggam suggested that a person's "race" was readily apparent; he did not identify the boundary between "the white races" and "the brown races." Wiggam also suggested that all "white" people should share his concern about their apparently declining numbers.

Nothing about this article, however, is more revealing than the fact that it was published in a widely read daily newspaper. This fact suggests that it was acceptable at this time for supporters of eugenics to express openly their beliefs about the superiority of "the white races" and the inferiority of "the brown races." Within two months, however, such explicit, general statements about racial superiority and inferiority became much less common or acceptable. As the next chapter will show, daily newspapers in Los Angeles continued to publish articles and editorials that emphasized what they depicted as the negative "racial" traits of people of Japanese ancestry. Officials, civic leaders, and journalists, however, increasingly tried to distance themselves from more general statements about the "racial" differences among groups of people.

Rioting in Los Angeles led to this change in the debate about "race." For a week in early June 1943, soldiers and sailors swept through downtown Los Angeles and some eastside neighborhoods, ostensibly looking for young men wearing zoot suits. These suits, according to most of the daily newspapers, were the uniform of young gang members who had previously assaulted some sailors and soldiers. Toward the end of the week, the soldiers and sailors were joined by mobs of civilians. These riots, which became known as the "Zoot-Suit Riots," were a turning point in the "race war" in Los Angeles during World War II. Chapter two demonstrated that people who believed that "race" determined a person's behavior had dominated the debate surrounding the loyalty of Japanese Americans in early 1942. Chapter three showed that a growing number of people came forward to attack this idea in the debate surrounding juvenile delinquency among Mexican Americans. Most of these people emphasized the threat to wartime unity and hemispheric solidarity posed by policies based upon what they described as a backward racial ideology. As this chapter will show, the violence on the streets of Los Angeles seemed to lend support to the arguments of those people who had warned about racial prejudice and discrimination's threat to wartime unity. Although some officials and journalists argued forcefully that the riots were not race riots, many also ended up having to agree with some people who insisted that the riots were the result of racial prejudice and discrimination. In the ongoing debates about the meaning of "race," it became increasingly difficult for people to argue that some groups of people were biologically inclined toward criminality. After the riots a number of civic leaders in Los Angeles established organizations designed to ameliorate racial tensions. In their public pronouncements, these organizations criticized discrimination, which they suggested was the result of outmoded beliefs about "race." The ideas of people such as Albert Edward Wiggam became increasingly invisible in the months that followed the riots.

"No Riot Here"

The Zoot-Suit Riots came as a surprise to many residents of Los Angeles. Although daily newspapers had devoted a good deal of attention to what they characterized as the problem of an increase in juvenile delinquency among Mexican Americans in the summer and fall of 1942, few articles and editorials about gang violence appeared in the newspapers in the first five months of 1943. Just before the rioting occurred, however, some African Americans mobilized in response to what they interpreted as racial prejudice on the part of Los Angeles Police Department officers. At the end of May 1943 a Los Angeles police officer shot and killed Lenza Smith, an African American shipyard worker. The shooting nearly led to a riot outside the house where Smith was shot. According to the *Times*, the police officer who shot Smith "was saved from manhandling by a crowd of more than 600 Negroes by the arrival of more than 20 policemen armed with sawed-off shotguns and tear gas equipment."[2] Other newspapers, including the African American weekly *California Eagle*, published similar reports.[3] Although the *Times* emphasized the fact that the crowd that gathered after Smith was shot was composed of African Americans, other newspapers did not depict the "near riot" as a racial situation. Neither the *Daily News* nor the *Examiner* reported that all of the people who gathered were African Americans. The *Eagle*, however, suggested that racial prejudice influenced the behavior of the police at the scene. One of the men who was arrested, William Harrison, told the *Eagle* that one of the officers who arrested him struck him and told him that "you are one of those smart Eastern n——s. You and the n——s down on Central avenue are listening to a bunch of Russian Communists who are trying to convince you that the American white people aren't treating you all right." The officer, whom the *Eagle* called a "storm trooper cop," said that "the white man would be treating the Negro right if he would kill all you smart n——s."[4]

Harrison's report of his treatment led African American community leaders to take action. The NAACP and the Negro Victory Committee sponsored a meeting on May 30, 1943, to protest both the killing and the arrests. Rev. Clayton D. Russell, the charismatic minister of the People's Independent Church of Christ, had formed the Negro Victory Committee in 1941. Its membership seems to have come largely from Reverend Russell's church, but it drew support from some other influential members of the community. The committee's initial goal was to end discrimination in defense employment, but it soon began protesting other forms of discrimination, racial prejudice more broadly, and even inadequate food distribution.[5] The *Eagle* reported that fifteen hundred people attended the meeting. According to the *Eagle*, speakers at the meeting described the Smith shooting, the arrests, and other recent events as "a deliberate effort to goad the Negro and Mexican people into rioting and bloodshed." Several of these speakers expressed anger at the way in which the daily newspapers reported incidents involving African Americans and Mexican Americans. They accused "the riot-baiters of metropolitan papers and large industries here" of trying to provoke "a racial outburst to camouflage a wholesale importation of Southern restrictions and segregation against the Negro and Mexican people." The meeting approved a resolution declaring that "there will be no riot in this community to divide and disrupt the war effort which must carry weapons to the black and white soldiers who offer blood sacrifices on every continent of the world."[6] Although this resolution did not explicitly say that "racial" characteristics were superficial, it did clearly imply that "racial" differences should not prevent people from different groups from working together in support of the war. An *Eagle* editorial echoed the sentiment expressed at the mass meeting. The editorial proudly declared that there had been "NO RIOT HERE." Despite the inflammatory rhetoric of the daily newspapers, police brutality, and the persistent indignity of employment and housing discrimination, the editorial stated, the killing of Lenza Smith "wrought a miracle of unity among Negroes, Mexicans, trade unionists and patriotic white citizens determined to draw the stiletto of police brutality out of the back of Los Angeles' all-out war production."[7]

The emphasis on discrimination "against the Negro and Mexican people" deserves closer scrutiny. None of the news reports indicated that Mexicans or Mexican Americans were involved in the "near riot" that occurred after Smith was shot. Nonetheless, Joe Marty, of the Citizens' Committee for the Defense of Mexican American Youth, spoke at the May 30 meeting. Marty told the audience that "Mexican people are facing the same problem with which Negroes are confronted." John Kinloch also spoke at the meeting. Kinloch reiterated the statements he had written for the *Eagle* for several months. He said that "police brutality against Mexicans and Negroes" and "crime stories in the metropolitan press" that emphasized the race of alleged criminals were "all part of a scheme to disrupt and divide the war workers of Los Angeles." Marty's and Kinloch's statements not only suggest that some Mexican Americans and African Americans had begun to see similarities in the treatment of the two groups by the daily newspapers, law enforcement officers, and employers, but they also reveal that members of both groups recognized that the groups were treated similarly because of racial ideology. According to people like Marty and Kinloch, law enforcement officers, the daily newspapers, and employers treated both Mexican Americans and African Americans as if they were biologically inferior to "white" people and by nature inclined to criminality and other antisocial behavior.

No one made the point that "race" should not matter more explicitly than Rev. Clayton D. Russell. A native of Los Angeles, Russell was born in 1910. After graduating from Jefferson High School, he attended the University of Southern California and Chapman College. He became the second pastor of the People's Independent Church of Christ in 1935.[8] In a statement published in the *Eagle*, the Negro Victory Committee leader pointed out that "never once did we raise the question of the races of the people involved in the unfortunate incidents." The NAACP and the Victory Committee did not argue that Smith was innocent just because he was an African American or that the officer who shot him was guilty just because he was "white," Russell noted. Instead, they called for a complete investigation. "We did say that if it was true that a police officer had stated that white police were going to shoot up black N——s, on the Eastside, that that officer was going beyond his line of duty and that if his words were the policy of the Police Force, then no Negro could feel safe in the city and the situation would have to be corrected."[9]

In retrospect, the pledges of African American community leaders and the *Eagle* that there would be no riot in Los Angeles appear especially ironic. The day this edition of the newspaper was published, riots erupted in Los Angeles. These riots, however, were not the kinds of riots that the speakers at the meeting or the editorial in the *Eagle* had feared. African Americans and Mexican Americans in the crowded neighborhoods of downtown and the eastside did not rise in revolt against the discrimination they had endured. Instead, gangs of soldiers and sailors, sometimes accompanied by "white" civilians, roamed through downtown and eastside neighborhoods, attacking young Mexican Americans and African Americans.

"Fights" or "Race Riots"?

The first reports of rioting in the daily newspapers tended to emphasize what historian Mauricio Mazón has described as the riots' "carnival-like atmosphere." They depicted the riots as "fights" that resulted from "zoot suiters"' assaults upon sailors and their wives and girlfriends. The *Los Angeles Times*, the *Examiner*, and the *Daily News* all reported that in these fights "the youthful hoodlums came off second best."[10] Some articles suggested that the fights were not even violent. One, for example, indicated that "groups of soldiers, sailors and marines stopped street cars, took off zoot suiters and left them suitless" and that "sailors and marines made fire of the zoot suits of two youths who were permitted to go their way in their underwear."[11] The light character of the *Times*'s early coverage of the rioting is reflected in an article about potential trouble at the beach. According to the article, Santa Monica lifeguards had been warned to "watch out for a

FIG. 5. *This photograph of a U.S. soldier being arrested during the Zoot-Suit Riots was published on the front page of the* Daily News. *The newspaper printed this caption: "Social Amenities Forgotten as Soldier Resists Arrest. 'Special agents' use clubs to force riot suspect into car at Second and Spring sts."* Daily News, *June 9, 1943, p. 1.* Los Angeles Daily News *Photographs (Collection 1386), Department of Special Collections, Charles E. Young Research Library, University of California, Los Angeles.*

zoot-suit gang" that might "cause trouble at the beach." The article quoted the captain of the beach lifeguards, Capt. George Watkins, who said that "some of them had long hair, which curled up at the back like a drake's tail, but their bathing togs weren't any different from those of the others so we were unable to tell just how many, if any, were gang members."[12]

Newspaper articles did not clearly and explicitly indicate that racial prejudice influenced these "fights" in any way. The *Times* implied that soldiers and sailors attacked only people who wore zoot suits, the gang uniform. As chapter three suggested, however, the term *zoot suiter* seems to have been used as a substitute for an ethnic or "racial" label. Articles in the *Examiner* and the *Daily News* suggested that these "fights" were in fact acts of racial violence. These newspapers, for example, used the term *pachucos* to describe gang members. It is possible that this term might have been used to describe people who were not Mexican Americans. *La Opinión* did not use the term *pachucos* to refer exclusively to Mexican Americans. An article published in *La Opinión* on June 11, for example, reported that "a gang of pachucos of the Negro race" assaulted a gas station owner and that the "Vigilantes of 1943" had broken down doors of houses "in a search for pachucos of whatever race."[13] The English-language newspapers, however, did not use the term in the same way that *La Opinión* did. There are no references in the daily newspapers to "Negro pachucos" or "white pachucos." The very use of the term served to emphasize the difference between *pachucos* and the mostly Anglo "juvenile gangsters" who had attracted some attention in 1941 and early 1942. Moreover, some articles suggested that "zoot suiters" were connected with certain neighborhoods. One article in the *Daily News*, for example, referred to "the zoot suit section in the east part of Los Angeles."[14] Again, while this reference to "the zoot suit section" of the city could be interpreted as an effort to connect the wearing of zoot suits to a section of the city inhabited mostly by working-class people, it seems to me to reflect more concern with "race" or ethnicity than with class. It would be a mistake, however, to ignore the ambiguity of the newspaper reports on the violence. Not all of the articles suggested that all "zoot suiters" were Mexican Americans. Some articles even took pains to point out that all "gangsters" were not Mexican Americans. One article in the *Daily News*, for example, noted that "records show that all the young gangsters are not zoot addicts. Nor are they of any single race or color."[15]

Only one daily newspaper, the Spanish-language *La Opinión*, suggested when the rioting began that the violence might be serious. *La Opinión* reported that the Mexican consul in Los Angeles had undertaken an immediate investigation of the riots and that "the authorities are frankly fearful of the repercussions that could come from these events and surely will use force to put an end to the situation." The newspaper, however, did not state explicitly that all of the pachucos who were attacked were Mexican Americans or that the sailors were motivated by racial prejudice.[16]

Despite the efforts of the Mexican consul and *La Opinión*, no local officials took action after the first night of rioting. For three nights the unrest seems to have increased in intensity. The increasing violence alarmed a number of Los Angeles residents. On the evening of June 7 the Citizens' Committee for Latin American Youth held its weekly meeting. The Los Angeles County Board of Supervisors had established this committee in late 1942 in response to concerns about gang activity among young Mexican Americans. Its members included law enforcement officials and several leaders from the Mexican American community.[17] Among the guests at the meeting were the consul general, the associate consul, and the vice-consul of Mexico, two representatives of the U.S. government's Office of the Coordinator of Inter-American Affairs, and Los Angeles County Supervisor John Anson Ford. As the meeting began the chair announced that "in view of the seriousness of the present situation further business of the Committee would be suspended so that all the remaining time might be given to consideration of the disturbances agitating the community at this time." The committee's chair, Probation Officer Stephen J. Keating, told the committee about a June 3 attack by a group of fifty sailors on a group of young Mexican Americans who had participated in a meeting with him, another probation officer, and a police officer. Eduardo Quevedo told the committee that he and Churchill Murray of the Office of the Coordinator of Inter-American Affairs had met with civilian and military law enforcement officials on June 5 and that these officials had assured them that the situation would be under control by the following night. The committee debated a motion to urge the navy "to punish to the fullest extent all sailors arrested for rioting" but in the end passed a substitute motion to "request an impartial community agency to study the situation and present an unbiased statement of fact."[18]

The Citizens' Committee meeting may have spurred John Anson Ford to action. The next day in the Board of Supervisors meeting he sponsored a resolution deploring "instances of lawlessness and racial discrimination."

Although Ford's resolution expressed concern about racial discrimination, it also argued that the riots did not indicate that racial discrimination was a serious problem in Los Angeles. The resolution insisted that "a generally cordial relation exists between residents of Anglo and Latin ancestry. . . . We do not believe that recent lawless outbreaks in any way indicate any change in that basic cordial and friendly relationship." Ford's resolution placed the blame for the riots on the "zoot-suiters." It pointed out that the Board and other public officials had taken steps to deal with juvenile delinquency and asked the public "to view the situation without prejudice toward any group, but as a problem aggravated by war conditions and calling for both a sympathetic understanding and a firm insistence on an impartial administration of justice." The Board of Supervisors passed the resolution.[19]

The Board of Supervisors' passage of a resolution against prejudice did not stop the violence. On the evening of June 8, a group of about 150 civic leaders met and called upon California Attorney General Robert W. Kenny, U.S. Sen. Sheridan Downey, and U.S. Attorney General Francis Biddle to investigate the riots. An article in the *Daily News* describing this meeting noted that a representative of these leaders spoke by telephone to both Kenny and Downey. Kenny told the representative that he would meet with Gov. Earl Warren and then come to Los Angeles to investigate. Downey said that he would consider initiating a congressional investigation. The leaders sent a telegram to Biddle. The telegram asked him to send a representative to Los Angeles. The article in the *Daily News* mentioned that "representatives of the Bar association, the Negro population, the Mexican communities, last year's grand jury, the CIO, the war manpower committee, and the studio unions were among those at the meeting," but it did not indicate that anyone had claimed that the sailors and soldiers who were rioting were motivated by their beliefs about "race."[20]

Some community leaders blamed the daily newspapers as well as the police for the rioting. Eduardo Quevedo, the chairman of the Coordinating Council for Latin American Youth, sent a letter to Elmer Davis and Alan Cranston of the Office of War Information and to President Roosevelt. Quevedo asked for the OWI to intervene with the local press in an effort to end its inflammatory coverage of the riots. Quevedo's letter was translated into Spanish and published in *La Opinión* on June 9. In addition to suggesting that the press had acted irresponsibly, Quevedo warned that the rioting would damage U.S. relations with Mexico and other Latin American nations.

In his letter to Davis and Cranston, Quevedo argued that the riots "will undoubtedly cause grave international repercussions distinctly harmful to the war effort and to our good neighbor policy."[21]

Although the resolution passed by the Board of Supervisors suggested that the riots were acts of racial discrimination, other officials and newspaper editors insisted that the riots were not race riots. The *Times*, for example, conceded that reports on the riots could damage U.S. prestige in Latin America but insisted that Mexican Americans had not been targeted because of their "race." An editorial in the June 9 issue of the *Times* stated that "there was, actually, no antiracial action and the affairs had no racial basis." The *Times* argued that the riots could not be race riots because "'zoot-suit' wearers" were not "confined to any one race or nationality."[22]

The *Times* editorial did not convince all elected officials that the violence "had no racial basis." California Governor Earl Warren appointed a committee to investigate the riots the day the *Times* editorial appeared and one day after the Board of Supervisors passed its resolution. Warren did not mention "race" in his first public statement about the riots, but his decision to include African American attorney Walter Gordon of Berkeley and Mexican American actor Leo Carrillo on the investigating committee seems to reflect some concern about the racial or ethnic dimensions of the riots. Warren appointed Joseph T. McGucken, an auxiliary bishop of the Roman Catholic diocese of Los Angeles, to chair the committee. The other two members of the committee were Willsie Martin, the minister of Wilshire Methodist Church, and Karl Holton, the director of the California Youth Authority.[23]

At the same time that some government officials expressed concerns about the "racial" dimension of the riots, others, most notably Los Angeles Mayor Fletcher Bowron, defended the rioters and police officers from the accusation that they had discriminated against young Mexican Americans on the basis of race. On June 9, Bowron issued a statement to the press about the riots and his actions in response to the violence. Bowron's statement is confusing, because it suggests that racial discrimination was only possible against immigrants. Although Bowron had argued that people of Japanese ancestry could never be "American," he insisted that people of Mexican ancestry who were born in the United States were not part of a racial group. "There is no question of racial discrimination involved," the mayor insisted, claiming that "98 per cent or more" of the members of the youth gangs "were born right here in Los Angeles." Bowron argued that too

FIG. 6. *The committee appointed by Gov. Earl Warren met on June 12, 1943, to investigate the recent rioting in Los Angeles. From left to right are California Attorney General Robert W. Kenny, Dr. Willsie Martin, pastor of the Wilshire Methodist Church, Karl Holton, the director of the California Youth Authority, Bishop Joseph T. McGucken, and Walter Gordon, Berkeley attorney. Actor Leo Carrillo, also a member of the committee, is not shown.* Herald-Examiner *Collection, Los Angeles Public Library.*

many Los Angeles residents "raise a hue and cry of racial discrimination or prejudice against a minority group every time the Los Angeles police make arrests of members of gangs or groups working in unison." The mayor insisted that all gang members "look alike to us regardless of color and the length of their coats." Bowron's words suggested a close relationship between racial ideology and gender ideology. He argued that officials had to respond to youth gangs with manly firmness rather than feminine permissiveness. The mayor promised "two-fisted action," not "powder puffs or slaps on the wrists," to keep the peace in Los Angeles. "If young men of Mexican parentage or if Negro boys are involved, it is regrettable," the mayor said, "but no one has immunity and whoever are the disturbers are going to be sternly dealt with." Churchill Murray, the Los Angeles representative of the Office of the Coordinator of Inter-American Affairs, seems to have agreed with Bowron. He argued that "the frequency of Mexican names among the 'zoot suit' element was without actual significance to relations between Mexico and the United States, because most of the civilian figures in the clashes with men of the armed services are American citizens."[24]

Like Mayor Bowron and Churchill Murray, Youth Correction Authority member Harold A. Slane argued that the "disease" of juvenile delinquency "is not confined to any race or color, but is infecting all groups." A column that Slane wrote for the *Daily News*, however, suggested that Mexican Americans were biologically inclined toward criminality. His explanation, for example, focused entirely upon people of Spanish or Mexican ancestry, not on "all groups." Slane insisted that delinquency could be traced "back to the days of the Dons, when there were two classes of Spanish speaking people here." Without explicitly explaining how class divisions in Spanish California fostered juvenile delinquency, Slane abruptly shifted his focus to Mexican migrant farm laborers. "The entire family worked in the fields," Slane observed. "The father taught his sons to work in the fields as soon as they were old enough to weed a beet or pick an orange." After relief became widespread in the 1930s, Slane argued, "the father no longer taught his sons to work." Contradictory messages in the U.S. school system compounded the demise of the work ethic, Slane argued. U.S. schools taught about democracy, but they did not teach that "freedom and liberties carry great responsibilities on the part of the individuals who enjoy them." This combination of forces left young Mexican American men with no respect for their parents and "not ready yet to accept the responsibilities of democracy." The politically immature Mexican American with no work ethic demanded attention. "Exhibitionism is a part of his very nature," Slane declared. "He expressed that desire by running in gangs with his fellows who were in a similar predicament." Slane insisted that "this was a natural result. The same result may be found in all nations and throughout the history of mankind."[25] Slane's words, then, depicted the rise of juvenile delinquency as a result of both "natural" characteristics of people of Mexican ancestry and government actions in the 1930s.

As the preceding paragraphs have shown, journalists, public officials, and community leaders disagreed about the causes of the violence and the character of the violence. As Bowron's words and Slane's column reveal, however, many officials focused on the "zoot suiters," suggesting that young Mexican Americans were to blame for the violence. Some of the participants in the initial debate surrounding the riots denied that "race" had influenced the rioting or the apparent increase in juvenile crime, while others suggested that race prejudice and discrimination were responsible both for the growth of juvenile gangs among Mexican Americans and for the sailors' and soldiers' attacks on "zoot suiters." This conflict grew more heated as people from different communities joined the debate.

"Time for Sanity"

On June 8 the navy declared the city of Los Angeles out-of-bounds for sailors and marines. Violence persisted in the city that night, but the naval order, combined with the mobilization of a large number of additional police officers, did end the rioting in the central area of the city on June 9. Some incidents occurred for a few more nights in Watts, several miles south of downtown, and in some suburban communities.[26] The debate about the rioting continued even as the violence itself abated. African Americans became active participants in the debate on June 10, when the *Eagle* was published for the first time since the violence erupted. Articles and editorials published between June 10 and June 15 make clear that the debate about the riot was, at its heart, a debate among people who disagreed about the meanings of "race."

Although many officials implicitly defended the soldiers and sailors when they turned their attention away from the riots in order to criticize juvenile delinquency, other people, especially those who depicted the riots as race riots, continued to focus on the unrest in Los Angeles. On June 10 the *Examiner* reported that Rafael de la Colina, an official in the Mexican embassy in Washington, had suggested that the Mexican government might file a formal protest about the riots. De la Colina described the riots as "mob violence" directed toward residents of the "Mexican colony" in Los Angeles, many of them "innocent Mexican bystanders." He also pointed out that the victims of the violence "have not been charged with any crime."[27]

The first post-riot issue of the *California Eagle* was published on June 10. The African American newspaper presented a number of opinions that had not been expressed in the daily newspapers. Clayton D. Russell, the minister of the People's Independent Church of Christ and the leader of the Negro Victory Committee, insisted that the riots were intended to hinder the war effort. He argued that "the whole riot situation is part of a giant defeatist conspiracy to disrupt war production." By suggesting that there was a conspiracy, Russell avoided accusing the sailors and soldiers of acting on their own racial prejudice. He depicted them as pawns of the "giant defeatist conspiracy." "It is certainly doing Hitler's job magnificently when the servicemen of this area can be organized to attack civilians whose brothers have fought gloriously on Bataan and Corregidor," he said.[28] Russell and other African American leaders, such as *Eagle* publisher Charlotta Bass, argued that people should not be attacked because of the kind of clothes they wore, but they also tended to depict the wearing of zoot suits as a symptom of a social problem. Discrimination led young men to wear these flashy clothes. Both Bass and Russell insisted that bad housing, poverty, and discrimination led some young men to wear zoot suits and engage in crime.[29]

Like Bass and Russell, *Daily News* columnist Ted LeBerthon suggested that if there were no discrimination Mexican Americans and African Americans would dress exactly the same as Anglo Americans. A San Francisco native who had worked for newspapers in New York and Chicago before he joined the *Daily News* in 1936, LeBerthon wrote frequently about race relations and jazz.[30] He devoted an entire column to the zoot-suit phenomenon. He explained to his readers that the "goshawful looking" zoot suit "is the garb of the young sport from any underprivileged stratum of society." These underprivileged people, whether they were "white, Negro, Mexican or Filipino," tended to be poor and as a result had "never known good taste in wearing apparel." The point of LeBerthon's column, however, was not to criticize paternalistically poor people who did not have "good taste in wearing apparel." The villains of LeBerthon's column were "white" people who treated African Americans, Mexican Americans, and Asian Americans as inferior. Many of the young people who wore zoot suits, he wrote, "have resented being treated as 'lower classes' by those who regard any dark skin as an indication of social inferiority." He also argued that zoot suiters were not unique to Los Angeles or even to the United States. People in many different nations resented the notion that they were inferior to white people. LeBerthon used his interpretation of the zoot suit to criticize "Fascistic and racist minded persons in our own country today who fan dangerous flames by coming out publicly for regarding the war itself as a war for maintaining white supremacy."[31]

While LeBerthon attacked white supremacists, the *Times* attacked people who "stirred up" racial prejudice by suggesting that discrimination existed. On the same day that LeBerthon's column appeared in the *Daily News*, the *Times* published a rare and important front-page editorial. The editorial's headline declared that it was "time for sanity." The insanity to which the editorial referred, however, was not the violence on the street. Instead, the editorial criticized the "hysteria and wild accusations" that had accompanied the violence. The editorial minimized the violence while placing the blame for the riots on the so-called zoot suiters. It declared that "a far greater danger than the gangsterism and its attendant flare-up of retributive violence lies in the perverted purposes to which reports of the difficulties here are being, and will be, put both at home and in other countries."

The *Times* was clearly more concerned with depictions of the riots "at home" than abroad. The editorial warned that "attempts by any group, faction or political philosophy to use the clashes for purposes of stirring up racial prejudice are unwarranted and are serving the aims of Axis propagandists." Although the editorial did not explicitly identify "any group, faction or political philosophy," it is clear from the editorial that the *Times* was attacking people who argued that racial ideology had influenced the events in Los Angeles in early June 1943. It characterized their arguments as efforts to stir up "racial prejudice," as if any acknowledgment of the existence of racial prejudice was in fact an effort to arouse prejudice. The *Times* suggested that racial prejudice did not really exist or was not widespread; it had to be "stirred up" by people whose motives the newspaper questioned.

The *Times* insisted that efforts to curb juvenile gangsterism "have had nothing whatever to do with race persecution, although some elements have loudly raised the cry of this very thing." In support of its claim that efforts to suppress juvenile crime could not have been "race persecution," the editorial noted that "at the outset zoot suiters were limited to no specific race; they were Anglo-Saxon, Latin and Negro." The editorial did acknowledge that zoot suiters later became "predominantly Latin," but this fact "was in itself no indictment of that race at all; the American-born boy gangs merely came from certain districts where the Latin population was in the large majority." This statement ignored the reasons why there were districts in which Mexican Americans constituted the majority of the population. It suggested that people could simply choose to live wherever they wanted and that discrimination did not affect housing options for Mexican Americans or members of other groups.

Although the *Times* suggested that racial discrimination was not a problem if it even existed in Los Angeles, it also distanced itself from some of the ideas expressed earlier by law enforcement officers. It declared that "no responsible person at any time condemned Latin Americans, as such, because some irresponsibles were causing trouble." In stating this, the *Times* seems to have declared that Ed Duran Ayres, Police Chief C. B. Horrall, and Capt. Vernon Rasmussen were irresponsible and that their ideas should not be considered seriously, for all of them had either expressed or endorsed the idea that Mexicans were biologically prone to criminality. In addition to ending "zoot suit gangsterism," the editorial stated, "the present pressing problem" was "to discourage as far as possible the loud and unthinking charges that the fault lies exclusively in racial prejudice, police brutality or Fascist tendencies of the constituted authorities."[32]

A few days later a *Times* editorial explicitly identified one group that it accused of "stirring up the racial prejudice." By claiming that Mexican Americans were the victims of racial persecution, the *Times* argued, "pressure groups" such as the Citizens' Committee for the Defense of Mexican-American Youth were actually spreading "the doctrine of racial hatred." This editorial repeated the suggestion that racial discrimination did not really exist and that people who said otherwise were simply stirring up prejudice. "There certainly can be no excuse for any group which deliberately seeks to spread the doctrine of racial hatred under the pious guise of 'safeguarding' the rights of the assertedly victimized minorities," the *Times* declared. Although this editorial attacked the Citizens' Committee for the Defense of Mexican-American Youth, it also expressed agreement with the Citizens' Committee's position regarding "race." "A criminal is not a criminal because of race," the *Times* admitted. "But the mere fact of race, on the other hand, cannot be allowed to shield the guilty."[33] Like the previous editorial that argued that "no responsible person at any time condemned Latin Americans," this editorial explicitly rejected the idea that "race" made people criminals.

In most of the articles published during the rioting, the daily newspapers did not quote any Mexican Americans. Once the rioting had begun to abate, however, they allowed a few Mexican Americans to express their perceptions of the riots. The *Times*, for example, devoted an entire article to the ideas of Rev. Francisco Quintanilla, the pastor of the Mexican Methodist Church in Watts.

This article reveals the complexity of the ongoing debate about the riots, as the article contradicts some of the statements in *Times* editorials. Unlike editorials that depicted people who expressed concern about racial discrimination as feminine "mollycoddlers," this article depicted Quintanilla as "a two-fisted man who commands the respect of even the toughest juvenile in Watts" because of his service in Pancho Villa's army during the Mexican Revolution.

Although the *Times* implicitly endorsed Quintanilla's warnings to young Mexican Americans, Quintanilla offered an interpretation of juvenile crime among young Mexican Americans that the *Times* had previously dismissed as "absurd." He argued that young Mexican Americans and African Americans attacked soldiers and sailors because they were "fed vicious propaganda by enemy agents who wish to stir up all the racial and class hatreds they can put their evil fingers on." Quintanilla blamed the riots on Mexican American and African American provocateurs who attracted the attention of sailors and soldiers and then ran "when the fighting gets hot," forcing "innocent Mexican and Negro youths . . . to bear the brunt of the mob fighting." He warned that "if the Mexican and Negro minorities want to gain the respect of the community, this rioting is not the way to go about it." He insisted that "you can't obtain respect by force—you're only digging your own grave."[34] Even though the *Times* insisted that the riots had nothing to do with "race," Quintanilla depicted the riots as racial riots, in which Mexican and African American men faced off against Anglo sailors and soldiers. Quintanilla was later invited to present his ideas

FIG. 7. *Rev. Francisco Quintanilla, the pastor of the Mexican Methodist Church in Watts. Quintanilla told the* Los Angeles Times *that young Mexican Americans and African Americans attacked soldiers and sailors because they were "fed vicious propaganda by enemy agents who wish to stir up all the racial and class hatreds they can put their evil fingers on." Quintanilla later appeared before the Tenney Committee.* Los Angeles Times *Photographic Archive (Collection 1429), Department of Special Collections, Charles E. Young Research Library, University of California, Los Angeles.*

before the California legislature's Joint Fact-Finding Committee on Un-American Activities.[35]

After hearing from a number of officials, including the chief of the Los Angeles Police Department and one of the department's deputy chiefs, the committee appointed by Gov. Earl Warren to investigate the riots issued its report on June 12. The committee members came from a wide range of backgrounds. Warren had appointed Holton, who had served as the chief probation officer of Los Angeles County since 1939, to head the California Youth Authority earlier in 1943. McGucken, who was born in Los Angeles in 1902, studied at the southern branch of the University of California (now UCLA) and at St. Patrick's Seminary in Menlo Park, California. He completed his training for the priesthood in Rome and was ordained in 1928. The next year Bishop John J. Cantwell appointed McGucken his private secretary. He continued to serve the diocese and later archdiocese in various administrative capacities before he was appointed an auxiliary bishop in February 1941.[36] McGucken later served as the Bishop of the Diocese of Sacramento (1955–1962) and as the Archbishop of the Archdiocese of San Francisco (1962–1977). He died in 1983.

Walter Gordon was born in Atlanta in 1894. His father, a Pullman porter, moved the family to Riverside when Walter was ten. Gordon graduated from high school in Riverside and entered the University of California in 1914. Gordon was a gifted athlete, and he served as an assistant football coach at the university for twenty-four years after he graduated. When Gordon graduated in 1918, he was hired as Berkeley's first African American police officer. Three years later he entered Boalt Hall, the law school at the University of California. When he completed law school, Gordon established his private law practice. For several years he was the president of the Alameda County NAACP. As an attorney in Alameda County he had come to know Warren when he was the district attorney for the county.[37]

Willsie Martin was born in Sherbrooke, Quebec, in 1876. He graduated from the University of California, in Berkeley, in 1900 and was ordained a Methodist minister in the same year. Martin served churches in Sacramento, Oakland, New York City (while he studied at Drew Theological Seminary in New Jersey), Chico, Alameda, and Boise, Idaho. In 1919 Martin returned to California, where he assumed the pastorate of the First Methodist Episcopal Church of Hollywood. Eight years later Martin became the minister at the Wilshire Methodist Episcopal Church. In the 1930s Martin became active in community affairs. He served on the city of Los Angeles's Committee on Governmental Reorganization in 1936, and he served as a mediator of two different strikes in the late 1930s. In the 1940s he served as a park commissioner for the city of Los Angeles, on the Los Angeles County Committee for Church and Community Cooperation, and on the Citizens' Committee for Latin-American Youth. Martin was a Republican.[38]

Leo Carrillo was born in Los Angeles in 1880. He was the great-grandson of Carlos Antonio Carrillo, who served as a governor of Alta California when it was part of Mexico. Carrillo attended Loyola University (now Loyola Marymount University) in Los Angeles and worked for the Southern Pacific Railroad and as a cartoonist before he took up acting. He worked in vaudeville and then acted on Broadway before he returned to California and worked in motion pictures. Often depicting stereotypical "Latin" characters, Carrillo had appeared in seventy movies, many of them westerns, prior to his being named to the governor's investigating committee. In 1942, when Warren was the Republican gubernatorial candidate, Carrillo traveled with him and introduced him at campaign stops.[39]

Although the members of the committee came from a wide range of backgrounds, they quickly agreed on a list of findings and recommendations. The committee's conclusions and recommendations reflected the statements both of those people who were concerned about racial prejudice and discrimination and of those people who denied the existence of prejudice and discrimination.[40] The committee concluded that there was no connection between nationality or "race" and gang membership. According to the committee, there were Anglo, Mexican, and African American gangs. In a rebuke to the *Times* and its allies, who argued that zoot suiters had been attacked because of their "weird dress," the committee concluded that gang members could not be identified by their clothing. The committee recommended an increase in the military and shore police, the establishment of a forestry camp for juvenile offenders, and the establishment of additional recreational facilities. Fully half of the committee's recommendations, however, addressed racial and ethnic tensions. The committee said that law enforcement agencies should not single out minority groups for arrest, that law enforcement officers who dealt with minority groups should have special training, and that "discrimination against any race in the provision or use of public facilities should be abolished."[41] In private correspondence with the governor, Bishop McGucken more explicitly challenged the idea that racial attitudes did not contribute to the violence. He wrote, "service men have been guilty of unprovoked assaults on not only 'zootsuiters' but innocent civilians, particularly those of minority groups."[42]

As the previous paragraphs suggest, a remarkable transformation occurred as rioting subsided in mid-June 1943. Although some of the daily newspapers and some elected officials continued to insist that there was no racial discrimination in Los Angeles, a committee appointed by the governor found that racial discrimination was a problem. More remarkable is the *Times*'s admission that "race" did not make someone a criminal. It is possible, of course, to place too much emphasis on the change in the *Times*'s position. Even as the newspaper admitted that Mexican Americans were not biologically prone to criminal behavior, the newspaper continued to insist that all people of Japanese ancestry were biologically prone to loyalty toward Japan.

The Silent Rioters

The early newspaper reports on the riots, the editorials, the statements of public officials, and even the private meetings of organizations that were concerned about the riots share a remarkable characteristic: few of them mention the words uttered either by the rioting sailors, soldiers, and civilians or by the so-called zoot suiters. One article in the *Examiner* quoted an unnamed sailor, who said: "we're going to do what the police haven't been able to. We're going to make the streets of Los Angeles safe for sailors, for sailors' girls, and for the general public."[43] Another article reported that a "battered pachuco at the hospital begged: 'Charge me with vagrancy or anything, but don't send me out there.'"[44] An article in the *Times* reported that one sailor shouted: "Give the cops. We'll go down the street and find another zooter. Come on gang, let's go."[45] Some articles quoted the victims of attacks by members of "zoot-suit gangs."[46] Most of the articles, however, simply described the violence on the streets of Los Angeles without quoting any of the people who were involved in the rioting.

The *Daily News* differed in this respect, as in many others, from the *Times* and the *Examiner*. Articles in the *Daily News* more often allowed some of the sailors and soldiers to speak for themselves. One article, for example, quoted in its entirety a telegram sent to the newspaper by "400 navy men" from San Pedro. This telegram, like the statement of the unidentified sailor quoted by the *Examiner*, insisted that the sailors were attacking "zoot suiters" to protect their wives and families. "Our intent of taking justice in our own hands was not an attempt to instill mob rule but only the desire to insure our wives and families safe passage in the streets." The telegram suggested that the orders prohibiting sailors from entering much of Los Angeles left the city in control of "the socalled zoot suiters."[47] Another article reported that "servicemen" descended upon Watts, shouting: "where are the zoot suiters? We'll fix those guys who hurt our buddies." The article also noted that these men "began to chant military tunes" when they did not find any zoot suiters.[48] Less frequently, the *Daily News* allowed some alleged gang members to express themselves. In a June 11 article, for example, the newspaper reported that one "slick chick" told a meeting of other women gangsters: "we won't quit. We'll keep it up until we're wiped out or they're wiped out." The article reported that another "girl, declaring she had paid $75 for her zoot suit," said "belligerently" that "nobody is going to take it off of me, either."[49] In a June 15 article about a meeting between "zoot suiters" in Watts and Los Angeles police officers, the newspaper reported that one young man asked, "Haven't we a right to wear the kind of clothes we want to?"[50] Even some of the articles that purported to explain the motivations and actions of gang members in the *Daily News*, however, often did not identify or quote any of these reputed "hoodlums."[51]

To a considerable extent, the early debate about the meaning of the riots depended upon the silence of all the people who were actually involved in the riots. The arguments of both sides could have been punctured by the actual words of the young Mexican Americans and African Americans or of the sailors, soldiers, and civilians who were involved in the rioting. Young Mexican Americans and African Americans might have and later did disagree with the people who suggested that racial prejudice and discrimination influenced both the behavior of these young people and the violence directed toward them. They did not say that they dressed in flashy clothes to compensate for the psychological damage done by discrimination. On the other hand, those who had argued that the riots were not race riots would have been proved wrong if sailors, soldiers, and civilian participants in the riots called their targets names such as "Mexicans," "Greasers," "Niggers," or other racial epithets.

The newspapers never reported what the participants in the rioting called each other, but it is possible to gather some sense of what was said during the rioting and in the events leading up to it from other sources. The navy conducted an investigation of attacks upon navy personnel, wives of sailors, and girlfriends of sailors by so-called zoot suiters before and during the riots. Records in the National Archives do not indicate that the navy investigated the attacks by sailors upon so-called zoot suiters, although the investigation of attacks upon navy personnel and their wives and girlfriends did sometimes indicate when attacks by "zoot suiters" led to retaliation by sailors. This report identified eighty-eight separate incidents involving conflict between "zoot suiters" and sailors from the armory in Chavez Ravine between August 1942 and June 8, 1943. Many of these reported incidents did not involve physical contact between "zoot suiters" and sailors. Although the navy report on these incidents cannot be accepted at face value, the information in the report raises some fascinating questions. The report clearly indicates that "zoot suiters" said things to sailors before and during assaults on them. Some of the incidents consisted entirely of verbal abuse. The report does not indicate, however, that the "zoot suiters" ever mentioned the race of the sailors. This could be interpreted in several different ways. It could, for example, be interpreted as evidence that "zoot suiters" never referred to the sailors as "white," or as "gringos," or as "crackers." It could also mean that the sailors in their reporting of these incidents did not mention the use of such racial terms. Finally, it could also mean that the officers who compiled the report could have deleted such terms. The omission of these terms could reflect the desire on the part of navy officers to downplay any racial undertones of these events. This report, however, was confidential, and navy officers appear not to have been reluctant to include examples of the "vile names" that "zoot suiters" hurled at sailors.

Even though "zoot suiters" did not apparently refer to the race of the sailors, the sailors frequently noted the race or ethnicity of the "zoot suiters." The descriptions of twenty-one of the eighty-eight incidents—nearly one-quarter—indicate that the people involved were "Mexicans" or, in one case, "Mexicans and Negroes." In some of these incidents, the assailants were identified as "Mexicans" rather than as "zoot-suiters." Some of the sailors who reported these incidents also distinguished between Mexicans who wore zoot suits and those who did not. One conclusion that can be drawn from these reports is that the sailors seem to have claimed the ability to determine who was Mexican and who was not—Mexican "race," nationality, or ethnicity appears to be self-evident. Since the names of the sailors were deleted from this report, it is impossible to determine if any of the sailors themselves had Spanish surnames. It is possible, since Mexican Americans were classified as "white" and were not subject to racial segregation within the military. So it is possible that the people who identified assailants as "Mexican" were themselves "Mexican" and were able to identify these assailants as such on some basis other than appearance. Only three of the incident descriptions mention people speaking "Mexican" or Spanish; in all the remaining incidents the assailants, some of whom were identified as "Mexicans," spoke English. Most commonly, the sailors reported that their antagonists called them "son of a bitch" or "sons of bitches" (thirteen times), "bastard" or "bastards" (twelve times), and "cock sucker" (three times).[52] While this report does offer some support for the *Times*'s argument that the riots were not "race riots," it also offers support for the arguments of many African American and Mexican American activists, in that it makes clear that the sailors involved in nearly one-quarter of all these incidents viewed their antagonists as "Mexicans." It is not clear what the sailors and soldiers yelled at the "zoot suiters." According to one woman who witnessed the rioting on June 7, 1943, military personnel driving past the intersection of Twelfth Street and Central Avenue "were hollering ugly names at the Mexicans and Negroes," but she did not repeat those names.[53]

After the rioting had subsided, the newspapers allowed a few "zoot-suiters" to speak. The *Times* and the *Examiner*, however, carefully restricted their readers' access to the statements of these young people. The Los Angeles County Grand Jury launched an investigation of the riots on June 15. The Grand Jury issued subpoenas to eighteen young men.

The *Times* briefly quoted two of them. Twenty-year-old Genaro Rojo, reputed to be the leader of the "Alpine Street Gang," told the jury that his gang had not been involved in the riots. He expressed the opinion that young people wore what the *Times* characterized as "their outlandish attire" because "they like it and have a right to wear it." An African American, John B. Thomas, "appearing in a bright green zoot suit with a gray 'rat-catcher' cap, exhibited his Army enlistment papers and asserted he had a right to wear his outfit until he dons khaki, which is scheduled for today." Thomas told the jury that he was not a gangster. "I just like this style," he said.[54] The *Examiner* article about the Grand Jury's investigation into "zoot suit gang warfare" mentioned only the testimony of Rojo and that of sixteen-year-old

FIG. 8. *The Los Angeles County Grand Jury conducted an investigation of "zoot-suit" crime soon after rioting ended. In this photograph, "zoot suiters" wait to appear before the grand jury on June 15, 1943.* Herald-Examiner *Collection, Los Angeles Public Library.*

Sylvester Rodriguez, who endorsed imprisonment. Rodriguez told the jury that his confinement on a farm for juvenile offenders "gave him opportunities denied him before."[55]

In one exceptional instance the *Examiner* offered one former zoot suiter the opportunity to express his beliefs about zoot suiters and the causes of the riots. Ignazio Martinez, a twenty-seven-year-old army paratrooper, told an *Examiner* reporter that "I used to wear zoot suits and so does my little brother." Many of his friends in the army also wore zoot suits before their induction, he said. "I lived on the east side all my life and I know all those kids. They're good kids and they're patriotic. But they used to get pushed around all the time and I guess that's what was behind the blowoff in the street riots here." Martinez contrasted the "pushing around" that Mexican American young people experienced with his treatment in the army. "Whatever the background causes of the riots—discrimination, inequality or lack of privileges—there's none of it in the Army." Martinez offered his suggestion for ending juvenile delinquency among Mexican Americans: "What these kids need is a place to play and hang around and a little consideration from the rest of the people. I hope while the rest of us are busy fighting the war the people on the home front give these kids this break."[56] Martinez's words, however, appeared in an article that was published on June 30, after news of the rioting had nearly disappeared from the pages of the daily newspapers.

In contrast to the *Times* and the *Examiner*, the *Daily News* offered the "zoot suiters" who appeared before the Grand Jury more of an opportunity to express themselves. The *Daily News* suggested that many of the young Mexican Americans who wore zoot suits were not gangsters but patriotic Americans awaiting induction into the armed services. The newspaper reported that "Raymond Serna, good looking 17-year-old zooter, proudly displayed his knee length Palm Beach coat and his acceptance notice from the marine corps." Serna told the Grand Jury that "zoot suits had nothing to do with recent fighting." "Soon I will wear the marine corps uniform," Serna said, "but until I do, nobody is going to make me take off this zoot suit." Twenty-year-old John B. Thomas told the Grand Jury that he had sold his zoot suit but that he was not delivering it to the purchaser until he was inducted into the army. "Racial prejudice, of citizens and police alike, is the real cause of the recent uprising, Mack Rojo, 22, and his brother, Genaro, said. Both work in war plants, both have only zoot clothes in their wardrobe, they said." Sixteen-year-old

Mac Wright told the jury about being attacked by "servicemen" during the riots. "He said he and another youth were en route to a theater one night when the sailors landed. A policeman stood nearby, and the two Negro lads appealed for help, but the officer turned the other way, he said."[57]

Some *Daily News* reporters also challenged the dominant depiction of young "zoot suiters." James Felton, for example, argued that "intelligent American soldiers" would not believe that "we ought to wipe out all those zoot suiters" if they knew about Mrs. Mercedes Abasta's son Frank, who lost his life and received a commendation for refusing "to leave a torpedoed merchant ship until all the sailors had left." If Frank were still alive and a civilian, Felton insisted, he would once again wear the "drape shape" of the zoot suit. Felton's article also mentioned Mrs. Abasta's other sons: sixteen-year-old Richard, who was working for a truck company; seventeen-year-old Edward and his older brother Trinidad, both of whom were working in an aircraft plant; and fourteen-year-old Joe, a junior high school student. "A zoot suit, or denim jeans, or war plant uniforms or old-fashioned black bloomers are not necessarily costumes of crime or robes of character," the article declared.[58]

As the preceding paragraphs indicate, the daily newspapers, particularly the *Times* and the *Examiner,* usually refused to allow the people who were involved in the rioting to explain their actions. When the young "zoot suiters" did have the opportunity to express themselves, they challenged all of the ways in which other people depicted them. These young men described themselves as patriotic Americans, not as criminals. They described the discrimination they had faced, but they did not say that they dressed in flashy clothes in order to compensate for that discrimination. Instead, they argued that their decision to dress as they did simply represented their individual tastes. The military personnel who participated in the violence in Los Angeles, however, had even fewer opportunities than "zoot suiters" to participate in the ongoing debate about "race."

Eleanor Roosevelt and the Conflict over Racial Discrimination

During the riots and in the first few days after the violence abated, community leaders, journalists, and public officials debated whether or not racial prejudice had motivated the attacks upon "zoot suiters." On June 17, however, the debates turned in a different direction. On that day Los Angeles newspapers published a statement made by First Lady Eleanor Roosevelt. In a press conference on June 16, Roosevelt said that she believed the riots resulted from "long-standing discrimination against Mexicans" in California and the Southwest. "For a long time I've worried about the attitude toward Mexicans in California and the States along the border," Roosevelt told reporters. She also indicated that the riots in California were related to events in other places: "race problems" were increasing in the United States and worldwide, and "we must begin to face it," the First Lady said.[59]

Roosevelt's words ignited a firestorm of protest from some prominent Californians who insisted that there was no discrimination against Mexican Americans in their state. On June 18 both the *Times* and the *Examiner* published a five-paragraph statement by Preston Hotchkis, the president of the California State Chamber of Commerce. Hotchkis began by insisting that "these so-called 'zoot-suit' riots have never been and are not now in the nature of race riots." Instead, he said, they grew out of "sporadic clashes between juvenile gangs in various parts of Los Angeles and environs, without regard to race or color." Hotchkis, however, did not simply assert that the riots were not race riots. He also answered Roosevelt's charge that Mexicans encountered discrimination in California. Hotchkis insisted that Roosevelt's statement "is untrue, unjust, and provocative of disunion among people who have lived for years in harmony." Hotchkis asserted that "the citizens of California" had never discriminated against "persons of Mexican origin." His distinction between "citizens of California" and "persons of Mexican origin" suggests that he did not see "persons of Mexican origin" as "citizens of California," but he later declared that California had treated Mexicans "with the utmost consideration, and many of their number are listed among the most prominent and most useful citizens of the State."[60]

The *Times* responded even more vitriolically to Roosevelt's words than did Hotchkis. An editorial in the *Times* accused the First Lady of "deliberately" trying "to create a vicious international racial antagonism without a foundation in fact." The editorial also attempted to connect Roosevelt with the Communist party. The *Times* characterized Roosevelt's statement that discrimination against Mexicans had influenced the riots as "untrue" and "dangerous." The editorial argued that Roosevelt's statement "shows ignorance" and "shows an amazing similarity to the Communist party propaganda, which has been desperately devoted to making a racial issue of the juvenile gang trouble here." Dismissing the words of people such as Ignazio

Martinez and Mack and Genaro Rojo, the *Times* declared that "the cry that Mexicans were being abused was not raised by Mexicans or persons of Mexican descent, but by pressure and political groups who always avidly seize upon any pretense to fan race discord." The editorial argued that "everybody here in a position to assay the facts—including Mexican leaders, officials, the Army and Navy and civic investigators—knows that the zoot suit fights were not based on racial antagonism at all." According to the *Times,* the sailors and soldiers who had participated in the riots "were not looking for Mexicans, Negroes, or Anglo-Saxons—they were looking for the weird costumes worn by the gangsters, who have included many races." The *Times,* like Hotchkis, insisted that Anglo Californians did not discriminate against Mexicans. The editorial argued that California "has always been rather ostentatiously proud" of its Spanish and Mexican heritage and had "paid homage and honor to the Californians of Mexican descent among us." Unlike Hotchkis, who simply asserted that many Mexican Americans "are listed among the most prominent and most useful citizens of the State," the *Times* provided specific examples. It identified Los Angeles County Sheriff Eugene Biscailuz, "proud scion of a California family," as "probably the most popular public official in Southern California." It also identified the "Jose Arias musical family," "worthy Mexican descendants," as "the most beloved entertainment group in California's famous fiestas." The editorial insisted that Anglo-Californians "enjoy fraternizing" with members of "the largest Mexican colony in the United States." Ignoring the repatriation movement of the early 1930s, as a result of which thousands of Mexican immigrants and their U.S.-born children were forced to leave southern California, the *Times* asserted that "we have been solicitous for their welfare in times of depression." The editorial concluded that Roosevelt, rather than the violence itself, had "contributed greatly toward misunderstanding with our Latin-American friends and allies."[61]

In contrast to Hotchkis and the *Times,* some Los Angeles community leaders applauded Roosevelt's statement. At its first meeting after the First Lady's statement, the Coordinating Council for Latin American Youth, whose membership included a number of Mexican Americans, approved a motion calling for the chair to write a letter to Roosevelt, "commending her statement as having been based upon accurate information and acknowledging our gratefulness and admiration for her bold and unequivocal stand, to the effect that race prejudice was the controling [*sic*] fundamental factor inciting the recent riots."[62] The action of the Coordinating Council, however, was not reported in the daily newspapers.

After Eleanor Roosevelt expressed her concern about discrimination against Mexican Americans, then, some people in Los Angeles endorsed her position. Others, most notably Hotchkis and the publisher of the *Times*, criticized her statement. The Spanish-language newspaper *La Opinión*, however, criticized both Roosevelt's statements and those of her critics as "simplistic." Neither Roosevelt nor her critics seem to have appreciated the complexity of the problem that led to the rioting, according to an editorial in the daily newspaper. The editorial in *La Opinión* disagreed with Roosevelt's argument that people had been attacked simply because they were Mexican. It agreed with Roosevelt that discrimination had contributed to the emergence of youth gangs, and it criticized Hotchkis and the *Times* for asserting that Mexicans faced no discrimination in Los Angeles. Mexicans in Los Angeles faced housing and employment discrimination, and Mexican American children endured school segregation, the editorial observed. But the fact that Hotchkis and the *Times* had begun to acknowledge the cultural and artistic legacy of Mexican California was a sign that discrimination might decline, the editorial suggested.[63]

The debate that followed Eleanor Roosevelt's statement reveals important characteristics of the larger debate about the meaning of "race" in Los Angeles in the aftermath of the Zoot-Suit Riots. In the conflict over Roosevelt's interpretation of the riots, people such as Preston Hotchkis and the publisher of the *Los Angeles Times* insisted that "Californians" or "citizens of California," terms they generally used to mean people who claimed to be "white," did not discriminate against "Mexicans" or "Californians of Mexican descent." In advancing this argument, Hotchkis and the *Times* dismissed the words of a number of elected and appointed officials—including the County Board of Supervisors, Governor Earl Warren's investigating committee, and the Mexican consul. The *Times* even argued that no Mexicans had suggested that they had endured discrimination. Yet the *Times* had obviously silenced the voices of the young Mexican American and African American "zoot suiters" who said that they had experienced discrimination in southern California. Moreover, both the *Times* and Hotchkis seem to have ignored the middle-class Mexican Americans who served on the Coordinating Council for Latin American Youth and who published *La Opinión*. These middle-class Mexican Americans agreed that discrimination against people of Mexican descent was a problem in Los Angeles. When Hotchkis and the *Times* argued that some Mexicans were among the "most prominent" residents of California, they suggested that the success of any members of a group demonstrated conclusively that no members of that group faced discrimination. In addition, by pointing to the prominence of the Arias family, the *Times* suggested that it was "natural" for Mexicans to work as entertainers and performers but that it might not be "natural" for Mexicans to engage in other kinds of endeavors.

African Americans and the Zoot-Suit Riots

While some Los Angeles residents focused their attention on Eleanor Roosevelt's words, other residents continued to debate the meanings of the riots. The June 17 issue of the *California Eagle* included several articles, columns, and editorials about the riots. In her column, *Eagle* publisher Charlotta A. Bass argued that the riots did not simply reflect local tensions in Los Angeles. Instead, she wrote, the riots were part of a Fascist conspiracy. Bass insisted that the rioting in Los Angeles was connected to events throughout the United States, such as "a Ku Klux Klan strike at the Detroit Packard plant" and conflict between New York police and African Americans. All of these events, Bass suggested, represented Fascist efforts to disrupt the war effort. The ultimate goal of these efforts, Bass wrote, "was a major race riot. It was to have broken out within the shipyards and aircraft plants of the city. It was to have disrupted all war production in the county for an indefinite period."

Bass and other *Eagle* staff members identified the publishers of metropolitan newspapers as participants in this conspiracy. In her column Bass wrote that "the greatest weapons of Hitler in America are the Hearst and Scripps-Howard newspaper syndicates." The Hearst and Scripps-Howard newspapers, she argued, "peddle Berlin's propaganda line day after day. They provoke attacks against minority groups; they urge class dissensions; they oppose vital government programs to an extent that amounts to treason." Bass insisted that the Hearst newspapers in Los Angeles had carried out a propaganda campaign against young Mexican and African Americans for more than a year. "It was simply done. As simple as this: Every crime story in which a Mexican or Negro youth was involved found the words 'zoot suit' attached thereto." Bass wrote that this smear campaign continued "day after day and week after week . . . mounting in fury and column inches per crime story." As a result of this campaign, she argued, "our city became convinced that a reign of terror had been launched by Mexican pachuco youth."[64]

Eagle editor John S. Kinloch agreed with Bass. In his column Kinloch bluntly declared about the rioting: "the Los Angeles metropolitan press started it." Kinloch wrote that "nothing, so help me, NOTHING on a newspaper happens by accident except upside down lines and then somebody accidentally gets fired." Kinloch quoted the report of the governor's investigating committee, which stated that "the increase of delinquency in the case of youths of Mexican families has been less than in the case of other national or racial groups and less than the average increase for the community." In claiming that Mexican "zoot suiters" constituted a menace to all of the law-abiding citizens of Los Angeles, "the papers WERE LYING," Kinloch wrote.[65]

In addition to accusing editors of the metropolitan papers of participating in a Fascist conspiracy, Bass compared the violence in Los Angeles with patterns of racial violence in Nazi Germany and the U.S. South. She argued that "while metropolitan papers assured the city that servicemen were restoring order," African Americans and Mexican Americans "were subjected to a terror spree reminiscent of Nazi mobs or the lynch fiends of Dixie America."[66]

Bass's depiction of the riots was similar to some other local and national leaders' descriptions of the violence. The Citizens' Committee for the Defense of Mexican-American Youth, which had been organized to support the Sleepy Lagoon defendants, issued a number of press releases after the riots. Although these releases were not published by the daily newspapers, they reflected the committee's efforts to participate in this debate. In one release, the Citizens' Committee declared that "behind the confusion created by the obvious disruptive forces in the last few days, lies a well thought-out Axis plan, carried out most successfully by Axis agents in our midst."[67] The committee argued that "Fascism never could make headway among a united people. Therefore its first aim is to cause discord and disunity among the races of man so that it can step in, crush unmercifully, and rule the groups exhausted with fighting each other."[68]

Like Bass, CIO President Philip Murray compared the rioting in Los Angeles to lynching in the South. Murray attributed the violence to the "lynch spirit" that had been "whipped up and directed against citizens of

Mexican descent and against Negroes." Murray also interpreted the rioting as part of a "conspiracy against our national unity." He called upon the president "to order the War and Navy Departments to undertake an educational campaign among the armed forces . . . to eradicate the misconceptions and prejudices that contributed to these attacks on their fellow-citizens."[69] Murray's words, unlike the words of Bass or other local African American leaders, were reported in the *Times*. Even though the *Times* was hostile to organized labor, however, it did not devote any editorial space to an attack on Murray comparable to its attack on Roosevelt.

African American writers argued that the riots made clear the need for changes in police procedures. An editorial published in the June 17 issue of the *Eagle* argued that the police should not treat all members of a "racial" group as if they were criminals. "Mass arrests, drag-net raids and other wholesale classifications of groups of people are based on false premises and tend merely to aggravate the situation," the editorial declared. "Any American citizen suspected of crime is entitled to be treated as an individual, to be indicted as such, and to be tried, both at law and in the forum of public opinion, on his merits or errors, regardless of race, color, creed OR THE KIND OF CLOTHES HE WEARS." When individuals were not treated as individuals, but were characterized as people typical of their race, color, or creed, race prejudice was fostered, and "the entire group accused wants revenge and vindication. The public is led to believe that every person in the accused group is guilty of crime," the editorial stated.[70]

Some officials were interested in African Americans' interpretations of the riots. Several African American community leaders appeared before the Grand Jury to discuss the riots. The daily newspapers, however, did not devote much space to the words of these leaders. Although the *Times* reported that a machinist named Paul Williams, NAACP President Thomas L. Griffith, Jr., and "several Negro ministers" appeared before the Grand Jury, it devoted only two paragraphs to Williams's testimony and ignored the testimony of the other African American leaders. Williams said that "a good deal of the gang problems can be traced" to inadequate housing in the African American district.[71] The *Examiner* correctly identified the Paul Williams who spoke as the "noted Negro architect," but Williams was the only African American mentioned by name in its four-paragraph article reporting that "county grand jurors yesterday heard the testimony of a number of Negro citizens and juvenile officers."[72]

The statements of African Americans deserve closer attention. From the vantage point of the early twenty-first century, the statements of Charlotta Bass and John S. Kinloch seem exaggerated. The *Times*, the *Examiner*, and the *Daily News* did not publish articles about "zoot suit" hoodlums on a daily basis. Nonetheless, to people who rarely saw African Americans or Mexican Americans mentioned in the daily newspapers, these negative articles certainly aroused suspicion and anger. African Americans, too, had reason to fear the possibility that discrimination would increase. Many long-term Los Angeles residents had experienced discrimination in housing, employment, and public accommodations. The migration of tens of thousands of additional African Americans to southern California threatened to exacerbate these discriminatory practices. Even more foreboding was the migration of tens of thousands of European Americans from the southern United States. Many African Americans encountered newcomers from the South who expected to find segregation in California as well as those who attempted to establish southern-style segregation in their new home. In one article the *Eagle* reported that "public recreation facilities, bowling alleys, dance halls, and restaurants all over the city have launched a campaign to prohibit Mexican and Negro attendance. This policy is in violation of state laws and at this time threatens national unity behind the war for survival."[73]

The Tenney Committee Investigates

As the preceding paragraphs indicate, a committee appointed by Governor Earl Warren and the Los Angeles County Grand Jury investigated the rioting soon after the violence abated. These investigations, however, did not satisfy all elected officials. On June 19 the newspapers reported that the California legislature's Joint Fact Finding-Committee on Un-American Activities, also known as the Tenney Committee because it was chaired by Sen. Jack B. Tenney of Los Angeles, would also conduct an investigation. Because this committee was devoted to the investigation of "subversive" activities, its hearings were intended to determine if "subversive elements fomented the outbreak." Tenney called a number of witnesses who would challenge the arguments advanced by community leaders such as Charlotta A. Bass and the Citizens' Committee for the Defense of Mexican-American Youth. These leaders had argued that Fascist agents had incited the violence. More importantly, however, the Tenney Committee directly challenged the statements of people who said that discrimination existed.

According to the daily newspapers and the Tenney Committee's report, the committee first heard from witnesses who rejected the idea that prejudice and discrimination had led to the violence on the streets of Los Angeles. On the first day of the hearings, for example, Tenney asked Police Chief C. B. Horrall if he believed that the riots "were principally due to racial prejudice and discrimination." Horrall answered that he did not.[74] Horrall maintained that "radical groups have been aggravating the situation here" and warned that "there seems to be a possibility trouble may be incited among the Negro population." Mayor Fletcher Bowron told the committee that the "zoot suit troubles" were caused by "a number of bad boys who have very little respect for the law," and he criticized Eleanor Roosevelt and "a number of busybodies" who "have been making a race issue out of it, whereas it's merely a matter of law enforcement."[75]

The Tenney Committee also heard from witnesses who identified the critics of racial prejudice and discrimination as Communists. Clyde C. Shoemaker, the former assistant district attorney who had prosecuted the Sleepy Lagoon case, for example, told the committee that the Citizens' Committee for the Defense of Mexican-American Youth was undoubtedly a Communist front organization.[76] Some Mexican Americans and African Americans appeared before the committee and said that they did not believe that prejudice and discrimination were the root causes of the violence in Los Angeles. Pedro B. Villaseñor and Martin Cabrera, two leaders of the Mexican nationalist Sinarquista movement, acknowledged that racial prejudice might have partially influenced some Mexican Americans' delinquency, but "the principal cause was the lack of proper education, particularly in the home, and the lack of home discipline."[77] The committee's "friendly" witnesses tended to agree with the committee and the *Times* that racial prejudice and discrimination did not simply exist but had to be "stirred up" by agitators. Le Roy R. Ingram, secretary-manager of the Eastside Chamber of Commerce, "a conservative, anti-Communist organization of colored people," told the committee that the *California Eagle* "had played a vital role in stirring up Negro and Mexican minorities by constantly declaring that both the Negro and Mexican population were being discriminated against and subjected to unfair treatment and police brutality." R. G. LaMar, the field secretary of the Eastside Chamber of Commerce, offered his opinion that the "National Negro Conference [*sic*] and the National Association for the Advancement of Colored People had been infiltrated by Communist Party members to such an extent that these organizations were presently little more than Communist fronts."[78]

The *California Eagle*'s reports on the Tenney Committee hearings differed dramatically from the daily newspapers' coverage. The *Times* and the *Examiner* briefly described exchanges between committee members and "unfriendly" witnesses such as Al Waxman and Carey McWilliams. They did not describe the questions mentioned in the *Eagle*'s reports. According to the African American newspaper, Sen. Hugh M. Burns of Fresno expressed the belief that all people thought that racial segregation was desirable or necessary in his questioning of *Eastside Journal* publisher Al Waxman. When Waxman argued that racial discrimination was a problem, Burns challenged him to identify "any discrimination against Negroes" in Los Angeles. When Waxman told of an African American friend who had been denied service at a restaurant, Burns insisted that such an incident was not discrimination. "Negroes have a rule not to impose on whites, and whites don't impose on Negroes," he said.[79]

In a similarly revealing exchange, Tenney asked McWilliams what he thought of miscegenation, and McWilliams replied that he thought "miscegenation statutes are a reflection of prejudice in the community" and that they should be abolished. Tenney followed with the question: "You think there should be free intermarriage?" McWilliams, referring to research by distinguished sociologists, argued that the laws had not accomplished their objectives. Tenney never explicitly expressed support for miscegenation laws, but his line of questioning suggested that any criticism of these laws was dangerously radical.[80] Another member of the committee, Assembly member Nelson S. Dilworth of Hemet, asked McWilliams, "Don't you believe segregation and discrimination are necessary for the Negroes and Mexicans?" According to the *Eagle*, "McWilliams hit the ceiling" and declared, "I most certainly do not."[81]

The fact that accounts of these questions did not appear in the daily newspapers is as significant as the questions themselves. There are, of course, a number of ways in which to interpret the fact that the newspapers did not report on these exchanges between the legislators and Waxman and McWilliams. It would be impossible to determine why the reporters wrote what they did and why editors edited the articles as they did. These questions, however, are less important than the implications of the reporting and editing. Considering all of the debate about "race" and the riots, and the explicit acknowledgment by the *Times* that "race" did not make someone a criminal, it seems likely that explicit defenses of segregation and other forms of racial discrimination—at least against Mexicans and African Americans—had become unacceptable.

People such as Carey McWilliams, Charlotta A. Bass, and John S. Kinloch depicted the racial ideology expressed by members of the Tenney Committee as outmoded. The *Eagle* mocked the Tenney Committee's apparent conclusion that the riots were the result of "a red plot."[82] The *Eagle* and Rev. Clayton Russell criticized African Americans who cooperated with the Tenney Committee. Russell labeled the committee "the sworn enemy of the Negro people and all minority groups." According to Russell, Tenney's goal was "to divide and weaken the Negro people." The leader of the Negro Victory Committee asked rhetorically in one speech, "Can't we understand that Negroes can no longer afford to fall into such traps?"[83]

New Organizations and Institutions

By the end of June, the debate about the rioting had largely disappeared from the pages of Los Angeles newspapers. When the Grand Jury issued its report on juvenile delinquency at the end of July, the *Times* did not even mention the riots in its article about the report.[84] The riots, however, stimulated a wave of organizational activity among people who were concerned with racial prejudice and discrimination in Los Angeles. The organizations that emerged after the riots challenged the dominant racial ideology of the time. These organizations worked to convince other Los Angeles residents to embrace their arguments that "racial" characteristics were superficial and that laws and public policy should not be based upon the outmoded "racist" ideology.

Some of this organizing began before the riots occurred. Just before the riots Ted LeBerthon reported on "plans for a general Los Angeles anti-discrimination committee" that would "oppose all forms of discrimination in any walk of life against any human being because of his or her race or creed." According to LeBerthon, this committee would include "outstanding leaders in religion, industry and labor" and "representatives of all anti-discrimination committees that have heretofore been representative of single social groups, such as Jews, Mexicans, Negroes and Filipinos."

LeBerthon indicated that the committee would oppose any act of racial or religious discrimination because such discrimination "is the very antithesis of democracy, which unifies" rather than divides. The organizers of the committee believed that they needed to clarify the meaning of "democracy," "so that democracy shall never imply the right to do a wrong and shall never be confused with any such nonsense as having the right to do as one pleases." The organizers also hoped to expand their "all inclusive anti-discrimination movement" throughout the United States.[85]

What became of this organizing effort is not clear. In his column, LeBerthon referred by name to only two of the organizers of this committee: Lester W. Roth and Dave Coleman. These names do not appear in the articles about the Committee for American Unity, which grew out of the meetings of citizens concerned about the riots. Carey McWilliams; Philip M. "Slim" Connelly, the president of the California CIO; Eduardo Quevedo; Charlotta Bass; Floyd L. Covington, the director of the Los Angeles Urban League; Harry Braverman; and Al Waxman had originally organized this committee. It expanded on June 20, when delegates representing various organizations with an estimated 500,000 members gathered at the Alexandria Hotel. The delegates at this meeting declared their opposition to "Fascist sympathizers" and their racial ideology. Delegates approved a resolution that insisted that these "Fascist sympathizers" since Pearl Harbor had "been trying to stop the fight against Hitler and increase a race war against the Japanese. Not a war against an aggressor, but a race war." The resolution further accused these "Fascist sympathizers" of seeking to increase racial antagonism toward the Japanese to the point that they could negotiate a peace agreement with Hitler. The delegates also called upon the governor's committee to investigate the Zoot-Suit Riots to implement its recommendations. If that committee failed to do so, the Unity Committee promised to launch its own program to eliminate discrimination and the "coloring of news both in the press and over the air in such a manner as to foster race prejudices and race hatred."[86] Young people also organized a junior division of the American Unity Committee.[87]

This Unity Committee seems not to have survived through the summer of 1943. The last article in the *Eagle* that referred to the committee was published on July 1, 1943.[88] Many of the activists who participated in the creation of the Committee for American Unity, however, participated in the formation of other committees designed to address discrimination and tension in Los

Angeles. In August 1943, for example, activists from the Jewish, Mexican, and African American communities, from labor unions, and from the Democratic party formed the Eastside Interracial Committee. The organizers of this committee included *Eastside Journal* publisher Al Waxman, labor attorney Ben Margolis, and *Eagle* publisher Charlotta A. Bass.[89] Committees such as the Eastside Interracial Committee repeated the statements made by their founders during and immediately following the riots. In inviting organizations and individuals to an interracial conference in August 1943, for example, the Eastside Interracial Committee argued that "the fifth column" had "opened a second front for Hitler" in Los Angeles and other cities.[90]

The riots troubled a married couple, William and Elizabeth Cummings, so much that they decided to begin publishing a newspaper, the *War Worker*, devoted to the improvement of race relations in Los Angeles. The *War Worker* began publication in July 1943. Elizabeth Cummings, an Anglo American, later wrote that her husband Bill, an African American, and she were disturbed by the daily newspapers' reporting of race relations. These newspapers "either tended to ignore the problem of race relations, or... tended to add to existing tensions by giving space primarily to the negative aspects of the problem—the incidents of friction and so on." "Minority group publications" were also unsatisfactory, she added. "We felt that an important morale-building, educational service could and should be performed through a publication directed toward all groups and which placed primary emphasis upon the positive aspects of the problem, at the same time giving wholly constructive, educational treatment to the negative aspects." According to Elizabeth Cummings, the *War Worker* was "based on a very simple but new tenet: the enemy says it can't happen—that we of different races and colors and creeds can work in harmony; we say not only that it can happen, but that it is happening—and we prove it through picture and feature material."[91]

As Elizabeth Cummings's words indicate, she and her husband did not exactly say that "racial" characteristics were superficial. They did insist, however, that different "races" could "live in harmony with others." In a long editorial in the first issue, Bill Cummings explained that "we are neither pessimists nor optimists, nor are we idealists in the popular sense of the word. We feel that races can and will work together in universal harmony." Even though the Cummingses suggested that "races" might be fundamentally different, they also rejected "race supremacy." Bill Cummings wrote in the first issue that "the bogy of race supremacy is just another symptom of our immaturity." He suggested that greater maturity could be achieved if people approached problems "objectively" rather than emotionally. In stating the policy of the *War Worker*, Bill Cummings wrote that "WW is unbiased. We are against injustices. Our aim is to view matters objectively and only objectively. We will not operate on the basis of emotional appeal to any particular group." The policy also stated that "our columns are open to all." According to the policy, the newspaper had no interest in "hearsay." Instead, "we want the facts of a story whatever race or races it concerns. WW will make certain that it has given all consideration to both sides of a story." Bill Cummings also promised that the newspaper would "remain non-partisan, non-political, and non-sectarian. We are strictly an educational newspaper."[92] The *War Worker*, whose name was changed to *NOW* in 1944, published a wide variety of articles, many of which did not relate directly to race relations. For example, it published articles about Hollywood and about sports. The newspaper did publish fewer articles and editorials about racial discrimination than the *California Eagle*, and it also published more articles that depicted people from different "racial" groups working in harmony. In 1944, for example, *NOW* regularly reported on the development of the Fellowship Church for All Peoples, in San Francisco. The church had an African American and an Anglo American pastor, and its congregation was nearly evenly split between African Americans and Anglo Americans.[93]

In addition to prompting some people to form new organizations and institutions, the riots renewed the zeal of some members of existing organizations. The members of the Citizens' Committee for the Defense of Mexican-American Youth had been working to overturn the conviction in the Sleepy Lagoon case since the verdicts were returned in January 1943. After the riots the committee frequently connected the Sleepy Lagoon case with the violence that erupted in June 1943. In a petition to Gov. Earl Warren, for example, the committee argued that "the way was paved for the Sleepy Lagoon case by the creation of a 'zoot-suit crime wave' by the defeatist press and other agencies interested in playing Hitler's game. The Sleepy Lagoon case in turn prepared the way for the later outbreaks of violence in Los Angeles, Beaumont, Detroit, and other parts of our country."[94] (Beaumont, Texas, and Detroit had experienced race rioting shortly after the Zoot-Suit Riots.) In a press release the committee declared that "the Sleepy Lagoon Case, viewed in the light of subsequent outbreaks of violence in Los

Angeles, Detroit, Beaumont and elsewhere, takes on a new and immediate national significance." The committee insisted that "the release of the 17 boys will be a guarantee to all the minorities in the nation that race hatred is being expunged from our country."[95] After the riots NAACP leaders depicted prejudice and discrimination as even more urgent problems than they were before the violence. These leaders frequently invoked the riots in their speeches and public statements. In urging all members of the NAACP Junior Council to attend a mass meeting "to form plans for youth mobilization against spreading race prejudice in the city," for example, President John S. Kinloch said, "this unification meeting of city-wide youth is the best way of fighting riot and provocation to riot."[96]

The leaders of this campaign against discrimination, however, did not simply demand action to prevent the recurrence of rioting. They also demanded an end to policies based upon what they depicted as an outmoded racial ideology. In one speech, for example, Rev. Clayton D. Russell demanded "a conference of daily press publishers, police officials, defense plant personnel managers and ministers at which a vigorous educational campaign may be launched to combat the fifth column incitement to riot which seizes upon every prejudice of our people to serve Hitler's end." Russell also insisted that African American leaders needed to stop fighting among themselves, "for when riot bullets fly the big shots and the little shots fall together." Moreover, Russell declared, "we must demand repeal of the Chinese Exclusion Act, barring citizenship to Chinese-Americans."[97] Russell's mention of the Chinese Exclusion Act suggests that he was interested in attacking and dismantling both the racial ideology on which discriminatory practices rested and those practices themselves.

In August and September 1943 the opponents of discrimination exulted in the actions of two officials. These opponents of discrimination declared that the actions of Los Angeles County District Attorney Frederick Howser and California Superior Court Judge Albert S. Ross represented the growing acceptance of their beliefs about "race." In early August Howser promoted Charles Matthews, an African American, to a high-ranking position within his office. The *Eagle* described Matthews's promotion not simply as a victory over racial discrimination but as a victory of a new racial ideology over an outmoded one. The *Eagle* stated that the fact that Matthews was an African American "is important in one way and unimportant in another." The attorney's biological characteristics were "not important in deciding whether he knew his job." This is the way it should be, according to the *Eagle*—biological factors, such as skin color, should not come into play in hiring and promotion decisions. At the same time, the *Eagle* declared, Matthews's promotion "is of immense importance to a nation at war. For here is an answer to the racists in our state. Here is a challenge to the 'Negro should stay in his place' gang. Here is a refutation of the fifth column agitation against the Negro people."[98]

Ross refused to uphold a covenant whose enforcement would have led to the eviction of the Mexican American family of Alex Bernal from its Fullerton home. The plaintiffs in the case argued that the presence of Mexican Americans in their neighborhood lowered "their social living standards" and the value of their property. Attorney David C. Marcus, who represented the Bernals, argued that the complaint "was taken from Hitler's 'Mein Kampf.'" Ross ruled against the plaintiffs, declaring restrictive covenants "unconstitutional and against public policy." Ross's decision made the front page of the *California Eagle*. The newspaper's coverage emphasized the fact that Ross rejected the arguments of the "white" neighbors who had said that a reduction in property values is "always caused by intermingling of peoples of other races with persons of the Caucasian race to the detriment of persons of the Caucasian race." The newspaper depicted the plaintiffs in the case as people who "had swallowed Hitler's theories of race superiority," and it depicted Ross as someone who had completely rejected "Hitler's theories." Ross's words themselves seem to support the *Eagle*'s depiction of him. His ruling stated that he did not believe that policies based on racial prejudice, such as the restrictive covenant he was asked to enforce, were "consonant with the United States." Ross further stated that his ruling was not simply related to the war. "I don't think we should consider things are different in time of war than in peace as far as these laws that come along are concerned." He also declared, "I would rather have people of the type of the Bernals living next door to me than Germans of the paranoic type now living in Germany."[99]

Official Action

Although opponents of racial prejudice and discrimination had formed a number of organizations during the summer and early fall of 1943, they also sought to convince elected officials to take action to alleviate racial tensions. The *California Eagle* connected the threat of more riots to the migration of people and attitudes from the South. "With a tremendous influx of Southerners, white and Negro, it is patently obvious that a vast educational program is necessary to prevent the Fifth Column from exploiting Dixie prejudices to the detriment of war production and national unity," an *Eagle* editorial declared at the end of September. The *Eagle* also insisted that "it is the job of our government to give the people ideological weapons with which to fight back the attack of race-haters." The newspaper endorsed "a sweeping state-wide program of mass rallies, radio broadcasts, and plant demonstrations."[100]

Perhaps because the Committee for American Unity seems not to have survived the summer of 1943, by October the *Eagle* and some of its allies had come to see official government committees as an important component of the solution to "racial" problems. They consistently encouraged local elected officials to create committees to promote "race unity." In one editorial, the *Eagle* argued that "race disorder" was not "spontaneous" and did not "grow from 'natural race enmity.'" Instead, the violence was cultivated by the "Ku Klux Klan, Silver Shirt and other fascist conspirators." The efforts of these groups, according to the *Eagle*, constituted "an ORGANIZED effort" "to bring Dixie to Los Angeles."[101] The *Eagle* pointed to the posting of a Ku Klux Klan membership application on the wall of a restroom at Consolidated Shipyards as evidence that the Klan was active in Los Angeles and that "race disorder" was not, as the daily newspapers suggested, a result of the actions of "the Negro hoodlum element." The *Eagle* argued that the "pro-Hitler gang" might use the "terrific influx of Southerners, white and black, . . . to set off a holocaust equaling anything that has to date disgraced our nation on the streets of Beaumont and Detroit." The *Eagle* insisted, however, that such violence could be prevented simply by "the recognition of the danger and the adoption of a vigorous propaganda campaign to combat it," backed by "the solution of some of the outstanding injustices suffered by the Negro and Mexican people of the city." Local elected officials bore "a grave responsibility" for promoting unity, the *Eagle* argued. "The mobilization of all the great democratic forces of Los Angeles can be best achieved only under the leadership of the people's elected representatives," the newspaper declared.[102] The *Eagle* also insisted that "the most logical form" for a "hard-hitting race unity program" was "a civic enterprise, pushed and organized by city and county officials." An editorial praised elected officials in San Francisco for their actions to promote "race unity," and it characterized Mayor Bowron's promise that he would expand an existing "all-Negro 'race unity' committee to include representatives of other minorities, labor, industry and the community generally" as a "welcome sign of civic awakening."[103] In November 1943 African American Assembly member Augustus F. Hawkins, speaking on behalf of the California State CIO, urged Governor Earl Warren to assist in "establishing in every community an official race relations commission with representation from labor, the church, community and minority groups. If these commissions are given the funds and power to act they can work out the details of this problem."[104]

In October 1943 Los Angeles Mayor Fletcher Bowron responded to the demands for a "race unity" committee by agreeing to expand a city committee that had previously dealt only with issues facing African Americans. Representatives of "whites," "other minorities," and organized labor would be added to the committee, which had previously consisted of four African American community leaders—Revels Cayton of the CIO; Norman O. Houston, the president of the Golden State Mutual Life Insurance Company; NAACP President Thomas L. Griffith; and Urban League executive director Floyd C. Covington.[105] The *Eagle* characterized the mayor's action as "a welcome sign of civic awakening."[106] The mayor's promise, however, went unfulfilled for at least a month. In mid-November Rev. Clayton D. Russell said, "the Mayor recently promised to expand his All-Negro race unity committee. No one has heard a peep about that."[107]

Opponents of prejudice and discrimination also called upon the city council to denounce restrictive covenants and to investigate people who had encouraged "white" property owners to insert these clauses into their deeds. In addition to expressing concern about the small number of homes available to African Americans and other "racial" groups, the opponents of restrictive covenants also declared their opposition to the racial ideology expressed by supporters of these deed restrictions. In one editorial, for example, the *Eagle* argued that the "chief threat" of restrictive covenants "lies in the revolting principle of race supremacy which is pumped into whole neighborhoods during the fascist drive to 'institute restrictions.'" The *Eagle* also declared that "the most elemental considerations of unity demand the swiftest suppression of all those within our country spreading the poison of anti-Semitism, anti-Negroism, and the whole line of race hatred visible day after day in the revolting Hearst press."[108]

The demands of people such as Charlotta Bass, Rev. Clayton D. Russell, and State Assembly member Augustus F. Hawkins moved some members of the city council to act.[109] In November 1943 the city council considered a resolution sponsored by the council's planning committee. The resolution stated that "at this time when our nation is at war and a state of emergency exists," residential race restrictions "are certainly not in public interest nor do they conform with the spirit of national unity." The resolution more specifically criticized the decision of developers to exclude African Americans from war worker housing to be built in Watts. "It is to be regretted that the owners of this subdivision have seen fit to exclude war workers in essential industries from needed homes because of their color. It is our opinion that the test of democracy is not in the freedom of its majority but in the freedom of its minorities."[110] The resolution provoked heated debate among council members. Carl Rasmussen told his colleagues that "racial tensions are mounting, and if we refuse to do something about it, we are failing our boys who are dying for freedom overseas." Charles "Cap" Allen, on the other hand, announced, "I have a large Negro constituency. I have done more for the Negroes in my district than I have done for the whites. I feel everybody is entitled to the same privileges. But it is none of anybody's business HOW I STAND ON RACE OR POLITICS!"[111] The city council rejected the resolution, but the vote was close: seven members of the fifteen-member body voted in favor of the resolution, and eight voted against it. Although the resolution's defeat left opponents of racial prejudice and discrimination disappointed and angry, the vote itself suggests that a growing number of elected officials had come to accept the idea that racial discrimination was undemocratic and should be condemned.

The city council refused to condemn residential race restrictions, but other prominent Los Angeles residents and organizations expressed public opposition to racial prejudice and discrimination in the fall of 1943. In December, for example, the board of directors of the Los Angeles Kiwanis Club adopted a resolution "demanding full equality of opportunity for all racial minorities, including Negroes, Jews and Japanese-Americans." In reporting on the resolution, the *Eagle* pointed out that the Kiwanians were not working-class radicals. Instead, the *Eagle* noted, the Kiwanis Club was "composed of generally wealthy and conservative business men." The Kiwanians accepted the argument that the Zoot-Suit Riots were "rooted in the race problem." Their resolution connected some European Americans' animosity toward African Americans with anti-Semitism and "the hysteria being whipped up against Americans of Japanese ancestry." The resolution recommended that Kiwanis members should "refuse to join in race hatreds, race-rumor mongering, or any other practices, involving any and all races, the effect of which is likely to add to the seriousness of the situation, but that Kiwanians insist on first having all the facts as the basis of study and decision." Finally, the Kiwanians endorsed the appointment of race relations commissions or boards at the national, state, and local levels. The Kiwanis resolution emerged from the Kiwanis Club's Public Affairs Committee, which was chaired by E. C. Farnham, who had emerged as a leading figure in the movement against prejudice and discrimination in Los Angeles.[112] Farnham was the executive secretary of the Church Federation of Los Angeles.

Farnham was also instrumental in the establishment of the Council for Civic Unity, which was organized in late December 1943. The representatives of civic, labor, and fraternal organizations who established the council indicated that they hoped to "avoid a repetition of such disorders as the 'zoot suit' riots which occurred in Los Angeles, or more grave disturbances such as the Detroit riot." According to a report in the *Eagle*, Farnham chaired the meeting and said that "it was desirable to mobilize public opinion in support of any constructive program dealing with means of abating racial discrimination and prejudice in employment, housing, transportation, etc." Farnham also said that he expected the Council for Civic Unity "to cooperate with similar councils to be appointed by the county supervisors" and by the mayor.[113] In the months following its formation, the Council for Civic Unity engaged in an anti-prejudice educational campaign.[114] Council members met with elected officials and with members of social, fraternal, and religious organizations in an effort to convince these officials and organizations to oppose prejudice and discrimination. They also sponsored public meetings designed to convince people to abandon their prejudices against other racial and ethnic groups. The Council for Civic Unity sponsored radio programs on KFWB four mornings per week. These radio programs included music designed to encourage listeners to appreciate "Negro, Mexican and Chinese music," "forums on racial issues," and dramatizations.[115]

The official race relations committee with which the Council for Civic Unity hoped to cooperate was finally established in January 1944, when the

Los Angeles County Board of Supervisors created the County Committee for Interracial Progress. The committee's name clearly reflected its purpose. The committee was composed of fifteen citizens from a number of civic organizations and the heads of eight county departments, including the sheriff, the district attorney, the superintendent of schools, and the probation officer. The committee was empowered "to take all actions necessary" to locate "the causes of racial tensions," "to eliminate these causes," and "to devise all possible means for the prevention of racial conflict." It was also supposed to "cooperate with any group or agency having similar interests."[116] Most of the citizens appointed to the committee were Anglo Americans, but two African Americans, State CIO Vice-President Revels Cayton and Rev. Clayton D. Russell, were appointed to the committee. Manuel Ruiz was also appointed to the committee.[117] In forming this committee, elected officials and community leaders in Los Angeles could look to many other communities for guidance. By November 1943, at least one hundred community interracial committees had been established, and the Rosenwald Foundation had made available information for people desiring to create such committees. County officials patterned the County Committee after a successful interracial committee already operating in the San Francisco area: the Bay Area Council against Discrimination.[118]

Conclusion: "A Titanic Political Conflict"

As a result of the debates that followed the Zoot-Suit Riots, overt expressions of racial prejudice became less acceptable in the public discourse in Los Angeles. The publishers of daily newspapers no longer warned their readers about the "danger" posed by the reproduction of members of the "brown races." Editorials in some of these newspapers even conceded that members of certain "races" were not genetically inclined toward criminality. This did not mean, however, that the publishers of daily newspapers actively campaigned against prejudice and discrimination. In fact, the publishers of the daily newspapers attempted to silence at least one writer who frequently condemned racial prejudice and discrimination. In September 1943 the *Daily News* fired columnist Ted LeBerthon. According to the *California Eagle*, the *Daily News* fired LeBerthon "because of 'too frequent' mention of discrimination against Negro people in his writings."[119] In one column Charlotta A. Bass elaborated on the relationship between the conflict over racial ideology and LeBerthon's dismissal. Bass argued that LeBerthon was fired because he had publicly questioned the "racist theories" espoused by *Los Angeles Times* publisher Harry Chandler. LeBerthon had denounced "race bias" at the Palladium ballroom, which Chandler partially owned. Bass interpreted LeBerthon's firing as the loss of "a great link in the chain of unity which has to date held us from the Fifth Column holocausts of Beaumont and Detroit." Chandler and the *Times*, which Bass characterized as "the sowers of disunity, race-hate, corruption and fascism," had silenced LeBerthon, she argued.

Bass used the occasion of LeBerthon's firing to make the point that "racial" differences were insignificant. "The hands that shape the guns, build the ships, the tanks, the airplanes used to fight this war are neither black nor white—just hands. Strong, honest hands," she wrote. "It is the sinister force of those in America who would set these hands at war with one another that has fired Ted LeBerthon." According to Bass, LeBerthon "said that men were created equal in the eyes of God. Try as he might, this writer could discern none of the mystic attributes of superiority which Los Angeles realty brokers ascribe to our 'white' populations. He could find no 'blood-theory' to ensure the profits of the Los Angeles Title and Guarantee Company."[120] Bass insisted that LeBerthon's firing reflected an agreement among the daily newspaper publishers to silence opponents of prejudice and discrimination. Bass declared that "the press should lead in the struggle to wipe out ancient race prejudices which serve today to divide and weaken our people. The press should incessantly clarify the issues of this war. The press should speak clearly for the unity of the nation and its allies." Instead, she argued, the Los Angeles press had fomented a race riot and "continually smeared both the Negro and Mexican-American communities."[121]

LeBerthon himself offered a slightly different explanation for his firing. In an open letter to Manchester Boddy, LeBerthon wrote that he was fired "on the grounds that I had failed to heed repeated warnings against overemphasizing my religious views and the inter-racial philosophy flowing from them."[122] LeBerthon's column in the *Daily News* did consistently criticize racial prejudice and discrimination, and it did so in a way that emphasized that such prejudice and discrimination ran counter to the tenets of Catholicism. During the Zoot-Suit Riots, for example, LeBerthon had published a column that attacked both the notion that a person's race was self-evident and the idea that some races were superior to others. LeBerthon expressed his opinion that not even Hitler, "that great race hater who has built a philosophy of conceit and a war motif around the socalled purity of race and breed," could say for certain "just what blood of just what race" flowed in the veins of his ancestors. According to anthropologists, LeBerthon reported, only one group of people, the "Negroes of the Andaman islands," could be considered racially pure, because they lived isolated from other peoples. All other races had been "crossed and recrossed" as a result of "conquests, colonizings, and migrations."

In the middle of this column, LeBerthon shifted abruptly to a discussion of "race" in Latin America. Racial mixing occurred frequently in Latin America, he pointed out, because the Catholic Church "does not recognize the existence of superior and inferior races." LeBerthon concluded this column by connecting the need for greater understanding of race with the war effort. "In our common military and political need to be good neighbors, and to stand together as United Nations, we Latin Americans and Saxon Americans are having to see each other truthfully," LeBerthon wrote. As these two groups of Americans saw each other more truthfully, LeBerthon argued, they would "also win that greatest of all freedoms, the freedom to be sincere brothers, brothers who have honestly cast away the last vestiges of Hitleresque racism."[123]

Despite the fact that LeBerthon no longer wrote for the *Daily News*, he continued to participate in the debate about "race" in Los Angeles. He spoke at a Hollywood Town Hall meeting in November 1943, and he wrote a column that appeared in the *War Worker* and *NOW*. Moreover, LeBerthon was joined by an increasing number of people who publicly expressed their opposition to racial prejudice and discrimination. The Sleepy Lagoon case and especially the Zoot-Suit Riots changed the debate about race in Los Angeles. African Americans who in late 1941 had narrowly opposed discrimination against African Americans had begun to acknowledge that discrimination against African Americans was not simply the result of prejudice against African Americans. Instead, a growing number of African Americans argued, this discrimination was more broadly the result of the acceptance of a racial ideology that appeared to many people to bear a striking resemblance to that embraced by Hitler and the Nazis. By autumn 1943 Charlotta Bass had come to characterize the emerging struggle in which she was participating as "a titanic political conflict." This conflict was not really over "Negro rights." Instead, it was "primarily a contest between progressivism and reaction." The forces of reaction, Bass argued, included the Ku Klux Klan, the National Rifle Association, and home owners' associations that drew "their ideological position directly from the 'master race' thesis of Mein Kampf and from the most backward American fascist elements of the deep South." The forces of progressivism, she suggested, included "the labor movement, both CIO and AFL, the Negro people, the Jewish and Mexican minorities." The "bulk of Americans," Bass admitted, were "in the middle." These people were "dangerously open to the fascist incitement of the racists, yet vulnerable to the arguments of national unity, willing to abandon prejudices in the common drive for victory."[124]

Many other African American community leaders, labor leaders, ministers, priests, and rabbis, and some politicians had come to agree with Bass.[125] They characterized their attacks on discrimination as part of a broader, "progressive" effort to eliminate what they described as an archaic and dangerous racial ideology. Some of the defenders of racial discrimination noted that these "progressive" leaders wanted to eliminate all distinctions based on "race." They tried to discredit their opponents by suggesting that people who protested discrimination did not perceive Japanese Americans as a threat. Former Assistant District Attorney Clyde C. Shoemaker, for example, told the Tenney Committee that "the same crowd is supporting the pachuco gangsters who want the Japs brought back here."[126] Despite Shoemaker's claim, most of the people who had protested discrimination against Mexican Americans and African Americans during 1942 and 1943 had said little about Japanese Americans. There were some signs, however, to indicate that some people acknowledged that the racial ideology that supported discrimination against African Americans and Mexican Americans was the same set of beliefs that had led to the incarceration and removal of Japanese Americans. In November 1943, for example, the *California Eagle* published an editorial that expressed "sincere penitence for past omissions" and that depicted Japanese Americans as unquestionably loyal to the United States. The *Eagle* declared that "persecution of the Japanese-American minority has been one of the disgraceful aspects of this People's War."[127] As the following chapter will show, at almost exactly the same time as this editorial was published, the debate about "race" in Los Angeles had returned to its focus on Japanese Americans. Throughout 1944 and 1945 the supporters and opponents of racial prejudice and discrimination continuously argued about the loyalty of Japanese Americans.

SIX

"The Long Day of the Jap-baiter in California Politics Appears to Have Ended"

Japanese Americans and "Race" in Los Angeles, 1943–1945

Only ten days after rioting in Los Angeles had abated, Los Angeles County District Attorney Frederick N. Howser spoke before a luncheon meeting of the Women's Christian Temperance Union. Howser's remarks did not focus on the violence that had engulfed parts of the city in early June. Instead, he told the assembled women that Japanese Americans should not be allowed to return to coastal areas. Howser suggested that soldiers and sailors who had served in the Pacific would naturally be filled with hatred toward all people of Japanese ancestry. "Anyone who realizes the attitude of the servicemen toward zoot-suiters should be able to see the reason for opposing the release of the Japs," Howser argued. The district attorney implied that the murder of people of Japanese ancestry might be justified on the basis of racial antagonism. "If you were called to serve as a juror at the trial of a serviceman who had murdered a Jap released on the Coast—a serviceman who perhaps had been bombed or strafed by Japs at Midway or Guadalcanal—how would you feel about enforcing the State law against murder?" Howser asked his audience. "The possibility of having to answer such a question, should Japs be allowed to return to the Coast, is the foremost reason for working now to see that they are kept out," he said. "We must create public opinion to the extent that officials back East who don't know and understand our problems regarding Japs will see just how dangerous their release might become," Howser declared.[1]

Howser's statement reveals a number of important points about the debate surrounding the meanings of "race" in wartime Los Angeles. It shows that the Zoot-Suit Riots, for all the words they generated, never thoroughly dominated the "war of words" in the city. Many people continued to focus their attention on Japanese Americans. Howser's statement also shows that he and other anti-Japanese leaders saw themselves as engaged in a concerted campaign to convince "officials back East" not to allow Japanese Americans to return to the Pacific Coast. The district attorney's words further reveal the continuing tendency of many anti-Japanese leaders to argue that there was no difference between lifelong residents of Japan and Japanese immigrants who had spent forty years or more in the United States or the U.S.-born children of those immigrants.

Soon after the rioting had ended in June 1943, many politicians and the editors of daily newspapers turned their attention away from "zoot suit gangsters" and returned to their attacks on Japanese Americans. From the Zoot-Suit Riots until the end of the war, the debate about the meanings of "race" focused largely on Japanese Americans. The organizations discussed in the previous chapter worked to address the concerns of Mexican Americans and African Americans, but most of their work occurred out of public view. Even African American newspapers did not consistently report on the activities of the Council for Civic Unity or the County Committee for Interracial Progress. As this chapter will show, a number of episodes in 1943, 1944, and 1945 demonstrate that the advocates of "fair play" gained greater public and official support for their statements against racial prejudice and discrimination against Japanese Americans. In part this resulted from the fact that fair play advocates presented their position as reasonable and cautious. In contrast, the words of many anti-Japanese leaders increasingly appeared irrational if not outlandish. *Time* magazine drew national attention to what it described as outrageous statements on the part of one anti-Japanese leader. At the same time, fair play advocates began pointing to the war record of Japanese American troops. The record of these soldiers undercut most of the arguments of anti-Japanese leaders, who had insisted that no person of Japanese ancestry could be loyal to the United States. The fact that anti-Japanese leaders had consistently depicted all Japanese Americans as men who could be mistaken for imperial Japanese troops also undermined their position when the army began allowing Japanese American women to return to the Pacific Coast.

"Un-American Activities"

As Howser's statement suggests, the rioting that occurred in early June 1943 did not long distract anti-Japanese politicians. A subcommittee of the House Committee on Un-American Activities conducted hearings in Los Angeles for several days in mid-June. The subcommittee was chaired by Rep. John M. Costello of Hollywood. News of these hearings shared the front pages of the daily newspapers with articles pertaining to the riots. Despite the fact that these articles appeared on the front pages of the newspapers, they presented information that did not match the rhetoric of "amazing revelations" that committee member J. Parnell Thomas had offered the month before. One front-page article from the *Times*, for example, simply reported that more than six hundred U.S. citizens of Japanese ancestry at Poston had not answered "yes" to the following question on a survey: "Will you swear allegiance to the United States and forswear allegiance to the Emperor of Japan or to any other foreign power?" Although the article interpreted any answer to this question but "yes" as evidence of disloyalty or "questionable loyalty," the *Times* itself had on numerous occasions challenged the idea that it was possible to determine the loyalty of Japanese Americans.[2] By publishing an article that accepted on some level the validity of a process designed to determine loyalty, the *Times* seems to have undermined its previous position. Moreover, the fact that six hundred of eleven thousand U.S. citizens at one camp had been found "openly disloyal" did not match the rhetoric of anti-Japanese leaders who had argued that no person of Japanese ancestry could be considered a loyal American.

Another article about the Costello subcommittee hearings revealed disagreement among War Relocation Authority administrators at Poston, but it did not produce substantial evidence that many Japanese Americans were disloyal or dangerous. A. W. Empie, the chief administrative officer at Poston, endorsed "segregation of the disloyal, the agitators and the troublemakers at the camp," and he pointed out that "a camp to handle troublemakers is getting under way" at Leupp, Arizona. Empie also told the subcommittee that "credit should be given to the many Japs who are sincere and are trying to understand the problem and to co-operate." Empie's stories of rule violations hardly made the incarcerated people appear to be threats to national security. He reported on "picnics at the river by evacues, [*sic*] high-handed action by some of the Japs, gasoline thefts and the appropriation of lumber at the camp by Japanese." The committee's chief investigator, James Steadman, referred to the "appropriation" of lumber as "stealing," but Empie pointed out that Japanese Americans had used the lumber "to build tables, chairs and shelves in their barracks. They said that those things should have been furnished by the government; they were needed." Empie revealed dissension among the WRA staff when he pointed out that Miss Nell Findley and John Powell in the social welfare and recreation departments supported Japanese Americans' use of the lumber, while other WRA employees, including himself, objected.[3] One day of testimony, then, led only to the depiction of Japanese Americans as people who thought they deserved furniture and who liked picnics. The testimony before the Costello subcommittee did not lead newspaper readers or elected officials to demand new or dramatic changes in federal policies toward Japanese Americans. None of the testimony prompted letters to the editor or editorials in the daily newspapers, although the *Examiner* on June 16 published an editorial criticizing the army for deciding to allow Japanese American soldiers on furlough into the coastal area.[4]

If Costello's hearings produced little evidence to support the claim that Japanese Americans were a threat to national security, they did allow anti-Japanese politicians and journalists to demean people who opposed what they saw as persecution of Japanese Americans. In its report on one Costello subcommittee hearing, the *Times* referred to one witness, Allen Hennebold, as a "pink-cheeked young man" who "said he never had been called by his draft board and had been classified as 4-E." According to the *Times*, Hennebold told the committee that he had met very few people "who were antagonistic or resentful of the Japanese living in America. He felt it was the press that was responsible for the ill-feeling." Costello asked Hennebold if he thought that "marines and sailors returning from Guadalcanal and the rest of the servicemen fighting with the Japs might have related experiences that stirred up the feelings of the people—like their barbarous treachery, calling for help and then shooting or bombing their would-be American helpers." Hennebold told Costello he did not think that the stories of veterans had aroused hostility toward Japanese Americans. He added that a friend who had experienced combat in the Pacific told him that "he never saw any of this so-called treachery."[5]

The *Times* identified another witness, Dr. Kirby Page, as "a Socialist" who "has been a pacifist and conscientious objector for years." Page was in fact an important figure in the pacifist movement. Born in east Texas in 1890, Page graduated from Drake University in Des Moines, Iowa, and was ordained a minister of the Disciples of Christ. He worked with Allied troops in Europe as a YMCA secretary during World War I. The horrors he witnessed helped to make him a pacifist. Page had edited the Christian socialist magazine *The World Tomorrow* from 1926 until 1934, and he published many books over the course of his life.[6] In response to questions from subcommittee members, Page said that "he would not have voted for a declaration of war following the attack on Pearl Harbor, nor would he have gone to war even if they had bombed Los Angeles." Costello told Page that "your viewpoint is astounding! Any American who would not resist the invasion of this country by Japan—when even your own churches would have become the victims of oppression and could not operate but would be under a pagan heel for centuries to come."[7]

Although legislators and the newspapers dismissed pacifists as naive if not dangerously deluded, they could not so easily demean or dismiss other people who supported "fair play" for Japanese Americans. A representative of the Church Federation of Los Angeles, for example, appeared before the Costello subcommittee and defended both Japanese Americans and the War Relocation Authority. Dr. S. Martin Eldsath told the subcommittee that the Church Federation did not support the return of Japanese Americans to the Pacific Coast during the war. The Federation, however, "feels that the W.R.A. should not be disrupted in its efforts to do a good job, for any but sound reasons." Eldsath said that the WRA was not pampering Japanese Americans. The Church Federation directly if politely challenged Costello's repeated statements that there was no way to determine the loyalty of a Japanese American. Eldsath said that the Church Federation believed that "a distinction can be made between the loyal and disloyal Japanese in America." Another minister, Dr. Allan A. Hunter, more directly challenged racial prejudice. A native of Canada, Hunter lived as a boy in Denver, Colorado, before moving to Riverside, California, where he graduated from high school. He attended Occidental College for a year but graduated from Princeton University in 1916. Like Page, Hunter had served with the YMCA during World War I. He also served with the American Red Cross in Palestine. After he earned an M.A. at Columbia, Hunter had spent a year in China and Japan. When he returned to southern California in 1926 he became the minister of the Mount Hollywood Congregational Church. Hunter agreed with the Church Federation that "we have the techniques" to determine whether or not a Japanese American is loyal to the United States, but, he added, "synthetic hatreds and prejudices are being generated."[8]

While the *Times* ridiculed some of the witnesses who appeared before Costello's subcommittee, the *Examiner* continued to attack Japanese Americans, the War Relocation Authority, and supporters of "fair play" for Japanese Americans in a series of editorial cartoons. These cartoons revealed the persistence of racial stereotypes and connections among politics, racial ideology, and gender ideology. One cartoon, "Relocation Center," repeated the claim that most Japanese Americans were loyal to Japan. The cartoon depicted two stereotypical Japanese people, with big teeth and narrow, slanted eyes, raising a flag. The flag depicts a rising sun fashioned from a U.S. flag; the remnants of the desecrated Stars and Stripes, a pair of scissors, and a spool of thread lie on the ground at the base of the flag pole. One of the Japanese people says, "We Good Americans—We Fry Stars and Stripes!" The caption says, "If the vast majority of the Japs in relocation centers were to show their real colors the result would be approximately the above. They would prefer the stripes on their flag radiating from a round center instead of our arrangement of the red, white and blue."[9]

This cartoon and others depicted WRA employees and supporters of "fair play" for Japanese Americans as feminine. In one, the *Examiner* depicted "silly sentimentality" as a weeping woman or a man dressed in women's clothing.[10] Another *Examiner* cartoon depicted "stupidity" as a weeping "Little Bo-Peep," presiding over the release of a flock of wolves in sheep's clothing from a "Japanese Relocation Center." In the cartoon, "Little Bo-Peep" says "they're such lambs."[11] "Relocation Center" depicted the WRA's "Molly Coddle Management" as a woman in petticoats, with tears in

Relocation Center

If the vast majority of the Japs in relocation centers were to show their real colors the result would be approximately the above.

They would prefer the stripes on their flag radiating from a round center instead of our arrangement of the red, white and blue.

FIG. 9. *"Relocation Center." This editorial cartoon, depicting the War Relocation Authority's "molly coddle management" as feminine, appeared in the* Los Angeles Examiner *on June 29, 1943.*

'Little Bo-Peep'

FIG. 10. *"Little Bo-Peep." This editorial cartoon, depicting War Relocation Authority "stupidity" as feminine, appeared in the* Los Angeles Examiner *on June 26, 1943.*

her eyes.[12] These cartoons, more graphically and explicitly than most statements, make clear that anti-Japanese leaders depicted their position as strong and "manly." People who suggested that Japanese Americans should be judged as individuals rather than as members of an "enemy race," by contrast, were weak, "sentimental," and "feminine."

The *Examiner*'s cartoons depicted all fair play advocates and WRA employees as "feminine," but the reports on the Costello subcommittee hearings suggested that a significant change had occurred in the debate about Japanese American loyalty. Despite their efforts, anti-Japanese leaders could not dismiss all of their opponents as naive if not dangerous "pacifists" or "socialists." Some of the people who had come before the subcommittee were respected ministers from mainstream Protestant denominations. It was unacceptable for newspapers to level attacks on these ministers and their ideas, which they presented as growing directly from their religious beliefs.

The Fair Play Movement

As the summer progressed, more people came forth to defend the loyalty of Japanese Americans and to call for "fair play." It is not clear why more of these people had not spoken out for fair play earlier in the war. It is possible that some of these people did defend Japanese Americans but the newspapers simply refused to print their statements. It is likely that some people did not raise objections to the policy of imprisonment and removal for the same reason that few Japanese Americans objected to the policy—it might have appeared unpatriotic to question military authorities during a time of war. By the summer of 1943, by contrast, many felt that a U.S. victory in the war was probable. More important, General DeWitt had exposed the racial prejudice on which his decisions rested, and the Zoot-Suit Riots had encouraged some officials to attempt to distance themselves from overt expressions of support for racial discrimination.

In calling for fair play for Japanese Americans, many people attacked anti-Japanese leaders. Japanese Americans themselves were among the most vocal critics of the anti-Japanese movement. Some Japanese American writers drew attention to the racial ideology that lay beneath the anti-Japanese campaign. *Pacific Citizen* columnist Bill Hosokawa, for example, argued that the programs of the Nazis and of the "California fascists" were "based on a similar argument: that race is conclusive of certain undesirable characteristics which must be purged from the national lifestream."[13] *Pacific Citizen* editor Larry Tajiri compared the anti-Japanese American campaign with white supremacists' efforts to intimidate African American in the South. Tajiri wrote that the anti-Japanese campaign "smacks of lynch law."[14] In another column Hosokawa noted that "the leaders of the Jap-haters are just as rabid about the issue as the politicians who keep Jim Crow alive."[15] Tajiri even expressed the opinion that an "unholy coalition" of anti-Japanese members of Congress from California and "the 'white supremacy' boys from the deep south" was beginning to emerge. Tajiri also noted that some anti-Japanese legislation had already been sponsored by members of Congress from the South.[16]

Other fair play advocates used words similar to those employed by Japanese Americans. Rev. Allan A. Hunter, for example, told a radio audience, "if we change the Constitution to make racial differences the basis of citizenship, we will be smashing at the essential spirit back of democracy which today is an issue of life and death." Hunter said that he imagined that if he were Hitler he would be happy with events in southern California, "for being Hitler, if I want to accomplish anything, it is to get across the idea everywhere that blood and race are what count." Like many other opponents of racial discrimination, Hunter cited anthropologists who denied "that race is a determinant of individual group character and behavior."[17]

Carey McWilliams expressed ideas similar to Hunter's in a July 1943 radio broadcast. McWilliams said that the anti-Japanese activists in the United States were doing "precisely what Tojo is trying to do; namely, to convince the colored people of the Far East that this is a race war." McWilliams also argued that anti-Japanese agitation in California "is being largely predicated, as in the past, upon dangerously irrelevant so-called racial considerations unsupported by a shred of scientific evidence." In this address McWilliams expressed his support for the return of loyal Japanese Americans to the Pacific Coast, but only after each Japanese American had endured "a searching and vigorous investigation."[18]

In addition to criticizing the ideas expressed by anti-Japanese leaders, McWilliams also questioned the support for their movement. In September 1943 McWilliams published an article in *Common Ground*, a journal edited by McWilliams's friend Louis Adamic and published by the Common Council for American Unity. In the article, McWilliams argued that only four or five organizations were responsible for the proliferation of anti-Japanese resolutions. "These resolutions are more or less identical in phrasing, and are always presented to the organizations for concurrence rather than having arisen spontaneously within particular groups."[19]

The growth of the "fair play" movement sparked new attacks from anti-Japanese leaders. Some of the anti-Japanese leaders insisted that the fair play movement's goal was not simply the restoration of Japanese Americans' rights. John M. Lechner, the executive director of the Americanism Educational League, told the Optimist Club that the Fair Play Committee's efforts to free "Japanese-Americans from war relocation centers is the spearhead move to an even more sinister purpose: a negotiated peace with Japan." The first phase of this effort, Lechner said, "is to so dramatize the plight of Japanese-Americans that the resistance to granting them unrestricted liberty will be termed 'race hatred' and broken down." The second phase "is to sell the American people on the idea that the war is a stalemate and a negotiated peace is the best way out."[20]

In October 1943, the California State Senate's Fact-Finding Committee on Japanese Resettlement convened hearings in Los Angeles. It heard from many witnesses who strongly opposed the return of Japanese Americans to the Pacific Coast during the war. Mayor Bowron told the committee that "stories of Jap atrocities" had "resulted in strong feelings against the Japanese race by many citizens." The mayor expressed his hope that "for their own good, not too many will return, even after the war. I know there will be strong objections to their return." The most shocking testimony came from District Attorney Fred N. Howser, who declared that he had "letters from three organizations informing me that their members have pledged themselves to kill any Japanese who comes to California now or after the war." Howser also said that he had "talked to servicemen who fought the Japs in the South Pacific and they tell me they will not hesitate to kill any Japanese they see here or anywhere else." Relatives of other soldiers and sailors said "the same thing," he reported.[21]

In the following days the Senate committee, chaired by Hugh P. Donnelly of Turlock, heard from other anti-Japanese leaders, such as Dr. John F. B. Carruthers, a navy chaplain during the First World War and the executive vice-president of the Pacific Coast Japanese Problem League. Carruthers attacked southern California ministers who had advocated the return of Japanese Americans to the coast. "I'm ashamed of the clergymen in many pulpits who think they can by-pass this problem, which amounts to Christianity versus paganism," Carruthers told the committee. Carruthers urged the committee to subpoena some of these clergy members. "If you're going to have a bunch of weasels in our pulpits, let's find them out," he declared.[22]

On its second day, however, the committee hearing became a reprise for the Tenney Committee's hearings following the Zoot-Suit Riots. This time, however, the daily newspapers reported briefly on revealing exchanges between the senators and the witnesses. After A. L. Wirin of the American Civil Liberties Union told the committee that "his organization favors the return of Japanese-Americans to the coastal area before the end of the war and of aliens who are 'loyal' afterward," Sen. Irwin T. Quinn of Eureka asked Wirin, "do you believe in racial integrity?" Wirin replied, "No, that is the worst folly and contrary to the basic principles of our country."[23] This brief exchange between Quinn and Wirin suggests that the debate about Japanese Americans was at its heart a debate about racial ideology.

Nobel Prize-winning novelist Pearl S. Buck also appeared before the Senate committee. In one article on the hearings, the *Examiner* printed sixteen paragraphs devoted to the testimony of anti-Japanese leaders before it discussed Buck's testimony. The newspaper, however, did publish a fairly detailed account of the exchanges between Buck and the state senators. According to the *Examiner*, Buck "opposed any discrimination against the Japanese at any time on a racial basis, contending that other Oriental nations will be antagonized." In response to her testimony, Senator Quinn demanded, "What are the Japs doing to our American citizens in Bataan?" Buck replied, "War is war. I'm not pleading for the Japanese. I'm pleading for America." Buck, then, was arguing that the United States should uphold its own principles, one of which was racial equality, and not sacrifice those principles to revenge. When Sen. Jess Dorsey of Bakersfield said that the Japanese government controlled Japanese Americans and asked if "we should consider these things in dealing with the Japs," Buck answered that "we should also consider the Japanese fighting in the U.S. armed forces—I am arguing that we treat our enemies on one basis and not on a race basis." Her words prompted Senator Donnelly to ask, "You're in favor of appeasement at all costs, then?" Buck replied, "No, if we discriminate even against an enemy in the Orient, it is going to work against us."[24] The exchanges between Buck and the senators, then, reveal the degree to which debates about the treatment of Japanese Americans were at root debates about the meanings of "race." Buck consistently opposed racial discrimination on principle, while the senators consistently offered reasons why Japanese Americans should be treated as part of a racial group with which the United States was at war.

The daily newspapers ignored the testimony of a number of people who defended the rights of Japanese Americans. The day after Howser argued that Japanese Americans should be kept away from the Pacific Coast because some people had threatened to kill them, Rev. Fred Fertig, the associate pastor of the All People's Christian Church, told the committee that "protective custody" was unfair and undemocratic. Reverend Fertig said that "the answer is not in Hitler's method, of taking the Japanese into protective custody. It is not the Japanese that are the lawless or disloyal element, but those who make this threat. They not only endanger the lives of Japanese but our whole system of law and order."[25]

The *Examiner* further ignored the testimony presented by Wirin and Fertig when it declared in an editorial that "one dominant fact, overwhelming all other testimony, emerged from the exhaustive hearings." That fact was that "West Coast citizens are irreconcilably opposed" to Japanese Americans' return to the Pacific Coast "at any time and under any conditions." The *Examiner* insisted that these "West Coast citizens, particularly Californians, will not endure the proximity of Japanese, now or in the future, for reason of their treachery, their brutality, their incompatibility with our morals, manners and standards of life." The editorial argued that "the long parade of witnesses" had observed firsthand proof of "Japanese greed, lust and barbarity." These witnesses "filled the record of the committee hearings with irrefutable accounts of wanton cruelty, plans of conquest, subversive activities, doubtful when not repudiated 'loyalty,' and a total incapacity of assimilation into American ideals and institutions." Insisting that the people of the West Coast wanted "nothing to do with the Japs beyond doing the utmost to drive them back and keep them where they belong, which is Japan and nowhere else," the editorial concluded by urging "the representatives and employees of the people" to heed their words.[26]

Tule Lake

Less than two weeks after the Donnelly Committee's hearings, a series of events occurred at the Tule Lake WRA camp in northern California that allowed anti-Japanese leaders to argue that they had been right all along and that Japanese Americans posed a threat to the nation's security. Reports of the events at Tule Lake appeared on the front pages of all the daily newspapers in Los Angeles. Anti-Japanese leaders dominated the response to the events at Tule Lake. They invoked the reports from Tule Lake to demand that the U.S. government base its treatment of all Japanese Americans upon the premise that all people of Japanese ancestry *as a race* were inclined to loyalty to Japan and posed a threat to the security of the nation, especially the Pacific Coast.

The trouble at Tule Lake began with a strike. A "segregation center" had been created at Tule Lake earlier in 1943 to house those people who had been deemed "disloyal" as a result of their answers on a "loyalty questionnaire." Some of these "disloyal" people had refused to work harvesting crops on the grounds that they were prisoners of war and could not be forced to work under international agreements. Los Angeles daily newspapers reported the strike on the front page, beneath banner headlines that exaggerated the extent of the strike. The headline in the *Examiner*, for example, blared: "15,000 DISLOYAL JAPS STRIKE AT WRA CENTER IN CALIFORNIA."[27]

The strike prompted members of Congress from California to repeat their demand that the army take over the control of the Tule Lake camp. Rep. John M. Costello of Hollywood, for example, continued his attacks on the WRA. "The dangerous situation now arising at Tule Lake is attributable to nothing else but the stubbornness of the War Relocation Authority, which has administered the evacuated West Coast Japanese with an unbelievable disregard of national security," Costello told the *Examiner*'s Washington correspondent.[28]

In an editorial, the *Times* connected the actions of any people of Japanese ancestry to all "members of their race." It warned that the people who had refused to harvest crops at Tule Lake "are storing up trouble for themselves and for other members of their race." Returning to one of the most common themes among anti-Japanese leaders, the editorial declared that "treatment of the Japs at Tule Lake may be contrasted with Japanese admissions of what happens to American war and civilian prisoners." The editorial then quoted from "intercepted Japanese language broadcasts": "Those who do not do their part are beaten by the Japanese guards.... Those who are hard to handle are severely beaten with rope which is similar to rope used by sailors."[29]

A few days later the newspapers reported much more dramatic events at Tule Lake. On November 3 the *Examiner* reported that U.S. Rep. Lowell

Stockman of Oregon had informed the press that "between 7000 and 8000 Japanese disloyalists staged a violent outbreak at the Tule Lake segregation center in Northeastern California yesterday, making prisoners of 100 Caucasian men and women, including War Relocation Authority Director Dillon S. Myer." According to Stockman, Myer and other WRA employees "were confined in a warehouse... by a destructive, screaming mass of Japanese."[30] Another article in the *Examiner*, relying on information from a "Northern California business man of unimpeachable veracity" who was at the camp at the time, reported that knives and clubs were used to threaten people who tried to leave the camp. "Young, burly Japanese, some displaying knives, hurried from point to point with clocklike precision. It was like a well rehearsed military operation, the eyewitness said."[31]

The *Times* offered a less sensational article. It reported that the residents of the small town of Tule Lake, near the camp, had organized and demanded "assurance of protection from disloyal Japanese." The residents said that they were concerned because "disloyal Japanese" had seized control of the camp for a few hours on November 1. Clark Fensler, an American Legionnaire and the head of the committee, told reporters that the "four Tule Lake residents were held prisoners by the Japanese for several hours." Fensler insisted that WRA officials in the camp had not called in the army guard stationed outside the camp and said that Tule Lake residents "feared the Japanese might attempt to break out of the camp." Ray Best, the camp director, and Dillon Myer, the head of the WRA, who was at the camp at the time, denied that Japanese Americans had seized control of the camp. Best and Myer told a reporter that "the Japanese had massed only to hear a speech by Myer and had disbanded peacefully after presenting several requests." The *Times* reported that Best also revealed the head of the camp's medical staff, Dr. Reece M. Pedicord, "was injured in a fight with a dozen Japanese at the relocation center."[32] In contrast with the *Times* and the *Examiner*, the *Daily News* did not publish reports of a confrontation or uprising at Tule Lake. Instead, it published an article that quoted an unnamed WRA official who had said that rumors of such events "were inspired by German agents."[33]

On November 4 the newspapers reported that the stories of WRA officials about what had happened at Tule Lake had begun to change. The *Times*, for example, revealed that the WRA's western field director, Robert Cozzens, "who yesterday said 'there is nothing to it,' when asked about reports of a disturbance at the center Monday," later admitted that the WRA had not summoned the camp inmates to hear Myers's speech. Instead, Cozzens said, "the Japanese themselves called the meeting." Another WRA employee, Orville Crays, told reporters that "several thousand Japanese, out of the 15,000 or so at the center surrounded the administration building, which houses 75 employees, for more than three hours." Although Crays stopped short of saying that the inmates were in control of the camp at the time, he did say that he "would have hesitated to have tried to leave the building without a good reason." Crays also said, however, "I wouldn't say the crowd ever was threatening. I saw no knives or clubs. I heard that two persons from the administration building tried to leave and were told (by the Japanese) that they couldn't. I heard other stories, too, but I don't know about them to my own knowledge." Cozzens also told reporters that a committee of the inmates "demanded more and better food, oiled streets, asked a change in some of the center's governing personnel, and asked what was to be done about the crops which the Japanese had refused to harvest."[34]

On November 5 the *Times* and the *Examiner* both reported that the army had taken control of the Tule Lake camp at 10:30 PM the night before. No details were available for the November 5 editions, but the papers published additional accounts of the events of Monday, November 1. Ernest Rhodes, who had served as the fire chief at the camp, told reporters on November 4 that on the previous Monday "all fire alarm telephones had been destroyed, sand and broken glass were tamped into hydrants, and automobiles were damaged, one having been scratched with the words: 'To hell with America.'" Rhodes also said that "Japanese firemen" in the camp had "made no attempt to reach the flames" in the last five fires that had broken out at the camp. Cozzens reported that a "contractor employee was 'roughed up' by disgruntled Japanese and his flashlight taken from him" on the night of November 3, and Pedicord spoke to reporters, telling of how "he was set upon by 15 Japanese who marched into his office at the center. One pulled off his glasses, he said, and he retaliated by knocking two of his assailants down, but then was beaten unconscious himself." The article also reported that "two women teaching at the center said in an interview they were so frightened that they wrote their wills while being held in the Administration Building."[35]

As new stories about the events of November 1 circulated, members of Congress demanded an investigation. Rep. Clair Engle, a Democrat from

Red Bluff who represented the northern California district in which Tule Lake was located, told the House that "the Japanese hauled down the American flag and ran up the Japanese flag in its place on the camp flagpole."[36] Engle also announced that "it is the considered opinion of the leadership of the Tule Lake community, which has been in a position to closely observe the operation of the camp, that the W.R.A. is thoroughly inefficient and incompetent and that the Japanese in the camp are beyond their control." In response to Engle's demand, the House Committee on Un-American Activities dispatched investigators to Tule Lake.[37]

On November 6 the *Times* reported that U.S. Army troops used tear gas to break up a "group estimated variously at from 250 to 1000 Japanese" who had "gathered apparently for a conference" on the evening of November 5. The article reported that the army's only statement was that "quiet has been restored." In discussing the previous incidents at the camp, the article emphasized the racial character of the incarceration. "Caucasians injured thus far include Dr. Reece N. Pedicord of Wheeling, W. Va., chief medical officer, and Edward Brobeck, W.R.A. internal security guard," the article noted.[38] In its article about the army's assumption of control at the camp, the *Examiner* also emphasized "race." When the army entered the camp, the newspaper reported, "white women living on the reservation, some carrying sleeping children in their arms, rushed to cars outside."[39]

The new stories emanating from Tule Lake led anti-Japanese politicians and newspaper publishers to attack both Japanese Americans and the War Relocation Authority. In a press conference on November 5, for example, California Gov. Earl Warren said that "I firmly believe there is positive danger attached to the presence of so many of those admittedly American-hating Japanese in an area where sabotage or any other civil disorders would be so detrimental to the war effort." Warren criticized the "attitude of the W.R.A. toward protecting the good name of even those violently un-American Japanese." The governor told reporters that he believed that the army "is the only agency thoroughly familiar with the Jap and his machinations which can tell what the situation is in relation to them."[40] An editorial in the *Los Angeles Times* declared that "serious-minded Californians who were willing to face realities have contended vigorously from the first that the Jap camps were no place for 'social experimentation' such as the New Dealish Myer and others like him have dealt in." The editorial also characterized WRA policies as "Myer's experiments in sweetness and light" and criticized Myer's "reluctance to believe evil of any Jap."[41] A southern California VFW post called WRA officials "theorist crackpots, who know nothing of the characteristics of the Japs" and demanded the agency's immediate abolition.[42] John R. Lechner, the executive director of the Americanism Educational League in Los Angeles, declared that pacifists were "largely responsible for the present sob-sister methods of the War Relocation Authority."[43]

The words of critics of the WRA make clear that racial ideology influenced how people described the events at Tule Lake. Those events were likely to be described as racial conflicts in part because the WRA itself relied upon racial terminology to distinguish between "Japanese" prisoners and "Caucasian" camp administrators. Although the WRA's terminology suggests that people of Japanese ancestry had been imprisoned because they were "racially" Japanese, the agency did not insist that all people of Japanese ancestry were disloyal to the United States. Leaders such as Warren and Lechner, however, argued that people of Japanese ancestry were, as a result of their race, inclined toward disloyalty to the United States. Moreover, most of these leaders argued that "Japanese" people were inferior to "white" people. Some statements make it appear that a primary concern of some anti-Japanese leaders was the fact that the "Japanese" did not accept the belief that they were racially inferior to "whites." One eyewitness to the events at Tule Lake, for example, reported that the "Japanese" prisoners "are insolent and worse to Caucasians. Their favorite indignity is to spit on white employees."[44]

In the two weeks following the tense confrontation at Tule Lake, Los Angeles newspapers published numerous front-page articles about conditions in the camp.[45] On November 9 the *Times* reported that two former WRA employees, one of them Ernest Rhodes, the former fire chief, had told the State Senate's Committee on Japanese Resettlement that inmates had "heaped oil-soaked sacks of straw about the administration building where they were holding 150 whites."[46] It is unclear why Rhodes did not make these claims or they were not reported earlier, after he had reported other acts of vandalism by the camp's prisoners. On November 10 the *Examiner* disclosed that the army had discovered radio sets, "caches of hundreds of knives, numerous pistols, supplies of gun powder and crude, but highly destructive, home-made bombs" in a search of the camp.[47] The *Examiner* played upon fears of miscegenation when it reported that "the War Relocation Authority encouraged white women employed at the Tule Lake segregation camp to entertain male Jap internees."[48] The *Times*, by contrast, did not suggest that the WRA had urged "white women" to entertain the prisoners. Instead, it reported that "Miss Seemah Battat, a W.R.A. secretary at the center, said that some women employees who were 'conscientious objectors in theory' had told the Japanese that they were 'justified at Pearl Harbor' and had sympathized with the Nipponese to the point of entertaining them in their homes."[49] U.S. Rep. Clair Engle later charged that prisoners at the camp operated brothels and trafficked in narcotics.[50]

In an editorial calling for the abolition of the WRA, the *Examiner* declared that the agency "has nullified the condition of security established by the United States Army in the early days of the war, when prompt removal of all Japanese from the Pacific Coast combat areas frustrated a well planned and powerfully organized program of sabotage." The editorial declared that the WRA "knows nothing about the Japanese and is unwilling to learn about them from a section of the nation that has had bitter experience with them for generations."[51] This editorial was accompanied by a cartoon, "Grapes of WRAth," which showed the female WRA, labeled "sob sister coddling," attempting to cajole a screaming infant, labeled "disloyal Jap internee," into eating his "nice hothouse grapes."[52] A later *Times* editorial repeated the argument that "the Army is the only agency that can be relied on to keep these disloyal aliens in line. A revamping of W.R.A. would merely put another crew of tender-minded heart-bleeders in charge."[53]

As the preceding paragraphs make clear, after the events at Tule Lake in early November 1943, anti-Japanese leaders grew more insistent in their demands for adoption of even more punitive policies toward all people of Japanese ancestry. In calling for more drastic measures, these leaders reiterated many of the claims they had made in the first ten months of the year. They continued to depict all people of Japanese ancestry as if they were loyal subjects of the Japanese emperor. They also repeated the charge that the WRA was "coddling" Japanese people in the camps.[54]

Anti-Japanese leaders, however, also leveled new, sensational charges at Japanese Americans, the War Relocation Authority, and President Franklin D. Roosevelt. The *Examiner*, for example, argued that President Roosevelt's inability to understand "the Japanese" had hindered the U.S. war against Japan. "What the President seems completely unable to understand is that there is no way of KNOWING whether a Japanese is loyal to the United States or not," an *Examiner* editorial declared. According to the editorial, Roosevelt

Grapes of WRAth

Abolish the War Relocation Authority

FIG. 11. *"Grapes of WRAth." This editorial cartoon, depicting "disloyal Jap internees" as spoiled children and the War Relocation Authority's management as feminine "sob sister coddling," appeared above an editorial calling for the elimination of the WRA in the* Los Angeles Examiner *on November 15, 1943.*

"has made it the policy of the United States to accept an avowal of loyalty by any Japanese against whom there is no record of disloyalty, and to grant such a man virtual freedom of movement in the country." Because of this policy, the *Examiner* argued, "the United States has for nearly two years failed to make effective war against Japan and is even NOW unable to make effective war against Japan."[55]

In its Sunday pictorial section, the *Examiner* claimed that U.S. citizens of Japanese ancestry had been trained as a Japanese military force before Pearl Harbor. This article, which reported on the "findings" of James Steadman of Los Angeles, the West Coast investigator for the Dies Committee, noted that "it can almost be said the United States Army made its first big troop capture of the war when it rounded up 107,000 West Coast Japanese residents and placed them in 'relocation centers.'" The article argued that "at least 10,000" Nisei "were Japanese military trainees under a specific system of instruction."[56]

The *Examiner* further insisted that Japanese Americans from Poston were "pouring into California in a virtual unchecked 'invasion' of the state going on under the eyes of authorities who are powerless to take action."[57] State Sen. Jack B. Tenney claimed, after a week-long survey, that "'hundreds' of Japs, unsupervised, were entering the State in automobiles and aboard trains 'for points unknown.'"[58] Some anti-Japanese leaders even suggested that Japanese American men represented a sexual threat to "white" women. The *Examiner*, for example, reported that a Blythe resident accused "arrogant Japanese interned in the Colorado River country" of attempting "to force their attentions on American girl swimmers."[59]

Anti-Japanese leaders argued that the reports from Tule Lake should convince everybody that all people of Japanese ancestry constituted a serious threat to the nation's security, that WRA officials had refused to acknowledge this fact, and that the army should assume permanent control of the concentration camps. Some expressed disappointment in members of Congress who had not jumped on the anti-Japanese, anti-WRA bandwagon. John R. Lechner of the Americanism Educational League, for example, insisted that "West Coast Congressmen who have failed to participate in positive action for the reform of the Japanese resident problem will find their attitude a principal issue at election time." Lechner complained that the "uprising" at Tule Lake, "one of the most hideous affairs ever conducted on American soil," had "stirred fewer than half a dozen West Coast Congressmen to action." "What has become of proud Americanism? What has become of the old-time American refusal to take insults of any kind from anyone, much less such ghastly insults as the scum at Tule Lake has hurled into our faces?" Lechner asked.[60]

In a related vein, an editorial in the *Examiner* lamented the fact that "there is an amazing lack of public interest in the mismanagement of the Japanese relocation program in the United States." The editorial suggested that the lack of public interest was a result of "an amazing lack of public understanding about the Japanese themselves." The editorial insisted that there should have been a "national protest" "against the fact that at least one thousand Japanese of unknown and undeterminable loyalty have been released from the relocation center at Manzanar in Southern California." The *Examiner* blamed the War Relocation Authority for the release of potentially disloyal people. According to the editorial, the WRA simply released people who claimed to be loyal, without understanding that "thousands of trained and ruthless Japanese saboteurs and spies known to be in the United States, but clever enough to have no evidence or records against them, are almost entirely within the group willing to profess loyalty to the United States." The editorial then attempted to inform "average Americans" about people of Japanese ancestry. According to the *Examiner,* all Japanese people were intensely loyal "to their homeland," and their loyalty was "ineradicable through many generations of residence in the United States." The editorial insisted that most Americans did not understand "the inscrutable mind of the Japanese" or "the instincts of the Japanese for treachery and cruelty, and their concepts of morality that are diabolical." The editorial argued forcefully that "the people of the United States should accept the judgment of the Japanese from those Americans who KNOW the Japanese. Particularly, they should require the administration of Japanese relocation by the military authorities who know the Japanese best of all, and not by a soft-headed Federal agency which knows them least of all."[61]

While the *Examiner* was concerned about public opinion, U.S. Rep. Clair Engle insisted that the problem was that elected officials were not responsive enough to anti-Japanese public opinion. Engle and other anti-WRA Democrats suggested that the administration's "continued protection of the War Relocation Authority" would cost it votes in the 1944 presidential election. Engle insisted that WRA Director Dillon S. Myer's resignation "will not satisfy the West Coast voters."[62]

The statements of Lechner, the *Examiner,* and Engle, as well as the sensational charges of other anti-Japanese leaders, may have reflected frustration over the fact that they were able to exert little influence over the actions of administration officials or the army. Even though Pacific Coast legislators gave Attorney General Francis Biddle, WRA Director Dillon S. Myer, and State and War department representatives "a stormy reception" when they met in late November 1943, their threats did not convince federal officials either to disband the WRA and allow the army to operate the concentration camps or to fire Myer and other top WRA officials. The army did not want to operate the camps, and State Department officials were concerned about the international ramifications of more punitive treatment of Japanese nationals.[63]

After it became clear that the army did not want to operate concentration camps, members of Congress from California demanded "the ouster of Director Dillon S. Myer and the installation of 'realistic' officials in the W.R.A."[64] These members of Congress claimed victory on December 7, 1943, when the *Examiner* reported that "the dismissal of Dillon S. Myer as director of the War Relocation Authority is certain."[65] A week later, however, the *Times* reported that "there appears to be little chance White House advisers will urge President Roosevelt to shake up the W.R.A. or create a new agency to supervise the 10 relocation camps."[66] Myer served as the agency's director until it was dissolved after the end of the war.

Federal officials' indifferent response to anti-Japanese leaders did not necessarily reflect changes in their beliefs about "race." State Department officials, for example, were probably more concerned with the possible ramifications of punitive policies toward Japanese aliens than they were with opposing racial discrimination. The fact that federal officials did not endorse the position taken by anti-Japanese leaders, however, seems to have emboldened "fair play" advocates in their verbal battles with anti-Japanese leaders. The intense, sensational anti-Japanese campaign that followed the events at Tule Lake sparked a more spirited response from advocates of "fair play" for Japanese Americans. Many of these "fair play" advocates, who included WRA officials, argued that unrelenting attacks on Japanese Americans were damaging the U.S. war effort. Many directly attacked the anti-Japanese leaders' racial ideology and insisted that racial prejudice should not limit the rights and responsibilities of U.S. citizens.

Although few articles defending the loyalty of Japanese Americans or the War Relocation Authority appeared in the two weeks following the events at Tule Lake, such articles did begin to see publication in mid-November.

On November 19, for example, the *Daily News* published an article that began by pointing out that some of the sensational "facts" presented in other newspapers earlier in the month were not supported by evidence. This article pitted the army, whom the anti-Japanese leaders had always claimed as an ally, against anti-Japanese politicians. It reported that the commanding general in charge of the troops at Tule Lake had "denied that any firearms or explosives were found" at the camp. The article also identified flaws in the logic of anti-Japanese leaders. For example, it criticized Los Angeles County District Attorney Fred Howser, who claimed to have sent WRA Director Dillon S. Myer a telegram asking for "clarification" of the WRA's plans for returning Japanese Americans to California. Myer told reporters that he had not received such a telegram. The article pointed out that "even if Myer had received Howser's telegram, the WRA director could not have answered it because the message, as released by the district attorney, didn't make sense." The article further stated, "Japanese were evacuated by the army, not by the WRA, everybody but Howser knows, and consequently the Japanese cannot return to coastal areas until the army revokes its exclusion order." The article referred to Howser's statements at a press conference as "a few more exhausted words—words that have been said again and again by the same people to create hypothetical dangers." In addition to criticizing Howser, the *Daily News* article reminded readers of the words of Charles F. Ernst, the director of the WRA's Topaz camp in Utah. On a trip to Los Angeles in May, Ernst had said that "those who criticize the relocation program, or who flatly declare 'a Jap's a Jap' are fanning the flames under the enemy's propaganda cauldron . . . by causing dissension and hysteria and mob hatred, disrupting the war effort, and sowing seeds of hate diametrically opposed to the principles for which we are fighting this war."[67]

Robert B. Cozzens, the assistant director of the WRA, who was based in San Francisco, lashed out at the "agitators of race hatred" whose verbal attacks on Japanese Americans, he argued, had led the Japanese government to break off negotiations for an exchange of Americans held in prison camps in Asia.[68] Cozzens's statement received some support from Warren H. Atherton, the national commander of the American Legion, who warned "that anti-Jap words and deeds should find expression only on the battlefronts or in production lines for war." Atherton told a Legion post in northern California not to "do or say anything in manifesting hate that would make it harder for our people at the mercy of the Japs to survive."[69]

"Send in Your Answer on the Jap Problem"

In its effort to convince officials throughout California and in Washington, D.C., that the vast majority of Californians supported drastic action against Japanese Americans, the *Los Angeles Times* asked readers to "send in your answer on the Jap problem." The survey asked readers to respond to eight questions, seven of which could be answered only with "yes" or "no." The questionnaire asked if the WRA had "capably handled the problem of Japanese in the United States;" if the army should assume control of the concentration camps; if "avowedly loyal Japanese" should be released so that they could "take jobs in the Midwest;" if Japanese should be "traded" for Americans held prisoner in Japan; if the Constitution should be amended to allow "the deportation of all Japanese;" if "American-born Japanese" should be allowed to remain in the United States; and if "all Japanese" should be excluded permanently "from the Pacific Coast States, including California." The final question asked, "do you have other suggestions to make?" All of these questions clearly rested on the assumption that all "Japanese" were loyal to Japan.[70]

A week after it printed its questionnaire, the *Times* reported that the response had been so overwhelming that it probably would not be able to publish the results as scheduled on December 6. The newspaper noted that "office girls have spent hours sorting the stacks of letters and a corps of tabulators has had to be called into service to compile the ballots." A photograph of two *Times* employees with a pile of letters accompanied the article.[71]

In the end, the "Jap Question Editor" did not need extra time to compile the results of the questionnaire. On December 6, 1943, the *Times* published these results. The readers who responded overwhelmingly supported the position already taken by the *Times*. Only 639 readers said that they thought that the WRA had "capably handled the problem of Japanese in the United States," while 10,773 said that they did not think that the WRA had done what it should have. More than 11,200 readers expressed support for "Army control of Japanese in this country for the duration," while 372 expressed opposition. More than 9,700 readers opposed the release of "loyal Japanese to take jobs in the Midwest," while 1,139 supported such a policy. More than 11,200 readers supported the "trading" of "Japanese now here for American war prisoners held in Japan," while only 256 opposed such an effort. Nearly 10,600 supported a "constitutional amendment after the war for the deportation of all Japanese from this country, and forbidding further

FIG. 12. *The* Los Angeles Times *published this photograph of Dolores Johnson and Jackie Peterman with some of the thousands of responses that the newspaper received to its "Jap questionnaire" in late November 1943.* Los Angeles Times, *Nov. 29, 1943, pt. 2, p. 1.* Los Angeles Times *Photographic Archive (Collection 1429), Department of Special Collections, Charles E. Young Research Library, University of California, Los Angeles.*

immigration," while 732 opposed such an amendment. Nearly 1,900 respondents, however, would have such an amendment apply only to Japanese aliens, not to "American-born Japanese." On the other hand, more than 9,000 respondents would have deported U.S. citizens as well as Japanese aliens. Finally, 9,855 readers supported the permanent exclusion of "all Japanese from the Pacific Coast States, including California," while 999 opposed such a policy.[72]

Most of the letters that the newspaper printed from readers supported its position. Many of these readers referred explicitly to "racial" differences between "Americans" and "Japanese." One reader, for example, wrote that the "American" and "Japanese" peoples should live apart. "It may be that there are inbred instincts and racial intuitions so strong and compelling that they are altogether beyond the control of those possessed of them. It may be the Japanese are like that. It looks that way. Why not recognize this fact and not attempt to do the impossible?"[73] Another reader stated that "the Japs have long been known as a two-faced race." She asked rhetorically, "How do you tell a loyal Jap? He will smile and bow at you and with one swift move knife you in the back."[74] A third letter argued that God placed the Japanese in Japan and intended them to stay there. "The amalgamation of races has resulted in failure wherever tried, so far as improvement is concerned," the author wrote.[75] Another writer argued that "there is not a Jap living that would not assist Japan against the United States if given an opportunity, were it not for the fear of getting caught, or knowing what to do. To release one of them is nothing short of a crime." The same writer expressed the opinion that "the Japanese, as a race, have forfeited every right or privilege they may have had to live and enjoy the freedom of this country."[76]

Some of the readers of the *Times*, however, responded to the "Jap Questionnaire" with letters that criticized the newspaper for its attempts "to inflame race hatred." One reader called the treatment of Japanese Americans "wanton, unfair, and un-American racial persecution" and declared that "it is disgraceful to see." This reader asked, "how can we hope to remain free and decent when such prejudiced statements are given by your paper?"[77] Even people who acknowledged negative feelings toward people of Japanese ancestry warned against some of the *Times*'s suggestions. One reader warned that "a constitutional amendment to revoke the citizenship of any group, because of their race, would place in jeopardy the citizenship of any individual or minority group in the United States." This reader insisted that Japanese

Americans should be treated as individuals. "If they are accused, tried and found guilty of treason, then action should be taken, but not on the basis of race."[78] A reader who expressed the belief that Japanese Americans "have forfeited all rights to ever return here to our West Coast" also acknowledged that "to indulge the feelings I have toward these people, many of whom are, of course, (maybe) loyal, would be un-American. We don't deal in European purges, even when we would like to."[79]

The editor of the *Westwood Hills Press*, a community newspaper in Los Angeles, also criticized the *Los Angeles Times* for its poll on "the Jap Question." The editor pointed out that the *Times* had offered no evidence that Japanese Americans or Japanese immigrants were disloyal to the United States. The newspaper also challenged the effort to label anyone who did not support persecution of Japanese Americans a "sentimentalist." An editorial in the *Press* concluded that "the Times poll will have no real effect in determining what really has become 'the Japanese Question.' There are too many Americans who don't like to see innocent people kicked around. Is that sentimentality, or is that part of what this war is about?"[80]

The "Jap questionnaire" episode reveals perhaps subtle but important changes in the debate about the loyalty of Japanese Americans. Anti-Japanese voices continued to dominate this debate, as the results of the questionnaire itself reveal. The ideas expressed by anti-Japanese readers of the *Times* reveal that most of these ideas reflected the belief that all people of Japanese ancestry possessed negative racial characteristics. At the same time, even the anti-Japanese *Times* agreed to print letters that challenged these statements and that criticized the newspaper for attempting to "inflame race hatred." The critics of the anti-Japanese position would continue to become more visible and more vocal as the end of the war approached.

The Gannon Committee Hearings

Some leaders of the anti-Japanese campaign responded to their apparent inability to influence federal policy by using their positions of authority to attempt to intimidate their opponents. Shortly after the events at Tule Lake, California State Assembly Member Chester Gannon of Sacramento announced that his Assembly Committee on the Japanese Problem would investigate groups that supported "fair play" for Japanese Americans.[81] In a

FIG. 13. *Members of the Gannon Committee. The Assembly Fact-Finding Committee on the Japanese Problem held hearings in Los Angeles in December 1943. In these hearings, Gannon attacked witnesses' beliefs about "race."* Los Angeles Times *Photographic Archive (Collection 1429), Department of Special Collections, Charles E. Young Research Library, University of California, Los Angeles.*

column he wrote before the hearings, Gannon lashed out at "Japanese sympathizers." Gannon ridiculed the efforts of "fair play" advocates, suggesting that they wanted Californians to "'kiss a Jap a day' just to prove our democratic principles." Gannon insisted that "kissing a Jap a day" "is not democracy—it is weakness, for such Jap-loving utterances are undermining our war spirit and are doing a job that Emperor Hirohito and his henchman would like to see accomplished." Gannon resolutely refused to accept that U.S. citizens of Japanese ancestry might not be Japanese. He referred to all people of Japanese ancestry as "our enemy" and argued that "it is high time we reappraise our enemy and get at the bottom of such groups or persons who are trying to tell the rest of us that hatred of our enemy is 'unethical' and that the Japanese are just poor, misguided souls who didn't know any better when they stabbed us in the back at Pearl Harbor."[82]

When the Gannon Committee began its investigation, it quickly became apparent that Gannon was interested in attacking people who opposed racial discrimination in general, not simply discrimination against Japanese Americans.

After Dr. Clinton J. Taft, the director of the Southern California American Civil Liberties Union, told the committee why he was in favor of the return of the Japanese to the Pacific Coast, Gannon asked Taft about his views about racial intermarriage. "When he testified that he believes in inter-marriage 'of any race who want to get married,' spectators in the State Building Assembly Room loudly hissed the witness," the *Examiner* reported. Ed Robbin, a columnist for the *People's World*, a radical San Francisco newspaper, told the committee that he believed in racial equality. Gannon asked him if he "would stop at the altar?"[83] Mrs. Maynard Thayer, the head of the Pasadena chapter of the Pacific Coast Committee on American Principles and Fair Play, told Gannon's committee that the Fair Play Committee did not support the return of people of Japanese ancestry to the coast before the end of the war. The committee, she said, "is merely interested in seeing to it that the constitutional rights of the Japanese were not trampled." Gannon asked Thayer "if she had ever smelled the odors that came from some of the Japanese homes." According to the *Times*, Gannon's question elicited "murmurs of protest from the contingent of Pasadena women in the audience."[84] Gannon also asked Thayer, "did Communists have anything to do with your organization?" According to the *Daily News*, Thayer bristled at the question, replying, "I am a registered republican, Mr. Gannon." Thayer's words indicate

FIG. 14. *Mrs. Maynard Thayer, a member of the Pasadena branch of the Pacific Coast Committee on American Principles and Fair Play, which called for "fair play" for Japanese Americans. The caption published in the* Times *pointed out that the Fair Play Committee did not endorse the return of Japanese Americans to coastal areas during the war. In response to her statement in favor of fair play and against racial prejudice, committee chair Chester Gannon of Sacramento asked Thayer "if she had ever smelled the odors that came from some of the Japanese homes."* Los Angeles Times *Photographic Archive (Collection 1429), Department of Special Collections, Charles E. Young Research Library, University of California, Los Angeles.*

FIG. 15. *Rev. Allan A. Hunter of the Mt. Hollywood Congregational Church. The* Times *reported that committee chair Chester Gannon "roared" at Hunter, "and you would go down to meet the Japanese invasion of this country with the Bible and a speech!" Hunter responded, "I would do as I thought Christ would do. I would try to do as Jesus did when He was crucified. I would probably be killed, but I hope I would be brave enough."* Los Angeles Times *Photographic Archive (Collection 1429), Department of Special Collections, Charles E. Young Research Library, University of California, Los Angeles.*

that the Fair Play Committee was concerned about racial prejudice and discrimination in general, not simply that directed toward Japanese Americans. She read a copy of a letter that described a meeting that took place on June 30, 1943, at Eliot Junior High School in Altadena. At that meeting, according to the letter, John R. Lechner gave a talk "calculated to instill hatred of all Americans of non-Caucasian ancestry."[85]

Gannon and other members of his committee engaged in a heated exchange with Rev. Allan Hunter, the pastor of the Mt. Hollywood Congregational Church and the Southern California chairman of the Fellowship of Reconciliation, a pacifist organization founded during World War I. According to the *Times*, "Assemblyman Gannon got so worked up over the debate that he stood up and Hunter stood up, although the latter retained his poise as he answered question after question and met argument with argument." The newspaper reported that Gannon "roared" at Hunter, "and you would go down to meet the Japanese invasion of this country with the Bible and a speech!" Hunter responded, "I would do as I thought Christ would do. I would try to do as Jesus did when He was crucified. I would probably be killed, but I hope I would be brave enough."[86]

In these hearings Gannon had hoped to discredit the "fair play" advocates. Instead, he ended up embarrassing the anti-Japanese movement. Gannon's treatment of Hunter and other witnesses led the *Times* to editorialize against Gannon's tendency "to browbeat and abuse witnesses and to get into hot arguments with them." The *Times* insisted that a legislative committee should not "seek to convert individuals to a particular point of view, or to turn itself into a prosecutor of what may currently be unpopular." Instead, legislative committees should simply "obtain facts or opinions on which legislation can be based," and in doing this they have "an obligation to be courteous to the witnesses they call and to remember that difference of opinion on public questions is an American privilege."[87]

The *Times* was not the only publication that criticized Gannon's zeal. *Time* magazine characterized the Gannon Committee's hearings as part of "the West's most violent racial hysteria since 'Yellow Peril' pioneer days." According to *Time*, "the 112,000 U.S. Japanese evacuated from the West Coast had become the object of hatred more intense than the anti-German-American feeling of World War I." The national news magazine reported that the witnesses who appeared before the committee outdid "each other in wild charges. Hearst's *Examiner* one day ran 62 inches of testimony, blazoning it high above the progress of the war in Russia, Teheran, and Italy." *Time* noted that the "evidence" presented included "stories of nude bathing parties in a river near Fresno," and "a missionary who said he had seen 'Japs take the body of a Chinese, cut out the heart and liver and eat it.'" The *Time* article also included excerpts of Gannon's grilling of Mrs. Thayer. *Time* noted the editorial published by the *Times,* concluding that "the Gannon investigation was too much even for the Los Angeles *Times,* which until then had been close behind the *Examiner* in retailing the committee's doings."[88] The responses to the Gannon Committee's hearings by both the *Times* and *Time* suggest that a growing number of people had come to see the increasingly shrill arguments of anti-Japanese leaders as illogical and outlandish.

At the same time the Gannon Committee was ridiculing witnesses for their belief in racial equality, the FBI revealed that many people of Japanese ancestry had already been allowed to return to Pacific Coast homes. Most of these people were women who were married to men who were not of Japanese ancestry.[89] The army had issued individual exemptions to its exclusion orders to these women. In allowing the reunification of families that had been separated by the exclusion orders in 1942, the army, probably unintentionally, had undermined the arguments of anti-Japanese leaders. These leaders had depicted all Japanese Americans as men as they argued that Japanese Americans were a threat to national security; they did not distinguish between men of Japanese ancestry and women of Japanese ancestry. This left them in the position of arguing that the return of these women to the Pacific Coast was a grave threat to national security even when the actual return of these women had generated no negative response.

When anti-Japanese leaders discovered that the army was allowing some Japanese Americans to return to the Pacific Coast, they expressed their opposition. U.S. Rep. John M. Costello reiterated the claim that people on the West Coast knew that "no examination can be given to Japanese that will bring absolute, indubitable proof of their loyalty."[90] The State Senate Fact-Finding Committee on Japanese Resettlement declared that "the relocation in this State of Japanese during the war will inevitably lead to violence and bloodshed."[91] Some participants in the anti-Japanese campaign refused to believe that the army would allow any people of Japanese ancestry to return to the Pacific Coast. The *Examiner,* for example, insisted that the army should be put in charge of the concentration camps because the army "understands the character of the Japanese enemy better than any civilian or political agency can possibly know it." Soldiers "could be relied upon to refrain from conducting social experiments with the Japanese," an *Examiner* editorial asserted.[92] None of these arguments, however, explained clearly why the release of a small number of Japanese American women would threaten the security of the Pacific Coast.

As the previous paragraphs suggest, by the end of 1943 anti-Japanese leaders were failing in their efforts to influence federal policies. Some supporters of "fair play," not satisfied simply with federal officials' refusal to act in accord with the anti-Japanese leaders' wishes, encouraged federal officials to take more definitive actions. Some Japanese American leaders called upon the Western Defense Command to consider relaxing "the restrictions which have been imposed upon American citizens of Japanese ancestry." They pointed out that some wartime orders, such as those requiring "dimouts," had been rescinded, and "everyone is agreed that the prospects of invasion by the Japanese forces are becoming more and more remote."[93]

Toward the Rescission of the Exclusion Order

In 1944 the debate about "race" and Japanese Americans' loyalty shifted decisively. In the weeks after the tense confrontation at Tule Lake, the words of anti-Japanese leaders filled the newspapers. Throughout 1944, however, supporters of "fair play" for Japanese Americans gained greater access to the newspapers. Powerful officials, including army officers, spoke out against discrimination against Japanese Americans. Some of these officials forcefully criticized their anti-Japanese opponents, particularly the beliefs about "race" that lay beneath their statements about Japanese Americans.

One of the most prominent officials who defended the WRA and its policies was Secretary of the Interior Harold L. Ickes. In an April 1944 speech in San Francisco, Ickes "called upon West Coast residents to quiet 'the clamor of those few among you who are screaming' for vengeance against former Pacific Coast area Japanese." Ickes insisted that the WRA, which had recently been moved under his jurisdiction "will not be stampeded into undemocratic, bestial, inhuman action. It will not be converted into an instrument of revenge or racial warfare." Ickes praised the WRA for not persecuting Japanese Americans and for not attempting "to punish those of a different race who were not responsible for what has been happening in the

Pacific." Ickes accused the WRA's opponents of wanting the agency to participate in "a lynching party."[94] Ickes argued that the United States should not punish Japanese Americans for the actions of the Japanese military. "To do this would be to lower ourselves to the level of the fanatical Nazis and Japanese warlords. Civilization expects more from us than from them." Ickes expressed his belief that the "overwhelming majority" of West Coast residents "believe in fair play and decency, Christianity, in the principles of America, in the Constitution of the United States." Ickes's criticism of West Coast attitudes rested firmly upon modernist racial ideology. He claimed not to understand what would have made Japanese Americans on the Pacific Coast, who had been removed from their homes, any different from Japanese Americans in other parts of the nation, who were not incarcerated. "I know of no virus in these three States which has infected them so that they must be treated differently than the Japanese Americans who reside in other States."[95]

"Los Angeles leaders" took "strong exception" to Ickes's statement, according to the *Examiner*. California's American Legionnaires unanimously called for Ickes to resign as head of the WRA.[96] Many of the leaders of the anti-Japanese movement insisted that they were not motivated by racial prejudice. In an editorial the *Los Angeles Times* insisted that "West Coast opposition to the return of persons of Japanese ancestry to this coast during wartime has a rational basis." The *Times* also stated that "the people who have been urging that the enemies of the United States be treated as enemies and not coddled or pampered are getting a bit tired of being accused of race prejudice every time the Ickeses and the Dillon Myers open their mouths."[97] The Lomita Post No. 1622 of the Veterans of Foreign Wars informed Ickes that "we men who have fought America's battles on foreign soil and on hostile waters cannot by any stretch of imagination be called race mongers, nor do we favor any bestial, undemocratic or inhuman action against the Japs in this state."[98]

The leaders of the anti-Japanese movement insisted that their efforts were motivated by their experience with and knowledge of people of Japanese ancestry, not by race prejudice. Bernard Hiss of the Native Sons, for example, said that "we feel that Japanese in this country are just as much our enemies as those in Japan proper and this feeling is based on past knowledge and experience." Hiss argued that "it is self-evident that if we are intolerant for opposing return of Jap evacuees to California, then our troops are intolerant for fighting the Japs in the Pacific."[99] The Lomita VFW post explained that its request that all people of Japanese ancestry be expelled from the United States was not undemocratic. "For years we have watched with apprehension the various activities of the Jap groups and we cannot subscribe to the theory there are any loyal Japs, nor can anyone else," the post's leaders wrote to Ickes. "They are all the product of teachings inculcated in them at Jap schools and their manifestations of loyalty are superficial."[100] Wallace L. Ware, a former Legion leader and a candidate for Los Angeles County District Attorney, declared that the Interior Secretary was "fresh from Washington and loaded with a strange love for a race with whom we are engaged in a life-and-death struggle."[101] As these examples suggest, anti-Japanese leaders insisted that there could be no meaningful difference between people who had lived their entire lives in Japan and Japanese Americans who had spent many years—some their whole lives—in the United States; both groups were "identical" in terms of "race." The protests by anti-Japanese leaders in California, however, had no effect on WRA policy.

Military officials continued to desert the anti-Japanese movement. In May of 1944 the *Los Angeles Times* reported that the army had allowed thirty-nine "Jap-American women, with their children," to return to the Pacific Coast since December 1943. These women were all married either to men who were not Japanese Americans or to U.S. soldiers. Lt. Gen. Delos C. Emmons, commanding general of the Western Defense Command, vouched for the security of the West Coast. "I personally have examined each individual case of Japanese-Americans being allowed to return to the area and I don't take any chances in having persons of Japanese descent who might jeopardize safety in restricted areas." He insisted that "we know that the ones permitted to return are no threat to military security."[102]

By the middle of 1944 the advocates of fair play for Japanese Americans had become more vocal and more visible. They also appear not to have attracted as much of a hostile response as they had in the past. In May the Los Angeles County chapter of the American Association of Social Workers "passed a resolution urging the Secretary of War to restore the full rights of American citizens of Japanese ancestry 'at the earliest possible date.'"[103] In June the Southern California-Arizona Methodist Conference passed a resolution supporting the right of Japanese Americans to return to the Pacific Coast "as soon as the military situation makes such a move feasible." The resolution urged "the people to exemplify the way of Christ by welcoming to our communities, our schools, our churches and our homes these victims of organized discrimination and wartime hysteria." To continue to exclude Japanese Americans from the West Coast "is contrary to every principle of fairness and indirectly violates the basic rights guaranteed by the Constitution."[104] Representatives of the Methodist churches in ten western states and the territories of Alaska and Hawai'i later approved a similar if not identical resolution.[105] Carey McWilliams, who at the time was working on his book *Prejudice: Japanese Americans, Symbol of Racial Intolerance,* published a pamphlet about Japanese Americans.[106] In a radio debate in early August 1944, McWilliams declared the views of two anti-Japanese American leaders "racist nonsense."[107] He argued that "race has nothing to do with being an American citizen. Race as a clue to character, capacity, or conduct is a myth,—one of Hitler's vital lies."[108] The Catholic Interracial Council of Los Angeles passed a resolution in September 1944 urging that "loyal Japanese-Americans and loyal Japanese aliens" be allowed to return immediately.[109]

By August 1944 the *Pacific Citizen* could declare that "there is an argument that west coast race-baiters cannot answer. It is the argument of the Japanese Americans in uniform, of the Nisei soldiers who have made a brilliant fighting record in the shell-pocked hills and rubble-strewn plains of Italy, and on islands and jungles wrested from the Japanese in the Pacific."[110] The valiant service of Japanese American soldiers did undermine many of the anti-Japanese arguments. Participants in the anti-Japanese campaign had argued that all people of Japanese ancestry were loyal to Japan, and some had opposed the army's decision to allow Japanese Americans to enlist. As reports of the exploits of Japanese American troops circulated, they rendered nonsensical the argument that Japanese Americans were not loyal to the United States.

After the events at Tule Lake in November 1943, some anti-Japanese leaders, most notably U.S. Rep. Clair Engle, had suggested that the public would only support anti-Japanese political candidates. The 1944 elections proved Engle wrong. Before the June primary election, the Civic Affairs Commission of the Church Federation of Los Angeles sent questionnaires to the 111 candidates for Los Angeles County's 31 state assembly seats. Only five of the forty-two candidates who responded indicated that they were definitely opposed to the return of Japanese Americans, and only one of these five was actually elected. Half of the sixteen candidates who favored the return of Japanese Americans "without question" were either elected or won their party's nomination. Republican Lee Bashore, who was reelected in the primary, noted on his questionnaire that "the Federal constitution grants them the right to live where they desire." Democrat Ernest Debs, who was also reelected, stated that citizens of Japanese ancestry "should be given privileges of all American citizens."[111] U.S. Rep. John Costello, one of the most prominent anti-Japanese politicians, failed in his bid for reelection. State Sen. Jack B. Tenney also failed to win the nomination for a U.S. Senate seat. In reporting on the electoral defeats of prominent anti-Japanese politicians, *Pacific Citizen* editor Larry Tajiri concluded that "race-baiting does not pay."[112] In the November general election, President Roosevelt handily won California even though he had ignored the warnings of anti-Japanese politicians. Moreover, U.S. Rep. Norris Poulson of Los Angeles, the author of an anti-Japanese article, lost his seat to Ned Healy, who had endorsed "fair play" for Japanese Americans.[113]

Esther Takei, Gender, and Modernist Racial Ideology

Anti-Japanese leaders did not abandon their campaign in the face of greater opposition from powerful officials and from some voters. Their efforts to convince officials to prevent Japanese Americans from leaving the camps and returning to the Pacific Coast, however, faced ever greater obstacles. The army continued to allow some Japanese American women to return to the Pacific Coast, and anti-Japanese activists continued to argue that these women were a threat to the security of the coastal area. Moreover, anti-Japanese leaders had to contend with concerted opposition from "fair play" advocates, including some veterans of World War II. The case of Esther Takei illustrates the growing support for "fair play" and the growing difficulties facing anti-Japanese leaders. In September 1944 the army granted the nineteen-year-old Takei permission to return to southern California to study at Pasadena Junior College. Even though a number of Japanese American women had been allowed to return to California prior to September 1944, the Los Angeles newspapers reported that Takei was the "first Japanese-American permitted to return" to the Los Angeles area.[114]

Takei's arrival in Pasadena sparked a protest from a "group of war mothers and other relatives of men and women in the armed services." This group, led by George L. Kelley, initially asked the Pasadena Board of Education to

FIG. 16. *Esther Takei, reportedly the first Japanese American woman allowed to return to the Los Angeles area, arrived in Pasadena in September 1944 to enroll in Pasadena Junior College. Anti-Japanese leaders called for her dismissal from the college and her removal from the area, but most students and community leaders supported Takei's right to remain.* Herald-Examiner *Collection, Los Angeles Public Library.*

expel Takei from the junior college. When the Board indicated that it had no power to expel Takei, Kelley sent a letter to U.S. President Franklin D. Roosevelt. The letter asked Roosevelt "to take personal action toward preventing Esther Takei . . . from attending classes at Pasadena Junior College." Kelley told reporters that "there is entirely too much pussyfooting going on in Pasadena." He said that "it is time we took a determined stand to prevent the return of nisei to our schools."[115] Other anti-Japanese leaders, such as Dr. John Carruthers, the president of the Pacific Coast Japanese Problem League, and the Native Sons of the Golden West, also protested Takei's return to the coastal area.[116] A number of Pasadena residents, however, actively supported Takei's right to live in Pasadena and enroll in the college. Dr. Leonard Oechsli, the district superintendent of the Methodist church, told the school board that Japanese Americans should be allowed to return. According to the *Daily News*, the audience at the board meeting applauded Oechsli's statement.[117]

Kelley's greatest obstacle was trying to convince officials in Pasadena and Washington that the presence of a nineteen-year-old woman in Pasadena threatened the nation's security. The statements of most people suggest that they refused to believe that it was dangerous for Takei to be in Pasadena. Gladys Rinehart, the president of the Pasadena Board of Education, told reporters that ninety-seven people had written to the board in support of Takei's admission to the junior college. Only one person, Kelley, had written to the board to oppose Takei's admission.[118] Takei's supporters insisted that it was unreasonable to think that a single Nisei woman who had been cleared by the army posed a threat to Pasadena. Dr. John A. Sexon, the superintendent of public schools in Pasadena, declared that the protests against Takei's admissions were "not in conformity with our American way or in accord with the dictates of reasonableness and sound judgment."[119] Sexon, drawing upon a poll conducted by the student newspaper, argued that 90 percent of the college's students supported Takei's enrollment.[120]

Kelley's efforts also encountered a determined campaign by the Fair Play Committee and other Pasadena organizations. Members of the Committee denounced Kelley's attacks on Takei's enrollment. Mrs. Willard J. Stone of the Fair Play Committee said that "when a citizen such as this girl is cleared by the military authorities, she has all the civil rights of all American citizens and such rights must be allowed."[121] The Assembly of the Southern California Council of Protestant Churches commended the position taken by the school authorities in Pasadena. The assembly passed a resolution urging "all citizens, public officials and churches to take the same attitude as the Pasadena School Board as the number of returning evacuees increases." The resolution insisted that all Americans should recognize that "the protection of citizenship rights is of the utmost importance at a time when we are fighting totalitarianism which would deprive citizens of their individual liberties."[122]

Anti-Japanese leaders had long argued that World War II veterans would fiercely oppose the return of Japanese Americans to the Pacific Coast. The Los Angeles County District Attorney had even argued that veterans who had fought in the Pacific had promised to kill any "Jap" they encountered in Los Angeles. The response of one group of veterans to Kelley's efforts to bar Takei from Pasadena, however, suggests that World War II veterans would not consistently participate in the anti-Japanese campaign. An organization of World War II veterans at UCLA passed a resolution that supported the right of loyal Japanese Americans to return to California. "We feel that Japanese-Americans who have shown their loyalty on the battlefields of Europe are as good Americans as any other citizens. We do not think that Japanese-Americans should be discriminated against on the basis of their race," Gordon Cleator, one of the group's members, said.[123]

The "fair play" efforts in Pasadena culminated in a speech by WRA Director Dillon S. Myer, who had been invited to speak by the Fair Play Committee.[124] Myer spoke before a standing-room-only crowd in the auditorium of the Pasadena Public Library. He argued that "facts have dispelled fear and ignorance." He directly attacked those people who argued that soldiers, sailors, and marines returning from the Pacific would attack any Japanese Americans they encountered. "The old story of the hate mongers, 'Wait till the boys come back,' simply is not founded on fact. The boys who already have come home tell stories of valor and of pride—not of hate."

According to the *Times*, the audience overwhelmingly agreed with Myer. The only person who disagreed with Myer was George L. Kelley, who "politely presented the speaker with his now familiar 'letter to the school board' which implored Gen. Bonesteel to alter his stand which allowed Esther Takei, 19-year-old Nisei, to return from Colorado to enroll at Pasadena Junior College."[125]

In a surprising development, Kelley changed his mind. According to the *Times*, Kelley resigned from the "Ban the Japs Committee" that he had established and "applied for membership in the Pasadena chapter of the

FIG. 17. *War Relocation Authority Director Dillon S. Myer. Anti-Japanese leaders frequently attacked Myer's policies throughout 1943 and 1944. By the end of 1944, however, some of the hostility toward him had abated. The anti-Japanese* Times *used positive terms to describe him in an article from the fall of 1944. He spoke in support of Takei and other Japanese Americans in Pasadena in September 1944.* Los Angeles Times *Photographic Archive (Collection 1429), Department of Special Collections, Charles E. Young Research Library, University of California, Los Angeles.*

Committee for American Principles and Fair Play." "When I'm wrong I'll admit it, and I was wrong," Kelley told a *Times* reporter. "That Dillon Myer fellow convinced me. Why, I have always felt just like they do only I didn't know it. They practice civil rights. At that meeting the people I'd been bucking invited me to sit on the platform with them."[126]

Myer's speech in Pasadena was part of a tour of California. As Myer's speaking tour continued, he drew favorable coverage from the *Los Angeles Times,* which had previously leveled personal attacks at him. After Myer spoke before the Friday Morning Club, an inter-faith organization, the *Times* characterized him as "handsome," and the newspaper identified him as "the man whose convincing eloquence caused George L. Kelley... to do an about face." In his speech, Myer "condemned racists and 'their tawdry appeal to fear and hatred' when they distort popular emotions by discrediting the ability of those of Japanese descent to accept the principles of American democratic life." Myer argued that public opinion toward Japanese Americans had changed because of "the magnificent combat record of Japanese-American boys in the uniform of the United States Army."[127]

"A Great Deal of Trouble Would Be the Inevitable Result"

As it became clear in 1944 that World War II veterans would not all side with the anti-Japanese leaders, these leaders quietly backed away from some of their claims. In the fall of 1944, some anti-Japanese leaders began to argue that Japanese Americans should not be allowed to return to the Pacific Coast because of the wartime changes that had occurred in the coastal areas. These arguments still reflected the assumption that all Californians would associate Japanese Americans with Japanese soldiers and the atrocities they had committed in the Pacific war, but they emphasized the inability of congested areas to accommodate tens of thousands of returning Japanese Americans. Los Angeles Police Chief C. B. Horrall argued that Japanese Americans should not be allowed to return because "depleted police personnel and a very bad crime situation caused by the war" would prevent the police from giving "24-hour daily protection to the Japs." Horrall predicted that "a great deal of trouble would be the inevitable result should a returned Jap start eviction proceedings against tenants, especially where a service man's family was involved." The police would be able to do "very little" "about the resultant violence, with our undermanned department," Horrall said.[128] The *Los*

Angeles Times editorialized against allowing Japanese Americans to return because of wartime congestion in Los Angeles. The *Times* argued that there was simply no place for people of Japanese ancestry to live in Los Angeles. "The space they occupied in this city has been solidly filled—rather more than solidly in the 'Little Tokyo' district—and so is no longer available," the editorial insisted.[129] Advocates of "fair play" vigorously attacked these new anti-Japanese arguments. The Catholic Interracial Council sent Horrall a letter that accused the police chief of attempting to "incite the lawlessness [of] a small number of Los Angeles residents who might believe in the law of Judge Lynch."[130]

Some anti-Japanese leaders offered increasingly far-fetched claims in support of their opposition to the return of Japanese Americans. When the army allowed fifty-four-year-old Tadayuki Todah to return to Los Angeles, for example, District Attorney Fred N. Howser told a group of Shriners gathered to observe Bill of Rights Week that "the second attack on Pearl Harbor has started!"[131]

Howser's statement appeared ridiculous to many people. Todah had operated City Hall Grill in downtown Los Angeles before his incarceration and had served in the U.S. Army during World War I.[132] In its article, the *Times* did not seem to suggest that Todah's return to Los Angeles posed a security threat to the United States or even that it would exacerbate problems related to wartime congestion. Howser, however, said, "I am wondering if it was just coincidence that this individual should be permitted to return one day before the anniversary of Pearl Harbor."[133] Howser also said, "we are taught to practice brotherly love, but the Jap is no brother of mine. To the Jap there are no human rights such as are guaranteed to us in the Bill of Rights which we are now commemorating." Howser's statements sparked public criticism from "fair play" advocates. The Catholic Inter-Racial Council sent Howser a telegram saying that "your ridiculous accusation in a public statement that one unnamed Japanese alien allowed to return to his Los Angeles home by military permit is a 'second Pearl Harbor invasion' befouls [the] Bill of Rights and insults the intelligence of the community."[134] The Fellowship for Social Justice of the First Unitarian Church of Los Angeles also criticized Howser. It sent the district attorney a telegram that said, "we regard your statement as un-American, un-Christian and calculated to encourage lawlessness and violence and the flaunting of constitutional rights of American citizens."[135]

FIG. 18. *Los Angeles County District Attorney Fred N. Howser told shriners that "the second attack on Pearl Harbor has started" after the newspapers reported on the return of fifty-four-year-old Tadayuki Todah to Los Angeles in December 1944.* Los Angeles Times *Photographic Archive (Collection 1429), Department of Special Collections, Charles E. Young Research Library, University of California, Los Angeles.*

At the same time as Howser was addressing the Shriners, Robert Cozzens, the assistant director of the War Relocation Authority, was speaking before a committee of the Junior Chamber of Commerce. Since it was Bill of Rights Week, Cozzens said that "it is difficult for me to understand how the Bill of Rights can function in 47 states and not in California." Cozzens also stated, "I want it made clear that the W.R.A. has no authority to relocate people on the West Coast who have been removed by military order, and that those who are returning are coming back without our assistance." The anti-Japanese agitators had argued that military authorities understood the Japanese better than the "tender-hearted" WRA employees did. Now that military authorities had begun to allow some Japanese Americans to return to coastal areas, Cozzens was able to employ an argument previously used by anti-Japanese agitators. He suggested that "the military authorities knew more about handling the Japanese problem than the agitators opposed to persons of Japanese descent."[136]

By the end of 1944 fair play advocates had begun to argue that the anti-Japanese movement had run its course. In early December 1944 *Pacific Citizen* editor Larry Tajiri wrote that "there is no large-scale opposition to the return of the evacuees." The opposition to a Japanese American return to the Pacific Coast, Tajiri argued, came from "a highly vocal, well-organized minority, paced by the Hearst newspapers." According to Tajiri, this minority "has abandoned any pretense of interest in the national security and have shown themselves in all their racist prejudice and naked economic self-interest." The "fascistic overtones" of the campaign waged by this small minority had embarrassed some people, such as Gov. Earl Warren, so that they decided "to issue statements upholding the rights of the Japanese American group." Tajiri argued that the position taken by groups such as the Native Sons "stems from their traditional antipathy toward all non-Caucasian minorities in the State" and therefore should concern not only Japanese Americans but all Americans, particularly other Asian Americans, Mexican Americans, and African Americans.[137] Roger N. Baldwin, the director of the American Civil Liberties Union, concurred with Tajiri. Baldwin, who had toured the West Coast, had concluded that "present evidence of hostility to Japanese-Americans on the Pacific Coast will disappear with the expected order permitting their return." Baldwin said that he had "found evidence of resistance with threats of violence are confined to farmer competitors in the agricultural valleys of California, Oregon and Washington."[138]

The Rescission of the Exclusion Orders

On December 17, 1944, the army rescinded the exclusion orders, effective January 2, 1945. Major Gen. Henry C. Pratt, temporary head of the Western Defense Command, said that the rescission of the orders reflected the "favorable progress of the war in the Pacific" and the fact that government agencies had studied carefully a vast quantity of information about Japanese Americans. "It is now possible to consider persons of Japanese ancestry on an individual basis rather than consider them as a group," Pratt stated. "I consider it of great importance that the people of the West Coast understand and appreciate that the most careful scrutiny of the vast amount of information now available has led to the conclusion that the great majority of Japanese-Americans have severed all connections with Japan, and are prepared to assume all the responsibilities of their situation as Americans," the general announced.[139] The fact that the army had now agreed completely with the proponents of "fair play" and the defenders of Japanese Americans' civil rights further undercut the position of the anti-Japanese leaders, who had long argued in their attacks on the WRA that the army was their ally.

Leaders of the anti-Japanese movement responded to the army's announcement in a variety of ways. Some, such as California Gov. Earl Warren, accepted the army's decision and encouraged all residents of California to honor and protect Japanese Americans' civil rights. "Any public unrest that develops from provocative statements, or civil disturbances that result from intemperate action will of necessity retard the war effort," Warren said.[140] Other leaders, such as Los Angeles Mayor Fletcher Bowron, declared that the army's decision was a "mistake." Some anti-Japanese leaders refused to believe that the army had deserted them. Walter H. Odemar of the Native Sons said that the army's decision was a "grave error caused, I believe, by the extreme pressure of idealists who believe in nice-sounding theories but fail to recognize cold, hard facts."[141] The *Los Angeles Times* agreed with Odemar. An editorial in the *Times* characterized the army's decision as "a grave mistake, due to snap judgment under political pressure from some nonmilitary source." The *Times* rejected Pratt's argument. "If Japs in large numbers on the Pacific Coast are dangerous under one set of wartime circumstances, they are dangerous under all sets of wartime circumstances," the *Times* insisted. The *Times* also criticized Pratt's statement that "no Jap known to be disloyal will be returned." Reiterating an earlier claim of the anti-Japanese movement, the editorial asked, "has some magic method suddenly been discovered whereby all the disloyal can infallibly be segregated from such a mass? Traditionally the most dangerous spies and wreckers are loudest in their protestations of fealty to their 'adopted' country." Despite the fact that veterans themselves had defended the rights of Japanese Americans, the *Times* claimed that relatives of soldiers and sailors would not offer "jobs and patronage and the spirit of equality" to "these tens of thousands of Japs." "Human nature simply isn't built that way," the editorial stated, suggesting that it was "natural" for Americans from a variety of ethnic backgrounds to hate all people of Japanese ancestry.[142] The Los Angeles Police Commission adopted a resolution protesting the army's decision to allow Japanese Americans to return to coastal areas. The resolution mentioned inadequate housing and wartime congestion. The resolution also stated: "we doubt the ability of any governmental authority to screen loyalty. Certainly a police force cannot do so, no matter how adequately it were equipped."[143]

Many people, however, expressed support for the army's decision. The Catholic Interracial Council "expressed confidence in the Army's policy on the Japanese and that California civil authorities will supply intelligent and sane leadership to the citizenry on the problem." William Carr of the Friends of the American Way in Pasadena said that "we are relieved that America no longer will banish people on a racial basis."[144] A *Pacific Citizen* editorial praised Warren's statement. "It is heartening to note that Mr. Warren, who has a record of racist statements against Americans of Japanese ancestry, placed statesmanship above his own personal prejudices when the chips were down," the editorial noted.[145]

The day after the army announced the rescission of the exclusion orders, the Supreme Court announced that it had decided that the federal government did not have the authority to detain American citizens who were loyal to the United States.[146] Japanese Americans and their allies celebrated their victory over the anti-Japanese movement. "The army and the government have repudiated the 'a Jap's a Jap' type of thinking in which at least one high military official as well as an unreasoning horde of racists and reactionaries, have indulged. The army's decision is an important victory in the unceasing war against racist thinking," Larry Tajiri declared.[147]

Despite the fact that both the army and the U.S. Supreme Court had rejected their arguments, anti-Japanese leaders did not abandon their efforts. Representatives of seven different anti-Japanese groups appealed directly to Japanese Americans to remain away from the Pacific Coast until after the war. These groups were the Native Sons of the Golden West, the Americanism Educational League, the Americans' League, the Native Daughters of the Golden West, the United Philippine War Veterans, the Sino-Korean People's League, and the "Ban-the-Japs" Committee. These groups insisted that "their opposition to the return of the evacuated Japanese was for security reasons and not racial or social."[148] Dr. John R. Lechner argued that "Japanese permitted to return to the West Coast on January 2 can best demonstrate their loyalty and a desire for America to win the war by remaining away for the duration."[149] The *Times* endorsed this position, saying that Japanese Americans "have an excellent opportunity to demonstrate their loyalty to the United States by seeking homes elsewhere than on the Pacific Coast until the war is over." In this editorial, the *Times* suggested that "every American" had made sacrifices comparable to the Japanese Americans, who had been imprisoned. "Very few are insisting on rights and constitutional privileges necessarily infringed because of the nation's danger." Japanese Americans should not demand their constitutional rights, the editorial suggested.[150]

The army's rescission of the exclusion order exacerbated divisions within organizations such as the American Legion. The Legion had played a prominent role in the anti-Japanese campaign throughout the war. After the events at Tule Lake, however, the Legion's national commander had warned California Legionnaires that their anti-Japanese statements could have negative repercussions for American citizens imprisoned by the Japanese in Asia.[151] After the army announced the rescission of the exclusion order, Los Angeles Post No. 8 of the American Legion adopted a resolution declaring that "there must be no discrimination whatever against any American citizen based solely on his Japanese ancestry." The resolution further deplored "any expression emanating from an American Legion source which refuses to accord any American ex-service man or service man the same rights, privileges and honors as any other citizen, solely because of his ancestry."[152] In January 1945 the Legion's Hollywood World War II Post, comprised of World War II veterans, admitted Harley M. Oka, a Japanese American veteran. After the Post inducted Oka, it passed a resolution condemning the Hood River, Oregon, Legion post, which had removed the names of sixteen Japanese Americans from its roll of honor. The Hollywood Post's actions sparked an investigation by P. A. (Dick)

Horton, the Legion's district commander.[153] Horton accused members of the Hollywood Post of attempting to sabotage the Legion and convince World War II veterans to join another organization for veterans.[154]

Despite their opposition to the return of Japanese Americans, some elected officials embraced fair treatment of Japanese Americans when they returned. In mid-January 1945, for example, Los Angeles Mayor Fletcher Bowron met with six Japanese Americans who had returned to Los Angeles. "Our citizens, whatever their origin, are Americans working together in a great common effort. Our democracy recognizes no distinction of race, color or creed," Bowron told them. "We want you, and all other citizens of Japanese ancestry who have located here, to feel secure in your homes, and in your community life. Everything which local government can do to make your relocation smooth and pleasant is being done. We want you to join in with us in our united effort for victory."[155]

In 1943 and 1944, racialists who had opposed the return of Japanese Americans to the coast had warned that members of other minority groups would attack Japanese Americans if they were allowed to return to congested cities such as Los Angeles. When Japanese Americans were allowed to return in early 1945, some friction did surface between African Americans who had moved into Little Tokyo and returning Japanese Americans. Both *Pacific Citizen* editor Larry Tajiri and African American leader Rev. Clayton D. Russell blamed the leaders of the anti-Japanese campaign for this friction. Tajiri argued that "race-baiters and the racist newspapers" were attempting "to provoke racial outbreaks among Los Angeles' war-increased Negro population against returning evacuees of Japanese ancestry." Tajiri compared these efforts to provoke outbreaks to "the pattern of the so-called 'zoot-suit' riots of 1943." Conditions in 1945 were different from those in 1943, however. "Men of goodwill in Los Angeles are far better organized than they were in 1943 to neutralize the racist dynamite which has been planted by the provocateurs." Tajiri also praised African American newspapers for their "magnificent work in dissipating fear propaganda."[156] Russell insisted that the people who were trying to arouse antagonism between African Americans and Japanese Americans "don't care if returning evacuees dispossess Negroes now living in Little Tokyo. Those same forces which would take property away from Japanese Americans would in turn take your property away from you."[157] African American leaders in Bronzeville, which had formerly been known as Little Tokyo, "pledged a welcome to the Japanese when

FIG. 19. *On January 14, 1945, Los Angeles Mayor Fletcher Bowron met with Japanese Americans who had returned to Los Angeles. "Our citizens, whatever their origin, are Americans working together in a great common effort. Our democracy recognizes no distinction of race, color or creed," Bowron told them. "We want you, and all other citizens of Japanese ancestry who have located here, to feel secure in your homes, and in your community life. Everything which local government can do to make your relocation smooth and pleasant is being done. We want you to join in with us in our united effort for victory."* Los Angeles Times, *Jan. 15, 1945, pt. 1, p. 7.* Los Angeles Times *Photographic Archive (Collection 1429), Department of Special Collections, Charles E. Young Research Library, University of California, Los Angeles.*

they return." Rev. Leonard B. Brown of the First Street Baptist Church, who had previously been depicted as an opponent of the Japanese Americans' return, told a reporter, "I have nothing against the return of the Japanese. I, among others, will welcome them." Brown elaborated: "I have nothing against any minority group. I'd be crazy if I did, considering that I am a member of a minority group myself."[158]

Conclusion

Although some anti-Japanese leaders, such as Mayor Bowron, backed away from their anti-Japanese positions when Japanese Americans were allowed to return to the Pacific Coast, others refused to change their position. Some still had the power to harass Japanese Americans. California state legislators, for example, took action throughout 1945 to continue their persecution of Japanese Americans. In April 1945 the Senate Judiciary Committee granted 200,000 dollars to the attorney general's office so that it could prosecute people of Japanese ancestry for violating the Alien Land Law. [159] In May 1945 the Senate's Fact-Finding Committee on Japanese Resettlement "reiterated its previous stand of 'vigorous opposition' to the return of persons of Japanese ancestry to California until after the end of the war." The committee also called for "stricter enforcement of the California Alien Land Act and a 'careful' scrutiny of Japanese language schools 'as they reopen with the return to California of evacuees of Japanese ancestry.'"[160] Later in May State Senator Hugh Burns of Fresno announced his intention to introduce legislation "to provide that an American citizen of Japanese ancestry may not own land in California if he is disloyal to the United States." Burns also introduced a bill that "would force 'disloyal citizens or aliens' to file an oath of allegiance to the United States before they could become plaintiffs in civil actions in California courts."[161] On June 4, 1945, State Sen. Jack B. Tenney introduced a resolution "urging the FBI and Army and Navy intelligence to scrutinize immediately the character and records of Japanese Americans returning to the West Coast from war relocation centers." Tenney argued that "federal civil service authorities had approved the employment of Japanese Americans 'against whom counterespionage cases may be filed at any time." Tenney also declared that "it is common knowledge that the FBI and the offices of Naval and Army intelligence have not been consulted by the WRA in reference to the character or loyalty or integrity of the persons being released."[162] In June 1945 the State Senate approved the submission to the voters "for ratification all amendments which have been placed in the California Anti-Alien Land Law, aimed at farmers of Japanese ancestry, since 1920." This measure appeared as Proposition 15 on the November 1946 ballot. The campaign surrounding this measure will be discussed in the final chapter.

Anti-Japanese politicians also continued to criticize the WRA. The Tenney Committee's June 1945 report, for example, declared that "the propaganda mill of the WRA indulges in the use of the terms 'loyal' Japanese Americans for the obvious purpose of raising by trick and device the question of the constitutional rights of citizens." The report also charged that Interior Secretary Harold L. Ickes and the WRA "had used deceptive and divisionary tactics in disseminating false and misleading information to the public in regard to the subject of evacuee relocation."[163] In July 1945 U.S. Rep. Harry P. Sheppard of Yucaipa lashed out at the WRA for "what amounts to an officially sponsored conspiracy which would have the effect of releasing Japanese and Japanese Americans from internment camps to engage in sabotage on the West Coast." Sheppard argued that the WRA "is carrying on a campaign of propaganda calculated to arouse sympathy for individuals of Japanese ancestry on grounds of persecution."[164]

In responding to the attacks of anti-Japanese leaders, "fair play" advocates took advantage of a remarkable turnaround. They, rather than their opponents, were able to claim the army as an ally. In a response to Sheppard's charge that the WRA was engaged in "an officially sponsored conspiracy," WRA Los Angeles Area Supervisor Paul G. Robertson pointed out that the army as well as the U.S. Supreme Court must also be involved in the conspiracy.[165] A number of army officers confirmed that they supported "fair play" for Japanese Americans. Two officers of the Japanese American 442nd Infantry Regiment, Capt. George H. Grandstaff of Azusa and Lt. Norman C. Mitchell of Los Angeles, criticized "witch hunting by fascistic and misguided groups in this country." Mitchell, who was recovering from combat wounds at the army's Birmingham General Hospital in Van Nuys, said that "the Nisei, the Negro and the Jewish soldiers at the hospital are treated as equals by all the men. There is no race feeling; it is real democracy."[166] Military officers also reiterated that they had "sole responsibility for determining which persons of Japanese descent may or may not return to Pacific Coast states." Gen. H. C. Pratt stated that he had "access to the records of the various intelligence agencies and am assisted by a large staff of experienced personnel. I feel, therefore, that I am able to determine which individuals may prove potentially dangerous... and such individuals are not allowed to return."[167]

Two episodes illustrate the extent to which the debate surrounding Japanese Americans and "race" had changed by the second half of 1945. In August 1945 the *Examiner* published photographs of what it described as a "dramatic meeting" of "returned Japs" and marines at Union Station.[168] An article describing this encounter claimed that "the Marines resented the contrast. They resented it with the deep resentment of men who may be about to die—and wonder if the people appreciate their sacrifice." The article did not indicate that the marines expressed this resentment verbally. Instead, it argued that "their resentment was written in their faces—in the hard, unbending way they returned the stares of the bewildered Japanese." The article described the Japanese Americans as "defiant." "Mrs. H. Kanow, Long Beach resident, pointed out testily that she had four sons with a Nisei regiment in Italy." Other people were "defiant" "because they had to make the seven-day trip from the relocation camp at Rohwer, Arkansas, by chair car." Despite the fact that the article quoted one woman who clearly pointed out that she was a U.S. citizen, its author attempted to perpetuate the notion that Japanese Americans were really Japanese. The Japanese Americans "will soon be enjoying normal American life and driving automobiles and earning salaries—while their countrymen are killing Marines," the article said. Some of these spoiled people "refused to leave the train at first because there were no red caps to help them with their luggage." The article also noted that "civilians at the depot stared unbelievingly at the sight of the Japanese returning here in carload lots at this time." An unidentified "civilian" said, "I thought there was a shortage of railroad cars and that civilians were almost banned from rail travel so the troops could move westward to finish off the Japs." The reporter insisted that "confused spectators" "couldn't figure out why the War Relocation Authority has started return of evacuated West Coast Japanese in trainload lots at the heaviest stage of the troop redeployment congestion."[169]

The *Times* also published an article and a photograph about this encounter between returning Japanese Americans and U.S. Marines. The *Times*, however, reported that the Japanese Americans were glad to be back in California. The *Times* reporter noted that the marines were "obviously

FIG. 20. *Japanese Americans returning from a WRA camp in Arkansas encountered U.S. Marines at Union Station in Los Angeles. In publishing similar photographs, the* Examiner *indicated that the marines looked at the Japanese Americans "with the deep resentment of men who may be about to die" and that the Japanese Americans were "defiant."* Herald-Examiner *Collection, Los Angeles Public Library.*

surprised at the sight of Nipponese in Los Angeles" and "gazed at them stonily and without comment." The reporter did not interpret the marines' looks as evidence of resentment. The *Times* noted that "several bystanders, some wearing service pins indicating loved ones at war, demanded to know from watching newspapermen why the Japs were being allowed to return while the war was still on." The *Times* also reported that "some of the Japanese complained because they had to travel by chair-car, and others looked vainly about for porters to carry their baggage." The reporter did not interpret these complaints or their looks as "defiance."[170] According to the *Pacific Citizen*, Hearst's International News Photos and King Features Service distributed this photograph with the caption "To a Pacific Vet, a Jap's a Jap." The *Pacific Citizen* also noted that people who witnessed the encounter said that "there was no situation to warrant such a caption."[171] The differences between the *Examiner*'s coverage of the scene at Union Station and the *Times*'s coverage are revealing. In order to claim military personnel as allies in its anti-Japanese campaign, the *Examiner* had to interpret the looks on the faces of the marines. The *Times* reporter, clearly less committed to an anti-Japanese position, offered a different interpretation.

Perhaps no event more clearly symbolizes the dramatic transformation of the debate about Japanese Americans and "race" than Gen. Joseph W. Stilwell's December 1945 visit to an Orange County farm. Even after the army rescinded the exclusion orders and allowed Japanese Americans to return to the Pacific Coast, anti-Japanese leaders had tried to claim the army as an ally. The army, they insisted, agreed with them that the Japanese were a treacherous race and had only rescinded the exclusion order under pressure from misguided politicians. Less than a year after the army allowed Japanese Americans to return to their Pacific Coast homes, however, one of the army's most respected generals traveled to Orange County to present the Distinguished Service Cross to the family of Kazuo Masuda. Stilwell's trip to Orange County was more than a medal presentation, however. It was a rebuke to the anti-Japanese movement. Mary Masuda had returned to Orange County in May 1945 to make preparations for her parents' return to their farm. While she was there, she was threatened by several of her neighbors. The WRA and the army arranged for the medal presentation and a rally to demonstrate that threats and intimidation were not acceptable.

The medal presentation ceremony itself was simple. According to the *Times*, "there was no fanfare." Stilwell arrived at the farm and, "after the reading of the citation, he conferred the military decoration on the Nisei's sister Mary." Stilwell told Masuda, "I've seen a good deal of the Nisei in service and never yet have I found one of them who didn't do his duty right up to the handle. The Distinguished Service Cross in itself is a small thing, but since it stands for gallantry in action, I hope you and your family will remember that Sgt. Masuda, in winning it, has also won the respect and admiration of all real Americans." Masuda, "struggling to keep back the tears," said to the general, "in accepting this distinction for my brother, I know that he would want me to say that he was only doing his duty as a soldier of our beloved country."[172] After the medal presentation, Stilwell spoke at a United America Day rally at the Santa Ana Municipal Bowl. At the rally, Stilwell said that "the amount of money, the color of one's skin . . . do not make a measure of Americanism. A square deal all around; free speech; equality before the law; a fair field with no favor; obedience to the majority;—an American not only believes in such things, but he is willing to fight for them." Stilwell then asked and answered the question, "Who, after all, is the real American? The real American is the man who calls it a fair exchange to lay down his life in order that American ideals may go on living. And judging by such a test, Sgt. Masuda was a better American than any of us here today." Stilwell was joined on the dais at the rally by three Hollywood celebrities. One of them, the thirty-four-year-old Hollywood actor Ronald Reagan, told the audience that "blood that has soaked into the sands of a beach is all of one color. America stands unique in the world, the only country not founded on race, but on a way—an ideal. Not in spite of, but because of our polyglot background, we have had all the strength in the world. That is the American way."[173]

At the end of 1945 Tajiri declared that "the long day of the Jap-baiter in California politics appears to have ended. For two generations the Yellow Peril has been a standard fixture in the political campaigns of the Land of the Native Sons but as things stand today the 'Japanese issue' is dead and the demagogues of 1946 will manage to work themselves into hysteria about other questions." Tajiri noted that "it is significant that Governor Earl Warren, whose political shrewdness is attested to by his opponents, has maintained a hands-off policy on matters regarding Japanese Americans, in sharp contrast to his behavior before 1944."[174]

The 1946 elections suggest that Tajiri's interpretation was accurate. No longer would anti-Japanese leaders gain much support in California politics. Although the advocates of fair play, which by 1945 included most WRA officials and many army officers, had largely discredited the anti-Japanese movement, however, they had not eliminated all racial prejudice and discrimination. The debate about the meanings of "race" continued throughout 1946.

SEVEN

"A Group of Termites Indoctrinated with an Atheistic, Totalitarian Foreign Ideology"

The Cold War and the Transformation of the "Battle for Los Angeles"

In the fall of 1945 the Los Angeles City Council considered the possibility of creating an Interracial Relations Committee. The proposal's sponsors envisioned a committee that would work to end discrimination in housing, recreation, education, and employment. Supporters also wanted the committee to engage in educational activities that would "lead to better interracial understanding and relations." Controversy immediately engulfed the proposal. At the city council meeting at which the proposal first surfaced, council member Lloyd Davies insisted that passage of the proposed ordinance would "create riots and more race discrimination."[1] Opponents of the proposed committee also claimed that its supporters wanted to eliminate restrictive covenants.[2] At a crowded hearing, city council members heard from both supporters and opponents of the proposed committee. Supporters of the ordinance included representatives of the African American community, several religious organizations, including the Church Federation of Los Angeles, and the Council for Civic Unity. They argued that the city needed the proposed committee to solve its interracial problems. The opponents of the proposal were mostly involved in real estate. They argued that "racial problems would work themselves out if they were not stirred up by politically interested groups." One opponent asserted that the "elimination of restrictive covenants would result in a 50 per cent reduction in real estate values and materially reduce tourist trade." At the end of the hearing, the council agreed unanimously to postpone consideration of the ordinance for two weeks.[3]

In the two weeks between the hearing and the city council's final consideration of the ordinance, proponents and opponents of the measure put their opinions before the public. In a long letter to the editor of the *Los Angeles Times*, Los Angeles attorney William C. Ring insisted that the ordinance was unneeded because no one in Los Angeles faced discrimination. Ring denied the existence of discrimination in every imaginable area—employment, politics, education, recreation, and "war," which he lumped together with education and recreation. "Jewish, Latin and Negro" children "intermingle indiscriminately in school, sports and war with those of other races," he wrote. Ring argued that Los Angeles, as a part of the United States, was a "free market," in which all people "are free to embrace the religion, join the political parties and engage in the professions and vocations of their choices." He declared that "free enterprise under our capitalistic system of fair competition draws no creed or racial lines." The success of Jewish people and "our Latin neighbors" proved that they did not face employment discrimination, Ring insisted. "The Jewish people operate most of our mercantile and small loan businesses, entertainment, theatrical and cinema enterprises," and "our Latin neighbors are traditionally imaginative, ingenious, energetic and thrifty and own some of the largest operations in the State," he wrote. Ring acknowledged that African Americans had not been as successful as "the Jewish people" and "our Latin neighbors," but he argued that any difficulties faced by African Americans were not the result of discrimination but of "the handicaps of illiteracy and a sense of dependency, resultant from slavery." Despite these handicaps, Ring suggested, African Americans had already begun to reap the benefits of the free market. He praised African Americans' advancement by stating that "no other race in history has so remarkably advanced in culture, science and private economy in so short a time." In the salubrious climate of the free market, Ring argued, "Jewish people have learned to do some things better than others. So have colored people. So have Latins. So have all Americans." The proposed ordinance, he claimed, would rob each group of the fruits of its labors.

Ring admitted that there were bigots who "prate the heresy of superior races," but he suggested that these "distasteful" people were not organized and had little or no influence over public policy. Legislative action would not change the minds of these bigots, Ring argued. Instead, virtuous behavior on the part of minority groups and competition among groups would convince bigots to abandon their heretical beliefs. Any legislative action would simply deprive Americans of "the opportunity afforded by life to enable men to emancipate themselves from their delusions, false beliefs and conceptions."

In defending the "color-blind" operation of the free market, Ring insisted that Communists wanted to interfere with the market. He accused the supporters of the ordinance of being Communists or "Red sympathizers" who wanted to capitalize on the "error" of bigotry "to exact the usury of organized evil." According to Ring, the Communists' "strategy would incite the descendants of all races and groups against each other until government becomes impossible without a dictator." Ring suggested that the debate about the proposed ordinance was part of a larger struggle that "involves precisely the same issue that Jesus, Washington, Lincoln and every great liberator of mankind faced in the great crisis of history. It is the eternal conflict between the flesh against the spirit; mob rule against free government; collectivist might against personal liberty; falsehood against truth."[4]

One week after Ring's letter appeared in the *Times*, the newspaper published a response from E. C. Farnham, the chair of the Council for Civic Unity. Farnham challenged the assumptions upon which Ring's arguments rested. He criticized Ring for dragging "the red herring of Communism and Fascism across the trail of a well-intended proposal." Farnham pointed out that the Council for Civic Unity was "opposed to both Communism and Fascism," and he stated that both of these ideologies "flourish where there is injustice." Farnham rejected Ring's argument that bigots were not organized or influential. Farnham insisted that "those with experience are only too well aware of vicious propagandistic activities to stir up race prejudice and antagonism." Farnham also took issue with Ring's interpretation of the proposed interracial committee. Ring had suggested that the committee would simply promote "racial tolerance." Farnham pointed out that "tolerance, at best, is a grudging attitude. It is not a final solution." He stated that the supporters of the proposed ordinance hoped that the new committee "can and will promote justice. This involves such matters as decent housing, fair opportunity for work and security, educational and cultural opportunities, and social appreciation." If relations between the majority and minority groups continued to be characterized by injustice, "our great metropolitan centers will be continuous tension centers, with increasing trouble," Farnham predicted. Farnham argued that Ring's insistence that "'merit and virtue' alone on the part of the underprivileged" would ease social tensions reflected "naivete or ignorance of the true conditions." These tensions were "largely due to the thoughtless traditionalism of the majority groups," Farnham insisted. "Majority groups must have the will to do justice and must deal with the real problems with knowledge and thought."[5]

Two days after Farnham's letter appeared in the *Times*, the city council returned to the proposal. At its meeting the council heard from opponents who restated Ring's arguments. Dr. Althea Briggs expressed bluntly her faith in "free market" ideology. Any effort to stifle competition among different groups of Americans, Briggs said, would represent an effort to "mollycoddle" African Americans.[6] City council member Charles A. Allen said that he was "convinced that this is a Communistic setup and that the fine people who have been associated with the effort have been misled."[7] The city council refused to pass the proposed ordinance.

The debate surrounding this proposed ordinance, particularly the letters by Ring and Farnham, suggests how the "race war" in Los Angeles changed after the end of World War II. Both the supporters and the opponents of the ordinance insisted that racial discrimination was undesirable. Supporters of the ordinance, such as Farnham, however, took for granted that African Americans, Mexican Americans, and Asian Americans in Los Angeles had all faced and continued to face discrimination. Their opponents, on the other hand, argued that members of these groups did not face discrimination. Instead, if they had not achieved material success equal to that of people of European ancestry, it was the result of deficiencies stemming from immigration or slavery. The opponents of the ordinance also interpreted legislative efforts to address racial tension as attempts to force bigots to become tolerant. Supporters of the ordinance, on the other hand, insisted that they were not trying to eliminate prejudice. Instead, their goals were to replace discrimination with justice. Finally, opponents of the ordinance argued that its supporters were either members of the Communist party or people who had been misled by Communists. The city council's rejection of the proposed ordinance demonstrates that opponents of racial discrimination, who had gained some powerful allies in their campaign for "fair play" for Japanese Americans, had not succeeded in their efforts to change many local, state, or federal policies.

In late 1945 and throughout 1946, opponents of racial discrimination continued to attack policies and practices whose supporters defended both as the natural social order and their rights as citizens. The newspaper articles and editorials about these struggles reveal how the end of World War II affected the ongoing debate about the meaning of "race." This chapter will examine those articles and editorials. It will argue that the end of the war limited the ability of opponents of racial prejudice and discrimination to challenge further the language—and the underlying ideology—employed by those who defended traditional beliefs and practices. During the war these opponents of discrimination had argued that World War II was a war against Hitler's racial ideology and for democracy. Their emphasis on the need for wartime unity seems to have led some people to disavow publicly racial discrimination and the belief that "race" made some people criminals. There appears to have been sufficient agreement among many public officials and newspaper editors and publishers that some statements did too closely resemble Hitler's words. By the fall of 1945, however, Hitler had been defeated. It was possible for some people to argue that national unity was no longer an urgent necessity. Moreover, by 1946 attention had shifted away from the need for unity to defeat Hitler and the Japanese militarists and toward the need for unity to confront and perhaps defeat Communism as embodied by the Soviet Union. Anti-Communism had never been suppressed forcibly during the war, but the words of anti-Communists were more subdued than they had been before the war and than they would be after the war. When the war ended and the relationship between the United States and the Soviet Union became characterized by growing tension, the defenders of the old racial order were able to employ a strategy in which they agreed in principle with their opponents but then attacked all of their policy proposals as "Communist-inspired" or disruptive. This rhetorical strategy allowed the beneficiaries of discrimination to continue to benefit from discrimination without having to defend themselves from the accusation that they were engaging in discrimination. In late 1945 and throughout 1946 the debates about "race" in Los Angeles focused on restrictive covenants, the revival of the Ku Klux Klan, and two propositions that appeared on the ballot in November 1946.[8]

Restrictive Covenants

As the war ended and members of minority groups sought to find housing wherever it was available, many European Americans organized and took action to prevent anyone but "Caucasians" from moving into many neighborhoods. Although most of the legal and extralegal actions taken by supporters of residential segregation were aimed at African Americans, some cases also involved Chinese Americans, Japanese Americans, and Korean Americans.[9] The opponents of racial discrimination did not choose to attack restrictive covenants—the deed restrictions that prevented African Americans, Mexican Americans, Asian Americans, and Jewish Americans from occupying houses in large portions of the city and county of Los Angeles. Instead, the campaign against restrictive covenants was largely a defensive struggle. African Americans and Asian Americans were always the defendants in suits filed by supporters of residential segregation.[10]

From the fall of 1945 until the election of 1946, when this study ends, Los Angeles newspapers published a number of articles about the conflict over restrictive covenants. Most of these articles appeared in the city's African American newspapers. On occasion, however, daily newspapers reported on the decisions in some of these cases. The fact that the daily newspapers, especially the *Times* and the *Examiner*, devoted little attention to the struggle over restrictive covenants deserves closer scrutiny. These newspapers were active participants in the other episodes examined in this book. They allowed some Japanese Americans to express themselves after Pearl Harbor, and they offered a platform for anti-Japanese leaders who called for the incarceration and removal of Japanese Americans from the coastal areas. The *Times* and the *Examiner* themselves published editorials supporting this course of action. The newspapers publicized the activities of "zoot-suit gangs" and editorialized about this phenomenon. They also reported on the riots and argued forcefully that they were not "race riots." The fact that they did not publish editorials defending restrictive covenants seems to suggest that overt statements defending racial discrimination had become less acceptable by late 1945 than they had been a few years earlier. The fact that they did not editorialize against covenants, however, seems to suggest that housing discrimination had not become any less desirable for those people who felt that they derived benefits from it. Moreover, the lack of coverage in the daily newspapers continued a trend—evident in the grand jury's investigation following the riots—of silencing African Americans. The *Times* and the *Examiner* rarely allowed African Americans to speak for themselves in news articles.

The daily newspapers' lack of attention to restrictive covenants also reflects the fact that people who encouraged European American property owners to use restrictive covenants and those who filed suit to enforce restrictive covenants made relatively few public statements about their actions. Some, like the realtor who spoke before the city council against the ordinance that would have created an interracial relations committee, simply asserted that property values would plummet if neighborhoods were integrated.[11] For the most part, however, supporters of restrictive covenants worked outside public view. They held meetings in private homes and meeting halls in which they promoted the use of covenants and plotted their legal strategy to preserve racial segregation. They were careful not to seek widespread publicity.[12] This seems to reflect a change in the debates about "race." Public statements in favor of discrimination had become increasingly unacceptable. Instead, the supporters of discrimination went door-to-door to encourage their neighbors to join their efforts.[13] Even the articles in the African American newspapers about the lawsuits filed by property owners seeking to enforce restrictive covenants rarely mentioned any arguments made by people who filed the suits.

The articles in the African American newspapers reveal that the struggle over restrictive covenants was part of the larger debate about the meaning of "race." The attorneys who represented the defendants in restrictive covenant cases and the journalists who reported on these cases emphasized that the deed restrictions rested on outmoded assumptions about "race." The African American attorney Loren Miller represented many African American defendants in a number of covenant cases. One of the most notable involved wealthy African Americans—including Hollywood actors Louise Beavers and

Hattie McDaniel—who had purchased homes in the fashionable "Sugar Hill" neighborhood. This neighborhood was bounded on the east by LaSalle Avenue, on the west by Western Avenue, on the north by Washington Boulevard, and on the south by Adams Boulevard. The case was ultimately decided by the California Supreme Court. In the trial in the superior court in Los Angeles, Miller argued that the covenants on the property were "based on the theory that only persons whose 'blood is entirely of the white race' may occupy property in the restricted area." He attacked this theory, arguing that "most scientists agree it is impossible to tell whether any given person's blood is 'pure' and unmixed in this day and age."[14]

When the Sugar Hill case was appealed to the California Supreme Court, Miller and his co-counsel, Harold J. Sinclair, also argued that covenants violated the United Nations Charter and the state and federal constitutions. In their brief Miller and Sinclair argued that "enforcement of the covenant would deprive Negro home owners of their property without due process of law and would deprive them equal protection of the law as provided in the Fourteenth Amendment and similar clauses in the State constitution."[15] California Attorney General Robert W. Kenny also argued that governments were violating the Fourteenth Amendment to the Constitution when they enforced restrictive covenants.[16]

The Sugar Hill case represented a great victory for the opponents of racial discrimination. In December 1945 Superior Court Judge Thurmond Clarke ruled in favor of the Sugar Hill defendants. Clarke's decision declared that the restrictive covenants on the Sugar Hill property were unconstitutional because they denied "to colored citizens of this state the equal protection of the laws."[17] Clarke also stated that "it is time that members of the Negro race be granted their full constitutional rights without evasion."[18] The judges who ruled in favor of the defendants in restrictive covenant cases, however, usually did not comment on the constitutionality of restrictive covenants or on the subject of racial ideology. For example, Superior Court Judge Frank M. Smith decided that an African American surgeon, Dr. Welles E. Forde, could live in the home he had purchased. Although Loren Miller had appealed to the United Nations Charter in his argument before the court, Judge Smith did not mention the charter or the U.S. Constitution in his decision. Instead, as the *Times* reported, he ruled that, "inasmuch as non-Caucasians, including Japanese, already are living in the section, the agreements were void."[19]

A number of judges explicitly rejected the idea that covenants were unconstitutional or in conflict with federal policies. Superior Court Judge Carl A. Stutsman, for example, rejected the argument that "race covenants were invalid under the constitution." Stutsman issued an injunction that prevented Mr. and Mrs. Henry C. Hutchins from occupying their home on west Fifty-sixth Street.[20] Superior Court Judge Joseph W. Vickers also ruled that "restrictions of this character are valid and not against public policy." Vickers issued an injunction to prevent two African American families from occupying homes they had purchased on Fifty-fifth Street.[21]

The most dramatic case in which a judge rejected the arguments of the opponents of racial discrimination involved Henry and Anna Laws. In November 1945 Superior Court Judge Allen W. Ashburn ruled that the Lawses' occupancy of their home on East Ninety-second Street violated a restrictive covenant and ordered them to vacate their home.[22] Ashburn's decision drew fire from opponents of restrictive covenants. The *Eagle* reported that Judge Ashburn ordered the family out of their home "after listening to a plea that would have stirred the sympathetic emotions of Hitler." This plea, however, left Ashburn "unmoved." The *Eagle* urged "every red-blooded American, of whatever racial extraction," to appear in Ashburn's courtroom "and by their presence, demonstrate that they disapprove the decision of this judge."[23]

In defending the Lawses, opponents of racial discrimination did not simply connect covenants with Hitler's racial ideology or argue that deed restrictions violated the U.S. Constitution. They also offered testimony from European Americans that challenged the idea that African Americans' "racial" characteristics made them undesirable neighbors. One article about the Laws family, for example, reported that the family's neighbors "have no objections to living as neighbors to a Negro family." Mrs. Foster, who lived next door to the Laws family, told the *Eagle* that "I would much rather have Negro neighbors than to see these dirty lots. In fact I would rather we had no restrictions in this tract." Mrs. Fowler, who lived on the other side of the Laws family, said that "the Laws are very good neighbors, as friendly and congenial as anyone could wish neighbors to be."[24]

The opponents of restrictive covenants also depicted the supporters of covenants as greedy. In one article, for example, the *California Eagle* reported that the family of Henry and Anna Laws had lived in their home without incident for more than two years. Then, however, "a couple of real

FIG. 21. *Demonstrators protest the jailing of Henry and Anna Laws in December 1945. The Lawses were jailed when they refused to obey a court order and leave their home, which was covered by a restrictive covenant preventing African Americans from occupying the property.* Los Angeles Daily News *Photographs (Collection 1386), Department of Special Collections, Charles E. Young Research Library, University of California, Los Angeles.*

estate hogs, seeing an opportunity to profit" from the housing shortage, "dug up an ancient restricted covenant on the Laws property, started agitation among some of the neighbors, and the Laws family was hauled into court to show cause why they should not be thrown out of their home."[25]

The conflict over restrictive covenants grew more intense when the Lawses decided to defy the court order and refused to leave their home. They were cited for contempt of court and were jailed on December 15, 1945.[26] The incarceration of Henry and Anna Laws sparked a demonstration and a mass meeting by the opponents of restrictive covenants.[27]

While the Lawses were in jail, a group that included Charlotta Bass and Rev. Clayton Russell visited the judge and asked him to release the Lawses. The protests and requests had no impact on Ashburn, who stated: "if I had the power to grant relief in these circumstances, I don't believe this is the proper case for it. I believe the Laws are guilty of contempt. I am satisfied the judgment of contempt is correct. It is the court's duty to see that the lawful orders of the court are obeyed." He added, "when the day comes that a court hasn't the courage to carry out its democratic responsibilities it will be a sorry day for democracy."[28] The Laws family was released from jail after five days.[29]

The articles about these court cases suggest how the debate about the meaning of "race" changed as a result of the end of World War II. Attorneys who represented the defendants in restrictive covenant cases argued that the deed restrictions reflected an outmoded racial ideology and violated the U.S. Constitution and international agreements. Some judges agreed. Other judges, however, were unmoved by comparisons between U.S. racial ideology and Hitler's beliefs about "race." This comparison seems to have lost some of its power after Hitler had been defeated.

The fact that the debate about restrictive covenants was largely a debate about the actions of judges and courts reveals to some extent why the opponents of racial discrimination often found it difficult to change government policies. In these cases judges did not have to address the relationship between racial ideology and restrictive covenants. Many judges sidestepped this issue in their rulings. Moreover, plaintiffs in these cases had an advantage over the opponents of racial discrimination, because the opponents of racial covenants had to defend themselves while at the same time arguing that the established social order was unjust and should be changed.

The Ku Klux Klan Returns

The debates surrounding housing discrimination became more charged in the spring and summer of 1946, when flaming crosses appeared on the lawns of African Americans and the letters "KKK" were burned into lawns and chalked and painted on sidewalks and the walls of houses. When these incidents first began, public officials and community leaders agreed that they represented a serious threat to the city. Within a few weeks, however, law enforcement officials and some elected officials began to express doubts about the existence of the Klan. As the following paragraphs will suggest, the cross burnings and defacing of property allowed the opponents of racial prejudice and discrimination to argue that prejudice and discrimination continued to constitute serious threats to law-abiding citizens. By arguing that reports of Klan activities were unsubstantiated or exaggerated, public officials suggested that racial prejudice and discrimination were not serious problems in Los Angeles.

When the cross burnings began, opponents of discrimination sponsored mass meetings and called upon elected officials to take action to suppress the organization.[30] Many opponents of discrimination interpreted the cross burnings and similar actions as efforts to strengthen residential segregation. The Home Owner's Defense Council, an organization associated with the *Los Angeles Sentinel*, for example, argued that "subversive groups" were "joining with other forces in an attempt to uphold restrictive covenants and agreements."[31]

Officials at first expressed concern about the appearance of the Klan. In April 1946, for example, California Attorney General Robert W. Kenny began investigating Klan activity after a cross burning occurred at Big Bear Lake in San Bernardino County.[32] Kenny's anti-Klan efforts received support from Los Angeles County Sheriff Eugene W. Biscailuz and District Attorney Fred Howser. In words that suggest that some elected officials had come to accept the argument that the war was against Hitler's racial ideology, Biscailuz said, "I believe it is to be especially regretted that the Klan movements should be undertaken at a time when the entire world is trying to recover from the wounds caused by bigotry and intolerance." Howser said that "the Ku Klux Klan has no place in our present day life.... If the Klan had its way there would be no district attorney's office nor the orderly processes of justice. Their method of singling out individuals and groups to terrorize cannot and will not be condoned by any conscientious

American citizen."[33] At an anti-Klan rally in April 1946 a representative of the district attorney's office declared that "many of our boys gave their lives to destroy the principles upon which the Ku Klux Klan operates, and we are not going to let them operate."[34] Kenny's anti-Klan efforts culminated in May 1946, when the attorney general demonstrated to the satisfaction of a superior court judge that the Klan had violated its charter. The judge's ruling effectively outlawed the Klan in California.[35] African American newspapers applauded Kenny's actions. The daily newspapers reported briefly that the Klan had been outlawed. The *Times*, for example, published a three-paragraph notice of this development.

In May Los Angeles Mayor Fletcher Bowron declared that cross burning "is not only abhorrent to any good American, but likely to lead into something far more serious." Bowron insisted that "no one is going to take the law into his own hands, stir up race prejudice or strike fear into the hearts of law abiding citizens of Los Angeles." Bowron promised that the police would take action to prevent further cross burnings, and the city council unanimously adopted a resolution "calling on law enforcement agencies to exercise diligence in prosecution of fiery cross burners."[36]

Some opponents of discrimination applauded the actions of elected officials but warned that the Klan's "bid for power cannot be defeated by punitive measure alone." The *Los Angeles Sentinel* argued that minority groups, labor unions, "and other democratic minded Americans" needed to challenge the Klan with strong support for "full employment legislation, a housing plan that will provide shelter for all, extension of social security measures, adequate old age pensions and increased veterans' benefits." According to the *Sentinel*, the success of such a legislative agenda would undercut the discontent on which "the Klan racket thrives."[37]

Although elected officials initially expressed alarm about evidence of Klan activity, some law enforcement officers expressed doubt that the Klan was responsible for cross burnings. After a cross was burned on the lawn of Mr. and Mrs. H. G. Hickerson of 134 West Fifty-sixth Street in May 1946, for example, the *Sentinel* reported that "police who appeared after Hickerson had extinguished the fire, seemed inclined to belittle the incident ... as the work of children or pranksters."[38] After the cross was burned, the Hickersons received a threatening letter. The letter said that "there's a place for colored folk, but not among whites—so get out before you get blown out and don't ever try to move into a white district again." The letter claimed that "you're getting just what you deserved for trying to mess round white people; I am not a KKK but if this is the only way you colored folks can get a lesson, I say more power to the Klan." J. L. Feinfeldt, the attorney representing the European Americans who had filed suit to evict the Hickersons from their home, told the *Sentinel* that he believed that the Hickersons and other African Americans had burned the cross "to create sympathy."[39]

By June 1946 some elected officials had begun to express doubts about the existence of the Klan in Los Angeles. Mayor Fletcher Bowron said that "the police so far have no information which could lead to the arrest of any persons responsible for the Klan terror acts."[40] In a revealing statement, the mayor also suggested that opposition to racial prejudice was equivalent to racial prejudice itself. The mayor told a group of anti-Klan activists that "we can't investigate people just because they're prejudiced. Why, you people here are prejudiced—against the Klan."[41] Bowron's statement elicited criticism from a number of opponents of discrimination, including William R. Bidner, the executive director of Mobilization for Democracy. This organization emerged from rallies and conferences in the summer of 1945. The organizers of Mobilization for Democracy included CIO State President Philip M. Connelly, G. Raymond Booth of the Council for Civic Unity, NAACP President Thomas L. Griffith, Jr., and Carey McWilliams.[42] Bidner called Bowron's statement a "contemptible attempt to cover up the police department's failure to solve Klan terror cases."[43] The American Civil Liberties Union, which posted a five-hundred-dollar reward for information about the cross burnings, insisted that the "reports that there has been a resurgence of the Ku Klux Klan" were "well-founded."[44]

A former police officer whose front walk was painted with the letters "KKK" also rejected the notion that "young pranksters" were responsible. "I don't believe it was a prank. I think this is the real thing," Homer L. Garrott said.[45] "I have had some experience in the police department. I was in the department for 27 years, and was a captain with the Newton street Detective Bureau. If I had thought the KKKs were child's play, I would not have called the police," Garrott told the *Sentinel*. Garrott also said that he believed that the act was related to efforts of "certain real estate interests" to restrict residence in the area in which he lived to European Americans.[46] The *Sentinel* compared the police response to acts of violence and intimidation to Mayor Bowron's slow response to the Zoot-Suit Riots in 1943. Because of Bowron's refusal to respond forcefully to the rioting, the *Sentinel* said, "a disgraceful episode that could have been halted in a few hours with a little firmness and with little or no damage dragged out until Los Angeles was held up to ridicule before the whole country." The newspaper warned that "the do-nothing attitude that the mayor and the city administration have assumed in reference to Klan antics are going to have the same untoward results. Nothing very serious has happened thus far and it is easy to laugh the whole thing off as the work of crack pots." The *Sentinel* predicted that "these crackpots are going to grow bolder with time and citizens, unable to get police protection, are going to get it into their heads that their only safety lies in counter measures and when that happens there is going to be trouble."[47] The *Eagle* reported as early as April 1946 that at least one officer of the Los Angeles Police Department was an organizer for the Klan.[48] In May 1946 the *Eagle* reported that Sheriff Biscailuz had taken action to dismiss a deputy who was "a close associate of Rev. Wesley A. Smith," a noted Klan leader based in Lancaster. Although opponents of prejudice and discrimination had urged the sheriff to fire the deputy for his association with the Klan, the sheriff reportedly took action after the deputy failed to report for duty.[49] In June the *B'nai B'rith Messenger* suggested in an editorial that the Los Angeles Police Department may not have identified any suspects in the Klan cases because some police officers were members of the Klan and were protecting the organization.[50]

Although most opponents of racial discrimination criticized Bowron's statement and the police department, the *Los Angeles Tribune* noted in an editorial that it agreed with the Los Angeles Police Department that there was "no evidence directly implicating the Klan." However, the *Tribune* stated, "unlike the police, we are not willing to scoff at the situation that has been created, nor to ignore the threat of serious danger to unprotected citizens." The *Tribune* recommended that "the department probe each KKK incident as thoroughly as if it had a first class murder mystery on its hands. It has every right to question and search residents in the vicinity of the outrages; and it has grounds in the fact that the victims generally are the objects of a race hate campaign to evict them from their homes."[51]

In September Bowron denied that there had been any "authentic instances of Ku Klux Klan activity in recent months." Bowron challenged Attorney General Robert W. Kenny to prove that the Klan had been active in Los Angeles and other parts of southern California. Bowron insisted that the police had thoroughly investigated "every one of the so-called Ku Klux

Klan incidents" and had found no evidence of "authentic Klan activity." Bowron reported that some of the incidents were "the work of pranksters," some of whom were juveniles, and he insisted that "in most instances the statements have not only been exaggerated but the facts deliberately misstated."[52]

Although Bowron doubted the existence of the Klan, some Los Angeles residents expressed support for the Klan and its activities. Some also insisted that they saw the Klan as an organization that could defend the United States and its residents from the threat of Communism. In June 1946, for example, Charlotta A. Bass published a letter she had received from Jennie Wainsworth of Los Angeles. Wainsworth was responding to a column in which Bass had asked "who is the enemy of the peace—the so-called 'Reds' or the Ku Klux Klan." Wainsworth wrote, "personally, I feel the Klan is doing a d— fine job of keeping you Negroes in your place." Wainsworth agreed with Rev. Jonathan Elsworth Perkins, who had recently spoken in Los Angeles. Perkins had told his audience that African Americans "were set apart and branded by God. It is wrong and sinful of us to mix with them." Wainsworth warned Bass, "don't you realize that your insistence to be placed on a basis of equality with white people in the United States will lead to the same fate experienced by the Jews in Germany?"[53]

In the same issue, the *Eagle* reported on Perkins's speech at the Embassy Auditorium. The article noted that "Perkins prefaced his remarks by telling how many friends he has among the Negroes, and what a great contribution the Negro race has made to the musical world through the Negro spirituals." Perkins continued, however, by insisting that "something has happened to the Negroes in America. They are turning toward Communism. They are going Red." In insisting that "God Almighty" had made "the Negro race" different from "the white race," Perkins dwelled on physical characteristics. "The Negro's skull is thicker. His lips are thicker, his hair is different, and he has different characteristics altogether." Perkins also referred to Communists as "Red crawling maggots that are infesting the body politic of America."[54]

Wainsworth's letter to Bass and the *Eagle*'s article about Perkins's speech help to illuminate the changes that were occurring in the debates about "race" in Los Angeles after the war. They expose the continued existence of people who insisted without apology that "racial" differences were created by "God Himself." Their voices were not commonly heard in the public debates about "race," for, as William Ring suggested in his letter to the *Times*, their statements were distasteful. When they were heard, these voices were usually amplified by people like Bass who opposed them. In a way, then, this seems to have lent credence to the statements of people such as Bowron, who were able to point out that opponents of discrimination kept drawing attention to the acts and words of these "racists." They suggested that these voices were marginal and would not have been heard by anyone if the opponents of discrimination had not allowed them access to the public debates about "race." Bass and other opponents of discrimination suggested that the ideas expressed by Wainwright and Perkins were the same ideas upon which discrimination rested. By suggesting that Wainwright and Perkins were marginal, however, some public officials ended up obscuring any possible ideological connections between these vocal racists and the quiet supporters of restrictive covenants and other existing patterns of discrimination.

In October 1946 State Senator Jack B. Tenney's Joint Legislative Committee on Un-American Activities initiated an investigation into Klan activities.[55] State Attorney General Robert W. Kenny told the committee that the Klan had engaged in violent acts and that its membership was growing. Four law enforcement officials, including Chief of Police C. B. Horrall, however, told the committee that "the Klan was not to blame in a single instance investigated." Tenney himself suggested that Communists had used reports of Klan activity to attract African Americans and Jews to the party.[56]

Even in reporting on the testimony of former Kleagle Ray J. Schneider, the *Times* and the *Examiner* downplayed the possibility that the Klan was a violent organization whose members continued to meet even after the organization had been outlawed by the state. Both newspapers reported that Schneider denied that the Klan had been involved with the cross burnings and other acts of vandalism in the spring and summer of 1946. They also noted that Schneider told the committee that former Klan members continued to meet in "Hearts and Hands" clubs. The *Times* made the Klan seem less threatening than it might have otherwise been by reporting that "Schneider raised a fuss at the beginning of his testimony because there was no Bible on which to swear." The *Times* also noted that Schneider's "sallies caused smiles to break across even the dour faces of the Communist-inclined members of the audience."[57] The *Daily News*, by contrast, depicted the Klan as more threatening than the other newspapers. According to the

FIG. 22. *Former Kleagle Ray Schneider in a Klan uniform. Although many public officials and law enforcement officers dismissed evidence of the Klan's revival in Los Angeles in 1946, the* Daily News *reported that Schneider told the Tenney Committee that "you cannot stop them, any way you try to do it."* Los Angeles Daily News *Photographs (Collection 1386), Department of Special Collections, Charles E. Young Research Library, University of California, Los Angeles.*

Daily News, Schneider "told the names of several past Klan officers, but refused to identify any current ones. The ones he gave, he said, were already publicly known, but his Klan oath forbade him to name other members." The *Daily News* also reported that Schneider told the committee, "you cannot stop them, any way you try to do it."[58]

At the same time as the Tenney Committee conducted its investigation, some members of the Los Angeles City Council suggested that people who demanded an investigation of the Klan rather than the Klan itself should be investigated. Council member Lloyd G. Davies, apparently relying upon the police chief's testimony before the Tenney Committee, reported to his colleagues that the police had determined that a member of Mobilization for Democracy was responsible for a cross burning.[59] Two other council members, L. E. Timberlake and Harold Harby, claimed that Davies had misrepresented the police chief's words and accused Davies of "dictatorial operation of a city council committee." A majority of council members, however, agreed with Davies that the council should not investigate Klan activities.[60]

In the year following the end of World War II, then, opponents of racial prejudice and discrimination had continued their efforts to connect restrictive covenants with Hitler's racial ideology and had argued that the appearance of Klan symbols in Los Angeles represented a serious social problem. They had convinced some judges to reject restrictive covenants, but many judges refused to accept their argument that covenants constituted illegal discrimination. At first many elected officials agreed with the opponents of prejudice and discrimination about the Klan. Within a few weeks, however, some elected officials publicly expressed doubts about the existence of the Klan. Some of these officials, such as State Sen. Jack B. Tenney, argued that Communism represented a much greater social problem than the Klan. The arguments about restrictive covenants and the Klan seem to suggest that the changes in the debates about the meaning of race that had occurred during the war had slowed or shifted afterward.

The November 1946 Election: Proposition 15

The "battle for Los Angeles" that began in 1941 culminated in the election of November 1946. For African Americans, Mexican Americans, and Asian Americans, the struggle against discrimination, of course, would continue. This struggle, however, would take place in a political environment that had been transformed by the conflicts between proponents of modernist racial ideology and their opponents. The debates surrounding the election reveal the degree to which wartime struggles over racial prejudice and discrimination had transformed the terms of further conflict over racial ideology. People on both sides of the issues in the 1946 election agreed that racial prejudice and discrimination were undemocratic and "un-American." This did not mean, however, that everybody embraced government action to eradicate discrimination. Instead, defenders of the status quo developed a number of arguments to explain how such governmental action would undermine other cherished rights and liberties. Moreover, even as defenders of existing policies and practices agreed that discrimination was undesirable, none explicitly argued that "racial" differences were superficial.

Some Los Angeles residents recognized that the November 1946 election would be a referendum on "the race issue." An editorial in the *Daily News*, for example, stated that Californians would have to "stand up and be counted on the race issue Nov. 5." The *Daily News* sided unequivocally with the opponents of prejudice and discrimination. Its editorial pointed out that "many people are a bit uneasy about their racial prejudices." On some level, the editorial suggested, they knew that "race is only an abstract image, the existence of which does not lie outside our brain." Because they had been taught since childhood "to classify human beings and set up arbitrary categories between them," however, "many folks just can't help reacting to their 'brothers under the skin' as if the latter were a species somewhat less than human." The editorial firmly embraced the goal of a "color-blind" society, stating that "building a society in which a man will no longer be classified by the color of his skin is the everlasting hope of those who want a better America and a better world." At the same time, like many opponents of legislation designed to create such a society, the *Daily News* argued that "we can't create such a society by law." If such a "color-blind" society were to emerge, it would "become a reality when the children who are to become the citizens of tomorrow can have a chance to grow to adulthood free of the superstition, ignorance and fear today's adults, in their childhood, had imposed upon them." After seeming to oppose legislative efforts to create a "color-blind" society, the *Daily News* insisted that "all of this does not mean the legislative contribution to racial justice should be ignored. Humane legislation can set the pattern. It can become a social lodestar, the far, glimmering light by which we fix our course and steer toward happier horizons." The *Daily News* implied that its readers should vote against "expressions against species or races or ethnic groups" and in favor of "expressions of the unity of humankind."[61]

Two of the propositions on the November 1946 ballot—Propositions 11 and 15—pertained directly to racial prejudice and discrimination. Proposition 15 was the earlier of these measures. As mentioned in the previous chapter, it originated in the summer of 1945, when state senators Jack B. Tenney of Los Angeles and Hugh Burns of Fresno proposed allowing California's voters to validate several of the legislature's amendments to the state's Alien Land Law. The legislature supported the proposal and placed the measure on the ballot. By the time of the election, Japanese Americans were no longer at the center of debates about race in Los Angeles. Proposition 15 generated considerable debate in the Central Valley and in the San Francisco Bay Area, but it received much less attention in Los Angeles. Tenney, one of the measure's sponsors, did not campaign actively for the measure. Neither the *Los Angeles Examiner* nor the *Los Angeles Times* published an editorial about the measure.

Even though the *Times* and the *Examiner* did not consider Proposition 15 worthy of attention, the Japanese American Citizens League and some of its allies waged an aggressive campaign against the measure.[62] Opponents of the measure offered several different arguments against Proposition 15. On one occasion the JACL attacked Proposition 15 on technical grounds. The JACL argued that the proposition was ambiguous and stated that "no voter should be asked to vote on a noticeably ambiguous amendment to the State Constitution."[63] Some of the measure's opponents argued that Proposition 15 represented an effort by greedy farmers to eliminate competition from Japanese American farmers and to acquire land already improved by Japanese Americans. In an editorial against Proposition 15, for example, the *Daily News* suggested that the measure might be "motivated by a desire to freeze minority groups out of business and property ownership to the advantage of selfish interests."[64] The JACL pointed out that lawsuits under the Alien Land Law could "enable interested parties to acquire valuable farm lands."[65]

The opponents of Proposition 15 frequently characterized the measure as an effort to persecute soldiers and veterans. Ex-Sgt. Akira Iwamura, who wrote a letter that was published in a number of California newspapers, including the *Daily News* and the *Times* in Los Angeles, noted that he and his brother had returned from military service to face prosecution under the Alien Land Law. The arguments for Proposition 15, Iwamura argued, sounded "like criminal indictments." He asked, "Why are we hounded like outlaws?"[66] Ex-Navy Lt. Commander Freeman Lusk, who had worked with Japanese American members of the U.S. Army Intelligence Service in the Pacific, declared that "it will be a sorry commentary upon the people of California if the valiant war service of our Nisei citizens is to be rewarded with discrimination, intolerance, ingratitude."[67] The Committee for Christian Democracy of the Congregational Churches labeled Proposition 15 "un-American," insisting that "returning Nisei soldiers should not face escheat cases and revived discriminatory legislation."[68]

Most often, however, the opponents of Proposition 15 simply insisted that the measure itself represented racial discrimination. The JACL, for example, insisted that Proposition 15, which would incorporate legislative amendments into the state constitution, would "make race discrimination constitutional."[69] ACLU attorney A. L. Wirin declared in a radio speech that Proposition 15 "is a race law, pure and simple."[70] The *Daily News* suggested that the proposition might be "motivated by simple, animal race prejudice."[71]

By simply pointing out that Proposition 15 represented racial discrimination, its opponents suggested that most Americans thought that racial discrimination was wrong and would reject it if it were pointed out to them. The JACL even deemed the Alien Land Law and the legislative amendments to the law "outdated."[72] Some of these opponents, however, elaborated upon their opposition to this "outdated" discrimination by invoking the German example. Wirin, for example, pointed out that "in Germany, the Jews, of whom I am one, have been the victims of race bigotry and cruelty. In our own South, persons of black skin are victims of discrimination and even lynching and now California is repeating its program of making the Japanese the butt of discrimination and prejudice."[73] Wirin insisted that California voters should ignore the "racist groups" that had led earlier anti-Japanese campaigns and "by a clear and overwhelming majority adhere to the commitment of our nation to the United Nations charter in which we made avowals of our concern the world over for 'human rights and fundamental freedoms for all, with no distinction as to race, sex, language or religion.'"[74] Daniel G. Marshall of the Catholic Interracial Council said that "the legal gibberish of this proposition is a crude restatement of the fundamental principle of Hitler's national socialism—the racist doctrine of white supremacy and non-white inferiority."[75]

The positions taken by some of the opponents of the measure clearly suggested that World War II had discredited "racism." Iwamura, for example, insisted that Japanese American soldiers had "died to prove Americanism is in the heart; looks and nationality don't count."[76] In a related vein, Masaoka said that "the Alien Land Law smacks [of] the kind of racism and facism [*sic*] which so many American soldiers of all nationalities had hoped to have destroyed overseas during World War II."[77]

Some of the opponents of Proposition 15 argued that Proposition 15, because it was "race legislation," would not simply affect Japanese Americans. Mike Masaoka, for example, depicted Proposition 15 as a threat to other minority groups. "Today, it is the Japanese Americans who are being singled out for special unkind treatment. Tomorrow it may be the Jews, the Catholics, the Negroes, the Mexicans, or any other group which can be identified or labeled because of their traits, religious beliefs, or their nationality," he said in one speech.[78] The *Los Angeles Sentinel*, in a brief editorial, told its African American readers that "we know, better than most Americans, that discrimination against one group can be used to justify other discriminations against other groups and all of us should vote 'No' on Proposition 15."[79]

Finally, some of the opponents of Proposition 15 argued that the "racism" represented by Proposition 15 was hindering and would continue to hinder U.S. foreign policy and the work of Christian missionaries. In a speech before YMCA members in Los Angeles, JACL leader Mike Masaoka said, "Unless Americans in general and Californians in particular demonstrate a little more real Christianity in their relations with their own minorities, the peoples throughout the world will continue to look with suspicion and distrust at our government and even the religion we profess."[80] The Committee for Christian Democracy of the Congregational Churches deemed the proposition "un-Christian," declaring that it "negates the Christian spirit and violates the program of the Church—local, national, world-wide" and "undermines American leadership in Asiatic affairs."[81] The *Daily News* referred to Proposition 15 as a "preposterous proposal" that would "announce to that vast society of submerged and colored peoples throughout our own nation and the world that this hopeful commonwealth had decided to return to the Ice Age."[82]

Few supporters of Proposition 15 responded publicly to the aggressive campaign waged by the JACL and its allies. The most visible supporter of the measure was Eldred L. Meyer, a past grand president of the Native Sons of the Golden West. Meyer tended to shy away from explicit appeals to racial prejudice. He even suggested that the Alien Land Law was not discriminatory. In a letter responding to ex-Sgt. Akira Iwamura, for example, Meyer insisted that "the California alien land law does not discriminate against the Japanese." Meyer sidestepped the question of whether or not a law that prevented "aliens ineligible for citizenship" from owning land discriminated against those aliens on the basis of race. He pointed out that the alien land law applied "to all aliens ineligible for citizenship—members of some 15 Asiatic groups in all." Meyer downplayed the significance of the proposition and at the same time implied his belief that World War II had not influenced racial ideology in California. He pointed out that voters were "only being asked in Proposition 15 to ratify two amendments to the law for the purpose of strengthening and more efficiently carrying out the people's purpose" as expressed in the alien land law, which was enacted by a vote of the people in 1920. Meyer further minimized the possibility that the Alien Land Law might be discriminatory by observing that "Oregon, Washington, Arizona, New Mexico, Utah, Wyoming and Kansas have also adopted legislation similar to and even more stringent than the California alien land law."

Meyer explicitly rejected the argument that the Alien Land Law was being used to persecute soldiers and veterans. He insisted that any violation of the law "should and must be prosecuted, even though it is against returned veterans, just as an action must be filed if the veteran committed murder or violated any other law—all laws of our State being equally sacred. Defense of our country has never granted license to violate any law."[83]

Although Meyer and some other supporters of Proposition 15 avoided the issue of "race," at times they inadvertently made clear their belief that all people of Japanese ancestry were racially Japanese and therefore rightly subject to discrimination. G. W. Farley of South Gate seemed unable to comprehend the fact that Iwamura was a U.S. citizen. Although Farley insisted that Iwamura "is entitled to and should be given every consideration that our American soldiers are given," he asked, "why should ex-Sgt. Iwamura squawk because he can't get privileges denied our own citizens?"[84]

On November 5, 1946, California's voters rejected Proposition 15. Some Japanese American leaders interpreted the measure's defeat as a victory for modernist racial ideology. JACL President Saburo Kido, for example, argued that voters had rejected Proposition 15 because "the loyalty of the Japanese Americans together with the contributions of the alien Japanese towards the war effort of this country" had proved that "Americanism is not a matter of race or blood ties, but of the heart and mind." Kido also suggested that the measure's defeat indicated that voters sought to "discourage the use of existing laws for racebaiting purposes."[85] Some Japanese Americans, however, depicted the defeat of Proposition 15 primarily as a victory for Japanese Americans rather than for modernist racial ideology. Mike Masaoka, for example, declared that "Proposition 15 was defeated because the voters of California were no longer impressed with appeals against the Japanese and most of them felt that the Nisei and Issei had earned the right to justice and fair treatment." Masaoka argued that "the lesson of the vote on Proposition 15 is that the war is over and the people of California will disprove [*sic*] of discriminatory treatment of those of Japanese ancestry," and he predicted "a new era of increased opportunities and greater social acceptability" for Japanese Americans.[86]

Proposition 11

One of the primary goals of the opponents of racial prejudice was the elimination of employment discrimination. Throughout the war Augustus Hawkins, the only African American in the California legislature, regularly introduced legislation to outlaw such discrimination. None of these bills passed. The arguments used by opponents of the legislation prefigured those used by later opponents of fair employment legislation. Rep. Jesse Kellems of Los Angeles led the opposition to Hawkins's 1943 bill, which nearly passed in the assembly. Kellems claimed that the proposed law "not only would serve to 'fan the flame' of race prejudice, but would attack 'the citadel of liberty.'" Kellems argued that "those actually behind these discrimination bills—those who profess to be the guardians of the underprivileged—do it in order to bring about bloodshed and chaos.'" Arthur Carlson of Piedmont argued that if the bill passed "California could expect increased racial hatreds or even race riots." Hawkins defended the bill, saying that it "fits in with the American ideal of fair play."[87] The arguments of Kellems and Carlson, then, fit perfectly with the arguments advanced by other members of the legislature in 1943. Many of these legislators, such as Hugh

Burns of Fresno (see chapter five), refused to believe that racial discrimination was a serious problem in California, despite the arguments presented by African Americans and members of other minority groups who had experienced discrimination.

In February 1946, after the legislature had refused to act on any of three different fair employment practices bills, Hawkins wrote that it had become clear that "any hope of passing an FEPC bill through this legislature is like believing in Santa Claus." He pointed out that Chester Gannon, who had defended racial segregation and its ideological foundations as the chair of the Assembly Committee on Japanese Problems, had argued that the passage of fair employment legislation "would result in 3,000,000 Negroes coming to California."[88] Because the supporters of fair employment legislation realized that the legislature would not enact such a law, in 1945 they launched a campaign to place a fair employment practices initiative on the ballot.[89] By June 1946 they had collected enough signatures to put their initiative, Proposition 11, on the November 1946 ballot.[90] The proposition would have made it illegal for an employer to "refuse to hire or employ or to bar, or to discharge from employment any person because of the race, religion, color, national origin or ancestry of such person." The measure also would have made it illegal for employment agencies and unions to discriminate on the basis of race, religion, color, or national origin.[91] The California Democratic Party, many AFL and CIO unions, and Protestant, Catholic, and Jewish groups endorsed Proposition 11. The NAACP, the National Lawyers' Guild, and the Catholic Interracial Council worked on behalf of the initiative.[92]

To many of Proposition 11's supporters, the need for fair employment legislation was self-evident. African Americans and members of other racial minorities had been denied access to many jobs. During the war, the President's Committee on Fair Employment Practice (also known as the Fair Employment Practice Committee or FEPC) had worked to discourage racial discrimination. After the war, as Augustus Hawkins observed, "with the war industries discontinued, the Negro people are forced to take low paying jobs and many find themselves out of a job."[93] Supporters of Proposition 11 also pointed out that racial discrimination affected many different groups. In a debate, Hawkins charged that "'the Associated Farmers and kindred groups' have used legislation to enact laws fostering discrimination against persons of Oriental ancestry in California."[94] The *Pacific Citizen* noted that discrimination "is practiced daily in employment against Americans because of their race, color or creed."[95]

Some supporters of Proposition 11 appealed to voters' sense of California as a "liberal" or "progressive" state and connected the measure to the principles embraced by such American icons as Abraham Lincoln and Franklin D. Roosevelt. Former Vice President Henry A. Wallace, in a luncheon on Central Avenue, said that California must "come through for Prop. 11" in order "to hold on to its record of progressivism in the eyes of the nation."[96] State Senator John F. Shelley of San Francisco, the Democratic candidate for lieutenant governor, insisted that the proposition "merely enforces constitutional rights as old as America."[97] To raise funds for the campaign, the California Committee for Fair Employment Practices sold "Freedom Bonds" that bore the images of Abraham Lincoln and Franklin D. Roosevelt and said that the purchaser "has invested in his country—and its people of every race, religion and national origin—with the full realization that the Fair Employment Practices Act will further the words of our founding fathers that 'all men are created equal.'"[98]

Some of the supporters of Proposition 11 argued that the initiative would help California's economy. The Los Angeles Democratic County Central Committee argued that "Proposition 11, by barring discrimination in employment, will help pave the way for fuller employment, higher pay and purchasing power and a more prosperous state."[99] Shelley said that prosperity was impossible "if large numbers of people are kept unemployed, or are continually paid substandard wages. In either case, purchasing power drops and eventually both business and labor, and profits, wages and jobs, will suffer severely."[100] Hawkins said that "we must pass the act if we are to have economic prosperity for all the people as well as members of minority groups in the crucial years ahead."[101]

Supporters of Proposition 11 frequently drew upon the rhetoric they had used during World War II. They depicted their opponents as Nazis. In one speech, for example, Augustus Hawkins declared that "the man who excludes a Negro from the privilege of this democracy, who sets up barriers against a human being because of his race and creed, is a Nazi."[102] The Los Angeles Democratic County Central Committee argued that Proposition 11 would "safeguard our state against the evils of race and religious hatred which were the cornerstones of the Axis philosophy and state which we have just defeated in a costly war."[103] Shelley declared that "we cannot look forward to a democratic, united nation if the disruptive evils of race and religious hatred are allowed to pit group against group in the manner that under Hitler brought ruin to Europe and death to millions."[104] When Gerald L. K. Smith, a vocal proponent of white supremacy, announced that he would campaign against Proposition 11, the initiative's supporters depicted their opponents as Fascists. Hawkins called upon all "true Americans to halt Smith's drive to promote fascism in America. Smith is here to master-mind the campaign against Proposition 11 and to rally all the forces of race and religious hatred against it."[105] Hawkins also said that "the anti-democratic groups are hoping to rely on Smith and his misled followers to stir up Hitler-like opposition to this Proposition 11, and to try to show to the rest of the country that race-baiters and religious bigots control California."[106]

Many business owners, chambers of commerce, veterans' organizations, some labor union leaders, and every English-language daily newspaper in Los Angeles opposed Proposition 11.[107] Newspaper opposition did not surface simply on the editorial page. News articles gave much more attention to the arguments advanced by the measure's opponents than by its supporters. One article in the *Times*, for example, reported that both supporters and opponents of the proposition had kicked off their campaigns. The article did not describe the position of the proponents of the measure, but half of the article was devoted to the arguments of the opponents of the measure.[108] The *Los Angeles Examiner* published "news articles" reporting that unnamed "major California and business groups" opposed Proposition 11 because "hidden jokers in the proposal" would create a "discriminatory, extra-legal agency with extreme dictatorial powers." Some of these articles did not identify a single source by name or by affiliation.[109] An ad hoc organization, the "Committee for Tolerance," coordinated opposition to the measure. The Committee for Tolerance claimed ninety members, but the chair of the committee, Frank P. Doherty, a former president of the Chamber of Commerce, issued most of the committee's statements.[110]

The campaign against Proposition 11 reveals the degree to which explicit defenses of racial discrimination had become unacceptable. Many of the opponents of Proposition 11 insisted that they were opposed to discrimination. The board of directors of the California Retailers' Association, for example, announced that it was "opposed to discrimination in any form."[111] Even State Sen. Jack B. Tenney, the chair of the California legislature's Committee on Un-American Activities, which had attacked the loyalty of Japanese Americans throughout the war, claimed that he was opposed to "all forms of racial and religious bigotry and intolerance."[112]

Even though many opponents of Proposition 11 claimed that they opposed discrimination, they offered a wide variety of explanations for their opposition to the initiative. Some argued that prejudice could not be outlawed. Efforts to outlaw prejudice, they argued, would only exacerbate racial tensions. Others insisted that Proposition 11 would deprive Americans of their rights and liberties. Some argued that Proposition 11 would undermine national security. Most of the initiative's opponents insisted that it was part of a Communist plot to destroy the United States.

Opponents of the measure depicted Proposition 11 not as an effort to eliminate discrimination but as an attempt to outlaw prejudice. They insisted that it was impossible to change people's beliefs through legislation. Committee for Tolerance chair Frank P. Doherty claimed that "experience has proved that tolerance cannot be enforced by law."[113] Methodist minister E. E. Helms stated that "the lesson that tolerance cannot be enforced by law has been proven over and over again."[114] The *Times* expressed the opinion that "prejudices by their very nature are matters of emotion rather than logic or reason; and when a State tries by ponderous legal machinery to interfere in matters of emotion it is treading on dangerous ground. Persuasion, education are suitable means for overcoming prejudice, but it cannot be eradicated by force."[115] State Sen. Jack Tenney argued that "an enlightened and educated civilization is the best antidote to bigots and rabble rousers."[116]

Efforts to "legislate brotherly love," the initiative's opponents argued, would only exacerbate the prejudices they were supposed to allay. The board of directors of the California Retailers' Association announced that Proposition 11 "will in fact create chaos and discontent."[117] Associated Farmers President Ray Badger said that Proposition 11 would not prevent employment discrimination. Instead, he argued, "the measure actually would inflame racial hatred and class distinction." The directors of the Los Angeles Chamber of Commerce also declared that Proposition 11 would "emphasize racial and religious cleavages rather than allay them."[118] Although most of these opponents simply asserted that the initiative would inflame prejudices without explaining how it would do so, the *Los Angeles Times* explained how Proposition 11 would increase racial tension. The *Times* insisted that "any man turned down for a job could threaten to appeal to the commission and thus extort money or a job from an unwilling employer." These "blackmail" attempts would lead to "the accentuation of prejudice and the disruption of productive industry."[119] State Senator Jack B. Tenney argued that Proposition 11 would whip the "flames of hope in the hearts of innocent and uninformed people for a Utopia of brotherly love . . . into a rising fury of racial and religious frictions and antagonisms."[120]

Opponents of the proposition frequently argued that it would deprive people of their civil liberties. The Chamber of Commerce, for example, claimed that the proposition authorized the "imposition of criminal penalties without trial by jury, one of our most valued constitutional rights."[121] The board of directors of the California Retailers' Association argued that the creation of a fair employment practices commission would "restrict the constitutional rights of individual citizens by the use of coercive powers granted in the act."[122] Committee for Tolerance chairman Frank P. Doherty argued that the initiative would deny people accused of discrimination a trial by jury, deny the courts the "power to restrain the commission set up by No. 11," deny the legislature the "power to amend or repeal the law," and compel citizens to testify against themselves.[123] A *Times* editorial tacitly acknowledged that other opponents of the measure lied about the role of the courts in enforcing the proposed law against employment discrimination. The editorial admitted that "the proposition appears to provide for a court appeal from any ruling made by the commission," but it argued that "the provision that the filing of an appeal does not stay the execution of the commission's order seems to make an appeal extra hazardous."[124] The Labor Committee against Proposition 11, led by Roy E. Center of the United Railroad Workers of America (CIO), Frank C. MacDonald, president of the State Building and Construction Trade Council, and William E. Burk, business representative of the International Association of Machinists, argued that the initiative "threatens more harm to organized labor and its members than to any other group of citizens." This committee repeated the claims made by other opponents—that the measure would deny people the right of trial by jury and compel people to testify against themselves. It also argued that Proposition 11 "empowers a political commission to subpoena union members, records, and private papers" and "authorizes the political commission to jail and fine union members."[125] Even the *Daily News*, which gave more thoughtful consideration to Proposition 11 than the *Times* or the *Examiner*, opposed the measure because of the threats it posed to "individual freedom." A *Daily News* editorial concluded that "the danger is too great that we would surrender long-cherished rights and liberties without gaining anything in return that could compensate us for the loss."[126]

In suggesting that Proposition 11 would deprive Californians of their rights, some of the initiative's opponents appealed to antibureaucratic sentiment among voters. The Chamber of Commerce, for example, claimed that the initiative would "set up a new bureaucracy with extremely broad and dangerous powers."[127] The board of directors of the California Retailers' Association argued that Proposition 11 would "create an uncontrolled bureaucracy in California."[128]

In arguing that Proposition 11 would deprive Californians of their rights, some of the initiative's opponents disagreed directly with the measure's supporters about the meaning of World War II. The measure's supporters argued that World War II had been a war against Hitler's racial ideology. Some opponents of Proposition 11, however, insisted that the war had been to "preserve individual liberty." "Individual liberty" apparently included the freedom to discriminate against fellow citizens on the basis of race or religion. VFW Commander J. E. Vanderclute, for example, said that "more than 10,000,000 soldiers and sailors of the United States have just waged a terrible war to smash totalitarianism and preserve individual liberty." Vanderclute argued that Proposition 11 "threatens to destroy the liberty to work for whom we will and the liberty to hire whom we will."[129] Vanderclute compared the opposition to employment discrimination with the "intolerance and shackles on freedom" represented by the enemies of the United States in World War II. "Now the same evil faces us in California," he said. "Every veteran and every citizen, for his own good and for the good of the country, should make it his first business to arouse every one of his friends to smash this measure."[130]

Some of the opponents of Proposition 11 argued that the initiative could undermine the security of the United States. Roy E. Center of the United Railroad Workers, for example, insisted that under one provision of the proposition "it could be a crime for a union to exclude from its membership someone who might actually be an undercover agent for a potential foreign enemy."[131] The Committee for Tolerance also emphasized this point in a pamphlet. It argued that "Proposition 11 could endanger national security," because the law would prevent employers from asking about "color, race, religion, national origin or ancestry." "In the event of a future war with any foreign power, this law could send an employer or any employee to jail for protecting the security of the United States from alien enemies."[132]

The argument employed most consistently by opponents of Proposition 11 was that the proposition was "Communist inspired." Frank P. Doherty, the chair of the Committee for Tolerance, argued that Communists supported the proposition and called it "unworkable, unconstitutional, undemocratic and un-American."[133] C. O. Hoober of the California Farm Bureau Federation called the authors of Proposition 11 "unwholesome and un-American. The same professional radicals who agitate night and day for disunity, chaos and confusion in the land are among those who sponsor this proposition."[134] Roy E. Center of the United Railroad Workers said that Proposition 11 "was conceived by enemies of everything American who are particularly enemies of the American labor movement." Center declared that "in plain language—this is one of those destructive schemes presented in the trappings of a 'popular' cause through which Communists and their fellow-travelers of the road to revolution hope to betray organized labor by subjecting it to dictatorial domination."[135] State Sen. Jack B. Tenney was, perhaps predictably, the bluntest in his attack on Proposition 11. He declared in a statewide radio broadcast a week before the election that the measure was "a Communist bill." Tenney said that "every voter in California should know that of the 63 sponsors and officers of the committee in favor of Proposition No. 11, more than half have been prominent in movements sponsored by the Communists and left-wingers." The "many fine Americans of good will, high ideals and the best of intentions" who supported Proposition 11 had been misled by "Communists and left-wingers," Tenney insisted. Tenney also described the authors of Proposition 11 as "a group of termites indoctrinated with an atheistic, totalitarian foreign ideology."[136]

As the preceding paragraphs suggest, most of the opponents of Proposition 11 avoided explicit appeals to racial prejudice. Few openly suggested that people should oppose Proposition 11 because the measure's approval would weaken white supremacy in California. Some of their statements, however, revealed their racialist beliefs. A Committee for Tolerance pamphlet, for example, suggested that people of certain ethnicities were concentrated in certain occupations as a result of biological differences rather than employment discrimination. The pamphlet pointed out that "Proposition No. 11 makes it against the law to specify a Japanese gardener or a colored porter or a Filipino fruit-picker or an English waiter or [*sic*] an English restaurant or a

Chinese cook or a French hairdresser or Swedish actress or an Italian singer or a Mexican dancer."[137] In a more subtle appeal to racial prejudice, the Committee for Tolerance suggested that "white" people were entitled to the positions they held. In one appeal to "white" voters, for example, the Committee for Tolerance declared that "you might lose your job or be demoted at the whim of appointed commissioners forcing another person into your place." Any person who believed that he had been "held back by his color, his race, his religion, his national origin or his ancestry, needs only to complain. The commission could force him into your job." Even though many opponents of Proposition 11 argued that discrimination did not exist, the Committee for Tolerance, in its appeal to "white" voters, subtly suggested that discrimination against members of minority groups was acceptable. The *possibility* of discrimination against "white" people, however, was not. "Your employer would be subject to political investigators dictating whom he may hire and whom he may promote," the Committee for Tolerance declared. "This political commission may discriminate against you."[138] The Committee for Tolerance more explicitly appealed to racial prejudice when it employed the image of African American men as threats to "white" women. It declared that the proposition "says that you, your wife, your daughter or your sister must work with anyone the commission directs regardless of color or race."[139]

The aggressive campaign waged by the opponents of Proposition 11 forced the measure's supporters to defend the initiative. In responding to the opponents of the proposition, Hawkins said that "Proposition Number 11 does not make the discriminatory practices themselves a crime, and no one is accused by the commission in any hearing of a crime. Any misdemeanor that results comes only from subsequent violation of the order of the courts. Hence FEPC hearings in no way impair the right of jury trial." Hawkins insisted that "judicial review is provided for" and that "the procedure is historically and legally in the American tradition. It will be oppressive only to those whose sole motive is to defeat the democratic rights guaranteed to people."[140] On more than one occasion Hawkins acknowledged that "prejudice cannot be eliminated by law."[141] He pointed out, however, that "prejudice is an opinion, which cannot be removed by law. But discrimination is a physical act of prejudice and clearly a fit subject for legislation."[142] Hawkins's statements, however, received little attention from the daily newspapers that published every statement issued by the Committee for Tolerance.

The *B'nai B'rith Messenger* lamented that the opponents' objections to Proposition 11 "are unanswerable" because "such objections are based on the very prejudices against which the Fair Employment Practices Act hopes to stand as a bulwark." The *Messenger* pointed out that "to say, as does the L.A. Times, that the act will promote race-prejudice, is to say that maintaining a force for defense will bring on a war; that taking medicine will increase disease, or that raising an umbrella in a drizzle will produce a storm." The *Messenger* also challenged the *Times*'s statement that the FEPC "was a good thing, but it was a war time measure, and should be discarded now." The *Messenger* insisted that "war has not ceased.... There is a war going on today between reactionary and progressive forces, that can break out at any moment into a shooting war. And such laws as Fair Employment Practice Acts can do much to avert such a calamity." The *Messenger* also declared that race hatred was a disease and compared fair employment legislation to public health measures designed to curb diseases. "If anti-Semitism is a disease, mental or psychological, why should it not receive the same treatment as a physical disease? Yes, let us try education for all its [*sic*] worth, but let us back it up with legislation, too."[143]

The *Sentinel* attacked the Chamber of Commerce for its opposition to Proposition 11. An editorial pointed out that the Chamber called for education rather than legislation and concluded that "the sham character of this opposition may be guaged [*sic*] from the fact that the State Chamber has never instituted, nor does it now have, any educational program of any kind directed toward the elimination of discriminatory practices in industry." The *Sentinel* insisted that "the truth is that these big business interests don't want an FEPC because they find it profitable to play race against race and group against group; the resulting antagonism makes it easier for these employers to beat down wages and maintain bad working conditions."[144]

Supporters of Proposition 11 urged voters to be wary of people who insisted that the measure was "Red" or "Communistic." *California Eagle* publisher Charlotta Bass, for example, wrote that "Negroes, in particular, should shy away from the 'Red' or 'Communistic' scare. If they will only realize that the people who shout 'Red' or 'Communism' at them are not their friends but their enemies, the better able will they be to understand the reasons behind these appellations [*sic*]."[145] Father George H. Dunne of Loyola University told the women's FEPC committee of the Catholic Interracial Council that most of the arguments advanced by Proposition 11's opponents "are lies by people who know they are lies, and the biggest lie of all is that FEPC is Communist-inspired."[146] The *Los Angeles Sentinel* pointed out that the FEPC law in New York passed with the support of Republican Gov. Thomas E. Dewey and a Republican majority in the legislature. "We're not yet convinced that Mr. Dewey is in the pay of Moscow or that Boss Stalin sent word down the line for the GOP in that state to thus undermine the foundations of the republic," the *Sentinel* stated in an editorial.[147]

On November 5, 1946, more than 70 percent of California's voters cast their votes against Proposition 11. Los Angeles County registered 758,641 votes against the initiative and only 294,938 in favor of the measure. It is impossible to determine exactly why people voted as they did. To some extent, however, the vote on Proposition 11, together with the vote on Proposition 15, can be considered a referendum on modernist racial ideology. As the debates surrounding Proposition 11 indicate, many people said that they agreed in principle that the United States should be a "color-blind" society. Discrimination on the basis of race or religion was wrong. The possibility that the government might act to prohibit racial discrimination in employment, however, was interpreted by many people as a threat to their rights. As Committee for Tolerance propaganda makes clear, many European Americans might say that discrimination was wrong, but that did not mean that they would agree to work alongside African Americans.

Conclusion

In the fourteen months between the end of the war and the November 1946 elections, then, Los Angeles residents continued to debate the meaning of "race" and the role that "race" should play in their city. Largely as a result of events during the war, most of the city's residents agreed that racial prejudice and discrimination were both morally wrong and socially undesirable. Many African Americans, Mexican Americans, and Asian Americans continued to encounter discrimination. They also continued their efforts to change discriminatory policies and practices. These efforts, however, often encountered resistance. Many Anglo Americans who said that they opposed discrimination consistently opposed efforts to dismantle residential segregation and to eliminate employment discrimination. Many of these Anglo Americans insisted, as did William Ring and Jack B. Tenney, that discrimination did not really exist. The end of the war also gave these defenders of existing practices a potent rhetorical weapon. During the war the U.S.-Soviet alliance had somewhat blunted attacks on "Communism." After the war, however, defenders of existing policies and practices were able to vilify without restriction anything that they could label as "Communistic." As I have pointed out throughout this book, it is impossible to determine whether or not many people truly believed that Communists wanted to outlaw discrimination in order to cause discord in the United States. The rhetoric of anti-Communism, though, did offer people who feared changes and who harbored prejudices a convenient way to deflect attention from those fears and prejudices, whether or not they truly believed that Communists lurked behind every "progressive" proposal.

Finally, the fact that both Proposition 15 and Proposition 11 failed deserves some comment. There seem to be many reasons why a majority of Californians rejected discriminatory legislation against Japanese Americans but refused to outlaw discriminatory actions against all groups of people. There were a relatively small number of Japanese Americans in California before World War II and an even smaller number in November 1946. It seems likely that few people saw Japanese American ownership of land as a serious economic or political threat. Even the proponents of Proposition 15 did not suggest that Japanese Americans posed an immediate or dire threat to California's economy or society. Also, the depiction of Japanese Americans as valiant soldiers, many of whom had given their lives for the United States, seems to have been nearly hegemonic by the fall of 1946. None of the supporters of Proposition 15 dared to suggest that Japanese Americans were disloyal in the face of these depictions.

In contrast, African Americans were the most vocal and visible proponents of Proposition 11, even though many labor unions and the Democratic party also endorsed the measure. Unlike Japanese Americans, whose presence in California had become less visible during the war than it had been before, African Americans' numbers had increased dramatically during the war. And while many Anglo Americans in California had argued that they knew Japanese Americans from their long experience with them, these same people rarely claimed that they knew African Americans. In the racial discourse of California in the 1940s, African Americans remained more exotic and more threatening than Japanese Americans. Moreover, policies of segregation within the U.S. military limited African Americans' ability to claim the status of war heroes. Most African American soldiers were assigned to frequently onerous and unpleasant tasks, and few were allowed to serve in the combat units on which most of the glory was showered. African American publications did draw attention to the heroism of African American soldiers, but the campaign for Proposition 11 was not dominated by the image of the heroic African American soldier.

The representation of men as soldiers also hints at a final explanation for the failure of both Proposition 15 and Proposition 11. As chapters four and six suggest, Japanese Americans were almost always depicted as male in the debates about "race" in Los Angeles during the war. The focus on Japanese American men as a threat to national security helps to explain why protests against the return of Japanese American women proved ineffective—Japanese American women had been invisible in the debate. In the debate surrounding Proposition 11, African Americans, too, were always depicted as men, at least by the initiative's opponents. Instead of being depicted as heroic soldiers, however, African American men were represented as sexual threats to "white" women. The debate surrounding Proposition 11 reveals that gender ideology as well as racial ideology worked to maintain patterns of employment discrimination in the United States in the mid-twentieth century.

Conclusion

Between Pearl Harbor and the election of November 1946, residents of Los Angeles debated the meanings of "race." Before the United States entered the war, many Los Angeles residents described "race" as something that played a vital role in determining who a person was. In prewar rhetoric, "race" signified a set of apparently biological characteristics that determined how a person looked, what a person believed, how a person behaved, which abilities a person possessed, and where a person fit into the social order. To people who described "race" in this way, there was no problem of racial discrimination in Los Angeles. The fact that people from certain "races" did not work in some occupations, live in certain neighborhoods, or interact with people from other "races" simply reflected the "natural" order, according to adherents of this traditional racial ideology.

To a growing number of people, however, "race" meant something different. It meant a set of distinct biological characteristics, but these characteristics determined only a person's outward appearance. They did not affect a person's beliefs, behaviors, abilities, or place in the social order. What I have tried to show in this book is how this second racial ideology—modernist racial ideology—spread through the public discourse about "race" in one place in a particular and important period of time. My goal has not been to trace changes in thought, which are only imperfectly captured by language, but to explore which words and metaphors were available to those people who argued about "race" and about policies and practices related to "race." I have also sought to explore the implications of the words and metaphors that people employed in their arguments about the relationship between the differences among people and U.S. society.

In chapter two I argued that the attack on Pearl Harbor intensified and transformed the ongoing debate about "race." Japanese Americans acknowledged that they belonged to the same "race" as the people in Japan who had become the enemies of the United States. They insisted, however, that their "race" did not make them loyal subjects of the emperor of Japan. Most Japanese Americans maintained that they were loyal to the United States, although many also indicated that there were people within the Japanese American community who were loyal to Japan. Although many public officials and some newspaper publishers expressed agreement with Japanese Americans in the aftermath of Pearl Harbor, most of these officials and publishers quickly abandoned the language of modernist racial ideology. Some continued to say that they believed that most Japanese Americans were loyal to the United States, but they also argued that "race" made it impossible to separate the loyal from the disloyal. Most of these leaders called for the incarceration of all people who were "racially" Japanese, as their "race" made it impossible for the United States to determine their loyalty. Few dissenting voices gained access to the press. Officials at the highest levels of the U.S. government decided to imprison and remove all people who were "racially" Japanese from areas close to the Pacific Coast. Although I would not argue that these officials were motivated only by traditional beliefs about "race," I do think that these beliefs, as reflected in the language used by these officials, were connected to the decision to relocate or evacuate all people of Japanese ancestry.

Chapter three argued that the verbal "battle for Los Angeles" shifted away from Japanese Americans in the summer of 1942 and toward the issue of juvenile delinquency among Mexican Americans. A critical episode in this portion of the debate actually occurred outside public view, but reports of this episode circulated and later became public. This episode was Lt. Ed Duran Ayres's statement before the Los Angeles County Grand Jury. Duran Ayres argued that "Mexicans," because of their Indian ancestry, were prone to violent criminality. Other law enforcement officials endorsed Duran Ayres's opinion. Two months later, however, scholars, public officials, and a representative of the Mexican government appeared before the Grand Jury to denounce the idea that Mexican Americans were by nature prone to violent criminal behavior. At the same time, African Americans, particularly *California Eagle* editors Charlotta A. Bass and her nephew John S. Kinloch, advanced the argument that there really was no "crime wave" among young Mexican Americans. The publishers of metropolitan newspapers, particularly William Randolph Hearst, they argued, had manufactured this "crime wave." These publishers, Bass and Kinloch maintained, were sympathetic to Hitler's racial ideology and afraid of the prospect of true democracy.

The interest in young Mexican Americans carried over into 1943, but from the end of 1942 until the end of the war, the debate about "race" focused on Japanese Americans more than any other topic. As chapter four showed, politicians and newspaper editors and publishers waged an anti-Japanese campaign from the time rioting erupted at the Manzanar camp in December 1942 until the end of the war. At the heart of this campaign lay traditional racial ideology. The participants in this anti-Japanese campaign insisted that all people of Japanese ancestry possessed negative "racial" characteristics and that most if not all were by nature loyal to Japan. Anti-Japanese leaders frequently called for harsh punishment for Japanese Americans' racial guilt. Until mid-1943 these anti-Japanese leaders faced little public opposition in Los Angeles. In April and May of that year, however, participants in the anti-Japanese campaign discovered to their dismay that they had lost the support of a critical ally—the U.S. Army. Despite the fact that the army continued to harbor officers such as John L. DeWitt, who unabashedly declared his belief in traditional racialism when he declared that "a Jap's a Jap," by April 1943 the army demonstrated that its primary concern was not the support of this ideology. Army officers decided to allow Japanese Americans to enlist, and then they decided that Japanese American soldiers on furlough would be allowed back into the Pacific Coast area. Anti-Japanese leaders protested loudly, but army officers rarely made public statements in support of the claims of the anti-Japanese leaders.

In chapter five I argued that the Zoot-Suit Riots of June 1943 critically transformed the debate about "race" in Los Angeles. Until the rioting occurred, explicit and general statements of support for traditional racial ideology were acceptable in this public debate. The riots presented a forceful challenge to the people who had suggested that Mexican Americans were biologically inclined toward violent criminality. U.S. and Mexican government officials and community leaders in Los Angeles chastised the press for their role in encouraging the riots; although newspaper editors and publishers denied that they had helped to incite rioting, they became more cautious and defensive in their statements about various "racial" groups, with the very important exception of Japanese Americans. The riots also encouraged people who opposed racial prejudice and discrimination to demand action from elected officials. They frequently argued that officials had an obligation to endorse educational efforts to reduce prejudice. Finally, because officials were slow to establish official committees to engage in these educational efforts, individuals who opposed discrimination created their own organizations and publications. These organizations and publications worked to dispel rumors and to convince people to question their prejudices.

Despite the establishment of these organizations and publications such as the *War Worker*, as chapter six showed, the Zoot-Suit Riots had little effect on the anti-Japanese campaign. Some of the elected officials who led this campaign continued their efforts soon after the rioting ended. From the middle of 1943 until the end of the war, politicians, patriotic and business organizations, and many newspaper editors and publishers argued forcefully that all people of Japanese ancestry were by nature loyal to Japan and a threat to national security. Despite their numerous pronouncements, articles, and editorials, however, they failed to prevent the return of Japanese Americans to the Pacific Coast. The anti-Japanese movement failed in its efforts to convince military officials and federal judges that U.S. policy should rest firmly on traditional racial ideology. The reasons for this failure are complex, but the effect of this failure is fairly simple: it served to delegitimate further the rhetoric of traditional racial ideology. One reason for the failure of the anti-Japanese movement deserves greater attention. The anti-Japanese movement's depiction of all Japanese Americans as men served to undermine the movement's arguments. Anti-Japanese leaders had asserted that the return of any Japanese Americans to the Pacific Coast would allow people who could not be distinguished from imperial Japanese soldiers and sailors into a sensitive military area. When military officials announced that they had already released Japanese American women on the Pacific Coast, and especially when Esther Takei returned to the Los Angeles area in the late summer of 1944, anti-Japanese leaders found themselves trying to depict young women as sinister threats to national security. In another place and time such a depiction may have resonated among a wider public. Because these anti-Japanese leaders had not presented such a possibility, however, the ones who did argue that Takei should be removed ended up presenting themselves and their arguments as unreasonable if not ridiculous. When the army lifted the exclusion order, anti-Japanese leaders looked more ridiculous because their dire predictions of sabotage and espionage did not prove correct. Japanese Americans did face acts of violence and intimidation, but they also received considerable support from federal officials in their efforts to withstand these acts.

Finally, chapter seven suggested how the "battle for Los Angeles" changed when the war ended. In late 1945 and 1946, opponents of racial prejudice and discrimination continued their efforts to end policies and practices that limited the opportunities of many African Americans, Mexican Americans, and Asian Americans. In these efforts they confronted opponents who said that they agreed that prejudice and discrimination were undesirable but who nonetheless defended prevailing policies and practices. In addition, the people who defended the status quo frequently accused the opponents of discrimination of being Communists or of doing the bidding of Communists.

The debates about "race" in Los Angeles during and immediately following the Second World War set the stage for later events and debates. Although some of the words and metaphors that had been used before the war became unacceptable in public debate, substantive change in Los Angeles came slowly. Many African Americans, Mexican Americans, and Asian Americans hoped that the apparently widespread support for the argument that the United States should be a "color blind" society would lead to new and improved opportunities. Yet prejudice and discrimination persisted.

Some of this discrimination probably persisted because wartime changes in the debate about "race" drove explicit statements of racial prejudice from public view. As these statements became less public, opponents of discrimination encountered the difficulty of convincing people that few African Americans were employed in certain occupations or lived in certain neighborhoods due to discrimination rather than "natural" tendencies and preferences. Perhaps because opponents of fair employment practices defended the "right" of employers rather than the state to determine whom to hire and fire and did not explicitly defend prejudice and discrimination, the state of California did not pass fair employment practices legislation until 1959.

Some change did occur, however, and it seems unlikely that change would have occurred if the war had not led to changes in the language that people employed to discuss "race." Some barriers to the employment of African Americans and Mexican Americans, for example, broke down in the years following World War II, even though California legislators refused to pass fair employment practices legislation. Because elected officials' words and actions were constantly exposed to public scrutiny, the greatest change in employment practices occurred in the public sector. Many elected officials had publicly expressed opposition to racial discrimination during the war. After the war, opponents of discrimination successfully pressed these officials to end some discriminatory practices. According to historian Josh Sides, the employment of African Americans in clerical jobs in the public sector made Los Angeles unusual among U.S. cities. In terms of percentages, nearly twice as many African American women worked in clerical jobs in Los Angeles than in other U.S. cities in 1960.[1]

The debates that occurred in Los Angeles during and immediately following the war, however, did not simply affect the history of Los Angeles or southern California. Similar debates also occurred in many other places across the country at the same time. These debates may simply be easier to follow in Los Angeles because of the unique set of circumstances that made several different issues resonate among residents of the city, most notably the size of the city's Mexican American and Japanese American communities and the fact that rioting occurred in Los Angeles during the war. Ultimately, I would argue that these debates about the meanings of "race" paved the way for the successes and the defeats of the civil rights movements of the 1950s, 1960s, and 1970s. If a growing number of people had not begun to depict "race" as a set of largely superficial biological characteristics and if such depictions had not spread during and after the war, it seems unlikely that these civil rights movements could have made such effective appeals to many Americans in later decades. Much of the rhetoric of these movements emphasized the notion that the only difference between African Americans, Chicanas and Chicanos, Asian Americans, and Anglo Americans was skin color. As Martin Luther King, Jr., said in his speech at the March on Washington in 1963, "I have a dream that my four little children will one day live in a nation where they will not be judged by the color of their skin but by the content of their character."

One important connection between the debates in Los Angeles during World War II and the civil rights movements is Earl Warren. When Warren was the attorney general and the governor of California during the war, as various chapters show, he tended to use the language of traditional racial ideology. Near the end of the war, however, perhaps because of the words and some of the efforts of opponents of racial discrimination, he tended to make statements defending the rights of U.S. citizens regardless of "race." Warren's position undoubtedly continued to evolve between 1946 and 1953, when he was appointed Chief Justice of the U.S. Supreme Court. The *Brown* decision does not explicitly address the meanings of "race," but it does suggest that racial differences among people are not significant enough to justify the segregation of children in public schools. By the time of the *Loving v. Virginia* decision of 1967, Warren had clearly embraced modernist racial ideology. Although it is impossible to know exactly how and why Warren's thoughts changed, it seems likely that his understanding of "race" was influenced by the debates examined in this book.

Notes

Introduction

1. Quoted in Ed Cray, *Chief Justice: A Biography of Earl Warren* (New York: Simon and Schuster, 1997), 115.
2. This discussion relies heavily on Cray's description of events following Pearl Harbor. See Cray, *Chief Justice*, 114–19.
3. See Cray, *Chief Justice*, 119. See also "Aliens Can Get Licenses," *Los Angeles Times*, Feb. 20, 1942, pt. 1, p. 10.
4. Quoted in Cray, *Chief Justice*, 121.
5. "State Council Opposes Any Plan to Return Japs," *Los Angeles Times*, May 22, 1943, pt. 1, p. 13. See also Cray, *Chief Justice*, 157–59.
6. See Cray, *Chief Justice*, 121.
7. "Warren Urges Public Support of Army Rule," *Los Angeles Examiner*, Dec. 18, 1944, pt. 1, p. 2. See also "Warren Urges People Support Army Decision," *Los Angeles Times*, Dec. 18, 1944, pt. 1, p. 1; "Safeguard Japs, Warren Plea," *Los Angeles Examiner*, Dec. 19, 1944, pt. 1, p. 1; "Climate on the Coast," *Pacific Citizen*, Dec. 30, 1944, p. 4; and Cray, *Chief Justice*, 157–59.
8. Earl Warren, *The Memoirs of Earl Warren* (Garden City, N.Y.: Doubleday, 1977), 149.
9. My thinking about "race" has been influenced by my reading in the history of sexuality. For some time historians have argued about when the concepts of homosexuality and heterosexuality emerged. Although "race" and sexuality differ, they both represent ways in which people give meaning to, maintain, and police differences among people. See Siobhan Somerville, "Scientific Racism and the Emergence of the Homosexual Body," *Journal of the History of Sexuality* 5, no. 2 (1994): 243–66; Jonathan Ned Katz, *The Invention of Heterosexuality* (New York: Dutton, 1995); George Chauncey, *Gay New York: Gender, Urban Culture, and the Making of the Gay Male World, 1890–1940* (New York: Basic Books, 1994); and Peter Boag, *Same-Sex Affairs: Constructing and Controlling Homosexuality in the Pacific Northwest* (Berkeley: University of California Press, 2003).
10. Peggy Pascoe, "Miscegenation Law, Court Cases, and Ideologies of 'Race' in Twentieth-Century America," *Journal of American History* 83, no. 1 (June 1996): 47.

11. For a thoughtful and provocative exploration of ideas about "race" among one group of intellectuals, the Chicago School sociologists, see Henry Yu, *Thinking Orientals: Migration, Contact, and Exoticism in Modern America* (New York: Oxford University Press, 2001).
12. George J. Sánchez, *Becoming Mexican American: Ethnicity, Culture, and Identity in Chicano Los Angeles, 1900–1945* (New York: Oxford University Press, 1993), 228.
13. "One Country—Neither Race Nor Creed Count," *Los Angeles Examiner*, Jan. 14, 1943, sec. 1, p. 12.
14. Quoted in Saburo Kido, "Timely Topics," *Pacific Citizen*, Feb. 12, 1944, p. 6.
15. "Protest Jewish Blood Bath," *Los Angeles Examiner*, July 11, 1944, pt. 1, p. 10.
16. Kido, "Timely Topics."
17. See Philip J. Ethington, *The Public City: The Political Construction of Urban Life in San Francisco, 1850–1900* (New York: Cambridge University Press, 1994); Karen J. Sawislak, *Smoldering City: Chicagoans and the Great Fire, 1871–1874* (Chicago: University of Chicago Press, 1995); Barbara Dianne Savage, *Broadcasting Freedom: Radio, War, and the Politics of Race, 1938–1948* (Chapel Hill: University of North Carolina Press, 1999); Elizabeth Vibert, *Traders' Tales: Narratives of Cultural Encounters in the Columbia Plateau, 1807–1846* (Norman: University of Oklahoma Press, 1997); and Frieda Knobloch, *The Culture of Wilderness: Agriculture as Colonization in the American West* (Chapel Hill: University of North Carolina Press, 1996).
18. Pascoe, "Miscegenation Laws, Court Cases, and Ideologies of 'Race,'" 48.
19. See Douglas Flamming, *Bound for Freedom: Black Los Angeles in Jim Crow America* (Berkeley: University of California Press, 2005); and Josh Sides, *L.A. City Limits: African American Los Angeles from the Great Depression to the Present* (Berkeley: University of California Press, 2003).
20. See Mark Wild, *Street Meeting: Multiethnic Neighborhoods in Early Twentieth-Century Los Angeles* (Berkeley: University of California Press, 2005); and Eric Avila, *Popular Culture in the Age of White Flight: Fear and Fantasy in Suburban Los Angeles* (Berkeley: University of California Press, 2004).
21. See Eduardo Obregón Pagán, *Murder at the Sleepy Lagoon: Zoot Suits, Race, and Riot in Wartime L.A.* (Chapel Hill: University of North Carolina Press, 2003); and Mauricio A. Mazón, *The Zoot-Suit Riots: The Psychology of Symbolic Annihilation* (Austin: University of Texas Press, 1984).
22. Dennis McDougal, *Privileged Son: Otis Chandler and the Rise and Fall of the L.A. Times Dynasty* (Cambridge, Mass.: Perseus, 2001), 7–152.
23. McDougal, *Privileged Son*, 40–41; Rob Leicester Wagner, *Red Ink, White Lies: The Rise and Fall of Los Angeles Newspapers, 1920–1962* (Upland, Calif.: Dragonflyer Press, 2000), 14, 20.
24. Alan Hensher, "No News Today: How Los Angeles Lost a Daily," *Journalism Quarterly* 47, no. 4 (Winter 1970): 684–86; Wagner, *Red Ink, White Lies*, 9, 21, 68–72, 86–89.

25. Takeya Mizuno, "Self-Censorship by Coercion: The Federal Government and the California Japanese-Language Newspapers from Pearl Harbor to Internment," *American Journalism* 17, no. 3 (2000): 34.
26. See Flamming, *Bound for Freedom*, 104–6. For additional information about Bass, see Kathleen Cairns, *Front-Page Women Journalists, 1920–1950* (Lincoln: University of Nebraska Press, 2003), 73–105.
27. See Flamming, *Bound for Freedom*, 366–67.
28. Ibid., 302–3.
29. For additional information about the *Sentinel*, see Roland E. Wolseley, *The Black Press, U.S.A.* (Ames: Iowa State University Press, 1971), 109–10.
30. Flamming, *Bound for Freedom*, 306.
31. Lee Finkle, *Forum for Protest: The Black Press during World War II* (Rutherford, N.J.: Fairleigh Dickinson University Press, 1975), 86.

Chapter One

1. "Klansmen March in Downtown Streets as Communism Protest," *Los Angeles Times*, Mar. 31, 1940, pt. 1, p. 1.
2. "Hooded Klan Marches through Downtown L.A.," *California Eagle*, Apr. 4, 1940, p. 1-A.
3. Charlotta A. Bass, "On the Sidewalk," *California Eagle*, Apr. 4, 1940, p. 1-A.
4. "The Klan Must Go!" *California Eagle*, Apr. 4, 1940, p. 4-B.
5. See Peggy Pascoe, "Miscegenation Law, Court Cases, and Ideologies of 'Race' in Twentieth-Century America," *Journal of American History* 83, no. 1 (June 1996): 47–48.
6. Ibid., 48.
7. Untitled script for radio broadcast, November 1939, "Bass, C. A.—Speeches, 1930s" folder, Box 1, Charlotta A. Bass papers, Southern California Library for Social Studies and Research, Los Angeles.
8. See Floyd C. Covington, "Biennial Report of the Executive Director, March 1, 1941 to March 1, 1943," "Urban League of Los Angeles" folder, Box 104, Series 1, Records of the National Urban League, Library of Congress, Washington, D.C., 3.
9. Mario T. García, *Mexican Americans: Leadership, Ideology, and Identity, 1930–1960* (New Haven: Yale University Press, 1989), 151.
10. Floyd C. Covington, "Political Activity Schedule," May 25, 1940, p. 5, Folder 7, Box 2, Los Angeles Urban League Records (Collection 203), Department of Special Collections, Charles E. Young Research Library, UCLA.
11. "The Negro Wage Earner," report prepared by Floyd C. Covington, Executive Director, Los Angeles Urban League, May 25, 1940, Folder 9, Box 2, Los Angeles Urban League Records.

12. See David Yoo, "'Read All About It': Race, Generation and the Japanese American Ethnic Press, 1925–41," *Amerasia Journal* 19, no. 1 (1993): 74.
13. Ibid., 80.
14. Quoted in Valerie Matsumoto, "Desperately Seeking 'Dierdre': Gender Roles, Multicultural Relations, and Nisei Women Writers of the 1930s," *Frontiers* 12, no. 1 (1991): 26.
15. Jere Takahashi, "Japanese American Responses to Race Relations: The Formation of Nisei Perspectives," *Amerasia Journal* 9, no. 1 (1982): 42–43.
16. "Every Nisei's Battle: Housing Restrictions at Issue," letter from John F. Aiso of Los Angeles to Mr. Togo Tanaka, English Section Editor, *Rafu Shimpo*, July 14, 1940, p. 4.
17. "Two Out of Every Ten," *Rafu Shimpo*, July 21, 1940, p. 14.
18. "Draft Program of the National Congress of Spanish Speaking People" (1939), Folder 9, Box 13, Ernesto Galarza Papers, Department of Special Collections, Green Library, Stanford University. See also David G. Gutiérrez, *Walls and Mirrors: Mexican Americans, Mexican Immigrants, and the Politics of Ethnicity* (Berkeley: University of California Press, 1995), 114.
19. Emma Tenayuca and Homer Brooks, "The Mexican Question in the Southwest," *The Communist*, March 1939, 266. See also Gutiérrez, *Walls and Mirrors*, 108, and García, *Mexican Americans*, 145, 154.
20. "Draft Program of the National Congress of Spanish Speaking People."
21. García, *Mexican Americans*, 151.
22. "Special Bulletin: Preparation for the Second Congress of the Spanish Speaking People in California, Dec 9, and 10, 1939," Folder 9, Box 13, Galarza Papers.
23. For general discussions of the creation and history of the FEPC, see Louis Coleridge Kesselman, *The Social Politics of FEPC* (Chapel Hill: University of North Carolina Press, 1948); Louis Ruchames, *Race, Jobs, and Politics: The Story of the FEPC* (New York: Columbia University Press, 1953); Herbert Garfinkel, *When Negroes March: The March on Washington Movement in the Organizational Politics for FEPC* (Glencoe, Ill.: Free Press, 1959); and Merl E. Reed, *Seedtime for the Modern Civil Rights Movement: The President's Committee on Fair Employment Practice, 1941–1946* (Baton Rouge: Louisiana State University Press, 1991).
24. "FEP Committee Schedules Hearing in L.A.," *California Eagle*, Sept. 18, 1941, p. 1.
25. For a general history of the NAACP, see Gilbert Jonas, *Freedom's Sword: The NAACP and the Struggle against Racism in America, 1909–1969* (New York: Routledge, 2005).
26. "Statement of Rev. J. L. Caston," in "Public Hearing in the Matter of Complaints of Discrimination in Employment in Defense Industries because of Race, Creed, Color or National Origin," Oct. 20, 1941, Records of

the FEPC, Record Group 228, 16–18. See also "Statement of Mr. George A. Beavers, Jr.," in "Public Hearing," 89–94.

27. "Local F.E.P. Committee Hearings Postponed," *California Eagle*, Oct. 2, 1941, p. 1-A.
28. "Gird for Battle," *California Eagle*, Oct. 2, 1941, p. 8-A.
29. "Who Are the FEPC Committee Members?" *California Eagle*, Oct. 9, 1941, p. 3-A.
30. John Kinloch, "FEPC Faces Big Task in Aircraft Bias Probe," *California Eagle*, Oct. 9, 1941, p. 3-A.
31. "State of the Nation," *California Eagle*, Oct. 9, 1941, p. 8-A.
32. "FEP Committee Hearings All Set," *California Eagle*, Oct. 16, 1941, pp. 1-A, 7-B.
33. "Graphic Pictures Portray FEPC Problem," *California Eagle*, Oct. 16, 1941, p. 3-A.
34. Charlotta A. Bass, "On the Sidewalk," *California Eagle*, Oct. 16, 1941, p. 7-B.
35. "Racial Bans in Jobs Here under Scrutiny of Federal Officials," *Daily News*, Oct. 10, 1941, p. 9.
36. "Fair Employment Hearings to Open," *Daily News*, Oct. 16, 1941, p. 31.
37. "Race Ban in Jobs to Be Told," *Daily News*, Oct. 20, 1941, p. 13.
38. "Bias in Defense Jobs to Be Aired," *Los Angeles Times*, Oct. 19, 1941, pt. 2, p. 1.
39. "Fair Employment Hearings to Open," *Los Angeles Examiner*, Oct. 16, 1941, sec. 2, p. 8; "Job Discrimination Hearing Slated," *Los Angeles Examiner*, Oct. 19, 1941, sec. 1, p. 25.
40. "Statement of Mr. Hugh Macbeth," in "Public Hearing," 62.
41. "Statement of Miss Dorothy Guinn," in "Public Hearing," 51.
42. "Statement of Mr. Hugh Macbeth," 66.
43. "Statement of Mr. Floyd Covington," in "Public Hearing," 133.
44. "Statement of Mr. Laurence F. La Mar," in "Public Hearing," 54–56.
45. "Statement of Rev. J. L. Caston," 20.
46. "Statement of Mr. Laurence F. La Mar," 57–59.
47. "Statement of Mr. C. E. Pearl," in "Public Hearing," 71–74.
48. "Statement of Baxter S. Scruggs," in "Public Hearing," 43.
49. "Statement of Rev. J. L. Caston," 20.
50. "Statement of Mr. Laurence F. La Mar," 54–57.
51. "Public Hearing," 59–60.
52. "Statement of Miss Jessie Terry," in "Public Hearing," 111–12.
53. "Public Hearing," 112–13.
54. "Statement of Miss Dorothy Guinn," 49–51.
55. "Statement of Rev. J. L. Caston," 20–22.
56. "Statement of Baxter S. Scruggs," 42.

57. “Statement of Mr. Hugh Macbeth,” 67.
58. See Takahashi, “Japanese American Responses to Race Relations,” 37.
59. “Statement of Mr. Mike Masaoka,” in “Public Hearing,” 80–82.
60. “Statement of Mr. Manuel Ruiz,” in “Public Hearing,” 99–101.
61. “Public Hearing,” 102.
62. Ibid., 103.
63. “Statement of Dr. Victor M. Egas,” in “Public Hearing,” 105–6.
64. “A Summary of the Hearings of the President’s Committee on Fair Employment Practice Held in Los Angeles, California, October 20 and 21, 1941, with Findings and Recommendations,” p. 1, in “Los Angeles Summaries” file, Box 464, Division of Field Operations, Office Files of Eugene Davidson, 1941–1946, Records of the FEPC, Record Group 228, National Archives, Washington, D.C.
65. Ibid., 2.
66. Ibid., 8.
67. Ibid., 2.
68. Ibid., 5.
69. Ibid., 6.
70. Ibid., 3.
71. Ibid., 3–4.
72. Ibid., 3.
73. Ibid., 8.
74. “Race Discrimination Denied by Three L.A. Plane Plants,” *Daily News*, Oct. 21, 1941, p. 12.
75. “F. D. R. Board Cites AFL Union for Racial Discrimination,” *Daily News*, Oct. 22, 1941, p. 14.
76. “Racial Prejudice Hearing Opens,” *Los Angeles Examiner*, Oct. 21, 1941, sec. 1, p. 8. See also “Race Discrimination Denials under Fire,” *Los Angeles Examiner*, Oct. 22, 1941, sec. 1, p. 15.
77. “Racial Prejudice Charged in Plants,” *Los Angeles Times*, Oct. 21, 1941, pt. 1, p. 18.
78. “F. E. P. Committee Flays Big Defense Industries,” *California Eagle*, Oct. 23, 1941, pp. 1-A, 3-A.

Chapter Two

1. “City Springs to Attention,” *Los Angeles Times*, Dec. 8, 1941, pt. 1, p. 1.
2. “Local Japs Declare They’re Loyal,” *Daily News*, Dec. 8, 1941, p. 3.
3. “Little Tokyo Carries on Business as Usual,” *Los Angeles Times*, Dec. 8, 1941, pt. 1, p. 2.

4. *December 7: The First Thirty Hours*, by the Correspondents of *Time, Life*, and *Fortune* (New York: Alfred A. Knopf, 1942), 116.
5. Ibid., 115.
6. "Local Japs Declare They're Loyal."
7. "Little Tokyo Gets Extra Police Guard," *Daily News*, Dec. 8, 1941, p. 3.
8. "Little Tokyo Carries on Business as Usual."
9. "Japanese Aliens' Roundup Starts," *Los Angeles Times*, Dec. 8, 1941, pt. 1, p. 1. See also "Hundreds of Japs Seized in L.A. Area," *Daily News*, Dec. 8, 1941, pp. 1, 29.
10. Mimeographed sheet produced by the Anti-Axis Committee of the Japanese American Citizens League, Southern District Council, n.d., Folder 6, Box 74, John Anson Ford Papers, Huntington Library, San Marino, Calif.
11. See Paul Spickard, "The Nisei Assume Power: The Japanese American Citizens League, 1941–42," *Pacific Historical Review* 52, no. 2 (May 1983): 158–59.
12. Mimeographed sheet produced by the Anti-Axis Committee.
13. "Japanese-Americans Ready to Aid Nation," *Los Angeles Times*, Dec. 9, 1941, pt. 1, p. 19; "Japanese Americans Pledge Aid in War," *Los Angeles Examiner*, Dec. 9, 1941, sec. 1, p. 8; "L.A. Nisei Pledge Allegiance to U. S.," *Daily News*, Dec. 9, 1941, p. 39; "Citizens Offer Loyalty Pledge to Flag," *Los Angeles Times*, Dec. 9, 1941, pt. 1, p. 19.
14. Minutes of Anti-Axis Committee Meeting, Dec. 8, 1941, Folder 6, Box 74, Ford Papers.
15. "County Declares State of Emergency Exists," *Los Angeles Times*, Dec. 10, 1941, pt. 1, p. 8.
16. "Little Tokyo Lid Clamped," *Los Angeles Times*, Dec. 14, 1941, p. D; "Japanese-Americans Ready to Fight Enemies," *Los Angeles Times*, Dec. 14, 1941, p. D.
17. "Nisei Students Vow Allegiance to America," *Los Angeles Times*, Dec. 10, 1941, pt. 1, p. 5.
18. "Japanese at UCLA Pledge Loyalty," *Daily News*, Dec. 11, 1941, p. 20.
19. "The Japanese American Citizens League Anti-Axis Committee Report of Activities, December 11, 12, and 13," folder 6, Box 74, Ford Papers. See also "Civilian Defense Plans Speeded Up," *Los Angeles Times*, Dec. 13, 1941, p. D.
20. "Death Sentence of a Mad Dog," *Los Angeles Times*, Dec. 8, 1941, p. A.
21. *Los Angeles Times*, Dec. 8, 1941, p. B.
22. See "Little Tokyo Banks and Concerns Shut," *Los Angeles Times*, Dec. 9, 1941, pt. 1, p. 4; "Roundup of Japanese Aliens in Southland Now Totals 500," *Los Angeles Times*, Dec. 9, 1941, pt. 1, p. 4; "Nipponese Store Taken under Federal Custody," *Los Angeles Times*, Dec. 9, 1941, pt. 1, p. 6; "Enemy Alien Restrictions Issued by U.S.," *Los Angeles Examiner*, Dec. 10, 1941, sec. 1, p. 3;

"Roundup of Aliens Called Nearly Over," *Los Angeles Times*, Dec. 11, 1941, pt. 1, p. 3; "Jap and Camera Held in Bay City," *Los Angeles Times*, Dec. 11, 1941, pt. 1, p. 3; "Two Japanese with Maps and Alien Literature Seized," *Los Angeles Times*, Dec. 11, 1941, pt. 1, p. 3; "Japs Seized after 'Survey,'" *Los Angeles Examiner*, Dec. 11, 1941, sec. 1, p. 14.

23. "Vegetables Found Free of Poisons," *Los Angeles Times*, Dec. 11, 1941, pt. 2, p. 2.
24. See, for example, "Japanese Fund Curbs Eased," *Los Angeles Times*, Dec. 16, 1941, pt. 1, p. 8; and "Japanese Funds Thawed by U.S.," *Los Angeles Examiner*, Dec. 16, 1941, sec. 1, p. 9.
25. "Suicide Reveals Spy Ring Here," *Los Angeles Times*, Dec. 19, 1941, pt. 1, pp. 1, 8; "L.A. Japanese Fifth Column Plots Probed," *Los Angeles Examiner*, Dec. 19, 1941, sec. 1, p. 1. The *Daily News* published a much shorter article about Senator Gillette's claims. See "Jap Suicide Linked with Alien Enemies," *Daily News*, Dec. 19, 1941, p. 26.
26. "Suicide Reveals Spy Ring Here."
27. "Roundup of Axis Aliens Jails 442," *Los Angeles Times*, Dec. 19, 1941, pt. 1, p. 8.
28. See "Hearings for Aliens Will Begin Here Monday," *Los Angeles Times*, Dec. 20, 1941, pt. 2, p. 7; and "Axis Aliens' Hearings Will Begin Monday," *Los Angeles Examiner*, Dec. 20, 1941, sec. 1, p. 13.
29. "Prove Our Loyalty," *Rafu Shimpo*, Dec. 23, 1941, p. 1.
30. "Human Kindness," *Rafu Shimpo*, Dec. 26, 1941, p. 7.
31. "Fight Together," *Rafu Shimpo*, Dec, 16, 1941, p. 1.
32. "Racial Identity," *Rafu Shimpo*, Dec. 22, 1941, p. 1.
33. "All for Defense," *Rafu Shimpo*, Dec. 18, 1941, p. 1.
34. "Filipinos Here Friendly to Resident Japanese," *Rafu Shimpo*, Dec. 26, 1941, p. 7.
35. "Perverted Patriotism," *Rafu Shimpo*, Jan. 4, 1942, p. 2. For reports on the killing and the efforts to apprehend the perpetrator, see "Man, Girl Held in Slaying of U.S. Japanese," *Daily News*, Dec. 24, 1941, p. 5, and "Killers 'Unknown' in U.S.-Jap Case," *Daily News*, Dec. 27, 1941, p. 24.
36. "New Chinese Emblem Issued for Autos, Stores and Homes," *Los Angeles Times*, Jan. 6, 1942, pt. 2, p. 3.
37. "Axis Aliens Must Turn in Radios and Cameras," *Los Angeles Times*, Dec. 28, 1941, pt. 1, pp. 1, 8. See also "U.S. Puts Stop to Possible Spying" and "Aliens Surrender Radios, Cameras," *Daily News*, Dec. 29, 1941, p. 3.
38. "Axis Aliens Surrender Radio Sets and Cameras," *Los Angeles Times*, Dec. 29, 1941, pt. 1, p. 1.
39. "Chinese Able to Spot Jap," *Los Angeles Times*, Dec. 28, 1941, pt. 2, p. 6.
40. "Two Japanese Arrested; Hissed President in Theater," *Los Angeles Times*, Jan. 3, 1942, pt. 2, p. 1. See also "2 Jap Youths Arrested as Woman Says One Spat on Her in Theater," *Los Angeles Examiner*, Jan. 3, 1942, sec. 1, p. 3.

41. "Unfinished Story, but it Could Happen Again!" *Rafu Shimpo*, Jan. 2, 1942, p. 1. *Rafu Shimpo* was reacting not to the *Times*'s coverage of the incident but to an article in the afternoon *Herald & Express*. Although there are some differences between the two articles, neither contained statements from the accused.
42. "Japanese Accused of Hissing Roosevelt Picture Released," *Los Angeles Times*, Jan. 11, 1942, pt. 2, p. 3.
43. "The Home Front," *Rafu Shimpo*, Jan. 4, 1942, pp. 2, 3.
44. "Dies Investigates Hiring of Japs," *Los Angeles Times*, Jan. 20, 1942, pt. 1, p. 9. The *Times* repeated these charges in greater detail two weeks later. See "Dies 'Yellow Paper' Reveals Jap Spying," *Los Angeles Times*, Feb. 5, 1942, pt. 1, pp. 1, 6.
45. "Dies and the Japs," *Los Angeles Times*, Jan. 23, 1942, pt. 2, p. 4.
46. "Eviction of Jap Aliens Sought," *Los Angeles Times*, January 28, 1942, part 1, pp. 1, 7.
47. "Japanese City Aides on Leaves," *Los Angeles Times*, Jan. 28, 1942, pt. 1, p. 7. See also "L.A. Officials in Quandary over Japs," *Daily News*, Jan. 28, 1942, p. 1; "L.A. Citizens, Officials Act to Oust Japs," *Los Angeles Examiner*, Jan. 28, 1942, sec. 1, pp. 1, 3; and "Mayor Explains Move," *Los Angeles Examiner*, Jan. 28, 1942, sec. 1, p. 3.
48. "Eviction of Jap Aliens Sought."
49. John Anson Ford, *Thirty Explosive Years in Los Angeles County* (San Marino, Calif.: Huntington Library, 1961), 28–29.
50. Memo from Wayne Allen to Mr. Spence D. Turner, forester and fire warden, Mr. E. W. Biscailuz, sheriff, Mr. J. F. Moroney, county clerk, and Mr. A. H. Adams, acting chief engineer, regional planning commission, Jan. 28, 1942, folder 7, Box 74, Ford Papers. This memo was quoted extensively in an article published in the *Los Angeles Times*. See "Terminal Island Issue Worries Officials Here," *Los Angeles Times*, Jan. 29, 1942, pt. 1, pp. 1, 6. See also "County to Urge Duration Leaves by Jap Workers," *Daily News*, Jan. 29, 1942, pp. 3, 17.
51. "Representative Ford Wants All Coast Japs in Camps," *Los Angeles Times*, Jan. 22, 1942, p. A.
52. LaRue McCormick, *Activist in the Radical Movement, 1930–1960: The International Labor Defense, the Communist Party*, an interview conducted by Malca Chall (Berkeley: University of California, 1980), 103.
53. "Legislature [*sic*] Asks Arrest of Bridges With Aliens," *Los Angeles Times*, Dec. 11, 1941, pt. 1, p. 3.
54. "Leland M. Ford in Group Held Tool of Nazi Agents," *Daily News*, Aug. 7, 1942, p. 18. See also "Ford Vote Record Shown Two Sided," *Daily News*, Aug. 10, 1942, p. 3.
55. "Representative Ford Wants All Coast Japs in Camps."

56. "Internment of Enemy Aliens in Western States Demanded," *Los Angeles Times*, Jan. 23, 1942, pt. 1, p. 6. See also "Native Sons Indorse Jap Evacuation Plan," *Los Angeles Examiner*, Jan. 24, 1942, sec. 1, p. 7.
57. "Terminal Island Japs Cause Worry for Navy," *Los Angeles Times*, Jan. 27, 1942, pt. 1, p. 7.
58. Wayne Allen to Board of Supervisors, Jan. 26, 1942, folder 7, Box 74, Ford Papers.
59. Resolution passed by the Los Angeles County Board of Supervisors, Jan. 29, 1942, folder 7, Box 74, Ford Papers. See also "Eviction of Jap Aliens Sought," *Los Angeles Times*, Jan. 28, 1942, pt. 1, pp. 1, 7; and "L.A. Citizens, Officials Act to Oust Japs," *Los Angeles Examiner*, Jan. 28, 1942, sec. 1, pp. 1, 3.
60. "Facing the Japanese Issue Here," *Los Angeles Times*, Jan. 28, 1942, pt. 2, p. 4.
61. Henry McLemore, "The Lighter Side," *Los Angeles Times*, Jan. 29, 1942, pt. 1, p. 6.
62. Kyle Palmer, "Coast Danger Spots Watched," *Los Angeles Times*, Jan. 29, 1942, pt. 1., p. 6.
63. "Dies Warns of Fifth Column Activities on West Coast," *Los Angeles Times*, Jan. 29, 1942, pt. 1, p. 6. See also "West Coast Periled by 'Enemy Within,' Dies Warns House," *Los Angeles Examiner*, Jan. 29, 1942, sec. 1, p. 1.
64. "Japanese Sad on Ouster Move," *Los Angeles Times*, Jan. 29, 1942, pt. 1, p. 6.
65. "Axis Aliens Ordered Out of Vital District Here," *Los Angeles Times*, Jan. 30, 1942, pt. 1, pp. 1, 8. See also "U.S. Orders Aliens Ousted," *Daily News*, Jan. 30, 1942, pp. 1, 14; and "U.S. Will Oust Japanese Here," *Los Angeles Examiner*, Jan. 30, 1942, sec. 1, p. 1.
66. "Moving Japanese," *Los Angeles Times*, Jan. 30, 1942, pt. 2, p. 4.
67. W. H. Anderson, "The Question of Japanese-Americans," *Los Angeles Times*, Feb. 2, 1942, pt. 2, p. 4.
68. McLemore, "The Lighter Side."
69. Anderson, "The Question of Japanese-Americans."
70. Kyle Palmer, "Californians Seek More Alien Curbs," *Los Angeles Times*, Feb. 3, 1942, pt. 1, p. 6.
71. "Bowron Asks Removal of All Japanese Inland," *Los Angeles Times*, Feb. 6, 1942, pt. 1, p. 1. See also "Bowron Bares Jap Plot Peril; Asks More Drastic Curb," *Los Angeles Examiner*, Feb. 6, 1942, sec. 1, pp. 1, 5.
72. "Mayor Suggests Japs Be Given Farm Work," *Los Angeles Times*, Feb. 8, 1942, pt. 1, p. 14.
73. "American Japs Removal Urged," *Los Angeles Times*, Feb. 3, 1942, pt. 1, pp. 1, 6.
74. Palmer, "Californians Seek More Alien Curbs."
75. See "Dies 'Yellow Paper' Reveals Jap Spying" and Warren B. Francis, "Japanese Here Sent Vital Data to Tokyo," *Los Angeles Times*, Feb. 6, 1942, pt. 1, p. 6. See also "Jap Attempt to Spy on Aqueduct Told," *Daily News*,

Feb. 6, 1942, p. 2; "Dies 'Paper' Tells of Jap Spying Here," *Los Angeles Examiner*, Feb. 5, 1942, sec. 1, pp. 1, 2; and "Jap Bid for L.A. Water Secrets in FBI Hands," *Los Angeles Examiner*, Feb. 6, 1942, sec. 1, p. 4.

76. "Dies on Jap Spy Activities Here," *Los Angeles Times*, Feb. 6, 1942, pt. 2, p. 4. See also "Dies 'Yellow Paper' Reveals Jap Spying."
77. "President to Be Asked to State Alien Policy," *Los Angeles Times*, Feb. 7, 1942, pt. 1, p. 6.
78. "Biddle, Freedom and Alien Restriction," *Los Angeles Times*, Feb. 7, 1942, pt. 2, p. 4.
79. "Newspaper Opinion," *Rafu Shimpo*, Feb. 15, 1942, p. 1.
80. *Rafu Shimpo*, Feb. 8, 1942, p. 2. The *Times* apparently refused to print Clark's letter.
81. "A. Nisei," "We Need Tolerance," *Rafu Shimpo*, Feb. 5, 1942, p. 7.
82. "Newspaper Opinion."
83. "United Citizens Call Mass Meeting at Maryknoll," *Rafu Shimpo*, Feb. 17, 1942, p. 1.
84. "What Are You Going to Do? Let's Get Organized!" *Rafu Shimpo*, Feb. 18, 1942, p. 1.
85. "United Citizens Federation Open to All Groups; 'Let's Get Organized,'" *Rafu Shimpo*, Feb. 19, 1942, p. 1.
86. "Nisei Launch Organization to Fight Coast Evacuation," *Los Angeles Times*, Feb. 20, 1942, pt. 1, p. 10.
87. "President Acts to End Menace," *Los Angeles Times*, Feb. 21, 1942, pt. 1, p. 1. See also "Army Controls All Coast Japs," *Daily News*, Feb. 21, 1942, pp. 1, 10.
88. "Immediate Evacuation of Japanese Demanded," *Los Angeles Times*, Feb. 25, 1942, pt. 1, p. 1.
89. "To Our Would-be Hitlers: 'We're Not a Bunch of Sheep!'" *Rafu Shimpo*, Mar. 13, 1942, p. 1.
90. "We're At War!" *California Eagle*, Dec. 11, 1941, p. 8-A.
91. "Target Jim Crow," *California Eagle*, Dec. 18, 1941, p. 12-A.
92. "Uncle Sam in Latin America: Bull in the Parlor?" *California Eagle*, Feb. 5, 1942, p. 8-A.
93. Charlotta A. Bass, "On the Sidewalk," *California Eagle*, Apr. 9, 1942, p. 8-A.
94. Text of radio address, February 1942, "Bass, C. A.—Speeches, 1940s" folder, Box 1, Bass Papers, Southern California Library for Social Studies and Research, Los Angeles.
95. "Back to the Farm?" *California Eagle*, Feb. 12, 1942, p. 8-A.
96. "Garden a Bit," *California Eagle*, Mar. 19, 1942, p. 8-A. See also "Back to the Farm—Again, Yes!" *California Eagle*, Apr. 30, 1942, p. 8-A.

97. "Minutes of Special Meeting," Feb. 16, 1942, "Annual Convention 1942 California Branch" folder, Box 24, Group IIA, Records of the NAACP, Library of Congress, Washington, D. C.
98. "False 'White' Farmer Story Angle in Local Daily Rapped," *California Eagle*, Feb. 19, 1942, p. 1-A.
99. "Resolution on: full participation in war production of allied aliens as voted upon and passed by the Coordinating Council of Latin-American Youth," June 24, 1942, Folder 2, Box 3, Manuel Ruiz Papers, M0295, Department of Special Collections, Stanford University Libraries, Stanford, Calif.

Chapter Three

1. "One Man Slain; Girls Join in Youthful Gang Forays Here," *Los Angeles Examiner*, Aug. 3, 1942, sec. 1, pp. 1, 5. See also "One Killed and 10 Hurt in Boy 'Wars,'" *Los Angeles Times*, Aug. 3, 1942, pt. 1, p. 1; and "11 Youths Jailed after Five Boys in Picnic Party Beaten by Gang," *Daily News*, Aug. 3, 1942, p. 4. The articles that appeared in the *Examiner* and the *Times* on August 3 were nearly identical, although the *Times* did not identify any of the gang members as "Mexicans." On the next day the *Examiner* reported that the victim of the Baldwin Park attack who was thought to have drowned "managed to drag himself from the pool and flee during the melee." "150 Rounded Up in Killing, Gang Terror," *Los Angeles Examiner*, Aug. 4, 1942, sec. 1, pp. 1, 3.
2. See Carey McWilliams, *North from Mexico: The Spanish-Speaking People of the United States*, updated by Matt S. Meier (1948; new ed., New York: Praeger, 1990), 207–17; Mauricio A. Mazón, *The Zoot-Suit Riots: The Psychology of Symbolic Annihilation* (Austin: University of Texas Press, 1984), 15–30; David G. Gutiérrez, *Walls and Mirrors: Mexican Americans, Mexican Immigrants, and the Politics of Ethnicity* (Berkeley: University of California Press, 1995), 121–30; Edward J. Escobar, *Race, Police, and the Making of a Political Identity: Mexican Americans and the Los Angeles Police Department, 1900–1945* (Berkeley: University of California Press, 1999), 207–28; and Eduardo Obregón Pagán, *Murder at the Sleepy Lagoon: Zoot Suits, Race, and Riot in Wartime L.A.* (Chapel Hill: University of North Carolina Press, 2003), 7–142. The Sleepy Lagoon case also inspired Luis Valdez's 1978 play *Zoot Suit*, which was made into a film in 1981.
3. Cultura Panamericana, Inc., Articles of Incorporation, in Folder 1, "Cultura Panamericana; Articles of Incorporation and By-laws, 1940," Box 2, Manuel Ruiz Papers, M0295, Department of Special Collections, Stanford University Libraries, Stanford, Calif. Biographical information about Ruiz is also included in Ruiz's papers.
4. Manuel Ruiz, Jr., secretary to trustees of Cultura Panamericana, Inc., to *Los Angeles Examiner*, Aug. 3, 1942, Folder 4, "Correspondence, June 1941–Oct 1942," Box 2, Ruiz Papers.

5. R. T. Van Ettisch, managing editor, *Los Angeles Examiner*, to Manuel Ruiz, Jr., Aug. 4, 1942, Box 1, Folder 3, "Correspondence, Fi-Lo," Ruiz Papers.
6. See "150 Rounded Up in Killing, Gang Terror"; "Gangs Warned 'Kid Gloves Off!'" *Los Angeles Times*, Aug. 4, 1942, pt. 1, p. 1; and "40 Arrested in Boy Gang Killing," *Daily News*, Aug. 4, 1942, p. 6.
7. Capt. Vernon Rasmussen to Ernest W. Oliver, foreman of the Grand Jury, Aug. 12, 1942, in Folder 7, "Los Angeles County Grand Jury Correspondence," Box 4, Sleepy Lagoon Defense Committee Records (Collection 107), Department of Special Collections, Charles E. Young Research Library, UCLA.
8. Gerald Woods, *The Police in Los Angeles: Reform and Professionalization* (New York: Garland, 1993), 202. See also Tom Sitton, *Los Angeles Transformed: Fletcher Bowron's Urban Reform Revival* (Albuquerque: University of New Mexico Press, 2005), 75.
9. C. B. Horrall, Chief of Police, to Ernest W. Oliver, Aug. 13, 1942, Folder 7, "Los Angeles County Grand Jury Correspondence," Box 4, Sleepy Lagoon Defense Committee Records.
10. For some biographical information on Duran Ayres, see "Death Takes Duran-Ayres," *Los Angeles Times*, Jan. 14, 1944, pt. 1, p. 10. See also "Es Necesario Aprobar una Ley en California que Ponga Fin a Todos Los Prejuicios Raciales [It is Necessary to Approve a Law in California that Puts an End to All Racial Prejudices]," *La Opinión*, Dec. 21, 1941, p. 2.
11. "Report of Ed. Duran Ayres," Folder 7, "Los Angeles County Grand Jury Correspondence," Box 4, Sleepy Lagoon Defense Committee Records.
12. Horrall to Oliver.
13. Rasmussen to Oliver.
14. Ibid.
15. "Report of Ed. Duran Ayres."
16. "Professional Mollycoddlers and the Gangs," *Los Angeles Times*, Aug. 4, 1942, pt. 2, p. 4.
17. Timothy G. Turner, "Significance of Zoot-Suit Gangsters," *Los Angeles Times*, Jan. 14, 1943, pt. 2, p. 4.
18. McWilliams, *North from Mexico*, 214.
19. See "Zoot Gangsters Knife and Rob More Victims," *Los Angeles Times*, Oct. 6, 1942, pt. 2, p. 2.
20. "Solution to Youthful Gang Violence Problem Sought," *Los Angeles Times*, Oct. 9, 1942, pt. 2, pp. 1, 3. See also McWilliams, *North from Mexico*, 214.
21. See Carey McWilliams, *The Education of Carey McWilliams* (New York: Simon and Schuster, 1978), 19–115.
22. "Obituaries: Harry Hoijer, 1904–1976," *American Anthropologist* 79 (1977): 105–8.

23. See Nunn's Curriculum Vitae and clippings in the archives of Occidental College, Los Angeles. I would like to thank Occidental College archivist Jean Paule for providing me with this material.
24. "Paper presented by Consul Aguilar" [to the Grand Jury], Folder 7, "Los Angeles County Grand Jury Correspondence," Box 4, Sleepy Lagoon Defense Committee Records.
25. "Testimony of Guy T. Nunn, Field Representative, Minority Groups Service, War Manpower Commission, before the Los Angeles County Grand Jury," Folder 7, "Los Angeles County Grand Jury Correspondence," Box 4, Sleepy Lagoon Defense Committee Records.
26. Harry Hoijer, "The Problem of Crime among the Mexican Youth of Los Angeles," Folder 7, "Los Angeles County Grand Jury Correspondence," Box 4, Sleepy Lagoon Defense Committee Records.
27. "Testimony of Carey McWilliams, Chief, Division of Immigration and Housing, Department of Industrial Relations, State of California, Before the Los Angeles County Grand Jury, October 8, 1942," Folder 7, "Los Angeles County Grand Jury Correspondence," Box 4, Sleepy Lagoon Defense Committee Records.
28. "Paper presented by Consul Aguilar."
29. "Testimony of Guy T. Nunn."
30. Hoijer, "The Problem of Crime."
31. "Testimony of Carey McWilliams."
32. "Paper presented by Consul Aguilar."
33. Ibid.
34. Hoijer, "The Problem of Crime."
35. "Testimony of Carey McWilliams."
36. Ibid.
37. Hoijer, "The Problem of Crime."
38. "Testimony of Guy T. Nunn." See also "Solution to Youthful Gang Violence Problem Sought."
39. "Solution to Youthful Gang Violence Problem Sought."
40. See Karl Holton, Kenyon J. Scudder, Heman G. Stark, and Kenneth S. Beam, *Earl Warren and the Youth Authority: Interviews conducted by Gabrielle Morris, Robert Knutson, Rosemary Levenson* (Berkeley: Regional Oral History Office, University of California, 1972), 1–5, 36–42.
41. "Gangs Called One of Cities' Second Generation Problems," *Los Angeles Times*, Oct. 29, 1942, pt. 2, p. 2.
42. Turner, "Significance of Zoot-Suit Gangsters."
43. Harry F. Henderson, chair of the Special Mexican Relations Committee of the Grand Jury, to Nelson D. Rockefeller, Jr., Coordinator of Inter-American Affairs, Nov. 12, 1942, in Folder 7, "Los Angeles County Grand Jury

Correspondence," Box 4, Sleepy Lagoon Defense Committee Records. See also Henderson to Elmer Davis, Director of the Office of War Information, Nov. 12, 1942, and Henderson to Henry Stimson, Secretary of War, Nov. 12, 1942, in the same folder.

44. Resolution adopted by 100 Mexican Employees of California Mill Supply, 4 September 1942, Box 28, John Anson Ford Papers, Huntington Library, San Marino, Calif.

45. "Plans Probe of Mexican 'Boy Gangs,'" *California Eagle*, Oct. 22, 1942, p. 1-A. See also press telegram from Tom Cullen to the *Daily People's World*, Oct. 22, 1942, Folder 1, "News Releases, Memeographed copies [*sic*]," Box 1, Sleepy Lagoon Defense Committee Records.

46. LaRue McCormick, *Activist in the Radical Movement, 1930–1960: The International Labor Defense, the Communist Party*, an interview conducted by Malca Chall (Berkeley: University of California, 1980), 1–30.

47. See Mario T. García, *Memories of Chicano History: The Life and Narrative of Bert Corona* (Berkeley: University of California Press, 1994), 32–107.

48. Press telegram from Tom Cullen to the *Daily People's World*.

49. Resolution adopted by 100 Mexican Employees of California Mill Supply.

50. Al S. Waxman, editorial, *Eastside Journal*, Jan. 20, 1943.

51. Press telegram from Tom Cullen to the *Daily People's World*.

52. Ibid.

53. Citizens' Committee for the Defense of Mexican-American Youth Public Relations press release, Mar. 2, 1943, Folder 1, "News Releases, Memeographed copies [*sic*]," Box 1, Sleepy Lagoon Defense Committee Records.

54. Resolution adopted by 100 Mexican Employees of California Mill Supply.

55. "We Have Just Begun to Fight," undated typescript, Folder 1, "News Releases, Memeographed copies [*sic*]," Box 1, Sleepy Lagoon Defense Committee Records.

56. "Jury's Gang-Case Verdict Disproves 'Persecution,'" *Los Angeles Times*, Jan. 14, 1943, pt. 2, p. 4.

57. For information about Jack B. Tenney and the California legislature's Joint Committee on Un-American Activities, see Ingrid Winther Scobie, "Jack B. Tenney and the 'Parasitic Menace': Anti-Communist Legislation in California, 1940–1949," *Pacific Historical Review* 43, no. 2 (1974): 188–211.

58. "Trial of Mexican Youths Used as Axis Propaganda," *Los Angeles Times*, Nov. 24, 1942, pt. 1, p. 1.

59. "Tenney Tells Inquiry Scope," *Los Angeles Times*, Dec. 19, 1942, pt. 2, p. 10.

60. "Sinarquistas Cleared by Tenney Committee," *Los Angeles Times*, Dec. 20, 1942, pt. 2, p. 7.

61. "Our Mexican Neighbors," *California Eagle*, Oct. 15, 1942, p. 8-A.

62. See "John S. Kinloch Killed in German Front Action," *California Eagle*, Apr. 26, 1945, p. 1. See also "A Lesser Light," *California Eagle*, Apr. 18, 1946, p. 6; and "John Kinloch Memorial a Tribute to Courage," *California Eagle*, Aug. 9, 1945, pp. 1, 2.
63. John Kinloch, "Mexicans Face Police Terror Round-Ups; Vile Press Slurs," *California Eagle*, Nov. 5, 1942, pp. 1-A, 7-B.
64. Ibid.
65. "Our Mexican Neighbors."

Chapter Four

1. "Pamphlet on Japs Stirs Legion Wrath," *Los Angeles Times*, Oct. 22, 1942, pt. 1, p. 6.
2. "Pamphlet Placed under Ban on Charge It Lauds Japs," *Los Angeles Times*, Oct. 23, 1942, pt. 2, p. 2. See also "Legion Booklet Attack Praised," *Los Angeles Times*, Oct. 25, 1942, pt. 2, p. 3.
3. See, for example, "Release of Stored Jap Farm Machinery Urged," *Los Angeles Times*, Jan. 22, 1943, pt. 1, p. 16; "Inquiry on Jap Cars Ordered," *Los Angeles Times*, Jan. 29, 1943, p. A; "Hearing Will Involve Owners of Stored Cars," *Los Angeles Times*, Feb. 4, 1943, pt. 1, p. 14; "Move Speeded to Obtain Use of Stored Jap Cars," *Los Angeles Times*, Feb. 16, 1943, pt. 2, p. 2; "Jap-Owned Farm Machines in Use," *Los Angeles Times*, Feb. 16, 1943, pt. 1, p. 7; "Japs' Farm Tools Sought," *Los Angeles Times*, Mar. 18, 1943, p. A; "Quick Action Promised on Jap Farm Tools," *Los Angeles Times*, Mar. 26, 1943, pt. 2, pp. 1, 2. See also "New Caches of Stored Jap Farm Tools Found," *Los Angeles Times*, Mar. 30, 1943, pt. 2, p. 12; "More Jap Farm Tools Discovered Rusting," *Los Angeles Times*, Mar. 31, 1943, pt. 2, p. 8; "Chester G. Hanson, "Bill for Taking Jap Farm Machines Being Drafted," *Los Angeles Times*, Apr. 3, 1943, pt. 1, p. 4; "Drive to Seize Jap Machinery Spurred," *Los Angeles Times*, Apr. 6, 1943, pt. 2, p. 3; "State Would Seize Jap Farm Machines," *Daily News*, Apr. 6, 1943, p. 3; "Senate Inquiry Planned on Jap Farming Tools," *Los Angeles Times*, Apr. 23, 1943, pt. 2, p. 8; "Help in Freeing Jap Machines Promised," *Los Angeles Times*, Apr. 27, 1943, pt. 2, p. 8; "Jap Farm Tools Use Proposed," *Los Angeles Times*, Apr. 29, 1943, p. A; "Jap Machinery Bill Completed," *Los Angeles Times*, May 9, 1943, pt. 1, p. 14; "Jap Machines to Be Seized," *Los Angeles Times*, May 23, 1943, pt. 2, p. 6; and "Jap Machine Survey Ends," *Los Angeles Times*, May 25, 1943, pt. 2, p. 1.
4. For information about Palmer, see Dennis McDougal, *Privileged Son: Otis Chandler and the Rise and Fall of the L.A. Times Dynasty* (Cambridge, Mass.: Perseus, 2001), 88–89, 141; and David Halberstam, *The Powers that Be* (New York: Knopf, 1979), 117–22.
5. Kyle Palmer, "Question of Jap Loyalty in Crisis Haunts Hawaii," *Los Angeles Times*, Feb. 5, 1943, pt. 1, p. 5.

6. Tom Hirashima, "A Nisei Viewpoint: Move to Take Away Citizenship Smells Just Like Hitlerism," *Pacific Citizen*, June 18, 1942, p. 5. See also "Native Sons and Fascism," *Pacific Citizen*, Nov. 5, 1942, p. 4; "Attacks on Nisei," *Pacific Citizen*, Nov. 12, 1942, p. 4; and "More Pity Than Fear," *Pacific Citizen*, Dec. 24, 1942, p. 4.
7. Larry Tajiri, "Nisei USA: Nisei and Race Prejudice," *Pacific Citizen*, Mar. 4, 1943, p. 4.
8. "Editorial: The Myth of Racial Superiority," *Santa Anita Pacemaker*, July 22, 1942, p. 6.
9. "Editorial: Translate Beliefs into Action," *Santa Anita Pacemaker*, Aug. 1, 1942, p. 6.
10. "Editorial: Fight for America in Our Way," *Santa Anita Pacemaker*, Aug. 12, 1942, p. 8.
11. "Girls Have 'Jam' Session: Southern Jamboree To Be Held On Monday at Recreation Hall," *Santa Anita Pacemaker*, Aug. 15, 1942, p. 5.
12. "More Japs Leave Arcadia," *Los Angeles Times*, Sept. 26, 1942, pt. 2, p. 1.
13. See Arthur A. Hansen and David A. Hacker, "The Manzanar Riot: An Ethnic Perspective," *Amerasia Journal* 2, no. 2 (1974): 112–57; Sue Kunitoni Embrey, Arthur A. Hansen, and Betty Kulberg Mitson, *Manzanar Martyr: An Interview with Harry Y. Ueno* (Fullerton, Calif.: Oral History Program, California State University, Fullerton, 1986); and Lon Kurashige, "Resistance, Collaboration, and Manzanar Protest," *Pacific Historical Review* 70, no. 3 (2001): 387–417.
14. "Beaten Jap Known for U.S. Loyalty," *Los Angeles Examiner*, Dec. 8, 1942, sec. 1, p. 3.
15. "Manzanar Boy Scouts Lauded," *Los Angeles Examiner*, Dec. 10, 1942, sec. 1, p. 11. See also "Flag Guarded at Manzanar," *Los Angeles Times*, Dec. 10, 1942, pt. 1, p. 22.
16. "Kindness to Alien Japs Proves Poor Policy," *Los Angeles Times*, Dec. 8, 1942, pt. 2, p. 4.
17. "Gen. DeWitt's Policy Vindicated Completely," *Los Angeles Times*, Dec. 9, 1942, pt. 2, p. 4.
18. "Don't Let It Happen Again!" letter to the editor from Peggy Keith, *Los Angeles Times*, Dec. 11, 1942, pt. 2, p. 4.
19. Warren B. Francis, "Manzanar Arson Case Disclosed," *Los Angeles Times*, Dec. 9, 1942, pt. 1, p. 13.
20. Ray Richards, "Congressmen Denounce Jap Camp Control," *Los Angeles Examiner*, Dec. 11, 1942, sec. 1, p. 7.
21. "Rigid Manzanar Control Sought," *Los Angeles Times*, Dec. 11, 1942, pt. 1, p. 21. See also Richards "Congressmen Denounce Jap Camp Control," and "Jap Camp Inquiry Sought by Leland Ford," *Los Angeles Examiner*, Dec. 14, 1942, sec. 1, p. 7.
22. "Rigid Manzanar Control Sought."

23. "Grand Jurors Back Ban on All Japanese," *Los Angeles Examiner*, Dec. 10, 1942, sec. 1, p. 11. See also "Jury Indorses Jap Farm Ban," *Los Angeles Times*, Dec. 10, 1942, pt. 1, p. 22.
24. Warren B. Francis, "Inquiry on Jap Camps Ordered," *Los Angeles Times*, Jan. 16, 1943, pt. 1, p. 1.
25. See Warren B. Francis, "Quiz on Jap Camps Near," *Los Angeles Times*, Jan. 23, 1943, pt. 1, p. 8.
26. "Change in Jap Camps Asked," *Los Angeles Times*, Apr. 1, 1943, pt. 1, p. 18. See also Ray Richards, "Chandler to Ask Cut in Jap Relocation Centers," *Los Angeles Examiner*, Apr. 1, 1943, pt. 1, p. 12.
27. "Closer Control of Japs Urged," *Los Angeles Times*, Feb. 12, 1943, pt. 1, p. 18.
28. "Manzanar Japs Rationed Too," *Los Angeles Times*, Jan. 28, 1943, pt. 1, p. 1.
29. Ray Richards, "Southern Congressman Demands Action against Japs," *Los Angeles Examiner*, Feb. 1, 1943, pt. 1, pp. 1, 7.
30. Ray Richards, "Hit Japs Now or Face Invasion, Says Rankin," *Los Angeles Examiner*, Feb. 4, 1943, pt. 1, pp. 1, 5. See also "'Coddling of Japs' Must End, Mississippi Legislator Warns," *Los Angeles Times*, Feb. 4, 1943, pt. 1, p. 6.
31. Richards, "Southern Congressman Demands Action against Japs."
32. "Total Warfare against Japan Should Be Waged NOW to Reduce Pacific Peril," *Los Angeles Examiner*, Feb. 22, 1943, sec. 1, p. 14.
33. "Army to Enlist Loyal Japs," *Los Angeles Times*, Jan. 29, 1943, p. A.
34. "On Military Service," *Pacific Citizen*, Feb. 4, 1943, p. 4.
35. "Army to Accept Loyal Japanese," *Los Angeles Times*, Feb. 6, 1943, pt. 1, p. 5. See also "Japs in State Get Chance to Fight for U.S.," *Los Angeles Examiner*, Feb. 6, 1943, sec. 1, p. 7, and "Army to Use Interned Japs," *Los Angeles Times*, Feb. 18, 1943, pt. 2, p. 12.
36. "Japs in Army Plan Protested," *Los Angeles Times*, Feb. 10, 1943, pt. 2, p. 3. See also "Jap Army Unit Plan Protested," *Los Angeles Examiner*, Feb. 10, 1943, sec. 1, p. 14. A Santa Monica parlor of the Native Sons passed a nearly identical resolution. See "Jap Soldier Unit Opposed," *Los Angeles Examiner*, Feb. 17, 1943, sec. 1, p. 16.
37. "Torrance Veterans Oppose Recruiting of Interned Japs," *Los Angeles Times*, Mar. 8, 1943, pt. 1, p. 12.
38. Richards, "Hit Japs Now or Face Invasion."
39. "Ban on Japs in Army Backed," *Los Angeles Times*, Feb. 19, 1943, pt. 1, p. 8.
40. "Army Duty Asked by 1000 Japanese," *Los Angeles Times*, Mar. 26, 1943, pt. 1, p. 3; "Nisei May Be Drafted for Military Service," *Los Angeles Times*, Apr. 3, 1943, pt. 1, p. 12.
41. "Japs in Coast Area Opposed," *Los Angeles Times*, Apr. 14, 1943, p. A. See also "DeWitt Fights Japs' Return to Coast Area," *Daily News*, Apr. 14, 1943, p. 32.
42. "Gen. DeWitt and Evacuation," *Pacific Citizen*, Apr. 15, 1943, p. 4.

43. Warren B. Francis, "Army Weighs Release of 'Loyal' Japs," *Los Angeles Times*, Apr. 17, 1943, pt. 1, pp. 1, 3. See also "American Army Japs to Enter Coast Area," *Daily News*, Apr. 19, 1943, p. 1.
44. "Costello Sees Peril in Return of Japs to State," *Los Angeles Times*, Apr. 18, 1943, pt. 1, p. 16. The *Los Angeles Times* later endorsed Costello's statements in an editorial. See "Gen. DeWitt Has Proved Wisdom in Jap Policy," *Los Angeles Times*, May 28, 1943, pt. 2, p. 4.
45. "Failure to Reduce Jap Victory Hit by Costello," *Los Angeles Examiner*, Apr. 18, 1943, pt. 1, p. 17.
46. "Ban on Japs in West Eased," *Los Angeles Times*, Apr. 19, 1943, pt. 1, p. 1. See also "DeWitt Relaxes Rules on Japs in U.S. Army," *Los Angeles Examiner*, Apr. 19, 1943, pt. 1, p. 1.
47. "Coast Furloughs for Japs Opposed," *Los Angeles Times*, May 6, 1943, pt. 1, p. 13.
48. "Lifting of Jap Ban Protested," *Los Angeles Times*, Apr. 21, 1943, pt. 1, p. 16.
49. "Stupid and Dangerous," *Los Angeles Times*, Apr. 22, 1943, pt. 2, p. 4.
50. "Coast Furloughs for Japs Opposed."
51. Kyle Palmer, "Not a Social Planning Problem," *Los Angeles Times*, May 9, 1943, pt. 2, p. 4.
52. "Fight to Bar Japs Pressed," *Los Angeles Times*, May 7, 1943, p. A. See also Warren K. Francis, "Coast Congressmen Fight Any Plan Allowing Japs' Return," *Los Angeles Times*, May 7, 1943, p. A.
53. "County Assured Army Japs Won't Jeopardize West Coast," *Los Angeles Times*, May 12, 1943, p. A.
54. "Southern California Christian Groups Oppose Discrimination," *Pacific Citizen*, Feb. 11, 1943, p. 2.
55. "Ickes Hires Japanese to Work on His Farm," *Los Angeles Times*, Apr. 16, 1943, pt. 1, p. 7. See also "Seven Japs Given Jobs by Ickes," *Daily News*, Apr. 16, 1943, p. 16.
56. "Group Demands Ickes Fire Japs Hired for Farm," *Los Angeles Times*, Apr. 27, 1943, pt. 2, p. 3. See also "Ickes' Hiring of Japs on Farm Is Insult to Patriotic Americans" and "Release of Interned Japs Menaces Nation's Safety, Says Woodman," *Los Angeles Examiner*, May 10, 1943, pt. 1, p. 14.
57. "Japanese-Americans' Segregation Criticized," *Los Angeles Times*, Apr. 17, 1943, p. A.
58. "Bleeding Hearts Discuss the Jap Problem," *Los Angeles Times*, Apr. 17, 1943, pt. 2, p. 4.
59. "Deny Japs U.S. Citizenship Bowron Asks," *Los Angeles Examiner*, May 27, 1943, pt. 1, p. 6. The *Times* reported on Bowron's statements as well. See "Bowron Stands Firm on His Views on Japs," *Los Angeles Times*, May 27, 1943, p. A. See also "Mayor Bowron Repeats Stand against Nisei," *Pacific Citizen*, June 3, 1943, p. 3.

60. Timothy G. Turner, "Mrs. Roosevelt Here to Visit Hospitals," *Los Angeles Times*, Apr. 27, 1943, pt. 2, p. 1. See also "Mrs. Roosevelt Pays Visit to Japs in Arizona Center," *Los Angeles Examiner*, Apr. 24, 1943, pt. 1, p. 4; and "Mrs. F.D.R. Here, Talks on Japs," *Daily News*, Apr. 27, 1943, p. 3.
61. "Mrs. Roosevelt and Japs," letter to the editor from Mrs. J. C. Thomas of Los Angeles, *Los Angeles Times*, Apr. 30, 1943, pt. 2, p. 4.
62. Ibid.
63. "Better for Japs," letter to the editor from W. C. Simmons of Long Beach, *Los Angeles Times*, Apr. 30, 1943, pt. 2, p. 4.
64. "Deep-Dyed Prejudice," letter to the editor from Wendell L. Miller, *Los Angeles Times*, Apr. 26, 1943, pt. 2, p. 4.
65. "Fanning Hatred's Flames?" letter to the editor from Leonora Vickland, *Los Angeles Times*, May 3, 1943, pt. 2, p. 4.
66. "Nisei's Viewpoint," letter to the editor from Tom Saki, Poston, Arizona, *Los Angeles Times*, May 3, 1943, pt. 2, p. 4.
67. "Jap Relocation Director Tells Job-Finding Aims," *Los Angeles Times*, May 12, 1943, p. A. See also "Conference Hears Jap Camp Director," *Daily News*, May 12, 1943, p. 3.
68. "Jap-Americans Being Shifted to War Jobs," *Los Angeles Times*, May 12, 1943, p. A.
69. "Church Council Raps Race Hatred," *Los Angeles Times*, May 16, 1943, pt. 1, p. 10.
70. "Jap-American League Condemns Executions," *Los Angeles Times*, Apr. 23, 1943, pt. 1, p. 5. See also "Jap-Americans Condemn Tokyo," *Daily News*, Apr. 23, 1943, p. 2.
71. Warren B. Francis, "Atrocity May Balk Release of 'Loyal' Japs," *Los Angeles Times*, Apr. 23, 1943, pt. 1, p. 6.
72. "Let's Ship Them Back," letter to the editor from Lou Manss, *Los Angeles Times*, May 3, 1943, pt. 2, p. 4.
73. "Bowron Hopes Jap-Americans Never Return to Los Angeles," *Los Angeles Times*, May 20, 1943, p. A.
74. "Deny Japs U.S. Citizenship Bowron Asks."
75. "Continue Being Saps!" letter to the editor from C. R. C., Seal Beach, *Los Angeles Times*, Apr. 26, 1943, pt. 2, p. 4.
76. "Let's Ship Them Back."
77. Francis, "Atrocity May Balk Release of 'Loyal' Japs."
78. "Let's Ship Them Back."
79. Letter to editor from Owen R. Stafford, M.D., *Los Angeles Times*, May 3, 1943, pt. 2, p. 4.

80. "Continue Being Saps!"
81. "Let's Ship Them Back."
82. "Jap Camp Proposals Deserve Consideration," *Los Angeles Times*, May 8, 1943, pt. 2, p. 4.
83. Palmer, "Not a Social Planning Problem."
84. "Gen. DeWitt Has Proved Wisdom in Jap Policy."
85. "Reports to Give New Light on Jap Centers," *Los Angeles Times*, May 19, 1943, p. A.
86. "Startling Jap Spy Activity Here Told," *Los Angeles Times*, May 20, 1943, pt. 1, p. 1.
87. "Representative Answers Pro-Jap Sentimentalism," *Los Angeles Times*, May 21, 1943, pt. 2, p. 4.
88. "State Council Opposes Any Plan to Return Japs," *Los Angeles Times*, May 22, 1943, pt. 1, p. 13.
89. "Gen. DeWitt Has Proved Wisdom in Jap Policy." The *Examiner* suggested that it was possible to determine if Japanese Americans were loyal to the United States but declared that "it is entirely too difficult to tell a good Jap from a bad Jap to ever take a chance on allowing these enemies of freedom anywhere." "I Predge Arregiance," *Los Angeles Examiner*, May 28, 1943, pt. 1, p. 10.
90. "Why Ignore Our Own War?" *Los Angeles Examiner*, May 13, 1943, pt. 1, p. 14.

Chapter Five

1. "Brown Race Danger Seen by Scientist," *Los Angeles Examiner*, May 10, 1943, pt. 2, p. 1.
2. "Negro Dies of Wounds in Clash with Officer," *Los Angeles Times*, May 25, 1943, pt. 2, p. 8.
3. See "3 Jailed on Riot Charge," *Los Angeles Examiner*, May 24, 1943, pt. 1, p. 26; "Near Riot in L.A. Shooting," *Daily News*, May 24, 1943, p. 22; and "Near-Riot as Cop Shoots Eastside Man," *California Eagle*, May 27, 1943, pp. 1-A, 3-A.
4. "Cops Curse, Beat Deacon, War Veteran," *California Eagle*, May 27, 1943, p. 1-A, 2-A.
5. See "Victory Body Meets Sunday," *California Eagle*, Apr. 9, 1942, p. 1-A; "Holy City Leader Rapped By Rev. Clayton Russell," *California Eagle*, May 28, 1942, p. 1-A; "Victory Committee Hits Food Distribution," *California Eagle*, Feb. 10, 1943, p. 1-A.
6. "Mass Meet Charges Attempt to 'Goad' Riot!" *California Eagle*, June 3, 1943, pp. 1-A, 4-B.
7. "Note To Disrupters: NO RIOT HERE," *California Eagle*, June 3, 1943, p. 8-A.

8. E. Frederick Anderson, *The Development of Leadership and Organization Building in the Black Community of Los Angeles from 1900 through World War II* (Saratoga, Calif.: Century Twenty One Publishing, 1980), 87.
9. Clayton D. Russell, "What the Victory Committee Thinks," *California Eagle*, June 10, 1943, p. 3-A. See also "Deacon Snags Cop Who Beat Him," *California Eagle*, June 10, 1943, p. 1-A.
10. The quotation is from "6 Zoot Suiters Sent to Hospital by Servicemen," *Daily News*, June 8, 1943, pp. 1, 3. See also "Zoot Suiters Learn Lesson in Fights With Servicemen," *Los Angeles Times*, June 7, 1943, pt. 2, p. 1; "Sailors Hunt Zoot-Suiters, 2 in Hospital," *Los Angeles Examiner*, June 5, 1943, pt. 1, p. 3; "'Zoot Front' Watched for Servicemen Raids," *Los Angeles Examiner*, June 6, 1943, pt. 1, p. 29; and "Navy-Battered Zoot Suiters Jailed by Police," *Los Angeles Examiner*, June 7, 1943, pt. 2, p. 1.
11. "6 Zoot Suiters Sent to Hospital by Servicemen."
12. "Lifeguards Can't Tell 'Zoot Suit' Bathers," *Los Angeles Times*, June 7, 1943, pt. 2, p. 1.
13. "Expidio importante llamado [Important call issued]," *La Opinión*, June 11, 1943, p. 1.
14. "44 Zooters Jailed in Attacks on Sailors," *Daily News*, June 7, 1943, pp. 1, 29.
15. "Zoot Suit Chiefs Girding Gangs for War on Navy," *Daily News*, June 8, 1943, p. 6.
16. "Batalla de marineros y pachucos en Belvedere [Battle of sailors and pachucos in Belvedere]," *La Opinión*, June 5, 1943, p. 1.
17. See "Committee for Latin-American Youth Selects Manuel Ruiz Jr.," *Los Angeles Times*, Dec. 3, 1942, pt. 1, p. 15.
18. Minutes of June 7, 1943, meeting, Citizens' Committee for Latin American Youth, Folder 6, "Citizens' Committee for Latin American Youth, 1942–1944," Box 4, Manuel Ruiz Papers, M0295, Department of Special Collections, Stanford University Libraries, Stanford, Calif.
19. "Statement on Behalf of Board of Supervisors, Presented by John Anson Ford," June 8, 1943, Folder 4, "1943," Box 51, John Anson Ford papers, Huntington Library, San Marino. See also "County Advises Public Against Racial Prejudice," *Los Angeles Times*, June 9, 1943, pt. 1, p. A.
20. "Federal, State Officials Asked to Delve into Riots," *Daily News*, June 9, 1943, pp. 1, 31.
21. Eduardo Quevedo to Elmer Davis, Alan Cranston, and President Franklin D. Roosevelt, n.d., Folder 11, "Correspondence, 1943," Box 1, Eduardo Quevedo papers, Department of Special Collections, Stanford University Library. A copy of Quevedo's letter was translated into Spanish and published in *La Opinión* on June 9, 1943. A copy of an English-language translation of the letter in *La Opinión* is in the Earl Warren papers, California State Archives, Sacramento.

22. "Strong Measures Must Be Taken against Rioting," *Los Angeles Times*, June 9, 1943, pt. 2, p. 4.
23. "Warren Orders Zoot Quiz; Quiet Reigns After Rioting," *Los Angeles Times*, June 10, 1943, pt. 1, pp. 1, A.
24. "Mayor Pledges 2-Fisted Action, No Wrist Slap," *Los Angeles Examiner*, June 10, 1943, pt. 1, p. 9. See also "Warren Orders Zoot Quiz"; "Issue Not Race Discrimination, Mayor Declares," *Los Angeles Times*, June 10, 1943, p. A; and "Mayor Decries Zoot 'Uproar,'" *Daily News*, June 10, 1943, p. 3.
25. Harold A. Slane, "Zoot Origins Are Traced," *Daily News*, June 10, 1943, pp. 3, 16.
26. See "Near-Martial Law in L.A. Riot Zone," *Daily News*, June 9, 1943, p. 1; "Zoot Suit Hunt on in Suburbs as Navy Clamps Ban on L.A.," *Los Angeles Examiner*, June 9, 1943, pt. 1, p. 1; "Warren Orders Zoot Quiz; and "Clashes Few as Zoot War Dies Down," *Los Angeles Times*, June 11, 1943, pt. 1, p. 1.
27. "U.S., Warren Act on Zoot Suits; New Outbreak of Gang Rioting," *Los Angeles Examiner*, June 10, 1943, pt. 1, p. 1.
28. "Eagle Demands Full Police Protection!" *California Eagle*, June 10, 1943, p. 1-A.
29. Charlotta A. Bass, "On the Sidewalk: An Open Letter to Fletcher Bowron," *California Eagle*, June 10, 1943, pp. 1-A, 3-A; and "Eagle Demands Full Police Protection!" See also "Hot or Cold, What Has a Grocery Store Got To Do With a Riot," advertisement for People's Victory Market, *California Eagle*, June 10, 1943, p. 8-B, and John S. Kinloch, "Kinloch's Corner," *California Eagle*, June 17, 1943, p. 1-B.
30. Rob Leicester Wagner, *Red Ink, White Lies: The Rise and Fall of Los Angeles Newspapers, 1920–1962* (Upland, Calif.: Dragonflyer Press, 2000), 186.
31. Ted LeBerthon, *Daily News*, June 11, 1943, p. 22.
32. "Time for Sanity," *Los Angeles Times*, June 11, 1943, pt. 1, p. 1.
33. "Who Is Really Stirring Up the Racial Prejudice?" *Los Angeles Times*, June 15, 1943, pt. 2, p. 4.
34. "Watts Pastor Blames Riots on Fifth Column," *Los Angeles Times*, June 11, 1943, p. A.
35. "Zoot Clash Held Riot Safety Valve," *Los Angeles Times*, June 23, 1943, pt. 2, p. 10.
36. Msgr. Francis J. Weber, "Archbishop McGucken: Hardworking Shepherd," *Catholic San Francisco*, Mar. 14, 2003. Available at http://catholic–sf.org/031403.html.
37. See Jonathan Wafer, "Remembering Berkeley's First Black Police Officer," *Berkeley Daily Planet*, Feb. 18, 2005, http://www.berkeleydailyplanet.com/article.cfm?archiveDate=02-18-05&storyID=20772.
38. *Who's Who in America*, vol. 23 (1944–45), 1359.
39. "Leo Carrillo Dies; Film Star Was 81," *New York Times*, Sept. 11, 1961, p. 27.

40. Carey McWilliams wrote that Kenny presented the committee a report that McWilliams had prepared and that the committee adopted it "with some modifications." See Carey McWilliams, *North from Mexico: The Spanish-Speaking People of the United States*, updated by Matt S. Meier (1948; new ed., New York: Praeger, 1990), 229.
41. "Report and Recommendations of Citizens Committee," June 12, 1943, file 2624, "Administrative Files, Department of Justice–Attorney General, Law Enforcement, 1943," Earl Warren Papers, F3640, California State Archives, Sacramento. See also the newspaper reports on the recommendations: "Punishment of All Urged to Break Up Zoot Suit War," *Los Angeles Times*, June 13, 1943, pt. 2, pp. 1, 2; "Remedies for Curbing Youth Gangs Offered," *Los Angeles Examiner*, June 13, 1943, pt. 1, p. 1.
42. Joseph T. McGucken to Earl Warren, June 21, 1943, file 2624, "Administrative Files, Department of Justice–Attorney General, Law Enforcement, 1943," Earl Warren Papers.
43. "Navy-Battered Zoot Suiters Jailed by Police."
44. "Downtown Crowds Storm Streets in Zoot Suiter Hunt," *Los Angeles Examiner*, June 8, 1943, pt. 1, p. 1.
45. "Riot Alarm Sent Out in Zoot War," *Los Angeles Times*, June 8, 1943, p. A.
46. See, for example, "Clashes Few as Zoot War Dies Down."
47. "Nazis Spur Gang War Here," *Daily News*, June 9, 1943, pp. 1, 6.
48. "6-Day Zoot War Hospitalizes 112," *Daily News*, June 10, 1943, p. 10.
49. "New Zoot Threat Hits War Workers," *Daily News*, June 11, 1943, p. 37.
50. Jack Cravens, "Zoot Suiters Pledge Police They'll Abandon Odd Garb," *Daily News*, June 15, 1943, p. 3.
51. See, for example, "6 Zoot Suiters Sent to Hospital by Servicemen."
52. Report on Attack on Naval Personnel by "Zoot-Suiters," June 10, 1943, Folder P8–5 (ZootSuit Gangs) 1943 [1/4], Box 296, Record Group 181, Records of Shore Establishments and Naval Districts; Eleventh Naval District, Records of the Commandant's Office, General Correspondence, 1924–55, National Archives, Laguna Niguel, Calif. See also the valuable discussion of this report and its implications in Eduardo Obregón Pagán, *Murder at the Sleepy Lagoon: Zoot Suits, Race, and Riot in Wartime L.A.* (Chapel Hill: University of North Carolina Press, 2003), 154–65.
53. "Affidavit of Mrs. Cruz Esquer," June 9, 1943, file 2624, "Administrative Files, Department of Justice–Attorney General, Law Enforcement, 1943," Earl Warren Papers.
54. "Jurors Hear 'Zooters' Defend Right to Garb," *Los Angeles Times*, June 16, 1943, p. A.
55. "Grand Jury Opens Zoot War Probe," *Los Angeles Examiner*, June 16, 1943, pt. 2, p. 1.

56. "Ex-Zoot Suiter Urges Place for East Side Youths to Play," *Los Angeles Examiner*, June 30, 1943, pt. 1, p. 15. These kinds of ideas were also expressed in private correspondence. See Rudy Sanchez to Eduardo Quevedo, June 6, 1943, Folder 11, "Correspondence, 1943," Box 1, Eduardo Quevedo Papers, Department of Special Collections, Stanford University Library.
57. "Jury Seeks Cause and Cure in Zoot Riots," *Daily News*, June 16, 1943, p. 16.
58. James Felton, "Mrs. Abasta's Son Was a Zoot Suiter, Too," *Daily News*, June 18, 1943, p. 2.
59. "First Lady Traces Zoot Riots to Discrimination," *Los Angeles Times*, June 17, 1943, p. A. See also "Mrs. FDR Hits Race Hatreds in Zoot War," *Los Angeles Examiner*, June 17, 1943, pt. 1, p. 4.
60. "Mrs. Roosevelt Challenged on Zoot Statement," *Los Angeles Times*, June 18, 1943, p. A. See also "Zoot Row Not Race Rioting, Mrs. FDR Told," *Los Angeles Examiner*, June 18, 1943, pt. 1, p. 15.
61. "Mrs. Roosevelt Blindly Stirs Race Discord," *Los Angeles Times*, June 18, 1943, pt. 2, p. 4.
62. Minutes, June 21, 1943 meeting, Coordinating Council for Latin American Youth, Folder 8, "Minutes, 1943," Box 3, Ruiz Papers.
63. "Sí Hay Discriminación [Yes there is discrimination]," *La Opinión*, June 21, 1943, p. 5.
64. Charlotta A. Bass, "On the Sidewalk," *California Eagle*, June 17, 1943, pp. 1-A, 5-B. An *Eagle* editorial published a week later reiterated some of the ideas that Bass expressed in her June 17 column. See "Bataan on the Home Front," *California Eagle*, June 24, 1943, p. 8-A.
65. John S. Kinloch, "Kinloch's Corner," *California Eagle*, June 17, 1943, p. 1-B.
66. Bass, "On the Sidewalk," *California Eagle*, June 17, 1943, p. 5-B.
67. Citizens' Committee for the Defense of Mexican-American Youth release, n.d., Folder 1, "News Releases, Memeographed copies [*sic*]," Box 1, Sleepy Lagoon Defense Committee Records (Collection 107), Department of Special Collections, Charles E. Young Research Library, UCLA.
68. Citizens' Committee for the Defense of Mexican-American Youth release, June 17, 1943, Folder 2, "News Releases Preliminary drafts (etc.)," Box 1, Sleepy Lagoon Defense Committee Records.
69. Lorania K. Francis, "Murray Appeals to Roosevelt in Zoot Rioting," *Los Angeles Times*, June 20, 1943, pt. 1, p. 14.
70. "Slums Manufacture Delinquency," *California Eagle*, June 17, 1943, p. 8-A.
71. "Negroes Testify at Hearings on Zoot Suit Riots," *Los Angeles Times*, June 24, 1943, pt. 2, p. 8.
72. "'Zoot' Jurors Hear Negroes," *Los Angeles Examiner*, June 24, 1943, pt. 1, p. 16.
73. "All Races Mobilize: American Unity Com. Juniors Move to Action," *California Eagle*, July 1, 1943, p. 1-B.

74. Joint Fact-Finding Committee on Un-American Activities in California, *Report* (Sacramento, 1945), 161.
75. "C.I.O. Ousted Shoemaker, Says Bowron," *Los Angeles Examiner*, June 24, 1943, pt. 1, p. 16.
76. Ibid.
77. "Zoot Suit Problem Here Studied by Tenney Group," *Los Angeles Times*, June 22, 1943, pt. 2, pp. 1, 2. See also "Tenney Body Opens Zoot Battle Probe," *Los Angeles Examiner*, June 22, 1943, pt. 1, p. 3.
78. Committee on Un-American Activities in California, *Report*, 208. See also "Zoot Clash Held Riot Safety Valve."
79. "Segregation OK Says Tenney Committee," *California Eagle*, June 24, 1943, pp. 1-A, 5-B.
80. Committee on Un-American Activities in California, *Report*, 194–95.
81. "Segregation OK Says Tenney Committee."
82. Ibid.
83. "Negroes Must Unify, Fight Riots—Russell," *California Eagle*, July 1, 1943, pp. 1-A, 8-B. See also "Segregation OK Says Tenney Committee"; "The Fifth Column Threat," *California Eagle*, July 1, 1943, p. 8-A; "Now Is the Moment . . . Now!" *California Eagle*, July 1, 1943, p. 8-A; and Charlotta A. Bass, "On the Sidewalk," *California Eagle*, Aug. 12, 1943, pp. 1-A, 8-B.
84. "Grand Jury Raps Officials for Rise in Juvenile Crime," *Los Angeles Times*, July 29, 1943, pt. 2, p. 1.
85. Ted LeBerthon, *Daily News*, June 1, 1943, p. 28.
86. "L.A. Power Bloc to Fight for Minorities," *Daily News*, June 21, 1943, pp. 1, 27. See also "Form City-Wide Anti-Bias Body; Sun. Meet," *California Eagle*, June 24, 1943, pp. 1-A, 5-B. This meeting was briefly described in the *Times*. See "Legislators Plan Zoot Suit Riot Inquiry Today," *Los Angeles Times*, June 21, 1943, pt. 2, p. 8.
87. "All Races Mobilize: American Unity Com. Juniors Move to Action."
88. Ibid.
89. Jeanette Cohen, "As I See It," *California Eagle*, August 26, 1943, p. 8-A.
90. East Side Inter-Racial Committee to All Organizations and Individuals, July 22, 1943, Folder 19, "Correspondence, in-coming, Di-Hu," Box 1, Ruiz Papers.
91. Elizabeth Cummings to Marshall Field, June 11, 1944, folder 4, "1944," Box 50, Ford Papers.
92. "The War Worker Makes Its Debut. There Is No Other Newspaper Like It," *War Worker*, July 1943, p. 10.
93. Rev. Albert B. Cleage, Jr., "Fellowship Church: Adventure in Interracial Understanding," *NOW*, first half October 1946, p. 4.
94. Petition to California Gov. Earl Warren, n.d., Folder 7, "Correspondence, Form letters," Box 2, Sleepy Lagoon Defense Committee Records.

95. Undated released, Sleepy Lagoon Defense Committee, Folder 2, "News Releases Preliminary Drafts (etc.), Box 1, Sleepy Lagoon Defense Committee Records.
96. "Mexican, Negro, White Youth Meet," *California Eagle*, June 17, 1943, p. 1-B.
97. "Negroes Must Unify, Fight Riots—Russell."
98. "Hitler Wouldn't Like Matthews' New District Attorney Position," *California Eagle*, Aug. 5, 1943, pp. 1-A, 8-B.
99. "Race Property Bars Held Illegal!" *California Eagle*, Sept. 2, 1943, pp. 1-A, 7-A.
100. "Why Not Fight the Fifth Column!" *California Eagle*, Sept. 30, 1943, p. 8-A.
101. "Race Unity Program City 'Must,'" *California Eagle*, Oct. 21, 1943, p. 8-A. See also, "Let's Stop the Next Riot!" *California Eagle*, Oct. 14, 1943, p. 1-A.
102. "Danger Signal: KKK Is Busy Here!" *California Eagle*, Oct. 21, 1943, p. 8-A.
103. "Race Unity Program City 'Must.'"
104. "'Speak Out!' Governor Asked: Hawkins Appeals To Warren," *California Eagle*, Nov. 4, 1943, pp. 1-A, 8-B.
105. "Mayor's Race Unity Body to Include Labor, Whites," *California Eagle*, Oct. 21, 1943, p. 2-A.
106. "Race Unity Program City 'Must.'"
107. "Halt Negroes at City Border–Mayor," *California Eagle*, Nov. 18, 1943, pp. 1, 2.
108. "Sit with City Council Tuesday AM," *California Eagle*, Nov. 11, 1943, p. 8-A.
109. See Charlotta A. Bass, "On the Sidewalk: Hitler's Helpers Spread Race Housing Bars!" *California Eagle*, Nov. 4, 1943, pp. 1-A, 8-B, and "Negroes, Labor Ask Drive on Racists," *California Eagle*, Nov. 4, 1943, pp. 1-A, 8-B.
110. Charlotta A. Bass, "On the Sidewalk: Mayor, Council Aid 5th Column!" *California Eagle*, Nov. 18, 1943, pp. 1, 12.
111. "Council Kills Race Unity Move," *California Eagle*, Nov. 18, 1943, pp. 1, 11.
112. "Kiwanis Club Raps Klan, Race Agitators," *California Eagle*, Dec. 9, 1943, pp. 1, 16.
113. "New Anti-Prejudice Group Formed," *California Eagle*, Dec. 30, 1943, p. 8. See also "New Council for Civic Unity Formed," *War Worker*, first half January 1944, p. 17.
114. Council for Civic Unity to Manuel Ruiz, Feb. 23, 1944, Folder 18, "Correspondence, in-coming, Ag-Co," Box 1, Ruiz Papers.
115. Everett Wile, "Bulletin," produced for the members of the Council for Civic Unity, n.d., Folder 3, "Council for Civic Unity," Box 5, Sleepy Lagoon Defense Committee Records.
116. In creating the committee, the Board of Supervisors approved recommendations advanced in a letter from Willsie Martin and Joseph T. McGucken to John Anson Ford, Jan. 7, 1944, Folder 3 "1944," Box 72, Ford Papers. The Board of Supervisors approved the course of action recommended by Martin and McGucken on Jan. 11, 1944.

117. Minutes of first meeting of Committee for Interracial Progress, Mar. 2, 1944, Folder 3, "1944," Box 72, Ford Papers.
118. "Statement," Folder 2, "1943," Box 69, Ford Papers.
119. "LeBerthon Gets Boot from News," *California Eagle*, Sept. 16, 1943, p. 1-A.
120. Charlotta A. Bass, "On the Sidewalk: LeBerthon Is 5th Col. Victim," *California Eagle*, Sept. 16, 1943, pp. 1-A, 8-B. See also "LeBerthon Gets Boot From 'News.'"
121. Charlotta A. Bass, "On the Sidewalk: Texas Mother–Courage Symbol," *California Eagle*, Sept. 23, 1943, p. 1-A.
122. *War Worker*, October 1943, p. 10.
123. Ted LeBerthon, *Daily News*, June 8, 1943, p. 32.
124. Charlotta A. Bass, "On the Sidewalk: Healthy Sign: N.A.A.C.P. Unity," *California Eagle*, Nov. 11, 1943, p. 1-A.
125. See, for example, "Citizens Emergency Group Launches Action Program," *California Eagle*, Dec. 2, 1943, p. 2.
126. "C.I.O. Ousted Shoemaker, Says Bowron."
127. "A Point Well Taken, We Think," *California Eagle*, Nov. 11, 1943, p. 8-A.

Chapter Six

1. Cecile Hallingby, "Violence Held Likely if Japs Return to Coast," *Los Angeles Times*, June 21, 1943, pt. 2, p. 5.
2. "Over 600 Nisei at Poston Found Openly Disloyal," *Los Angeles Times*, June 9, 1943, pt. 1, p. 1.
3. "Firmer Control of Japs Urged by Poston Chief," *Los Angeles Times*, June 10, 1943, pt. 1, p. 1.
4. "Muddlers: Roosevelt Administration Obstinate About Japs," *Los Angeles Examiner*, June 16, 1943, pt. 1, p. 12.
5. "Arizona Fears Rioting if Japs Settle There," *Los Angeles Times*, June 16, 1943, pt. 1, p. 1.
6. See Charles DeBenedetti, Introduction to *An American Peace Policy*, by Kirby Page (New York: Garland, 1971), 5–6.
7. "Arizona Fears Rioting if Japs Settle There."
8. Ibid.
9. "Relocation Center," *Los Angeles Examiner*, June 29, 1943, pt. 1, p. 13.
10. "Japandora," *Los Angeles Examiner*, June 18, 1943, pt. 1, p. 12.
11. "'Little Bo-Peep,'" *Los Angeles Examiner*, June 26, 1943, pt. 1, p. 10.
12. "Relocation Center," *Los Angeles Examiner*, June 29, 1943, pt. 1, p. 13.
13. Bill Hosokawa, "From the Frying Pan: Coast Fascists' Campaign Parallels Hitler's," *Pacific Citizen*, June 24, 1943, p. 5. See also Larry Tajiri, "Nisei USA: Naziism Is a Nasty Word," *Pacific Citizen*, Aug. 7, 1943, p. 4.

14. Larry Tajiri, "Nisei USA: The Nisei Are Not Alone," *Pacific Citizen*, June 17, 1943, p. 4.
15. Bill Hosokawa, "From the Frying Pan: It Is Time We Started Swinging Back," *Pacific Citizen*, June 17, 1943, p. 5.
16. Larry Tajiri, "Nisei USA: The Unholy Coalition," *Pacific Citizen*, Aug. 14, 1943, p. 4.
17. "L.A. Pastor Defends Citizenship Rights of Nisei in Radio Talk," *Pacific Citizen*, June 24, 1943, p. 2.
18. "Carey McWilliams Expresses Hope for Relaxing Ban against Return of Evacuees to Coast," *Pacific Citizen*, July 24, 1943, p. 5.
19. "McWilliams: Reactionary Bloc Sponsors Anti-Oriental Drive," *Pacific Citizen*, Sept. 4, 1943, p. 1.
20. "Lechner Gives Jap Warning," *Los Angeles Examiner*, July 30, 1943, pt. 2, p. 1.
21. "Howser Sees Bloodshed if Japs Return," *Los Angeles Times*, Oct. 19, 1943, pt. 1, p. 1. See also "Peril of Japanese Return Told State Senate Group," *Los Angeles Examiner*, Oct. 19, 1943, pt. 2, p. 8.
22. "Clergy Who Want Japs Back Scored," *Los Angeles Times*, Oct. 20, 1943, p. A.
23. Ibid.
24. "More Voices Heard against Japs' Return," *Los Angeles Examiner*, Oct. 22, 1943, pt. 1, p. 3. See also "Pearl Buck's Plea for Fair Treatment of Minority Upsets California State Senate Hearing," *Pacific Citizen*, Oct. 30, 1943, p. 7.
25. "Right of Evacuees to Return to Coast Upheld by Witness," *Pacific Citizen*, Oct. 23, 1943, p. 8.
26. "Jap Return Plans Condemned," *Los Angeles Examiner*, Nov. 2, 1943, pt. 1, p. 12.
27. "15,000 Disloyal Japs Strike at WRA Center in California," *Los Angeles Examiner*, Oct. 29, 1943, pt. 1, p. 1. The *Times*'s headline was smaller and more subdued: "Tule Lake Japs Refuse to Work," *Los Angeles Times*, Oct. 29, 1943, pt. 1, p. 1. For other historical interpretations of the events at Tule Lake, see Gary Y. Okihiro, "Tule Lake under Martial Law: A Study in Japanese Resistance," *Journal of Ethnic Studies* 5, no. 3 (1977): 71–85; and Michi Weglyn, *Years of Infamy: The Untold Story of America's Concentration Camps*, updated edition (Seattle: University of Washington Press, 1996), 156–216.
28. Ray Richards, "Congressmen Assail Coddling Japs at Tule," *Los Angeles Examiner*, Oct. 30, 1943, pt. 1, p. 14.
29. "The Strike at the Tule Lake Segregation Center," *Los Angeles Times*, Oct. 30, 1943, pt. 2, p. 4.
30. Ray Richards, "8000 Japs at Tule Riot, Seize Citizens," *Los Angeles Examiner*, Nov. 3, 1943, pt. 1, p. 1.
31. "Japs Brandish Knives, Clubs in Tule Riot, Says Witness," *Los Angeles Examiner*, Nov. 3, 1943, pt. 1, p. 2.

32. "Jap Outbreak at Tule Lake Causes Alarm," *Los Angeles Times*, Nov. 3, 1943, pt. 1, p. 1.

33. "Nazi Agents 'Started' Nip Riot Reports," *Daily News*, Nov. 3, 1943, p. 11.

34. "Tule Lake Japs' Actions during Melee Disclosed," *Los Angeles Times*, Nov. 4, 1943, p. A. See also "WRA Verifies Tule Lake Japanese Riot after Denial," *Los Angeles Examiner*, Nov. 4, 1943, pt. 1, pp. 1, 9; and "Jap Mob Act at Tule Lake Told by WRA," *Daily News*, Nov. 4, 1943, p. 2.

35. "Army Takes over Tule Jap Camp," *Los Angeles Times*, Nov. 5, 1943, pt. 1, pp. 1, A. See also "Nips Blockade Mail at Tule Lake; U.S. Flag Hauled Down," *Los Angeles Examiner*, Nov. 5, 1943, pt. 1, p. 1; "Auto Marked 'To Hell With America,' Report," *Los Angeles Examiner*, Nov. 5, 1943, pt. 1, p. 8; and "Army Takes over Tule Jap Center," *Daily News*, Nov. 5, 1943, pp. 1, 46.

36. "Nips Blockade Mail at Tule Lake."

37. Warren B. Francis, "House Orders Inquiry into Tule Lake Riot," *Los Angeles Times*, Nov. 5, 1943, p. A. See also "Dies Investigators Sent to Tule Lake," *Los Angeles Times*, Nov. 5, 1943, pt. 1, p. 1; and "Nips Blockade Mail at Tule Lake."

38. "Tear Gas Routs Tule Lake Japs," *Los Angeles Times*, Nov. 6, 1943, pt. 1, p. 1. See also "Army Quells Tule Lake Japs; 16 Hurt," *Daily News*, Nov. 6, 1943, pp. 1, 4; and "Army Takes over Tule Jap Center."

39. "Army's Tear Gas Quells Japs in New Tule Lake Outbreaks," *Los Angeles Examiner*, Nov. 6, 1943, pt. 1, pp. 1–2.

40. "Japs Constitute Peril to State, Warren Declares," *Los Angeles Times*, Nov. 6, 1943, pt. 1, p. 2.

41. "Tule Lake Jap Riots Prove Myer's Incompetence," *Los Angeles Times*, Nov. 6, 1943, pt. 2, p. 4.

42. "Veterans Urge Control by Army," *Los Angeles Examiner*, Nov. 5, 1943, pt. 1, p. 8. See also "Army Rule of Camps Asked in Resolution," *Los Angeles Times*, Nov. 5, 1943, p. A.

43. "Disorders Laid to Pacifists," *Los Angeles Examiner*, Nov. 5, 1943, pt. 1, p. 8.

44. "Uprising Details Told by Aide," *Los Angeles Examiner*, Nov. 5, 1943, pt. 1, p. 8.

45. See "Tule Lake Jap Sabotage, Plot to Destroy Buildings Bared," *Los Angeles Examiner*, Nov. 9, 1943, pt. 1, pp. 1–2; "Plan of Tule Lake Japs to Burn Building Related," *Los Angeles Times*, Nov. 9, 1943, pt. 1, pp. 1, A; and "Tule Lake Japs Armed with Stolen Knives, Solons Told," *Daily News*, Nov. 9, 1943, pp. 1, 11.

46. "Plan of Tule Lake Japs to Burn Building Related."

47. "Radio Sending Sets Found by Army at Tule Lake Jap Camp," *Los Angeles Examiner*, Nov. 10, 1943, pt. 1, p. 1. See also "Bombs and Knives Found in Jap Camp," *Los Angeles Times*, Nov. 10, 1943, pt 1, pp. 1, A; and "Tule Lake's Future Control Discussed," *Daily News*, Nov. 10, 1943, p. 6.

48. "White-Jap 'Brotherly Love' at Tule Bared in State Probe," *Los Angeles Examiner*, Nov. 11, 1943, pt. 1, p. 1.

49. "Continued Army Control of Tule Lake Japs Urged," *Los Angeles Times*, Nov. 11, 1943, pt. 1, p. 5.
50. "Jap Vice Traffic in Tule Camp Bared," *Los Angeles Examiner*, Nov. 13, 1943, pt. 1, p. 1. See also "Engle Urges Dies Inquiry on Tule Lake," *Daily News*, Nov. 15, 1943, p. 3.
51. "Abolish the War Relocation Authority," *Los Angeles Examiner*, Nov. 15, 1943, pt. 1, p. 12.
52. "Grapes of WRAth," *Los Angeles Examiner*, Nov. 15, 1943, pt. 1, p. 12.
53. "Gov. Warren Right about Army Control at Tule Lake," *Los Angeles Times*, Nov. 24, 1943, pt. 2, p. 4.
54. "What! No Caviar?" *Los Angeles Examiner*, Nov. 18, 1943, pt. 1, p. 12.
55. "A Policy of Ignorance," *Los Angeles Examiner*, Nov. 20, 1943, pt. 1, p. 10.
56. "U.S. West Coast 'Loaned' to Japs for Training Soldiers before War," *Los Angeles Examiner*, Nov. 21, 1943, pictorial review.
57. "Jap Evacuees Pour into State; Supplied with Rifles, Autos," *Los Angeles Examiner*, Nov. 30, 1943, pt. 1, pp. 1, 9.
58. "Jap Internees Entering State, Tenney Charges," *Los Angeles Times*, Nov. 30, 1943, pt. 1, p. 1.
59. "Japs Molest Girl Bathers," *Los Angeles Examiner*, Dec. 3, 1943, pt. 1, p. 8.
60. "WRA Seen as Election Issue for West Coast," *Los Angeles Examiner*, Nov. 12, 1943, pt. 1, p. 11.
61. "Americans Should Know Their Enemy," *Los Angeles Examiner*, Dec. 2, 1943, pt. 1, p. 10.
62. Ray Richards, "Myer Will Testify on Tule Lake Riots," *Los Angeles Examiner*, Nov. 24, 1943, pt. 1, p. 10.
63. Warren B. Francis, "Stormy Session Reported at Jap Camp Inquiry," *Los Angeles Times*, Nov. 28, 1943, pt. 1, p. 1. See also Ray Richards, "New Dealers Make Last Try to Save WRA," *Los Angeles Examiner*, Nov. 28, 1943, pt. 1, p. 13, and "Army against Tule Lake Rule," *Los Angeles Times*, Nov. 29, 1943, pt. 1, p. 7.
64. "Congress Group Will Ask Change in Jap Control," *Los Angeles Times*, Dec. 4, 1943, pt. 1, p. 2.
65. "New Deal May Discard Myer for Jap Blunders," *Los Angeles Examiner*, Dec. 7, 1943, pt. 1, p. 12. See also "Myer on Way Out as WRA Director," *Los Angeles Examiner*, Dec. 8, 1943, pt. 1, p. 1; and "West Coast Congressmen Ask Ouster of Dillon Myer," *Pacific Citizen*, Dec. 18, 1943, p. 2.
66. "Federal Officials Cool toward W.R.A. Changes," *Los Angeles Times*, Dec. 15, 1943, pt. 1, p. 3.
67. "Army and WRA Debunk Roar Created over Jap Internees," *Daily News*, Nov. 19, 1943, p. 2.
68. "W.R.A. Official Blames Race Hatred Agitators," *Los Angeles Times*, Dec. 16, 1943, p. A.

69. "Legion Chief Warns on Jap Hate Program," *Los Angeles Times*, Dec. 16, 1943, p. A.
70. "The Japs—What to Do?" *Los Angeles Times*, Nov. 22, 1943, pt. 2, p. 4.
71. "So Sorry! 'Jap Question Editor' Deluged by Storm of Mail," *Los Angeles Times*, Nov. 29, 1943, pt. 2, p. 1.
72. "Here Are Results of Jap Questionnaire," *Los Angeles Times*, Dec. 6, 1943, pt. 2, p. 4.
73. "A Way Out," letter from Paul E. Stillman to the editor of the *Los Angeles Times*, Dec. 6, 1943, pt. 2, p. 4.
74. "The Two-Faced Japanese," letter from Louise Eldridge King to the editor of the *Los Angeles Times*, Dec. 6, 1943, pt. 2, p. 4.
75. "Three Reasons," letter from L. V. Shepherd to the editor of the *Los Angeles Times*, Dec. 6, 1943, pt. 2, p. 4.
76. "Military Handling Urged," letter from M. T. Speer and George A. Howell to the editor of the *Los Angeles Times*, Dec. 6, 1943, pt. 2, p. 4.
77. "'Disgraceful,'" letter from Edna N. Ingham to the editor of the *Los Angeles Times*, Dec. 6, 1943, pt. 2, p. 4.
78. "More than 'Yes' or 'No,'" letter from "D. C. H." to the editor of the *Los Angeles Times*, Dec. 6, 1943, pt. 2, p. 4.
79. "'Forfeited All Rights,'" letter from Mrs. E. H. Horner Sr. to the editor of the *Los Angeles Times*, Dec. 13, 1943, pt. 2, p. 4.
80. "From the Westwood Hills Press: The Los Angeles Times and the 'Hate Campaign' against Japanese Americans," *Pacific Citizen*, Dec. 18, 1943, p. 5.
81. Robert C. Weakley, "Jap Sympathy Probe Slated," *Los Angeles Examiner*, Nov. 25, 1943, pt. 1, p. 10. See also "Pasadena Committee Called 'Pro-Japanese,'" *Los Angeles Times*, Nov. 25, 1943, p. A.
82. "Gannon Flays 'Kiss a Jap a Day' Theory," *Los Angeles Examiner*, Nov. 25, 1943, pt. 1, p. 10.
83. "Jap Brutality Told in State Quiz Here," *Los Angeles Examiner*, Dec. 9, 1943, pt. 1, pp. 1, 9. See also "Pasadenans Face Solons in Jap Inquiry," *Daily News*, Dec. 9, 1943, pp. 3, 20.
84. "Conflicting Testimony Features Jap Hearing," *Los Angeles Times*, Dec. 9, 1943, p. A.
85. "Pasadenans Face Solons in Jap Inquiry."
86. "Rioting Predicted in Event Japs Return to California," *Los Angeles Times*, Dec. 10, 1943, pt. 2, p. 1. See also "Dr. Millikan Heard on Jap Problem," *Daily News*, Dec. 10, 1943, pp. 2, 15; and "California Assembly Committee Investigates Groups Favoring Fair Play for Evacuees," *Pacific Citizen*, Dec. 18, 1943, p. 2.
87. "Legislative Committees Should Not Be Bullies," *Los Angeles Times*, Dec. 11, 1943, pt. 2, p. 4.

88. "Inquisition in Los Angeles," *Time*, Dec. 20, 1943, pp. 18–19. See also "Agitation on Pacific Coast Against Japanese Americans Described in 'Time' Article," *Pacific Citizen*, Jan. 8, 1944, p. 2; and Saburo Kido, "Timely Topics," *Pacific Citizen*, Jan. 8, 1944, p. 2.
89. "Japs Here under Permit," *Los Angeles Examiner*, Dec. 9, 1943, pt. 1, p. 9. See also "Twenty Japanese Live Here Legally," *Los Angeles Times*, Dec. 9, 1943, pt. 1, p. 1.
90. Ray Richards, "Movement of Japs back to West Coast Started," *Los Angeles Examiner*, Dec. 11, 1943, pt. 1, p. 7.
91. "State Senators Ask President Retain Jap Ban," *Los Angeles Times*, Dec. 12, 1943, pt. 1, p. 3. See also "Japs Coming Back to Coast, Board Hears," *Los Angeles Times*, Dec. 9, 1943, pt. 1, p. 1.
92. "Let the Army Take Over," *Los Angeles Examiner*, Dec. 27, 1943, pt. 1, p. 10.
93. Saburo Kido, "Timely Topics: Restrictions Still Bind Loyal Nisei," *Pacific Citizen*, Nov. 27, 1943, p. 6.
94. "Ickes Assails Coast Stand on Japanese," *Los Angeles Examiner*, Apr. 14, 1944, pt. 1, p. 4.
95. "Ickes Assails Jap Camp Critics as 'Bloodthirsty,'" *Los Angeles Times*, Apr. 14, 1944, pt. 1, pp. 1, 8. See also "Ickes Denounces West Coast Hate Mongers," *Pacific Citizen*, Apr. 15, 1944, p. 1.
96. "Legion Urges Ickes Quit," *Los Angeles Examiner*, Apr. 17, 1944, pt. 1, p. 1. See also "Legion Leaders Denounce Ickes for Nisei Views," *Los Angeles Times*, Apr. 17, 1944, pt. 1, p. 1.
97. "Secretary Ickes Assails Straw Men at San Francisco," *Los Angeles Times*, Apr. 14, 1944, pt. 2, p. 4.
98. "Veterans Flay Ickes' Speech," *Los Angeles Examiner*, Apr. 21, 1944, pt. 1, p. 9.
99. "We Don't Want Japs Back, Say L.A. Leaders," *Los Angeles Examiner*, Apr. 14, 1944, pt. 1, p. 4. See also "Ware Assails Jap Coddling by Ickes, WRA," *Los Angeles Examiner*, Apr. 15, 1944, pt. 1, p. 6, and "Wallace Ware Assails Stand on Japs by Ickes," *Los Angeles Times*, Apr. 15, 1944, pt. 1, p. 8.
100. "Veterans Flay Ickes' Speech."
101. "Criticism Mounts against Ickes' Plan for Nip Relocation in West," *Los Angeles Examiner*, Apr. 22, 1944, pt. 1, p. 12.
102. "Emmons Allows Jap Women to Return to Coast," *Los Angeles Times*, May 16, 1944, pt. 1, p. 2. See also Larry Tajiri, "Nisei USA: Evacuation and Intermarriage," *Pacific Citizen*, June 3, 1944, p. 4.
103. "L.A. County Social Workers Urge Return of Nisei to Coast at 'Earliest Possible Date,'" *Pacific Citizen*, May 27, 1944, p. 2.
104. "Loyal Japs Return Asked," *Los Angeles Times*, June 28, 1944, pt. 2, p. 1.
105. "Methodists Ask Return of Loyal Japs to Coast," *Los Angeles Times*, July 16, 1944, pt. 1, p. 7.

106. "Carey McWilliams to Present the Case of Japanese Americans," *California Eagle*, June 1, 1944, p. 1.
107. "McWilliams Raps Anti-Evacuee Views as 'Racist Nonsense,'" *Pacific Citizen*, Aug. 5, 1944, p. 3.
108. "Can 'Japanese' Be Assimilated? Ask America's Fighting Men, Suggests Carey McWilliams at Town Meeting of the Air," *Pacific Citizen*, Aug. 5, 1944, p. 5.
109. "Catholic Group Advocates Return of Loyal Jap Aliens," *Los Angeles Examiner*, Sept. 25, 1944, pt. 1, p. 3. See also "Group Supports Return of Japs," *Los Angeles Times*, Sept. 25, 1944, pt. 2, p. 1.
110. "Telling the Racists," *Pacific Citizen*, Aug. 5, 1944, p. 4.
111. Larry Tajiri, "Nisei USA: Twilight of the Demagogues," *Pacific Citizen*, May 27, 1944, p. 4.
112. Larry Tajiri, "Nisei USA: Race-Baiting Does Not Pay," *Pacific Citizen*, May 20, 1944, p. 4. See also Saburo Kido, "Timely Topics," *Pacific Citizen*, May 20, 1944, p. 6; and Larry Tajiri, "Nisei USA: The Failure of Race-Baiting," *Pacific Citizen*, June 17, 1944, p. 4.
113. Larry Tajiri, "Nisei USA: The People at the Polls," *Pacific Citizen*, Nov. 11, 1944, p. 4.
114. "U.S. Japanese Girl Returns to Southland," *Los Angeles Examiner*, Sept. 13, 1944, pt. 1, p. 7. See also "First Nisei Returns Here," *Los Angeles Times*, Sept. 13, 1944, pt. 2, p. 1.
115. "Ban on Jap Girl Asked," *Los Angeles Examiner*, Sept. 21, 1944, pt. 2, p. 1. See also "Pasadena School Board Rules Nisei Girl Must Be Accepted," *Los Angeles Times*, Sept. 21, 1944, pt. 1, p. 1.
116. "Storm Raging over Nisei Girl," *Los Angeles Examiner*, Sept. 23, 1944, pt. 1, p. 3. See also "W.R.A. Attempts to Make Jap Return Test Case Condemned," *Los Angeles Times*, Sept. 23, 1944, pt. 1, p. 6, and "School Board in Row over Jap Student," *Los Angeles Examiner*, Sept. 27, 1944, pt. 2, p. 2.
117. "Pasadena Torn over Return of Jap Girl to Junior College," *Daily News*, Sept. 20, 1944, p. 36.
118. "Nisei Student Battle Raging," *Los Angeles Times*, Sept. 27, 1944, pt. 2, p. 1. See also "'One-Man Crusade,'" *Pacific Citizen*, Sept. 30, 1944, p. 4.
119. "Pasadena School Head Aroused by Protests," *Daily News*, Sept. 26, 1944, p. 8.
120. "'Poll Conductor' Led Off Campus in Nisei Rumpus," *Los Angeles Times*, Sept. 28, 1944, pt. 2, p. 1.
121. Ibid.
122. "Pasadena Stand on Nisei Hailed by Church Group," *Los Angeles Times*, Sept. 29, 1944, pt. 2, p. 16.
123. Ibid.
124. "'Poll Conductor' Led Off Campus in Nisei Rumpus."

125. "Pasadena Hears W.R.A. Director Defend Policies," *Los Angeles Times*, Sept. 30, 1944, pt. 2, p. 8.
126. "'Ban Japs' Head in Flip-Flop to Opposing Side," *Los Angeles Times*, Oct. 1, 1944, pt. 1, p. 3.
127. "Relocation Head Speaks for Japanese-Americans," *Los Angeles Times*, Oct. 3, 1944, pt. 2, p. 1.
128. "Police Oppose Japs' Return," *Los Angeles Examiner*, Nov. 29, 1944, pt. 2, p. 1.
129. "Clear Explanation of Jap Situation Is Needed," *Los Angeles Times*, Dec. 3, 1944, pt. 2, p. 4.
130. "Church Group Raps Horrall," *Daily News*, Dec. 1, 1944, p. 19.
131. "Howser Wonders if Jap Returns by Coincidence," *Los Angeles Times*, Dec. 8, 1944, pt. 1, p. 6.
132. "Naturalized Japanese Returns to Home Here," *Los Angeles Times*, Dec. 6, 1944, pt. 1, p. 1. See also "Japanese Back; Happy to Hear 'They Miss His Pie,'" *Daily News*, Dec. 6, 1944, p. 2.
133. "Howser Wonders if Jap Returns by Coincidence."
134. "Contrasting Views Heard on Calif. Japs," *Daily News*, Dec. 8, 1944, p. 2. See also "Catholic Council Hits Howser Statement," *Los Angeles Times*, Dec. 8, 1944, pt. 1, p. 6.
135. "Howser Rapped for Voicing Opposition to Japs Return," *Daily News*, Dec. 11, 1944, p. 16.
136. "Contrasting Views Heard on Calif. Japs." See also "Attempt to Bar Japs Scored by W.R.A. Official," *Los Angeles Times*, Dec. 8, 1944, pt. 1, p. 6.
137. Larry Tajiri, "Nisei USA: West Coast Hate Bunds," *Pacific Citizen*, Dec. 2, 1944, p. 4. For more on Warren's statement, see Bill Hosokawa, "From the Frying Pan," *Pacific Citizen*, Dec. 2, 1944, p. 4.
138. "Japanese-American Hostility Held Fading," *Los Angeles Times*, Dec. 6, 1944, pt. 1, p. 1.
139. "Japs' Return to Coast OK'd," *Los Angeles Examiner*, Dec. 18, 1944, pt. 1, p. 1. See also "Army Lifts Ban on Japs' Return," *Los Angeles Times*, Dec. 18, 1944, pt. 1, p. 1, and "Open West Coast to U.S. Japanese," *Daily News*, Dec. 18, 1944, p. 1.
140. "Warren Urges Public Support of Army Rule," *Los Angeles Examiner*, Dec. 18, 1944, pt. 1, p. 2. See also "Warren Urges People Support Army Decision," *Los Angeles Times*, Dec. 18, 1944, pt. 1, p. 1; "Safeguard Japs, Warren Plea," *Los Angeles Examiner*, Dec. 19, 1944, pt. 1, p. 1, and "Climate on the Coast," *Pacific Citizen*, Dec. 30, 1944, p. 4.
141. "Troops Should Be Sent to Guard Returning Japs, Protests Bowron," *Los Angeles Examiner*, Dec. 18, 1944, pt. 1, p. 2.
142. "We Shan't Pretend to Like It," *Los Angeles Times*, Dec. 19, 1944, pt. 2, p. 4.
143. "Families of Soldiers First Japs to Return," *Los Angeles Examiner*, Dec. 20, 1944, pt. 1, p. 11.

144. "Troops Should Be Sent to Guard Returning Japs." See also "Officials Fear Crisis in New Order on Japs," *Los Angeles Times*, Dec. 18, 1944, pt. 1, p. 1; "'Protect Japs' Policy Urged for Southland," *Los Angeles Examiner*, Dec. 19, 1944, pt. 1, p. 6; "Southland Uneasy Over Japs' Return," *Los Angeles Times*, Dec. 19, 1944, pt. 1, p. 1; and "Climate on the Coast."

145. "Climate on the Coast."

146. "Supreme Court Rules Loyal Nips Held Illegally," *Los Angeles Times*, Dec. 19, 1944, pt. 1, p. 1. See also "High Court Backs Return of Nisei," *Daily News*, Dec. 19, 1944, pt. 1.

147. Larry Tajiri, "Nisei USA," *Pacific Citizen*, Dec. 23, 1944, pt. 2. See also "Supreme Court Decisions," *Pacific Citizen*, Dec. 23, 1944, pt. 2; and Bill Hosokawa, "From the Frying Pan: The Army's Revocation Orders," *Pacific Citizen*, Dec. 23, 1944, pt. 2.

148. "Japs Advised to Stay Away," *Los Angeles Times*, Dec. 22, 1944, pt. 2, p. 1.

149. "Loyal Japs Advised to Shun Coast," *Los Angeles Examiner*, Dec. 23, 1944, pt. 2, p. 2.

150. "Japanese-Americans Have Chance to Show Loyalty," *Los Angeles Times*, Dec. 23, 1944, pt. 2, p. 4.

151. "Legion Chief Warns on Jap Hate Program," *Los Angeles Times*, Dec.16, 1943, p. A.

152. "Loyal Japs Advised to Shun Coast."

153. "Legion Aides Differ on Jap," *Los Angeles Examiner*, Jan. 26, 1945, pt. 1, p. 5. See also "Intra-Legion Battle Rages," *Los Angeles Times*, Jan. 25, 1945, pt. 2, p. 1.

154. "Smear Plot Seen in Legion Post Row over Nisei," *Los Angeles Times*, Jan. 26, 1945, pt. 1, p. 2.

155. "Bowron Talks with Nips Here," *Los Angeles Examiner*, Jan. 15, 1945, pt. 2, p. 1. See also "Mayor Gives Greeting to Japanese-Americans," *Los Angeles Times*, Jan. 15, 1945, pt. 1, p. 7.

156. Larry Tajiri, "Nisei USA: Blueprint for Race Riot," *Pacific Citizen*, Jan. 6, 1945, p. 4. See also Larry Tajiri, "Nisei USA: Undoing the Evacuation," *Pacific Citizen*, Jan. 13, 1945, p. 4.

157. "Pastor Warns of Forces Inciting Negro-Nisei," *NOW*, first half February 1945, p. 13.

158. "Negroes O.K. Japs' Return," *Los Angeles Examiner*, Jan. 20, 1945, pt. 1, p. 6.

159. "Approve Fund for Land Law Prosecutions," *Pacific Citizen*, Apr. 7, 1945, p. 1.

160. "California State Senate Group Raps Return," *Pacific Citizen*, May 5, 1945, p. 3.

161. "California Senate Gets Bills to Restrict 'Disloyal' Citizens," *Pacific Citizen*, May 26, 1945, p. 7. See also "Weasel Words," *Pacific Citizen*, May 26, 1945, p. 4.

162. "Tenney Wants Closer Watch on Returnees," *Pacific Citizen*, June 9, 1945, p. 3.

163. "Tenney Committee Reverses Stand, Opposes Return of Evacuee Group to West Coast," *Pacific Citizen*, June 23, 1945, p. 3.

164. "Rep. Sheppard Raps WRA for Relocating Nisei," *Pacific Citizen*, July 21, 1945, p. 2.

165. "WRA Official Counters Charge of 'Conspiracy' by Legislator," *Pacific Citizen*, July 28, 1945, p. 2.
166. "Returned 442nd Officers Act to Fight West Coast Racism," *Pacific Citizen*, July 21, 1945, p. 3.
167. "Army Arbiter on Jap Return," *Los Angeles Examiner*, July 31, 1945, pt. 1, p. 9.
168. "Japs Return to Southland as Marines Leave for Pacific," *Los Angeles Examiner*, Aug. 1, 1945, pt. 1, p. 12.
169. "Vets Meet Returning Japanese at Depot," *Los Angeles Examiner*, Aug. 1, 1945, pt. 2, p. 10.
170. "Jap-American Group Back From Arkansas," *Los Angeles Times*, Aug. 1, 1945, pt. 1, p. 8.
171. "Vagaries: No Incident," *Pacific Citizen*, Aug. 11, 1945, p. 5.
172. "Stilwell Pays Tribute to Nisei Killed in Italy," *Los Angeles Times*, Dec. 9, 1945, pt. 2, pp. 1, 5. See also "DSC Presented to Family of Kazuo Masuda," *Los Angeles Examiner*, Dec. 9, 1945, pt. 1, p. 3.
173. "General Stilwell Pins DSC on Sister of Nisei Hero in Ceremony at Masuda Ranch," *Pacific Citizen*, Dec. 15, 1945, p. 2.
174. Larry Tajiri, "Nisei USA: The Yellow Peril in 1946," *Pacific Citizen*, Dec. 15, 1945, p. 4.

Chapter Seven

1. "Ordinance Sought as Aid To Group Understanding; Public Hearing Oct. 31," *California Eagle*, Oct. 18, 1945, p. 1.
2. "Interracial Issues Stir Up Council Battle," *Los Angeles Times*, Oct. 31, 1945, pt. 1, p. 2. See also "Ordinance Sought as Aid to Group Understanding."
3. "Action Delayed for Two Weeks on Racial Plan," *Los Angeles Times*, Nov. 1, 1945, pt. 2, p. 14. See also "Council Hears Public Demand For Race Bill," *California Eagle*, Nov. 1, 1945, p. 1.
4. "Wrong Road to 'Tolerance'?" letter from William C. Ring to the editor of the *Los Angeles Times*, Nov. 5, 1945, pt. 2, p. 4. The tone of Ring's letter to the *Times* is calm and dispassionate. Ring, however, might best be described as a zealous anti-Communist. In the summer of 1945 he had sent a letter to Charlotta Bass accusing her of "moral treason" for warning "the colored people of propaganda 'against the Soviet Union.'" Ring also wrote: "I am forwarding a copy of this letter to Congressman Rankin with the request that you and other Negro rodents be examined by the Anti-Subversive Committee to ascertain the need for appropriate legislation concerning such activities, including the more recent subversive alliance between certain Negros [*sic*] and Russian Jews." See Charlotta A. Bass, "The Sidewalk: Threaten to Turn Eagle Editor over to Sen. Rankin," *California Eagle*, July 26, 1945, p. 1.

5. "The Tolerance Issue," letter from E. C. Farnham to the editor of the *Los Angeles Times*, Nov. 12, 1945, pt. 2, p. 4.
6. "City Council Shelves Bias Bill," *California Eagle*, Nov. 15, 1945, pp. 1, 2.
7. "Interracial Plan Dropped," *Los Angeles Times*, Nov. 15, 1945, pt. 2, p. 1.
8. Some readers might think that the case of *Mendez v. Westminster* was a critical case in the "battle for Los Angeles." In reality, few newspapers devoted much attention to this case. Moreover, the decision in the case clearly stated that "it is conceded by all parties that there is no question of race discrimination." See "Ruling gives Mexican Children Equal Rights," *Los Angeles Times*, Feb. 20, 1946, pt. 1, p. 1. See also "Federal Judge Rules Race Segregation in Schools Violation of Constitution," *California Eagle*, Feb. 21, 1946, p. 1; and "Segregated Schools," *Pacific Citizen*, Apr. 6, 1946, p. 4.
9. See, for example, "Plague of Covenant Lawsuits," *Pittsburgh Courier*, Dec. 22, 1945, pp. 1, 4; "Los Angeles Civil Rights Group Will Investigate Suit to Oust Japanese American from Home," *Pacific Citizen*, Nov. 2, 1946, p. 7; and "Move to Evict Japanese from Harvard Home Fought," *Los Angeles Tribune*, Oct. 26, 1946, p. 1. This and all subsequent references to the *Pittsburgh Courier* refer to the West Coast edition.
10. This is a point that seems to have escaped even well-informed observers. In February 1946 Carey McWilliams, an attorney, pointed out in an article in *Negro Digest* that "more suits contesting the validity of restrictive covenants were filed by Negroes in Los Angeles than by Negroes in all the rest of the nation." McWilliams concluded from this fact that "the pattern of racial segregation in American cities will be broken down first in Los Angeles." In actuality, more suits seeking to enforce restrictive covenants were filed in Los Angeles than "in all the rest of the nation." See "Uncle Toms Suffer Quick Death in L.A., Says McWilliams," *Los Angeles Tribune*, Feb. 23, 1946, p. 3.
11. "Action Delayed for Two Weeks on Racial Plan."
12. A revealing description of one such meeting in 1947 was written by Evelyn R. Mathews, who wrote the description for the American Civil Liberties Union. See "'Minutes' of meeting of property owners in area bounded by Wilshire Blvd. (N), Western Avenue (E), Pico Blvd. (S), and Crenshaw Blvd. (W); called the 'Southwestern Wilshire Protective Association,'" in "Race—Housing and Landownership" Folder, Box 33, American Civil Liberties Union of Southern California Records, Department of Special Collections, Charles E. Young Research Library, UCLA.
13. For a description of how this process operated, see "Restrictive Covenants . . . How Property Owners Are Propagandized into Signing Them," *NOW*, second half October, 1944, p. 4.
14. "Celebrities in Spotlight as 'Sugar Hill' Trial Begins," *California Eagle*, Dec. 6, 1945, p. 4. See also "'Sugar Hill' Covenant Fight Opens Wednesday," *California Eagle*, Nov. 29, 1945, p. 1; and "Movie Stars Seek Right to Live in Homes," *Pittsburgh Courier*, Dec. 1, 1945, p. 1.

15. "Sugar Hill Case Appealed," *Los Angeles Sentinel*, Sept. 5, 1946, pp. 1, 3.
16. "Covenants Branded as Illegal," *Los Angeles Sentinel*, Sept. 19, 1946, pp. 1, 2.
17. Atty. Willis O. Tyler, "Defense Attorney Analyzes Historic 'Sugar Hill' Decision," *California Eagle*, Dec. 13, 1945, pp. 1, 24. European American homeowners appealed the decision allowing African Americans to move into Sugar Hill. See "Negro Restriction Case Goes to Supreme Court," *Los Angeles Times*, June 7, 1946, pt. 2, p. 3. The State Supreme Court heard oral arguments in the case in October 1946. See "Race Zoning Case in Supreme Court," *Los Angeles Times*, Oct. 3, 1946, pt. 2, p. 3.
18. "'Sugar Hill' Cases Slated for Hearing on Oct. 2; No Date on Laws' Appeal," *California Eagle*, Sept. 5, 1946, p. 1.
19. "Negro Wins Right to Live in New Home," *Los Angeles Times*, Jan. 18, 1946, pt. 2, p. 3.
20. "Judge Upholds Race Covenants," *California Eagle*, Feb. 7, 1946, p. 1.
21. "Court Decision Bars Negroes from Homes They Bought Here," *Los Angeles Times*, Feb. 28, 1946, pt. 1, p. 2. See also "Upholds Racial Covenants; to Oust Families," *California Eagle*, Feb. 28, 1946, p. 1.
22. "Laws Family Ordered to Quit Home," *California Eagle*, Nov. 22, 1945, p. 1.
23. "Citizens Urged to Fight Laws Case Verdict," *California Eagle*, Nov. 29, 1945, pp. 1, 2.
24. "White Neighbors Like the Laws Family, Survey Shows," *California Eagle*, Dec. 6, 1945, p. 1.
25. "Citizens Urged to Fight Laws Case Verdict."
26. "Mass Meeting Sunday Will Protest Racist Covenants," *California Eagle*, Dec. 20, 1945, p. 1. See also "Hearing Denied; Family Ordered to Vacate Home," *California Eagle*, Dec. 13, 1945, p. 1.
27. "Mass Meeting Sunday Will Protest Racist Covenants."
28. "Judge Refuses to Free Negroes in Restriction Case," *Los Angeles Times*, Dec. 18, 1945, pt. 1, p. 7.
29. J. Cullen Fentress, "Case to State Supreme Court," *Pittsburgh Courier*, Dec. 29, 1945, pp. 1, 4.
30. "Mass Meeting Sun. to Press Action on Klan," *California Eagle*, Apr. 11, 1946, pp. 1, 8.
31. "Homeowners Act to Oust KKK Covenants," *Los Angeles Sentinel*, May 2, 1946, p. 4.
32. "Kenny Queries Law Officers in KKK Hunt," *Los Angeles Sentinel*, Apr. 11, 1946, pp. 1, 2. See also "Kleagle Seeks to Deny Klan's Lurid Record," *Los Angeles Sentinel*, Apr. 18, 1946, p. 1.
33. "California's Att'y General Seeks to Revoke State's KKK Charter," *Pittsburgh Courier*, Apr. 20, 1946, pp. 1, 4. See also "California Sues Klan," *Pittsburgh Courier*, Apr. 27, 1946, pp. 1, 4; and "Actor Joins War on Klan; Asks Damages," *Los Angeles Tribune*, Apr. 20, 1946, pp. 1, 24.

34. "Mass Rally Demands Outlawing of Klan; Backs Kenny's Probe," *California Eagle*, Apr. 18, 1946, pp. 1, 8.
35. "Court Outlaws Ku Klux Klan," *Los Angeles Times*, May 22, 1946, pt. 1, p. 2. See also "KKK Probed in California," *Pittsburgh Courier*, Apr. 13, 1946, p. 1; "State Brings Suit to End Hooded Outfit," *California Eagle*, Apr. 18, 1946, p. 1; "Ku Klux Klan Case Headed For Court Test," *Los Angeles Sentinel*, May 9, 1946, p. 1; and "Klan Loses Legal Sanction in State," *Los Angeles Sentinel*, May 30, 1946, p. 4.
36. "Council Backs Mayor's Slap at Cross Burner," *Los Angeles Sentinel*, May 23, 1946, p. 12.
37. "The Klan Is Crawling Out," *Los Angeles Sentinel*, Apr. 11, 1946, p. 7. See also "Hoods and Hoodlums," *Pacific Citizen*, May 4, 1946, p. 4.
38. "Burning Cross Linked to L.A. Race Housing Fight," *Los Angeles Sentinel*, May 16, 1946, p. 1. See also Charlotta A. Bass, "On . . . the Sidewalk," *California Eagle*, May 16, 1946, pp. 1, 20.
39. "Letter Threatening Hickersons With Bodily Harm Mis-Fires," *Los Angeles Sentinel*, May 23, 1946, pp. 1, 2.
40. "Police Can't Find Vandals," *B'nai B'rith Messenger*, June 7, 1946, pp. 1, 18. See also "No Arrests Made in K.K.K. Lawlessness," *Los Angeles Sentinel*, June 6, 1946, p. 1.
41. "Bowron Whitewashes Klan Terror; Sees No Cause for Police Probe," *California Eagle*, June 6, 1946, p. 2.
42. See "'Mobilization for Democracy' Meet Aug. 6th," *California Eagle*, Aug. 2, 1945, p. 13; "'Mobilization for Democracy' Conference Set for Aug. 26th," *California Eagle*, Aug. 16, 1945, p. 12; "Democracy Mobilization Rally to Be Held Sunday," *California Eagle*, Aug. 23, 1945, pp. 1, 2; "Citizens Mobilize to Fight Bias," *California Eagle*, Aug. 30, 1945, pp. 1, 2. See also the material in "Olympic" folder, Box 19, Carey McWilliams Papers (Collection 1319), Department of Special Collections, Charles E. Young Research Library, UCLA.
43. "Bowron 'on Pan' for Klan Whitewash," *Los Angeles Tribune*, June 15, 1946, pp. 1, 24.
44. "$500 Reward Posted for Cross Burning Information," *Los Angeles Tribune*, June 29, 1946, p. 1. See also "$500 Reward for Information on Cross Burnings," *Los Angeles Sentinel*, June 27, 1946, p. 1.
45. "Former Police Captain Not Frightened by KKK Branding," *Los Angeles Tribune*, June 29, 1946, p. 2.
46. "Ex-Police Captain Victimized by KKK," *Los Angeles Sentinel*, June 27, 1946, p. 13.
47. "Encouraging the Ku Klux Klan," *Los Angeles Sentinel*, July 4, 1946, p. 7.
48. "LA Policeman Solicits for Hooded Order," *California Eagle*, Apr. 25, 1946, p. 1.
49. "Ousts Deputy Linked to Klan," *California Eagle*, May 2, 1946, p. 1.
50. "The Klan and the Police Force," *B'nai B'rith Messenger*, June 7, 1946, p. 4.

51. "Herewith, One Pound of Cure," *Los Angeles Tribune*, June 29, 1946, p. 12.
52. "Bowron Challenges Kenny to Prove Klan Activity Here," *Los Angeles Times*, Sept. 13, 1946, pt. 1, p. 2. See also "Kenny Asked to Probe Klan Activity—If Any," *Pittsburgh Courier*, Sept. 21, 1946, p. 22.
53. Charlotta A. Bass, "On the Sidewalk," *California Eagle*, June 27, 1946, p. 1.
54. "Racist Preacher Fears Negro Ready to Strike Back; Attacks the Eagle," *California Eagle*, June 27, 1946, pp. 1, 17.
55. "Tenney Inquiry on Klan Calls High Officials," *Los Angeles Times*, Oct. 3, 1946, pt. 1, p. 2. See also "Tenney Says He Will Help to Break KKK," *Los Angeles Tribune*, Oct. 5, 1946, p. 23.
56. "Reds Use Klan Scare to Build Party, Charge," *Los Angeles Examiner*, Oct. 8, 1946, pt. 2, p. 1.
57. "Tenney Acts on Witnesses," *Los Angeles Times*, Oct. 9, 1946, pt. 2, p. 1.
58. "Tenney Hunts for Reds in Negro Groups," *Daily News*, Oct. 8,1946, p. 2.
59. "Council Shelves Pleas for Klan Investigations," *Los Angeles Times*, Oct. 11, 1946, pt. 1, p. 2. See also "City to Probe Complaints of Group Charging KKK Acts," *Los Angeles Examiner*, Oct. 11, 1946, pt. 1, p. 3.
60. "Councilman Blasted in Klan Debate," *Daily News*, Oct. 14, 1946, p. 8. See also "Klan Issues Stir Council," *Los Angeles Times*, Oct. 16, 1946, pt. 2, p. 1.
61. "What California Wants," *Daily News*, Oct. 8, 1946, p. 27.
62. See "JACL Starts Campaign to Eliminate Alien Land Law," *Rafu Shimpo*, Aug. 5, 1946. See also "Statewide Committee Planned to Campaign for Defeat of Alien Land Law Amendments," *Pacific Citizen*, Aug. 10, 1946, p. 2.
63. "Arguments against Alien Land Law Filed by JACL," *Rafu Shimpo*, Aug. 17, 1946.
64. "What California Wants."
65. "Arguments against Alien Land Law Filed by JACL."
66. "Ex-Sgt. Akira Iwamura Is Puzzled," *Los Angeles Times*, Oct. 14, 1946, pt. 2, p. 4. See also "An Answer for Akira," *Daily News*, Oct. 22, 1946, p. 24.
67. "Ex-Navy Man Raps Land Law; Cites Nisei Heroism," *Rafu Shimpo*, Oct. 30, 1946.
68. "Church, Civic Groups Support FEPC, Oppose Alien Land Law," *Pacific Citizen*, Oct. 26, 1946, p. 2. See also "Proposition 15," *Pacific Citizen*, Oct. 5, 1946, p. 4.
69. "Arguments against Alien Land Law Filed by JACL." See also "Leading California Citizens Oppose Proposition No. 15," *Pacific Citizen*, Aug. 24, 1946, p. 2.
70. "Proposition 15."
71. "What California Wants."
72. "Arguments against Alien Land Law Filed by JACL."
73. "Proposition 15."

74. "Proposition 15."
75. "Church, Civic Groups Support FEPC."
76. "Ex-Sgt. Akira Iwamura Is Puzzled."
77. "Proposition 15 Is Another Form of Facism [*sic*], Says Ex-GI," *Rafu Shimpo*, Oct. 25, 1946.
78. Ibid.
79. "Defeat Proposition 15," *Los Angeles Sentinel*, Oct. 31, 1946, p. 7.
80. "Raps Alien Land Law as unChristian, Undemocratic," *Rafu Shimpo*, Oct. 22, 1946. For a similar argument advanced by columnist and correspondent Selden Menefee, see "United States Prestige in Asia Undermined by Discrimination against Japanese Americans," *Pacific Citizen*, Sept. 28, 1946, p. 6.
81. "Church, Civic Groups Support FEPC."
82. "What California Wants."
83. Letter to the editor from Eldred L. Meyer, *Los Angeles Times*, Oct. 21, 1946, pt. 2, p. 4. See also "Farmer Group Claims FEPC Act Red Inspired," *Los Angeles Examiner*, Oct. 13, 1946, pt. 1, p. 5.
84. Letter to the editor from G. W. Farley, *Los Angeles Times*, Oct. 21, 1946, pt. 2, p. 4.
85. Saburo Kido, "Election Significance: Defeat of Proposition 15 Shows Opposition of Voters to Race-Baiting Legislation," *Pacific Citizen*, Nov. 9, 1946, p. 2.
86. "'50-yrs of Anti-Orientalism End' with Rejection of 15," *Rafu Shimpo*, Nov. 7, 1946.
87. "Racial Job Bill Beaten in Assembly," *Los Angeles Examiner*, Apr. 7, 1943, pt. 1, p. 8.
88. Augustus Hawkins, "An Editorial: The Truth about the FEPC Bill," *California Eagle*, Feb. 21, 1946, p. 1.
89. "Group Maps Plan for State FEPC Initiative Campaign," *California Eagle*, Nov. 1, 1945, p. 3. See also "Unite In Fight—Win State FEPC," *California Eagle*, Nov. 22, 1945, p. 13; and Hawkins, "An Editorial: The Truth About The FEPC Bill."
90. "FEPC Initiative Petition Placed On Nov. Ballot," *California Eagle*, June 27, 1946, p. 1. See also "People Get Chance to Vote on FEPC Bill," *Los Angeles Tribune*, June 22, 1946, p. 1; and "FEPC Officially Placed on Ballot," *Los Angeles Sentinel*, June 27, 1946, pp. 1, 2.
91. Jean Simon, "FEPC Front: Proposition No. 11," *Los Angeles Sentinel*, Sept. 12, 1946, p. 3.
92. Frank Observer, "Daily News Hears Citizens Committee Backing FEPC," *Daily News*, Nov. 2, 1946, p. 6.

93. "Hawkins Warns Existence of Local Concerns Depends on FEPC Victory in November," *California Eagle*, Aug. 8, 1946, pp. 1, 9. See also "Not Only Pass It But Make It Work," *California Eagle*, Aug. 29, 1946, p. 6.
94. "Anti-Oriental Laws Cited as FEPA Sought," *Pacific Citizen*, Sept. 7, 1946, p. 7.
95. "Notes on a Fascist," *Pacific Citizen*, Nov. 2, 1946, p. 4.
96. "FEP Hopes Fade," *Los Angeles Tribune*, Nov. 2, 1946, pp. 1, 24.
97. "Sen. Shelley Urges Yes Vote on FEPC; Endorsements Grow," *California Eagle*, Sept. 26, 1946, p. 2. See also "FEPC Front: Labor Groups Endorse FEPC Proposition 11," *Los Angeles Sentinel*, Sept. 26, 1946, p. 3.
98. "Californians Sell 'Freedom Bonds' in FEPC Brive [*sic*]," *Los Angeles Sentinel*, Aug. 15, 1946, p. 3.
99. "FEPC Will Help Build Civic Unity, Buying Power, Prosperity, Says L.A. Democratic County Committee," *California Eagle*, Sept. 19, 1946, p. 16.
100. "Sen. Shelley Urges Yes Vote on FEPC."
101. "Vote Registration Drive in Eastside this Weekend Proposition No. 11," *Los Angeles Sentinel*, Sept. 12, 1946, p. 4.
102. "Hawkins Blasts Enemies of FEPC; Warns Growth of Bigotry Hurts State," *California Eagle*, Sept. 5, 1946, pp. 1, 19.
103. "FEPC Will Help Build Civic Unity."
104. "Sen. Shelley Urges Yes Vote on FEPC."
105. "G. L. K. Smith Returns to Los Angeles to Lead Fight On FEPC, Rep. Helen Douglas," *California Eagle*, Sept. 12, 1946, p. 1. See also "Notes on a Fascist." In August 1946 Charlotta Bass had referred to some of the groups that worked against Proposition 11 as "Fascist-type" organizations. See Charlotta A. Bass, "On the Sidewalk," *California Eagle*, Aug. 22, 1946, pp. 1, 2.
106. "FEPC Opponents Using G.L.K. Smith," *Los Angeles Sentinel*, Sept. 12, 1946, p. 3.
107. For a list of individuals and organizations opposed to Proposition 11, see "Workers Told of Danger in Proposition 11," *Los Angeles Times*, Oct. 20, 1946, pt. 2, p. 3.
108. "Employment Act Campaign Opens," *Los Angeles Times*, Oct. 8, 1946, pt. 1, p. 6.
109. "Hidden Jokers in State FEPC Act Arouse Fears of Dictator Agency," *Los Angeles Examiner*, Oct. 6, 1946, pt. 1, p. 11.
110. "Group Fights State FEPC," *Los Angeles Examiner*, Oct. 22, 1946, pt. 2, p. 12.
111. "Proposition 11 Hit by Retailers," *Los Angeles Times*, Oct. 17, 1946, pt. 2, p. 12.
112. "Proposition No. 11 Called Communistic by Tenney," *Los Angeles Times*, Oct. 30, 1946, pt. 1, p. 4.
113. "Fair Employment Act Debated by Leaders," *Los Angeles Times*, Oct. 16, 1946, pt. 1, p. 7.

114. "State Retailers and Pastor against Proposition No. 11," *Los Angeles Examiner*, Oct. 17, 1946, pt. 1, p. 7.
115. "Promotion of Race Prejudice," *Los Angeles Times*, Oct. 27, 1946, pt. 2, p. 2.
116. "Proposition No. 11 Called Communistic by Tenney."
117. "Proposition 11 Hit by Retailers."
118. "Farmer Group Claims FEPC Act Red Inspired," *Los Angeles Examiner*, Oct. 13, 1946, pt. 1, p. 5. This language was nearly identical to that used in a Committee for Tolerance pamphlet. A copy of this pamphlet is in "FEPC Progress–California" Folder, Box 32, ACLU of Southern California Records.
119. "Promotion of Race Prejudice."
120. "Proposition No. 11 Called Communistic by Tenney."
121. "C. of C. Opposes Proposition 11," *Los Angeles Times*, Oct. 11, 1946, pt. 1, p. 2.
122. "Proposition 11 Hit by Retailers." See also "State Retailers and Pastor against Proposition No. 11."
123. "Fair Practices Act Assailed as Public Menace," *Los Angeles Times*, Oct. 27, 1946, pt. 2, p. 2. See also the Committee for Tolerance pamphlet.
124. "Promotion of Race Prejudice."
125. "Labor Group Fights No. 11," *Los Angeles Examiner*, Nov. 1, 1946, pt. 1, p. 8. See also "Unionist Raps Proposition 11," *Los Angeles Examiner*, Nov. 2, 1946, pt. 1, p. 5.
126. Frank Observer, "Daily News Urges: Vote 'No' on Propositions 2 and 11," *Daily News*, Oct. 25, 1946, pp. 16, 33.
127. "C. of C. Opposes Proposition 11."
128. "Proposition 11 Hit by Retailers." See also "State Retailers and Pastor against Proposition No. 11."
129. "Vets Fight FEPC Move," *Los Angeles Examiner*, Oct. 8, 1946, pt. 1, p. 9.
130. "Employment Act Campaign Opens."
131. "Rail Union Aide Hits FEPC Plan," *Los Angeles Examiner*, Oct. 28, 1946, pt. 2, p. 1.
132. Committee for Tolerance pamphlet.
133. "Fair Employment Act Debated by Leaders." See also "Employment Act Campaign Opens" and "Farmer Group Claims FEPC Act Red Inspired."
134. The Watchman, "Farm Bureaus in State Oppose Proposition 11," *Los Angeles Times*, Oct. 29, 1946, pt. 1, p. 5.
135. "Rail Union Aide Hits FEPC Plan."
136. "Proposition No. 11 Called Communistic by Tenney."
137. Committee for Tolerance pamphlet.
138. "Workers Told of Danger in Proposition 11." This language was identical to that in the Committee for Tolerance pamphlet.
139. "Fair Practices Act Assailed as Public Menace."

140. "Hawkins Blasts Enemies of FEPC." See also "FEPC Argued in Public Debate," *Los Angeles Tribune*, Oct. 19, 1946, p. 7.
141. "Anti-Oriental Laws Cited as FEPA Sought." See also "Hawkins Blasts Enemies of FEPC."
142. "Hawkins Blasts Enemies of FEPC." See also "Anti-Oriental Laws Cited as FEPA Sought."
143. "Fair Employment," *B'nai B'rith Messenger*, Nov. 1, 1946, p. 4.
144. "Get Ready for the Battle," *Los Angeles Sentinel*, Aug. 22, 1946, p. 7. See also "Remember Proposition 11," *Los Angeles Sentinel*, Oct. 10, 1946, p. 7.
145. Bass, "On The Sidewalk," Aug. 22, 1946.
146. "Local Catholics Told to Lead Fight for FEPC," *Los Angeles Tribune*, Oct. 12, 1946, p. 9.
147. "The Times Is at It Again," *Los Angeles Sentinel*, Sept. 5, 1946, p. 7.

Conclusion

1. See Josh Sides, *L.A. City Limits: African American Los Angeles from the Great Depression to the Present* (Berkeley: University of California Press, 2003), 91–92.

Index

Page numbers for illustrations appear in italic type. The letter *n* following a page number refers to an endnote. The number following the *n* is the number of the note on that page.

WITHDRAWN
U. C. BERKELEY LIBRARIES
C079634788